Matthew

INTERPRETATION
A Bible Commentary for Teaching and Preaching

INTERPRETATION
A BIBLE COMMENTARY FOR TEACHING AND PREACHING

James Luther Mays, *Editor*
Patrick D. Miller, Jr., *Old Testament Editor*
Paul J. Achtemeier, *New Testament Editor*

DOUGLAS R. A. HARE

Matthew

INTERPRETATION

A Bible Commentary
for Teaching and Preaching

John Knox Press
LOUISVILLE

Scripture quotations from the Revised Standard Version of the Bible are copyright 1946, 1952, © 1971, 1973 by the Division of Christian Education of the National Council of the Churches of Christ in the U.S.A. and are used by permission.

NRSV quotations are from the New Revised Standard Version of the Bible, copyright © 1989 by the Division of Christian Education of the National Council of the Churches of Christ in the U.S.A. and are used by permission.

NEB quotations are from *The New English Bible,* © The Delegates of the Oxford University Press and The Syndics of the Cambridge University Press, 1961, 1970. Used by permission.

REB quotations are from *The Revised English Bible,* © Oxford University Press and Cambridge University Press, 1989. Used by permission.

TEV quotations are from the *Good News Bible* — Old Testament: Copyright © American Bible Society 1976; New Testament: Copyright © American Bible Society 1966, 1971, 1976.

NIV quotations from the *The Holy Bible, New International Version.* Copyright © 1973, 1978, 1984 International Bible Society. Used by permission of Zondervan Bible Publishers.

Library of Congress Cataloging-in-Publication Data

Hare, Douglas R. A.
   Matthew / Douglas R. A. Hare.
       p.   cm. — (Interpretation, a Bible commentary for
teaching and preaching)
   Includes bibliographical references.
   ISBN 0-8042-3126-5 (alk. paper)

   1. Bible. N.T. Matthew—Commentaries.   I. Title.   II. Series.
BS2575.3.H34   1993
226.2'07—dc20   92-17838

© copyright John Knox Press 1993
This book is printed on acid-free paper that meets the American National Standards Institute Z39.48 standard. ∞
10 9 8 7 6 5 4 3
Printed in the United States of America
John Knox Press
Louisville, Kentucky 40202-1396

SERIES PREFACE

This series of commentaries offers an interpretation of the books of the Bible. It is designed to meet the needs of students, teachers, ministers, and priests for a contemporary expository commentary. These volumes will not replace the historical critical commentary or homiletical aids to preaching. The purpose of this series is rather to provide a third kind of resource, a commentary which presents the integrated result of historical and theological work with the biblical text.

An interpretation in the full sense of the term involves a text, an interpreter, and someone for whom the interpretation is made. Here, the text is what stands written in the Bible in its full identity as literature from the time of "the prophets and apostles," the literature which is read to inform, inspire, and guide the life of faith. The interpreters are scholars who seek to create an interpretation which is both faithful to the text and useful to the church. The series is written for those who teach, preach, and study the Bible in the community of faith.

The comment generally takes the form of expository essays. It is planned and written in the light of the needs and questions which arise in the use of the Bible as Holy Scripture. The insights and results of contemporary scholarly research are used for the sake of the exposition. The commentators write as exegetes and theologians. The task which they undertake is both to deal with what the texts say and to discern their meaning for faith and life. The exposition is the unified work of one interpreter.

The text on which the comment is based is the Revised Standard Version of the Bible and, since its appearance, the New Revised Standard Version. The general availability of these translations makes the printing of a text in the commentary unnecessary. The commentators have also had other current versions in view as they worked and refer to their readings where it is helpful. The text is divided into sections appropriate to the particular book; comment deals with passages as a whole, rather than proceeding word by word, or verse by verse.

Writers have planned their volumes in light of the requirements set by the exposition of the book assigned to them. Biblical books differ in character, content, and arrangement. They also differ in the way they have been and are used in the liturgy, thought, and devotion of the church. The distinctiveness and use of particular books have been taken into account in decisions about the approach, emphasis, and use of space in the commentaries. The goal has been to allow writers to develop the format which provides for the best presentation of their interpretation.

The result, writers and editors hope, is a commentary which both explains and applies, an interpretation which deals with both the meaning and the significance of biblical texts. Each commentary reflects, of course, the writer's own approach and perception of the church and world. It could and should not be otherwise. Every interpretation of any kind is individual in that sense; it is one reading of the text. But all who work at the interpretation of Scripture in the church need the help and stimulation of a colleague's reading and understanding of the text. If these volumes serve and encourage interpretation in that way, their preparation and publication will realize their purpose.

The Editors

PREFACE

One of the deepest frustrations of ministers, seminary students, and lay Bible teachers is that scholarly commentaries so often provide answers for questions they are not asking and fail to address their basic question concerning the theological meaning of the text. Scholarly commentaries are indispensable. The church has learned the hard lesson that there is no shortcut to meaning; if we are serious about discovering what the biblical authors are trying to say, there is no escape from the careful questioning undertaken by such studies. This commentary is by no means intended as a substitute for these. Its intention is to supplement their work by emphasizing what each passage means to Matthew and, by extension, to the modern church.

Efficiency in the fulfillment of this purpose requires that bibliographical notes be kept to a minimum. In the bibliography at the end of this volume are included a few of the available commentaries on Matthew as well as works cited. It is not feasible, however, to include references to the many scholars, ancient and modern, who have contributed indirectly to this commentary. I must be content to register here my gratitude for all I have learned from them.

Quotations from Scripture are usually taken from the Revised Standard Version. If a quotation departs from the RSV and its source is not indicated (NEB, REB, NRSV, TEV, etc.), the translation is my own.

I am grateful to the editors of the Interpretation series for inviting me to write this volume and to the staff of John Knox Press for their helpfulness in preparing the manuscript for publication. My thanks are also due to President C. Samuel Calian and the Board of Directors of Pittsburgh Theological Seminary for granting me two one-term sabbaticals in 1989 and 1991 for work on this project. As usual, the staff of the seminary's Barbour Library has been graciously efficient in providing needed resources. My final word of gratitude must go to my students who for thirty years have stimulated my study of Matthew by asking provocative questions concerning the meaning of texts.

This volume is affectionately dedicated to my wife and daughters, Ruth, Jennifer, and Laurie.

CONTENTS

PART THREE
The Messiah's Obedient Submission to Death
Matthew 16:13—28:20

Introduction

From its first appearance Matthew has been treasured as the Gospel of the Sermon on the Mount. This justly famous compendium of Jesus' teachings sets Matthew apart from the others. While much of the material in the sermon is found also in Luke, the First Gospel has been so popular that most Christians are more familiar with Matthew's version of the Beatitudes, the Lord's Prayer, and the Golden Rule (to take only a few obvious examples) than Luke's.

This is not to say that the rest of the Gospel is merely a cradle in which the Sermon on the Mount has been placed. It is important to remember that the author could have chosen to write a book entitled "The Teachings of Jesus" in which narrative played no part. No, the sermon is set in a *gospel*, that is, a passion narrative with an extended introduction (Martin Kähler's characterization of the genre). The Sermon on the Mount is important to the Evangelist precisely because it derives from the Messiah, the Son of God, whose death on the cross constituted "a ransom for many" (20:28).

What has made Matthew so precious to generation after generation of Christians is thus its fusion of gospel and ethics, of faith and morality. The dominant characteristic of the First Gospel is its moral earnestness. The Evangelist sets himself severely over against those who claim that accepting Jesus as Lord and Savior is all that is required of them. The concluding warning of the Sermon on the Mount thus sounds the note that will dominate this Gospel: "Not everyone who says to me, 'Lord, Lord,' will enter the kingdom of heaven, but only the one who does the will of my Father in heaven" (7:21, NRSV). We can hear the echo of this clarion call in the Great Commission with which the Gospel ends: "Go, enlist all the Gentiles as disciples . . . , *teaching them to observe everything that I commanded you*" (28:19–20). It is remarkable that in this commissioning scene there is no reference to preaching the gospel and no demand for faith as a precondition for baptism. Matthew can assume that the gospel will be proclaimed and that converts

1

who undergo baptism will confess faith in Jesus, but he cannot take for granted that they will take seriously Jesus' moral imperatives. The "mixed state of the church" causes him great concern; there are too many in the church whose lives do not conform with their confession. The purpose of his writing is to convince Christians that a genuine faith in Christ must be demonstrated in daily obedience to the way of life he proclaimed. Faith and ethics, Matthew insists, are two sides of the same coin, or the coin is counterfeit.

Because this commentary will focus primarily on the meaning of each passage for the benefit of preachers and teachers, no attempt will be made here to survey the scholarly debates concerning the author, the location of the church for which he writes, the date of his writing, and the relationship between this Gospel and the others. Readers interested in the ongoing discussions of such issues may consult one of the recent scholarly commentaries listed in the bibliography or a good Bible dictionary. It will be sufficient to indicate the position here taken. In what follows, it will be assumed, in agreement with the current consensus, that the First Evangelist composed his work by using two primary sources, the Gospel of Mark and a collection of sayings and parables (referred to as Q) upon which Luke also drew. In addition, he incorporated oral traditions found in no other Gospel. Although I will follow the custom of referring to the author as "Matthew," I assume that his dependence on Mark indicates that he was not the tax collector but a later Jewish Christian, living in a diaspora city, perhaps Antioch, where he wrote for a church that contained Christian Jews but that was already largely Gentile Christian in composition. On the basis of 22:7 it will be assumed that the Gospel was written a decade or so after the destruction of Jerusalem in 70 C.E.

The Gospel's Structure

An obvious feature of Matthew's structure that distinguishes it from Mark and Luke is the author's arrangement of much of the teaching material in five great discourses, each of which concludes with the formula "And when Jesus finished these sayings" (7:21, and with slight variations 11:1; 13:53; 19:1; 26:1). In each of the five the Evangelist locates material from his various sources on a topical basis. Because these discourses are obviously of great importance to Matthew, it has been proposed that his intention was to compose a new "Pentateuch" modeled on the Five Books of Moses, in which narrative and

2

legal material alternate. A number of commentators have taken this as the fundamental clue to the structure of the First Gospel and have organized their own studies accordingly. There are serious weaknesses in the theory, however. Most important is the comparative neglect of the Markan story line, which is every bit as fundamental to Matthew as it is to Mark. The five-book hypothesis fails to give sufficient emphasis to the passion narrative, which can by no means be reduced to the status of an epilogue.

The ingenious chiastic structure that some have found in Matthew will also not do, since it likewise builds on the primacy of the five discourses. In this hypothesis the middle discourse indicates the central focus of Matthew's writing; each discourse and narrative preceding it has a corresponding discourse or narrative in the second half of the book. It is indeed probable that early sections or verses often foreshadow later ones in the author's intention, but one fears that the chiastic proposal subjects the First Gospel to a Procrustean violence it does not deserve.

A third proposal, suggested briefly by several scholars but developed most fully by Jack Kingsbury in *Matthew: Structure, Christology, Kingdom,* notes that the formula "From that time Jesus began . . ." occurs at two significant junctures, 4:17 and 16:21. The first marks the transition from the preliminary material (infancy, baptism, temptation) to the public ministry proper. The second signals the preparation for the passion. Kingsbury suggests that Matthew has employed the formula to divide his book into three main sections that can be entitled "The Person of Jesus Messiah," "The Proclamation of Jesus Messiah," and "The Suffering, Death and Resurrection of Jesus Messiah." It is possible that this places more weight on the transitional formula than Matthew intended, but Kingsbury's proposal has the virtue of taking seriously Matthew's dependence on Mark's story line. In this commentary it will be maintained that the narrative of Peter's confession and the subsequent passion announcement together constitute the basic turning point or "hinge" in Matthew just as they do in Mark.

Matthew's Christology 3

Matthew skillfully employs narrative to tell us who Jesus is. Even the Sermon on the Mount becomes a christological statement in his presentation. He also uses traditional christological titles, chief of which are "the Christ"—that is, the Anointed or the Messiah—and "the Son of God." As we shall see, these two ways of speaking about Jesus are largely equivalent for Matthew. They are used together in two critical passages (16:16; 26:63). "The Son of God" (and its abbreviated form, "the Son") emphasizes Jesus' unique relationship to God (see esp. 3:17; 11:27; 17:5). "The Lord" is also an important term for Matthew, but it occurs primarily as a form of address used by Jesus' followers when speaking to him. It does not add specific content to the Christology implied by Matthew's use of "the Son of God."

Earlier commentaries often found special christological meaning in the phrase "the Son of man." On the hypothesis that this title designated a heavenly figure in certain Jewish apocalyptic writings (Dan. 7:13–14; *IV Ezra* 13; *I Enoch* 37–71), it was proposed that Matthew uses the title as a way of indicating that Jesus is the incarnation of a supernatural being. This is most improbable in view of the way Matthew uses the phrase. It consistently appears as Jesus' self-designation without arousing any response from the narrative audience, whether followers or enemies—that is, no one perceives it as implying an unusual claim. This is particularly evident in 16:13, where Jesus asks, "Who do people say that the Son of Man is?" (NRSV). If the phrase means something like "the heavenly Messiah," Jesus provides the answer in the question (since he has already spoken of himself as the Son of man in 8:20; 9:6; etc.), and there is no reason to pronounce a special blessing on Peter. It is impossible to discover what meaning, if any, the phrase had for Matthew, since at no point does he interpret it for us. It functions in his Gospel as a mysterious name that sets Jesus apart without betraying his significance. For an extended treatment of this problem, see chapter 5 of my monograph *The Son of Man Tradition*.

PART ONE

Who Is Jesus?

MATTHEW 1:1—4:11

The Genesis of Jesus Christ

MATTHEW 1:1-25

Matthew 1:1-17
The Royal Genealogy

Who is Jesus Christ? The question haunts us still. Ultimately the answer is extremely personal. To the extent that we have been drawn into the fellowship of the church, however, the answer we appropriate must participate in the definitions that belong to the shared faith of ancient and modern Christians.

The First Gospel constitutes one of the earliest attempts to articulate a comprehensive answer. Matthew does not begin with a theological definition and proceed to elucidate it by means of the gospel story. Instead, he begins with an important but incomplete definition that must be corrected by amplification in the course of his book until we reach the climactic conclusion of 28:18–20.

The initial definition is given by means of a genealogy. No other Gospel author thought it helpful to begin the story in this way (Luke's version of the genealogy constitutes an appendix to his account of Jesus' baptism at Luke 3:23–38). It was, of course, appropriate to begin a biography with a statement concerning the subject's family background, but why start with a genealogy of over forty generations?

5

Matthew's intention is indicated by the opening verse: "The book of the genealogy of Jesus Christ, the son of David, the son of Abraham." Three messages are here enunciated. First, Jesus is declared an authentic king. As David's descendant he is no usurper but is the legitimate ruler of God's people. This truth is underscored when the Evangelist traces the descent from David through the glorious Solomon instead of through his little-known brother Nathan, as is done by Luke 3:31 (see II Sam. 5:14; I Chron. 3:5). For further emphasis Matthew divides Jesus' ancestors into three groups of fourteen. The number is clearly schematic. To obtain a grouping of fourteen in the period from David to Jeconiah, Matthew omits three kings between Joram and Uzziah (also known as Azariah; see I Chron. 3:11–12). It is widely believed that Matthew is making a wordplay. Hebrew consonants must do double duty as numbers. The Hebrew "D" stands for the number 4, the "W" (or "V") represents 6; thus DaViD has the numerical value of 14 (4 + 6 + 4). By structuring the Davidic posterity in this way, Matthew announces that Jesus is not just *a* son of David (as is said of Joseph, 1:20) but is the long-awaited Messiah, David's ultimate successor.

Second, Jesus is presented as an authentic Jew. This is, of course, implicit in "son of David." Lest Gentile Christians somehow evade the point, however, Matthew makes it explicit: Jesus, like all Jews, is a son of Abraham. For the Evangelist, Jesus was not a disembodied bearer of a divine message; rather, he was the ultimate Jew, the Jew in whom Israel's deepest hopes would find fulfillment.

It is in this second message that we are to find the meaning of the strangest feature of Matthew's genealogy. Contrary to custom, four women are included as ancestresses of the Messiah. One might not be surprised to find the names of Sarah, Rebekah, and Leah listed, but it is not these but four questionable women who are mentioned: Tamar, who played the harlot with Judah (Gen. 38:15); Rahab, the Canaanite harlot (Josh. 2:1); Ruth the Gentile (Ruth 1); and Bathsheba, with whom David committed adultery (Matt. 1:7 identifies her simply as "the wife of Uriah"). Two of the four are clearly non-Jewish; the other two, Tamar and Bathsheba, were frequently so regarded in Jewish tradition. Their inclusion in the Messiah's genealogy reminded the Jewish and the Gentile readers of the Gospel that God's great plan of salvation included Gentiles, even unrighteous Gentiles.

6

The third message is still more subtly communicated. Scholars have long debated whether the opening line was meant to serve as title for the genealogy only, for the first two chapters, or for the Gospel as a whole. The answer depends on how the second word is translated. It is certainly correct that the Greek word *genesis* can mean "genealogy," and so it is rendered in the RSV. The word had other meanings, however. It recurs in Matt. 1:18, where the RSV employs "birth" as its equivalent. Since other words for "genealogy" (I Tim. 1:4) and "birth" (John 9:1) were available, it is possible that *genesis* is chosen precisely because it can be used with overlapping meanings in these two verses. We must seek a rendering that will refer both to ancestry and to conception. "Origin" is a viable candidate. But why did Matthew choose *genesis* as the key noun in the opening lines of these first two paragraphs? Worth pondering is the possibility that he wished this word to evoke associations with the first book of the Hebrew Scriptures. Not only was the book referred to among Greek-speaking Jews as *Genesis* but also his phrase "the book of the *genesis* of Jesus Christ" is strongly reminiscent of the Greek version of Gen. 5:1, "the book of the *genesis* of human beings," and Gen. 2:4, "the book of the *genesis* of heaven and earth." By imitating these two phrases, Matthew intended perhaps to remind his readers that in Jesus Christ, God had made a new beginning. To borrow from the language of Hollywood, the First Gospel could be billed as "Genesis II, the Sequel."

Two problems present themselves to modern readers of Matthew's genealogy: How can Matthew's report of Jesus' ancestry differ so sharply from Luke's? (even Joseph's father is differently named), and why is Joseph's ancestry relevant, since he is not regarded by Matthew as Jesus' father? Students of the Scriptures, ancient and modern, have struggled valiantly to solve these two puzzles. It has been proposed, for example, that Joseph was the offspring of a levirate union as prescribed by Deut. 25:5–10; Luke traces Joseph's line through his biological father, whereas Matthew names his mother's deceased husband as his scriptural father. This is hardly acceptable, since the substitute parent was supposed to be "near of kin," whereas the two lists suggest that the relationship, if known, was a very distant one. The second problem is in some respects still more baffling. Why did Matthew take such pains to supply Jesus with Joseph's genealogy if his physical descent must be regarded as maternal only? Would it not have been more to the point to show that Mary was descended from David?

7

Our answer to these two questions must be based on a single observation: apparently they posed no serious problem to Matthew and, by extension, to his first readers. The details of the genealogy were obviously of secondary importance to the Evangelists, as Matthew shows by his intentional deletion of three generations of Judean kings. What was important to him was that Jesus was truly David's son. He was this not by the natural process of male procreation but by the direct will of God. How God's intention was effected in this instance is the topic of the next passage.

Matthew 1:18–25
The Supernatural Conception and Naming of the Messiah

In this passage Matthew continues to tell us who Jesus is by describing God's preparation for his birth and explaining that the Messiah's advent is in accordance with Scripture.

The most obvious feature of this narrative and the narratives that succeed it in Matthew 2 is that Joseph, not Mary, is the primary human actor. In Luke 1—2, Mary is dominant and Joseph is but a shadow in the background. The traditional explanation—namely, that Luke was in touch with traditions stemming directly from Mary, whereas Matthew knew only stories reported by Joseph—is unsatisfactory; it is most improbable that any family would so rigorously separate its traditions. It is more likely that the Evangelists selected and embellished traditions in accordance with the distinctive messages they wished to communicate. By focusing on Mary, Luke emphasizes the essential passivity of the human response to God's action: "Let it be to me according to your word" (Luke 1:38). Matthew, on the other hand, by selecting Joseph as his leading actor, stresses the active component in the human response. Three times Joseph is instructed by an angel in a dream, and three times he must *do* something. This is fully in keeping with Matthew's understanding of the Christian religion. For him as for Paul, God is the supreme actor in the drama of salvation; God's grace (although Matthew never uses this Pauline term) is prevenient.

The First Evangelist, however, insists that the human response to saving grace must be active and not merely passive. As we shall see, the key to his perception is found at the climax of the Sermon on the Mount: "Not every one who says to me, 'Lord, Lord,' shall enter the kingdom of heaven, but he who *does* the will of my Father who is in heaven" (7:21).

In Matthew's story of the miraculous conception ("virgin birth" is the traditional but less accurate designation), Joseph becomes aware of the pregnancy before he learns the cause. His immediate response is that of a "just" man: he must divorce her. That is, it is not out of anger that he resolves to terminate the relationship but out of deep religious conviction. No matter how much he still loves Mary, it is his religious obligation to annul the marriage contract, because she is apparently guilty of fornication, a capital crime according to Deut. 22:23–24. It is not his prerogative to forgive her and act out that forgiveness by consummating the marriage. In this instance, however, justice is tempered by mercy; although he must divorce her in order to demonstrate that his love for God is stronger than his love for Mary, he determines to do it secretly, so as not to cause her public humiliation. Joseph lives in accordance with the principle dear to Matthew, "I desire mercy, and not sacrifice" (Hos. 6:6, quoted at both 9:13 and 12:7).

Joseph's purpose is annulled by the Lord's angel, who addresses him as "son of David." From this salutation we are alerted to the fact that Joseph's role in the story has to do with his Davidic descent. It also reminds us that the miraculous conception announced to Joseph has to do with Jesus' Messiahship.

Perhaps the greatest difficulty that we modern Christians have in appropriating this narrative (and the parallel in Luke 1:26–35) is that we inevitably read it in the light of the Nicene Creed: "Very God of Very God, begotten, not made." The miraculous birth is seized upon as "proof" of the divinity of Jesus. We surely ought to confess our faith in the incarnation of the Second Person of the Holy Trinity, but it is a mistake to buttress our confession with this narrative. To Matthew and his readers the story of the miraculous conception did not involve incarnation as we understand it in the light of Nicaea.

Although the evidence is fragmentary, scholars point to documents that seem to espouse the idea that Moses was miraculously conceived. The same seems to have been claimed for Isaac. The book of *Jubilees* hints that God, not Abraham, was responsible for Sarah's pregnancy ("And in the middle of the sixth month the LORD visited Sarah and did unto her as He had spoken and she conceived," *Jub.* 16:12). In each of these other instances (if valid) the motif of the miraculous birth is concerned not with the *nature* but with the *function* of the man so conceived: it identifies him as one who has a major role to play in God's salvation-historical drama. Just as God had miraculously created Isaac as the one through whom the people of God would come into existence, so now God raised up Jesus as the new Isaac, the one in whom the renewed people of God would cohere. Just as God had miraculously created Moses to be his people's deliverer, so now God raised up Jesus to be the new and greater Moses, the ultimate savior.

Such an understanding of the miraculous conception seems to be supported by Matthew's use of Isa. 7:14. Many English translations, including the RSV, are misleading: "Behold, a virgin shall conceive." Matthew's Greek is *ho parthenos* (*"the* virgin") (correctly rendered by NIV, NRSV), a phrase he takes directly from the Septuagint. It may be permissible to ignore the article in Isaiah's Hebrew phrase, "the young woman"; it seems less appropriate in a rendering into English of the Septuagint version, where the force of the article must be taken seriously. One can, of course, attempt to explain the Greek article as the result of zealous literalism on the part of the Alexandrian translators—they are simply reproducing the Hebrew—except for one obvious fact: zealous literalism did not induce them to translate *'almah* ("young woman") with its nearest Greek equivalent. If we can guess what prompted them to select *parthenos* ("virgin"), we may be able to understand what the definite article meant to them.

Although Isaiah's Hebrew is ambiguous (is the young woman already pregnant or is she to become pregnant soon?), the Greek translators employed the future: "Behold, the virgin will be pregnant and will give birth to a son." Does their selection of the future tense indicate that they regarded the prophecy as still to be fulfilled? If this were the case, we could understand their choice of "the virgin" for the role. In the Hebrew Scriptures, Israel is often referred to as a young woman and sometimes specifically as a virgin. One of the classic instances is Amos 5:2: "Fallen, no more to rise, is the virgin Israel" (see also II Kings 19:21; Isa. 37:22). Firm evidence is lacking, but we can speculate that the translators saw in Isaiah's words a messianic prophecy and proposed that Virgin Israel would give birth to the Messiah. This postulated state of affairs would make it easier to understand why Isa. 7:14 was selected by Matthew (or by earlier Christians) as an important text for understanding who Jesus was. Accordingly, Mary represents Virgin Israel, who cannot bring forth the Messiah without God's direct intervention.

However we interpret the story of the miraculous conception, it is most important that we not lapse into paganism by taking it as presenting Jesus as a demigod, half human by virtue of birth from a human mother, half god since begotten by a god. Matthew's environment was full of such stories. Zeus and other Olympians were credited with the procreation of numerous progeny through union with mortal women. Matthew and his Christian readers would surely have been angered by the suggestion that Mary's conception through the agency of the Holy Spirit placed her son in the same category. This is a Jewish, not a pagan, story and must be interpreted as such.

In 1:21 we have the New Testament's only attempt to find meaning in the name "Jesus." The name was not uncommon among first-century Jews. *Iēsous* had been adopted as the Greek rendering for "Joshua," and it occurs as such at Acts 7:45; Heb. 4:8 (where the KJV reads "Jesus," not "Joshua"). The intertestamental book Ecclesiasticus was written by Jesus son of Sirach, and we hear of a Christian Jew named Jesus in Col. 4:11. A popular etymology related the Hebrew *Yehoshua* ("Joshua") and its later form *Yeshua* to the verb "save" and the noun "salvation." While an inexact etymology, such wordplays were popular in Judaism, as witnessed in Ecclus. 46:1: "Joshua the son of Nun . . . became, in accordance with his name, a great savior of God's elect." Although the same etymology is employed in Matthew, the meaning of salvation has dramatically changed; whereas Jesus son of Nun saved Israel from their Gentile enemies, Jesus son of Joseph will save his people from their sins.

Many Christians are uncomfortable with the expression "Jesus son of Joseph," because it sounds to them like a denial of the virgin birth. For Matthew, it was essential that Jesus be recognized as truly the son of Joseph, because only so was he an authentic descendant of David. But how could Matthew simultaneously deny and affirm the paternity of Joseph? Apparently for Matthew, God's miraculous action in causing the pregnancy *included* the miraculous incorporation of the child into Joseph's

11

family. Joseph's role was simply to acknowledge this part of the miracle by naming the child. It was common for women to name their babies (cf. Luke 1:31). Joseph's naming of Mary's baby constituted in this instance an acknowledgment that, by God's will and act, the boy is authentically his son.

Jack Kingsbury has called Matt. 1:23 "Matthew's thumbnail definition of his Son-of-God christology" (*Matthew: Structure, Christology, Kingdom,* p. 137). In a remarkably succinct way the full significance of Jesus' life and work is caught in this functional definition of who Jesus is. In Hebrew, *immanu* means "with us"; *El* is a short form of the word for "God." Again, we must be careful not to read this through Nicene glasses. In its Matthean context it focuses not on Jesus' *essence* but on his *function* in the divine plan of salvation. At no point in his Gospel does Matthew betray any interest in the philosophy of incarnation. It remained to the Fourth Evangelist to ponder the metaphysical implications of the conviction that God was in Christ reconciling the world to himself and to articulate this deepest mystery of the Christian faith in his startling declaration: "And the Word became flesh and dwelt among us" (John 1:14).

The Infant Messiah's Exodus

MATTHEW 2:1–23

Matthew 2:1–12
Contrasting Responses to the New King

Matthew's sublime story of the adoration of the Magi has often been better understood by poets and artists than by scholars, whose microscopic analysis has missed its essence. Our task as Christian scholars, preachers, and teachers is to seek a deeper understanding of the story through study of its narrative details without losing our wonderment at the story as a whole.

In this particular segment of "the genesis of Jesus Christ"

12

(1:18) the Holy Family is entirely passive. Joseph is not even mentioned! Mary is seen but not heard. Especially to be noted is the fact that the miraculous child does nothing. He does not miraculously speak, as occasionally is the case in ancient birth narratives of extraordinary persons. He is not rendered more awesome by being given flames of fire to eat, as is done to the infant Elijah in *The Lives of the Prophets* 21:2 (a document roughly contemporary with the Gospel). Despite his supernatural conception, the child is here portrayed with great restraint. No literary halo is placed over his head.

The primary actors in the story are the nameless strangers from the east and Herod the king. Matthew refers to the visitors as *magoi*. The word had several distinct uses. In Acts 13:6, 8 it means "magician," and this seems to be its predominant meaning in later Christian literature. It could also designate the Magians, a Persian priestly caste, possibly Zoroastrian. A scholarly consensus seems to favor a third meaning for this context: astrologers. The practice of astrology was popularly derived from "the east." Since the visit of the *magoi* is prompted by their observation of the stars, this seems to be the probable meaning. Their question, as well as their origin and occupation, suggests that they are Gentiles: they must be told that David's great successor is to be born in David's town. When the visitors come into the presence of Mary's child they do obeisance to him, unwittingly anticipating that day when every knee shall bow and every tongue confess that Jesus Christ is Lord (Phil. 2:10–11).

Much has been derived from Matthew's brief report that the Magi presented gifts of gold, frankincense, and myrrh. First, the number of gifts suggested that there were three visitors, although the text need not be taken as implying this. Eventually the three were viewed as kings, perhaps under the influence of such Old Testament texts as Isa. 60:3: "And nations shall come to your light, and kings to the brightness of your rising." Later they were given names: Melchior, king of Persia; Gaspar, king of India; and Balthasar, king of Arabia. Still later they were identified as descendants of Shem, Ham, and Japheth, the progenitors of the three races of humankind. Such pious embellishment of the story may help us to enter into the spirit of Christmas, but we must remember that it goes well beyond the text.

In the same way, the three gifts were given spiritual mean-

13

ings. It was natural to associate gold with monarchy. Articles of gold have from earliest times been regarded as fit for a king (see I Kings 10:2, 25). Fragrant substances, often imported from distant lands at great expense, were also royal favorites. Myrrh appears on the gift list of I Kings 10:25. In S. of Sol. 3:6–7 we read that the king's litter was "perfumed with myrrh and frankincense." In addition to such functions, myrrh was also employed in the high priest's anointing oil (Exod. 30:23–33). It is possible that royal oil contained the same ingredients. In this case it would have been seen as particularly appropriate that the one to be known as "the Anointed One" (the Christ) should receive a gift of myrrh at his birth. According to Exod. 30:34, frankincense was employed in the holy perfume used in the sanctuary and nowhere else. Did the Evangelist see the gift of frankincense as anticipating the time when the risen and glorified Messiah would be worshiped with the Father? Another possible symbolic function for myrrh is suggested by John 19:39, where we read that Nicodemus brought "a mixture of myrrh and aloes, about a hundred pounds' weight," for the preparation of Jesus' body for burial. It is this use which prompted the view that the gift of myrrh in the Christmas story ties the Messiah's birth to his death. Jesus is the rejected king who must die before he reigns. Again, these pious reflections may enhance our appropriation of the story, but they are additions to the text, not necessary inferences from the text. For Matthew, the gold, frankincense, and myrrh may be nothing more than gifts fit for a king.

A major role in the story is played by the star, but its significance is far from clear. Various attempts have been made to "explain" its presence. It has been identified as Halley's comet, which was sighted in 12 B.C.E. Others have proposed that the extraordinary star resulted from a mistake in perception: it represented the congruence of several bright stars. All such attempts are futile. Matthew intends to report not a natural but a supernatural phenomenon. The star is perhaps intended to remind the reader of the Balaam prophecy of Num. 24:17: "A star shall come forth out of Jacob, and a scepter shall rise out of Israel." That this was viewed as a messianic prophecy is evidenced not only by the Dead Sea Scrolls (e.g., War Scroll 11:6) but by the fact that Bar Koziba, leader of the Jewish revolt of 132–135 C.E. and hailed as messiah by Rabbi Akiba, was nicknamed Bar Cocheba, "Son of the Star." The Christmas star identifies Mary's baby as the long-awaited Messiah.

14

Herod's role can be more fully appreciated when we compare Matthew's story of the nativity with Luke's. The Lukan narrative contains no negative element; the exclusion of the Holy Family from the inn is due to full occupancy, not hostility, and the account of Jesus' circumcision on the eighth day suggests a peaceful sequel. In Matthew, however, the circumstances attending the Messiah's birth include the murderous jealousy of King Herod. This theme will be investigated more fully in the next section. For the moment it will suffice to note that the opening passage of Matthew 2 sharply contrasts the acceptance of the new king by Gentile strangers with the violent rejection of him by the Jewish ruler. *For Matthew,* this undoubtedly symbolized the future rejection of Jesus by his own people and the acceptance of the gospel by Gentiles. *For us,* the contrast can serve to symbolize the internal contrast between that part of the inner self which willingly and joyfully accepts the Lordship of Christ our king and that darker side of the self which firmly and persistently rejects his right to rule. Scoff not at Herod until you have acknowledged the Herod in yourself!

Matthew 2:13–23
"Out of Egypt I Have Called My Son"

In this half chapter Matthew presents three distinct scenes, each interpreted as a fulfillment of Scripture. It was axiomatic among early Christians that Christ's coming constituted a fulfillment of Scripture, and all the Gospel writers employ the verb "fulfill" in this way, but Matthew more often than all the others together. The three instances in this passage are instructive concerning his understanding of scriptural fulfillment.

To modern Christians the application of Hos. 11:1 to Jesus' sojourn in Egypt (v. 15) seems very forced. Surely it must have been as clear to Matthew as to us that Hosea was here speaking of Israel's exodus from Egypt ("When Israel was a child, I loved him, and out of Egypt I called my son"). Undoubtedly Matthew would fully agree that in the first instance Hosea's statement had this meaning, but he would insist that the text could well have a second reference: it looked backward and forward. Just as in the advent of Jesus there was a new genesis, so was there

15

also a new exodus. Hosea points to the inconclusiveness of the first exodus: "The more I called them, the more they went from me; they kept sacrificing to the Baals, and burning incense to idols" (Hos. 11:2). Jesus in his own person represents Israel, but in a unique way; by his obedience, set over against Israel's disobedience, he alone is worthy to be called by God "my Son." (See the discussion of 4:1–11 below.) Hosea's statement is thus transformed by early Christian faith into a messianic text and related to Jesus' function as the Son of God who is summoned out of Egypt to the Promised Land not to be served but to serve and to give his life as a ransom for many (20:28).

In the second scene Jeremiah is drawn upon to provide a fulfillment text but with a significant difference in the introductory formula. Whereas verse 15 employs the conjunction of purpose, *hina*, "in order that" (RSV paraphrases: "This was to fulfil what the Lord had spoken by the prophet"), verse 17 has simply a temporal conjunction, *tote*, "at that time" (RSV: "Then was fulfilled what was spoken by the prophet Jeremiah"). By this subtle change Matthew suggests that the slaughter of the innocents fulfills Scripture but is not directly willed by God. The All-knowing foresees the atrocities that humans commit in defiance of his will, but we must not negate human responsibility by attributing Herod's massacre or any in our time to God's intent. The conundrum of divine sovereignty and human free will must not be so superficially resolved.

Place-names play a role in all three fulfillment texts, as in the earlier instance in 2:5–6, but the significance of Ramah is not immediately apparent. Perhaps the importance of Ramah lies in its association with the Babylonian captivity, since in Jer. 40:1 Ramah is specified as the place where Jeremiah parts from the exiles who are being taken by their captors to Babylon. The allusion to Rachel weeping for her children at Ramah (Jer. 31:15) undoubtedly referred also to the Babylonian captivity. The woeful oracle about Rachel is set, however, in a chapter that is full of hope for the future, including the promise of the new covenant (Jer. 31:31–34). Possibly Matthew intends the Ramah oracle to evoke such associations. As in Jeremiah 31, so in Matthew 2 the Ramah oracle is set in the midst of passages full of hope for the new exodus that the Messiah will provide for the reconstituted people of God.

16

The scriptural fulfillment to which the third scene refers is of a very different order. The formula is modified again. Instead of *hina* ("in order that"), we find *hopōs* ("in such a manner that"). Here the emphasis seems to lie on result rather than purpose. This is appropriate, since the subject of verse 23*a* is Joseph, whereas the fulfillment refers to Jesus: Joseph settled in a town called Nazareth, with the result that scriptural testimony about Jesus was fulfilled.

The problem with the fulfillment text in verse 23 is that such a statement can nowhere be found in the Old Testament. That Matthew is treating Scripture differently in this instance is indicated by his choice of the plural "prophets" instead of the customary singular. That is, the statement "He shall be called a Nazarene" is attributed to the prophets collectively, since it is not to be found in any individual's statement. We can only speculate concerning the various prophetic texts Matthew had in mind. He appears to be employing a complicated wordplay, in which *Nazōraios* (inhabitant of Nazareth) is taken as a pun on both *Nazir* (Nazirite, one consecrated to God; see Numbers 6) and *Netzer* (branch, as in Isa. 11:1, a messianic text). There were undoubtedly members of the synagogue who stoutly resisted the Christian claim that the Messiah had been an inhabitant of the insignificant town of Nazareth (see John 1:46; 7:41). In his scriptural wordplay Matthew defends the providence of God.

In addition to these three explicit appeals to Scripture, there are probable allusions. Herod's murder of the infant boys of Bethlehem is strongly reminiscent of Pharaoh's treatment of the male offspring of his Hebrew slaves (Exod. 1:22). Jesus, the ultimate redeemer, is rescued from this fate just as was Moses, the first deliverer. Joseph is informed that he can return with Jesus to his people because "those who sought the child's life are dead," just as Moses is instructed in Exod. 4:19, "Go back to Egypt; for all the men who were seeking your life are dead." Matthew's use of the plural, despite the fact that Herod alone is reported as seeking Jesus' death, suggests that he may be echoing Exodus.

The Commissioning of the Messiah

MATTHEW 3:1—4:11

Matthew 3:1–12
The Messiah's Herald

It is a striking fact that, while only two of the Gospels begin with stories about Jesus' birth, all four preface the narrative of Jesus' ministry with an account of John the Baptist. That it was regarded as essential to begin the gospel story in this way is suggested by the speech attributed to Peter in Acts 10:36–37: "You know the word which he sent to Israel, . . . beginning from Galilee *after the baptism which John preached.*"

Confirmation of the importance of John the Baptist is provided by Josephus, who, after praising John's piety and religious leadership, notes that Herod did away with him out of fear that political upheaval might result from John's ministry (*Antiquities* 18.5.2). It is clear that John's contemporaries by no means viewed him simply as Jesus' forerunner. Like the prophets of old, John threatened Israel with divine judgment and summoned all to repent and amend their ways. Unlike his predecessors, he offered a sacrament of repentance. As far as can be determined from the evidence available, John's once-and-for-all water lustration was without precedent in the Jewish world. Later it found a parallel in proselyte baptism which Gentile converts underwent as an admission requirement. Whereas the lustrations at Qumran and in other Jewish groups were frequent and symbolized the continual washing away of sins, John's baptism was apparently a sacramental sealing of those who responded to his preaching and, through repentance, joined the faithful remnant of those who would survive the fiery judgment.

18

Since John the Baptist's movement was in some sense a competitor of early Christianity, offering Jews an alternative way to eschatological security, it may seem surprising that the

Evangelists chose to emphasize John's role instead of ignoring it. Their motive was not simply historical accuracy—Christianity did in fact emerge out of the Baptist's movement, and some of Jesus' first followers had been John's (see John 1:35–37)—but the desire to present the famous prophet as Jesus' herald.

John seems to have proclaimed to his followers the imminent appearance of a human but supernaturally empowered Messiah as anticipated by Isa. 11:1–5: "and he shall smite the earth with the rod of his mouth, and with the breath (*pneumati*, "spirit") of his lips he shall slay the wicked" (cf. Matt. 3:11). The political implications of such preaching would explain the drastic action taken by Herod Antipas.

While Jesus had not yet played such a role, his followers insisted that he had been supernaturally empowered to perform "mighty works and wonders and signs" (Acts 2:22), and through resurrection had been raised to the right hand of God, from which he would come as judge of the living and the dead (Acts 10:42; 17:31). Whether or not John himself originally knew it (see Matt. 11:2–3), the Messiah he proclaimed was none other than Jesus of Nazareth.

Two features distinguish Matthew's treatment of John the Baptist from that of Mark and Luke. First, Matthew draws John and Jesus closer together by ascribing to them the same message: "Repent, for the kingdom of heaven is at hand" (3:2; see 4:17). Similarly, opponents are addressed by both John and Jesus as "You brood of vipers" (3:7; 12:34; 23:33). This is another subtle way of presenting John as a witness to Jesus. The second feature is not so transparent. Whereas Luke 3:12, 14 has tax collectors and soldiers humbly approach John with the question, "What shall we do?" in Matthew's version it is Jesus' future opponents, the Pharisees and the Sadducees, who are specifically mentioned. The conjunction of Pharisees and Sadducees, repeated by Matthew four times in a later passage (16:1, 6, 11, 12), is found nowhere else in the New Testament. For all their vaunted distinctiveness, these two parties, by virtue of their opposition to Jesus during his lifetime and resistance to the gospel following the resurrection, showed themselves as belonging to a single group.

This passage is scheduled by some lectionaries for the second Sunday of Advent. In parts of the modern church, Advent has become almost exclusively preparation for Christmas, that is, a time of pondering the meaning of the incarnation. It was not so earlier. The four Sundays preceding the Feast of the

19

Nativity focused attention on the awesome second coming of Christ as judge as well as on his first coming in humility.

It is wise to retain the twofold accent of Advent, lest our concentration on the Christmas baby become empty sentimentality void of awe. We must not speak of God's love coming down at Christmas without remembering that the divine love is fierce in its judgment of those who resist love's demands. John the Baptist warns us that repentance must not be procrastinated.

The Christian equivalent of "We have Abraham as our father" is "We have Christ as our Savior." While trust in Christ's salvation is a first requirement, it is not the last. Even Paul, mistakenly perceived by some as substituting grace for human responsibility, soberly reminded his converts at Corinth, "For we must all appear before the judgment seat of Christ, so that each one may receive good or evil, according to what he or she has done in the body" (II Cor. 5:10).

Matthew 3:13–17
Baptized for Service

Distinctive of Matthew's treatment of the baptismal narrative is the insertion of a dialogue between Jesus and John that is found in no other Gospel. The tone is clearly apologetic. Perhaps Matthew wished to defend Jesus against the supposition that he too was guilty of prebaptismal sin and came to John to have it washed away. Perhaps Matthew was piqued by followers of the Baptist who claimed that Jesus must be inferior to John since he had submitted to baptism by John. The Evangelist sets matters straight with the words attributed to the Baptist: "I need to be baptized by you, and do you come to me?" (v. 14).

Jesus' answer has puzzled students of the New Testament from the church fathers to the present day: "Let it be so now; for thus it is fitting for us to fulfil all righteousness." Some contemporary scholars stress "fulfil," pointing out that in the First Gospel this verb normally refers to scriptural fulfillment; by undergoing baptism, Jesus is submitting to scriptural necessity. This is hardly satisfying, since no text is adduced that might suggest that the Messiah must be baptized. Others point out that *plēroun* ("fulfill") is used in the passive when referring to scriptural fulfillment, whereas here it is found in the active. It is preferable, therefore, to understand the statement as meaning: "It is required that you and I fulfill God's will by allowing me to be baptized."

Why would Matthew regard it as God's will that the Messiah be baptized? The most likely answer to this question stresses Jesus' solidarity with sinners. The one who will save his people from their sins (1:21) by submitting to a baptism of annihilation (20:22) must here consecrate himself to his vocation by joining the sinful multitude in the waters of the Jordan. As the one destined to be their lord and king he accepts the sacrament of the renewal of God's people. In so doing, however, he takes the first step on the road to Calvary.

All four Gospels report the descent of the Holy Spirit. Where Mark 1:10 and John 1:32 have "as a dove," which is intensified by Luke's "in bodily form" (Luke 3:22), Matthew has "like a dove." That is, while the others allow for the possibility that a real bird served as the vehicle of the Spirit, Matthew suggests that the Holy Spirit assumed a visual appearance that resembled that of a dove. It is not at all clear why the pre-gospel tradition presented the investiture of Jesus with the Spirit in this way, since there are no parallels for so conceiving the Spirit. It may perhaps have been prompted by Gen. 1:2, which describes God's Spirit as "hovering" over the waters. In any event, the dove imagery avoids a misconception of the relationship of the Spirit to Jesus: the Messiah is not seized by the Spirit as was Samson (Judg. 14:6).

What does the coming of the Spirit to Jesus mean to Matthew? Although no fulfillment text is cited, we can assume that the Evangelist would have regarded messianic texts such as Isa. 11:2 as apposite: "And the Spirit of the LORD shall rest upon him." The same text is probably alluded to in the messianic psalm attributed to Solomon: "For God has made him powerful in Holy Spirit" (*Pss. Sol.* 17:37). Similarly, Isa. 42:1, perceived as messianic by later targums, may well have been so understood in the first century: "Behold my servant, whom I uphold, my chosen, in whom my soul delights; I have put my Spirit upon him, he will bring forth justice to the nations." While for Matthew Jesus was already Messiah at his conception, here at the Jordan, after he has consecrated himself to the messianic task, he receives divine empowerment through the visible conferral

21

of Holy Spirit. By this power he will be able to attack Satan's forces and thereby exhibit the proximity of the kingdom of heaven (Matt. 12:28). The words of the heavenly voice, "This is my Son, *the Beloved, in whom I am well pleased,*" confirm the application to Jesus of the prophecy of Isa. 42:1: "Behold, my servant whom I have chosen, my *Beloved, in whom* my soul is *well pleased.*"

As Jack Kingsbury has emphasized (see Introduction), the opening section of the Gospel is devoted primarily to the question, Who is Jesus? Incomplete answers have been provided: Jesus is son of Abraham and ultimate Son of David, and as such the Christ (Messiah). His special relationship to God has been referred to in two scriptural quotations, Isa. 7:14 and Hos. 11:1, but here finally the identification is made explicitly by God himself, who acknowledges Jesus as "my Son, the Beloved."

As modern interpreters of the First Gospel, we can treat this utterance in two ways, both valid. For the sake of historical accuracy we must be careful not to turn the First Evangelist into a Nicene theologian. There is no evidence anywhere in his Gospel of the incarnational thought and Logos Christology of the Fourth Gospel. It seems probable, therefore, that "my Son" was understood by him in functional, not metaphysical, terms. It referred not to the nature of the Second Person of the Trinity but to the messianic task, echoing as it does the Nathan prophecy of II Sam. 7:14: "I will be his father, and he shall be my son."

As Christian believers, however, we see this text in the full context of the canon as a whole. In this wider setting the divine declaration attains a profounder meaning than that intended by Matthew. At this second level of appropriation the Matthean text is rightfully co-opted for the incarnational Christology that more satisfactorily articulates the meaning of Christ. The one here identified as "my Son, the Beloved" is the Word become flesh for our salvation.

Matthew 4:1–11
The Testing of the Messiah

This passage is not to be reckoned a historical narrative in the strict sense. Its intent is not to convey objective, biographi-

cal data. This we understand by comparing it with similar rabbinic stories. It constitutes a piece of haggadic midrash, that is,
it is a fanciful story whose purpose is to interpret Scripture.
There may well be an underlying kernel of historical truth,
since other passages suggest that Jesus regarded himself as involved in a struggle against Satan (see Matt. 12:29; Luke 10:18).
In its present form, however, the story is less involved with the
vanquishing of Satan than with the meaning of Jesus' divine
Sonship. It is, in effect, a theological meditation on the baptismal narrative, addressing the question: What is implied in the
heavenly declaration, "This is my Son, the Beloved, in whom I
am well pleased"? This is suggested by the fact that the first two
temptations both begin with the premise, "Since you are the
Son of God." (The "If" of the RSV and other translations is a too
literal rendering of the Greek *ei*, which was often used with the
meaning "since," "in view of the fact that," as in Matt. 6:30.
There is no indication in the narrative that Satan is seeking to
establish Jesus' identity.)

A second, critically important connecting link is provided
by "the Spirit." The Spirit that descended upon Jesus at the
Jordan now leads him into the wilderness with the express purpose of subjecting him to a confrontation with the devil (Matthew employs an infinitive of purpose, where Luke has simply
a participle, "being tempted by the devil"). The infinitive is
normally translated "to be tempted." This is not incorrect; the
Greek verb *peirazein* is often so used, and Satan is sometimes
referred to by means of the participle as "the tempting one,"
that is, the tempter (v. 3). *Peirazein* also means "to test," however, as in John 6:6 and (in a compound form) in our passage,
Matt. 4:7: "You are not to put the Lord your God to the test"
(NEB; see also I Cor. 10:9; Heb. 11:17). In Matt. 4:1 the verb
clearly has both meanings. God, through the Spirit, intends to
test Jesus; Satan, God's indirect agent, seeks to *tempt* the Messiah designate. (A similarly ambiguous use of the verb occurs in
Rev. 2:10.)

Because God's intention must be regarded as taking priority over Satan's, the passage is to be seen as a story about the
testing of God's Son. It has a parallel in God's testing of Abraham (Gen. 22:1). In this case, however, Jesus is both Abraham
and Isaac; eventually he must lay his own life on the altar. (Some
scholars trace a connection with the Genesis story through the
use of "the beloved" in the Septuagint of Gen. 22:2 and in Matt.

23

3:17.) The content of the passage, however, suggests that a closer parallel can be found in Israel's testing by God in the wilderness. The "forty days and forty nights" of verse 2 is reminiscent not only of Moses' fast (Exod. 34:28; Deut. 9:9, 18) but also of Israel's forty-year wilderness sojourn. The responses to the temptations are all drawn from Deuteronomy (Deut. 8:3; 6:16, 13). The three temptations in Matthew's order reflect the chronological order of three tests faced by Israel. Whereas Israel, called "son" by God (Hos. 11:1; see Deut. 8:5), failed each of the tests, Jesus demonstrates his worthiness to be the Son of God by responding to the tests with resolute faithfulness.

The first temptation has its point of departure in Jesus' hunger. The parallel here, of course, is Israel's hunger prior to the gift of bread from heaven (Exod. 16:1–4). The nature of the test is described in Deut. 8:2–3: "Remember the whole way by which the LORD your God has led you these forty years in the wilderness to humble and test you, and to discover whether or not it was in your heart to keep his commandments. So he afflicted you with hunger and then fed you on manna . . . to teach you that people cannot live on bread alone, but that they live on every word that comes from the mouth of the LORD" (REB). Although in this instance God's grace prevailed over strict justice in the gift of manna, the grumbling of Exod. 16:3 reveals utter faithlessness; God's son Israel does not trust God to provide and thus betrays the covenant relationship that requires confident trust in God's readiness and ability to fulfill his self-imposed covenant obligations (see Gen. 15:6). By contrast, the latter-day Son of God refuses to give way to mistrust by exploiting the Spirit's power and thus providing himself with bread from stones instead of confidently awaiting bread from heaven (see v. 11). He draws strength to resist the temptation from Deut. 8:3: Human beings possess life not by consuming bread but simply and solely because it is God's will that they live. ("Every word from the mouth of God" includes not only Scripture but God's will as it pertains to each human life.) Jesus faithfully remembers that he is totally dependent upon God.

The point of the second temptation is to be similarly inferred from Jesus' response, which quotes Deut. 6:16: "You must not put the LORD your God to the test as you did at Massah" (REB). The sorry affair is related in Exod. 17:1–7, which concludes with an etymology of the place-names: "He named the place Massah and Meribah, because the Israelites had disputed with him and put the LORD to the test with their question, 'Is the LORD in our midst or not?' " (REB; cf. Deut. 9:22; 33:8; Ps. 95:8; Heb. 3:8). The rebellious people challenges its covenant partner, the Lord God, to fulfill his covenant obligations and, in so doing, proves itself unworthy of the covenant. Jesus, on the other hand, refuses to demonstrate God's presence with him by leaping from the "wing" of the temple (the location of the *pterygion* is a matter of pure speculation). He refuses, not because of any lack of faith in God's power and providential care (this faith has been amply demonstrated in his first response to the tempter), but because honoring God excludes every kind of manipulation, including putting God to the test. Later the Son of God will indeed leap into the abyss, but only because he is convinced that it is God's will that he do so (see Matt. 26:39, 53; 27:46).

The concern of the third temptation is idolatry, as seen in the sequel to Jesus' deuteronomic response. Immediately following the command, "You shall fear the LORD your God; you shall serve him, and swear by his name," we read, "You shall not go after other gods, of the gods of the peoples who are round about you" (Deut. 6:13–14). Despite this and many other warnings, Israel repeatedly "played the harlot" with other gods (Exod. 32:1–6; Judg. 2:17; etc.). Their love for the Lord their God (Deut. 6:4) was "like a morning cloud, like the dew that goes early away" (Hos. 6:4).

The connection between the third temptation and idolatry was probably clearer to Matthew's first readers than it is to us. First, the gods of the Greco-Roman pantheon were regarded by Jews as demons (see I Cor. 10:20) and hence as Satan's minions. Second, idolatry was a genuine temptation for many Jews who wished to participate fully in the politics and economics of the Greco-Roman establishment. A classic case, well known to Jews of the day, was provided by Tiberius Alexander, nephew of the famous Jewish philosopher Philo, who apostatized from Judaism to enter Roman service. There were probably many others who did not abandon Judaism but who were willing to accept "a pinch of idolatry" to further their personal careers. It is unlikely that any of Matthew's readers believed that Jesus had been so tempted. They were well aware, however, of the compromises that public office seems to require of even the best-intentioned. What kind of king would Jesus have become? For good ends would he have sacrificed the means? The third scene in the

25

triptych assures us of Jesus' undivided loyalty. He will not ride two horses. He will worship and serve God only. Here is the purity of heart so prized by Kierkegaard: to will one thing.

This passage (4:1–11) is often appointed by lectionaries for the first Sunday of Lent. The presumption is that the narrative is of direct relevance for Christians as they enter a period of penitence. Ordinary Christians are unlikely to perceive it so, and with good cause. The story does not correspond with our experience; we do not hold conversations with a visible devil, nor are we whisked from place to place as Jesus is in the story. Moreover, the temptations that Jesus faces are peculiar to him; they seem very remote from those we face day by day. This passage may in fact prompt some to doubt the validity of Heb. 4:15: "For we have not a high priest who is unable to sympathize with our weaknesses, but one who in every respect has been tempted as we are, yet without sin." What did Jesus know of the temptations that are faced daily by the recovering alcoholic and substance abuser? the lonely divorcée? the struggling business owner? the teenager who covets peer acceptance above all? There is, however, a common denominator that links all of these with the temptations ascribed to Jesus. The basic, underlying temptation that Jesus shared with us is the temptation to treat God as less than God. We may not be tempted to turn stones into bread (we are more apt to turn butter into guns), but we are constantly tempted to mistrust God's readiness to empower us to face our trials. None of us is likely to put God to the test by leaping from a cliff, but we are frequently tempted to question God's helpfulness when things go awry; we forget the sure promise, "My grace is sufficient for you, for my power is made perfect in weakness" (II Cor. 12:9). Pagan idolatry is no more a temptation for us than it was for Jesus, but compromise with the ways of the world is a continuing seduction. It is indeed difficult for us to worship and serve God only. We should be continually grateful that we have a great high priest who, tempted as we are, was able to resist all such temptations by laying hold of Scripture and firmly acknowledging that only God is God.

PART TWO

The Messiah's Ministry to Israel

MATTHEW 4:12—16:12

The Messiah of Word and Deed

MATTHEW 4:12—9:38

Matthew 4:12–25
The Messiah Begins His Ministry

The three paragraphs of Matt. 4:12–25 serve to prepare the readers for the Sermon on the Mount, the Messiah's inaugural address. The first emphasizes that the Messiah's ministry will fulfill Scripture by bringing light to those in darkness. The call of the four fishermen prepares for the fact that the sermon will be addressed especially to disciples, although in the hearing of the crowds. The third subsection stresses that the Messiah's healing ministry, despite its great significance, is strictly subordinate to his teaching and preaching.

Jesus Begins to Preach (4:12–17)

Matthew suggests that the inauguration of Jesus' public ministry occurs as the direct result of the violent interruption of the Baptist's renewal campaign: "Now when he heard that John had been arrested . . . " It is not clear why Matthew selects the verb "heard." Does he wish to suggest that Jesus was not a

27

follower of John and had no contact with the Baptist apart from the moment of his baptism? In this respect Matthew seems to parallel the curious little report of John 4:1–3: "Now when the Lord knew that the Pharisees had heard that Jesus was making and baptizing more disciples than John, . . . he left Judea and departed again to Galilee." That is, in both the First and the Fourth Gospels Jesus is aware of John's activity and reacts to it but does not himself share that activity. Jesus and John have parallel but independent ministries.

Most English renderings of Matt. 4:12 refer explicitly to John's arrest, but the underlying Greek verb, *paradidonai,* is not normally so translated. It is usually rendered "deliver up" or "hand over" (see 5:25; 10:17, 19, 21) and becomes a semitechnical term in the announcements of Jesus' passion (17:22; 20:18; 26:2). In its participial form it becomes a fixed epithet for Judas Iscariot, "the one handing [him] over," that is, the betrayer (26:25, 46, 48; 27:3). Here, as in the passion announcements, the verb is used in the passive. Here, as there, we are dealing with the divine passive, that is, a statement in which the presumed actor is God but where the divine name is not explicitly mentioned because of a desire to show due reverence. Just as Jesus' passion conforms to God's plan of salvation, so also does John's arrest.

Matthew alone among the Gospels explicitly suggests that Jesus transferred his residency from Nazareth to Capernaum. The reason is not given. Perhaps a source anterior to Matthew and Luke placed the rejection at Nazareth at the beginning of Jesus' ministry (see Luke 4:16–31; contrast Mark 6:1–6). It was not necessary for Jesus to leave Nazareth in order to fulfill the prophecy of Isa. 9:1, since Nazareth appears to have been situated in the tribal area of Zebulun. Possibly the tribal boundaries had become very blurred by Matthew's day, and he thought of Nazareth as belonging to Asher's territory.

The quotation of Isa. 9:1–2 is truncated. Matthew omits the verbs of verse 1, retaining only the geographical terms, which are set by him in a series that climaxes in "Galilee of the Gentiles." Although the point is implicit only, we are surely on safe ground in assuming that Matthew's quotation is intended to remind his readers that the preaching ministry begun by Jesus in Galilee in fulfillment of Scripture would eventually issue in the mission to the Gentiles (28:18–20). Matthew does nothing further in his Gospel to develop the motif of Jesus as the light of the Gentiles, but it is possible that his substitution of "sat" for "walked" and "dwelt" in his rendering of Isa. 9:2 is meant to be reminiscent of Isa. 42:6–7, where the Servant of 42:1 (see Matt. 3:17; 12:18), the "light of the Gentiles," ministers to "those who *sit* in darkness."

The words "From that time Jesus began . . ." occur only here and in 16:21. From these respective contexts we learn that in each case the formula signals the opening of a new section in the First Gospel (see Introduction). Whereas the first three and a half chapters were concerned with the genesis, consecration, and testing of the Messiah, and thus with the question, "Who is Jesus?" the next section, which will continue up to 16:12, presents the Messiah's ministry to his people.

Matthew radically edits Mark's summary of Jesus' preaching, omitting both "the time is fulfilled" and "believe in the gospel" (Mark 1:15). He also omits the identification of this proclamation as "the gospel of God" (Mark 1:14). In place of "the kingdom of God," Matthew substitutes "the kingdom of heaven." Although Matthew occasionally retains the phrase "the kingdom of God" unchanged (compare 19:24 with Mark 10:25), he normally alters it to "the kingdom of heaven," apparently out of a desire to show reverence for the divine name (the ancient rabbis exhibit the same tendency). Since the verb here rendered "is at hand" refers normally to temporal rather than spatial proximity, we are justified in seeing in "the kingdom of heaven" a reference to the full establishment of God's rule. That is, in most occurrences of the phrase, "the kingdom of heaven" refers not to the space where God rules, "God's territory" (which one can "enter," 19:23–24), but to the activity of ruling itself. Jesus, repeating the warning uttered by John the Baptist (3:2), announces that God is about to establish his rule among those who have treated his sovereignty with disdain.

Called to Fish (4:18–22)

In this narrative of the call of the first disciples, Matthew carefully chooses his words so as to emphasize Jesus' regal authority. Luke's very different version of the event is placed by him at a different point on the story line. In Luke 5:1–11 Simon, James, and John (Andrew is not mentioned) are overwhelmed by Jesus' fish miracle and are thus moved to leave everything to follow the master. Moreover, there is preparation for the

29

event; Mark's story of the healing of Peter's mother-in-law is placed by Luke *before* the call story (Luke 4:38–39) and Jesus is already famous for his miracles (Luke 4:37) before he challenges Peter with the announcement, "From now on you will be catching people" (Luke 5:10, REB). Similarly, preparation is evident in John's version; Andrew is induced to follow Jesus by the testimony of John the Baptist, and he in turn convinces his brother by announcing, "We have found the Messiah" (John 1:35–41).

Matthew's story, taken over with only minor changes from Mark 1:16–20, presents a stark contrast to Luke's and John's. No attempt whatsoever is made to prepare for the event. We are not informed that the four fishermen were among those who heard Jesus proclaim the imminence of the kingdom (4:17). No summary statement concerning Jesus' miracles has yet been given. Nor is interest shown in any psychological reaction to Jesus on the part of those he confronts (contrast Luke 5:8–9). The call story is here reduced to its barest essentials: Jesus summons with irresistible authority, and the men respond with radical obedience.

Because of the important roles the fishermen had in the early history of the church, this story could have been framed as an explanation of their selection as leading apostles. The three call stories in Acts concerning Paul are clearly so designed: despite variations, all are intended to present Paul as the Apostle to the Gentiles par excellence (Acts 9:1–22; 22:3–21; 26:2–23). The call of the four in Matthew serves no such purpose. The word "apostle" is nowhere to be found. There is no hint of their future importance. Instead, they seem to represent all future believers whom Jesus irresistibly summons to follow him. It may not be necessary for all to leave professions and possessions behind (see the comments on 19:16–30), but all must leave their world behind and enter the new world into which Jesus invites them.

Implicit in the peremptory "Follow me!" is a profound theological perception, articulated by the Fourth Evangelist at John 15:16: "You did not choose me, but I chose you and appointed you that you should go and bear fruit and that your fruit should abide." It was customary for rabbinic students to seek a master and then choose to learn from him. At a certain level of reality it is undoubtedly true that we choose Jesus as our master. We choose to be present where he is proclaimed and his words studied. We choose to read the Gospels and ponder their sig-

30

nificance. At a deeper level of our being, however, we acknowledge, if only in retrospect, that the reverse has been true. In all our searching we were being sought. The one whom we choose is the one who first chose us.

The metaphor "fishers of men and women" is natural to the context. When Jesus confronted farmers, perhaps he challenged them to plant the seed of the gospel. Fellow carpenters may have been invited to build the community of faith. The metaphor of fishing has a raw edge, however. In Jer. 16:16 it seems, because of its parallel to hunting, to be a negative image, an image of judgment. In fact, if it were placed by Matthew beside 19:28, "You who have followed me will also sit on twelve thrones, judging the twelve tribes of Israel," we might well take it in the same way. It is far more likely, however, that it is intended positively; the fishermen are to catch men and women as fellow disciples of the master. As in the parable of 13:47, they are to spread the gospel net broadly and capture as many as they can for Christ and his church.

If modern readers feel some ambivalence in response to this metaphor, it is with good reason. It seems to encourage manipulation. We are probably more sensitive than prior generations to the evils of manipulation because we are aware of the subtleties of advertising's "hidden persuaders" and the role of "public image" in convincing others. There is no need for us to press the metaphor so far, however. It summons us to evangelism, and for evangelism to be real it must be nonmanipulative. People cannot be coerced into the kingdom. Our task is to share a faith that is exciting enough to be contagious.

Teaching, Preaching, Healing (4:23–25)

For Matthew, Jesus' teaching is of much greater significance than his miracles. Indeed, teaching takes precedence even over preaching the gospel of the kingdom. The First Gospel is less a manual on evangelism than a treatise on church life. Matthew is deeply concerned about the mixed state of the church. There are too many Christians whose lives do not match their profession. They have heard the gospel but have not heeded Jesus' teaching; they are quick to cry "Lord! Lord!" but slow to do what Jesus said (7:21–27). For the health of the church, Jesus' teaching about life in the kingdom must be given the fullest emphasis.

In Mark's Gospel the call of the first disciples is followed

31

immediately by the first miracle story, the exorcism of an "unclean spirit" (Mark 1:21–28). It is unlike the many other miracle stories in Mark in one respect: it emphasizes that the miracle worker is a teacher. As an introduction to the miracle, Mark reports that Jesus went into the Capernaum synagogue to *teach* and that "they were astonished at his *teaching*, for he *taught* them as one who had authority, and not as the scribes" (Mark 1:22). Mark makes no attempt whatsoever to illustrate this by quoting Jesus' teaching, however. Instead, he documents Jesus' authority as a teacher by relating the exorcism. Again the crowd is amazed, and again the amazement is related to his function as teacher: "What is this? A new *teaching!* With authority he commands even the unclean spirits, and they obey him" (Mark 1:27).

Matthew apparently disagreed vigorously with Mark's manner of presenting Jesus as a teacher, for this miracle story in the Second Gospel prompts Matthew's first major departure from Mark. Matthew omits the exorcism, retaining only Mark 1:22, which he places at the end of chapter 7. In its place he puts the Sermon on the Mount, the greatest compendium of Jesus' teaching to be found in the First Gospel. Only then, in chapters 8–9, does Matthew include miracle stories, most of which are taken from Mark. It is as if Matthew were saying to Mark: "Yes, you are right in emphasizing Jesus' authority as a teacher, but you are absolutely wrong in making that authority dependent on his miracle-working power. Miracles do not certify teaching; it is the other way round! In themselves miracles are ambiguous events. It is the authenticity of Jesus' teaching that renders his miracles significant. He is Messiah of Word before he is Messiah of Deed." Mark's statement concerning the amazement of the synagogue audience is consequently transferred by Matthew to the multitude on the mount: "Now when Jesus had finished saying these things, the crowds were astounded at his teaching, for he taught them as one having authority, and not as their scribes" (7:28–29, NRSV; cf. Mark 1:22).

This theological point is reinforced by the summary statement Matthew creates (partially in dependence on Mark 1:39) to introduce and conclude the five chapters containing the Sermon on the Mount and the miracles collection: "And he went about all Galilee, *teaching* in their synagogues and *preaching* the gospel of the kingdom and *healing* every disease and every infirmity among the people" (4:23). This summary is repeated with only minute changes at 9:35: "And Jesus went about all the cities and villages, *teaching* in their synagogues and *preaching* the gospel of the kingdom, and *healing* every disease and every infirmity." These identical statements bracket the two major sections, chapters 5–7 and chapters 8–9, and confirm the priority of teaching over healing. The priority is further confirmed by a significant change that Matthew makes at 11:4. In the Lukan parallel Jesus tells John's disciples, "Go and tell John what you have *seen* and *heard:* the blind receive their sight, the lame walk, lepers are cleansed, and the deaf hear, the dead are raised up, the poor have good news preached to them" (Luke 7:22). In Matthew, however, the order is reversed: "Go and tell John what you *hear* and *see.*" Since Luke's order is more appropriate to the context, which speaks of seeing miraculous events before hearing good news, it is probable that Matthew wishes to emphasize again that hearing must be given precedence. Only those who truly *hear* Jesus will be able to *see* the miracles as signs of the kingdom.

Matthew 5:1—7:29
The Messiah's Inaugural Address

The Sermon on the Mount, Matthew's first and longest collection of Jesus' teachings, plays a fundamental role in the First Gospel. Just as Jesus' sermon at Nazareth (Luke 4:16–30) is the frontispiece of Luke's two-volume work, setting the tone for the entire history, the Sermon on the Mount serves as the frontispiece of Matthew. It presents Jesus as Israel's ultimate, God-authorized teacher and sternly warns the readers that believing in Jesus means doing what he says (7:21–28). It thus anticipates the Great Commission with which the Gospel concludes, in which the apostles are charged: "Go, enlist all the Gentiles as *disciples, . . . teaching* them to observe everything I commanded you" (28:19–20). They are to be enlisted as disciples, not simply as believers, because their faith in Jesus must be actualized in their behavior.

The basic structure for the sermon was provided by Q, the double tradition used independently by Matthew and Luke (see Introduction). When Matthew's expanded version is compared

33

with Luke's brief Sermon on the Plain (Luke 6:20–49), it is clear that their common source contained a five-part discourse:

Blessings (and Woes?)	Matt. 5:1–12	Luke 6:20–26
Love of Enemies	Matt. 5:38–48	Luke 6:27–36
Judging Others	Matt. 7:1–5	Luke 6:37–42
Trees and Their Fruits	Matt. 7:15–20	Luke 6:43–45
Parable of the Builders	Matt. 7:24–27	Luke 6:46–49

From this outline it can be observed that nothing in the middle chapter of the Sermon on the Mount derived from the Q sermon. Certain passages, such as the Lord's Prayer, may have been drawn from elsewhere in Q, since they are found in other contexts in Luke.

The Setting (5:1–2)

Matthew's treatment of the Q sermon gives it more weight than it has in the Third Gospel. Luke places it at a less prominent point on his story line. Immediately following the appointment of the Twelve, Jesus comes down from the hills, stands "on a level place," engages in healing, and then addresses his disciples (Luke 6:17–20). By contrast, Matthew not only makes the sermon Jesus' first important act but he gives it a special significance by placing it on "the mountain." As we shall see in the comments on 28:16, the definite article is to be taken seriously in both passages. Although the Moses typology is not pressed by Matthew, because he regards Jesus as far greater than Moses, he apparently wishes his readers to see the Sermon on the Mount as a definitive interpretation of the Torah delivered to Moses on Mount Sinai.

The weightiness of the sermon is further emphasized by the introductory language: Jesus *sits*, the disciples *approach* him, and he *opens his mouth* and *teaches*. In these subtle ways Matthew indicates that he intends the Sermon on the Mount to be a *christological statement*. It not only tells Christians how to live but emphasizes the importance of Jesus. He is not simply "one of the prophets" (an opinion held by some, according to

34

16:14) but is the Messiah. He sits like a king on his throne, his disciples approach him like subjects in a royal court, and the king delivers his inaugural address, in which he lays out in considerable detail what life in his kingdom will be like.

It has consequently been proposed that the mountain of 5:1 is reminiscent of Zion, David's seat, rather than Sinai. Perhaps neither mountain is intended. In any event, it is important to recognize that Matthew does not represent Jesus as a lawgiver; Jesus does not annul the Mosaic law by substituting a new legal code. As we shall see in the antitheses of 5:21–48, the Matthean Jesus does not abrogate Torah but "fulfills" it by providing its proper interpretation.

The Beatitudes (5:3–12)

The question whether the beatitudes are best described as *eschatological warnings* or *entrance requirements* for those who wish to participate in the kingdom is still vigorously debated. Are they indicatives, testifying to God's grace, or imperatives, demanding obedient action? If scholars have difficulty reaching a consensus, it is probably because truth lies on both sides of the issue. We should understand Matthew's beatitudes both as expressions of eschatological grace and as implicit commands.

It is difficult to find an adequate translation for the word *makarioi,* the first word in each of the beatitudes. In Homer's Greek it was used to describe the immortals of Mount Olympus, but it gradually came to be used more commonly in secular ways with the meaning "How fortunate is . . ."—much as we might say, "How lucky are the wealthy!" On the basis of the secular usage, some modern translations and commentators render the word as "happy," as, for example, TEV: "Happy are the pure in heart" (5:8). It is even suggested that the original force of the word would be better captured in English by rendering it as "congratulations"—"Congratulations to the pure in heart, because they are going to see God!"

While such a nuance cannot be fully excluded in a Greek gospel, it is important to remember that Jesus spoke in a Semitic context. The meaning he intended in the original beatitudes undoubtedly reflects the function of *ashrē* in the Hebrew Scriptures, for example, Ps. 1:1, where the happiness is less subjective than objective. The man or woman who walks not in the

35

counsel of the wicked but delights in the law may or may not be happy in the sense in which this word is normally used in the secular world. The happiness derives from a right relationship with God (cf. Ps. 33:12, where such happiness is attributed collectively to the nation whose God is the Lord). For this reason it is probably better to retain "blessed" as the English rendering because of the word's religious associations.

The Poor in Spirit (5:3)

Because of the normal secular use of *makarios,* the opening beatitude in Luke's series must have sounded particularly paradoxical to Greek ears: "How happy are the poor" (Luke 6:20). What the beatitude means to say, of course, is that the poor, despite their present evil circumstances, will joyfully participate in the grand reversal that will occur when God's rule fully arrives. This is made more explicit by the corresponding woe given in Luke 6:24: "But woe to you that are rich, for you have received your consolation."

In Matthew's version the first beatitude is turned in a very different direction by the additional phrase "in spirit." Perhaps life experience convinced the Evangelist that the dichotomy of pious poor and wicked rich was a gross oversimplification. Despite the powerful tradition in Israel contrasting the piety of the poor and the godless arrogance of the wealthy, the wise did not forget that poverty too can breed injustice (Prov. 28:3) and disobedience to the commandments (Prov. 30:8–9).

At the heart of the poverty-piety equation lies a profound insight, however. The proud self-reliance that is fed by prosperity all too easily prompts forgetfulness of our dependence upon God (see Deut. 8:11–18). The poor, to whom less is given, are more likely to remain aware of the givenness of life than are the well-to-do who so naturally come to regard their blessings as deserved.

Matthew's version, although less "revolutionary" than Luke's, does not automatically *include* the rich, as if the beatitude read "Blessed are the humble, whether rich or poor." Neither, however, does it *exclude* them as in Luke's contrasting beatitude and woe. It can therefore be appropriated by the wealthy in an indirect fashion: "Blessed are the affluent who regard themselves as if they were poor, remembering humbly their dependence upon God and their subservience to his will."

"Poor in spirit" thus refers neither to those who are poor for

36

religious reasons (the voluntarily poor) nor to those who are deficient with respect to spirit (the dispirited) but rather to those poor who manifest the attitude (the "spirit") appropriate to their condition, namely, humble dependence on God's grace. An instructive parallel is provided by Isa. 57:15, where it is declared that God dwells with "the lowly of spirit" (see also Ps. 51:17).

"Theirs is the kingdom of heaven," an assurance granted both to the poor and to the persecuted (v. 10), brackets the main group of beatitudes and is perhaps to be considered as implicit in all of them. Modern readers need to be reminded that Matthew's "kingdom of heaven" is no more otherworldly than Luke's kingdom of God. Matthew simply prefers the reverential paraphrase that omits "God." Both Evangelists recognized that, while God's rule in heaven was eternal, that rule was not yet fully actualized on earth, and consequently the "coming" of God's kingdom on earth must be the burden of continual prayer ("Thy kingdom come," Matt. 6:10; Luke 11:2). The "poor in spirit" are "blessed" not only because of their *future* participation in God's kingdom but because of their *present* assurance of that blessedness. In this respect Jesus' beatitudes are performative: they not only speak of blessing but convey it because of the authority peculiar to Jesus.

Those That Mourn (5:4)

The Lukan parallel, "Blessed are you that weep now, for you shall laugh" (Luke 6:21, which is third in Luke's series), is defined by its opposing woe, "Woe to you that laugh now, for you shall mourn and weep" (v. 25). As in the first beatitude, Luke's version contrasts the haves and the have-nots, whose condition will be reversed in the coming kingdom. Again we are tempted to charge Matthew with domesticating Jesus' revolutionary rhetoric; in his version there is no longer any hint that the mourning concerns the plight of the oppressed poor. It has become customary for us to remove the beatitude farther from the world of economic struggle by individualizing its application. The recipients of the blessing are seen as those who mourn the death of loved ones or as those who mourn their own sins.

Here as elsewhere in Jesus' teachings the key to interpretation lies in the Hebrew Scriptures. The antecedent to this second beatitude, as to the first and perhaps to the series as a whole, is Isa. 61:1–4, where one is anointed with the Spirit to

37

bring good news to the poor and "to comfort all who mourn; to grant to those who mourn in Zion—to give them a garland instead of ashes, the oil of gladness instead of mourning, the mantle of praise instead of a faint spirit. . . . They shall build up the ancient ruins." From the context it is clear that this post-exilic prophecy was addressed to those who mourned the devastation of Israel and mourned therewith the disobedience that brought such punishment upon the nation (see Isa. 60:10).

The land of Israel was not devastated in Jesus' generation; indeed, it was reasonably prosperous. The prosperity was not equally shared, however. The enormous tax burden fell most heavily on those who could least support it. It was not uncommon for a poor farmer or a day laborer to sell members of his family into slavery to pay his debts. As in our own age, it was easy for the affluent to be unconcerned about the agony of the poor. There were many, nonetheless, who mourned the injustice of a system rigged in favor of the rich and powerful. In this beatitude the one anointed with the Spirit at the Jordan fulfills his God-appointed task of assuring the mourners that the God of justice is not asleep. The devastations wrought by human avarice and thirst for power will be remedied.

It is perhaps harder for modern Christians to appropriate this assurance, since the poor have continued to suffer for two millennia. We are too aware of the depth of human sinfulness to be optimistic that we can easily change their condition. But we are too convinced of God's bias in favor of the poor to abandon the effort. As we mourn our shared sinfulness, we receive assurance that our struggle for justice is not futile.

The Meek (5:5)

Since the third beatitude finds no parallel in Luke, it is possibly a "commentary word," added by Matthew as a means of interpreting the preceding beatitudes. It must have been easily recognized as a quotation of Ps. 37:11: "But the meek shall possess the land, and delight themselves in abundant prosperity." Here "meek" renders the Hebrew *anawim*. This word was often used as a virtual synonym for "poor" (and is so understood by the Greek translators of Isa. 61:1; see Luke 4:18). Such was not its basic meaning, as we see in Num. 12:3, where the adjective is used to describe Moses: "Now the man Moses was very meek, more than all men that were on the face of the earth." The corresponding Greek word *praus*, used to translate

38

Num. 12:3 and as a description of Jesus in Matt. 11:29; 21:5, defines the recipients of the third beatitude. Like Moses and Jesus, the meek who will inherit the earth are nonviolent people, who are humble and gentle in their dealings with others because they have humbled themselves before the greatness of God.

Probably Ps. 37:11 originally promised tenant farmers and the owners of small plots of ground that the oppression of the wicked rich would be terminated and they would gain their fair share of the soil. In Matthew's context the ambiguous term *gē* (soil? land? earth?) was probably understood in its broadest sense: "The meek will come into possession of the whole inhabited earth."

Whether this beatitude was intended to be taken so literally, however, may be doubted. Matthew himself seems to believe that the full establishment of God's kingdom will occur only after the dissolution of life as we know it (see 24:29, 38–41). He may therefore have understood "inherit the earth" as synonymous with "for theirs is the kingdom of heaven."

Hungering and Thirsting for Righteousness (5:6)

It is customary to regard "righteousness" here as a reference to personal ethics (hence the TEV rendering: "Happy are those whose greatest desire is to do what God requires"). There is much to be said in favor of this understanding. The First Gospel places heavy emphasis on personal righteousness (see 5:20; 7:21–24). Two considerations, however, count against it. First, it seems a little presumptuous to understand this beatitude as promising perfect righteousness to those who work hard at achieving it (TEV: "God will satisfy them fully"). Second, the metaphors of hungering and thirsting seem more apt with reference to a righteousness that is not subject to our willing and doing, the righteousness of God. Here we should think not of the "right-wising" righteousness of the ungodly of which Paul writes so eloquently in Romans but of God's saving righteousness as proclaimed by the prophets. "My righteousness [RSV: "deliverance"] draws near speedily, my salvation has gone forth" (Isa. 51:5). Isaiah 51:1 must be understood in the same way: "Listen to me, you that pursue righteousness [RSV: "deliverance"], you that seek the LORD" (NRSV). It is not their own righteousness that is the object of their yearning but God's.

If it is correct to understand the beatitude in this way

39

("Blessed are those who yearn for the manifestation of God's saving righteousness"), the distance between Luke's version and Matthew's is greatly diminished. In the Lukan parallel it is clear that this beatitude, like the first, refers to those who are literally hungry. The corresponding woe promises the well-fed that they will exchange places with the undernourished (Luke 6:21, 25). Like Luke, Matthew yearns for the establishment of social justice.

Among those who long for God to set things right are both those who themselves suffer hunger pangs and those who mourn over an inequitable distribution of goods and services that allows millions to starve on a planet capable of providing food sufficient for all. "How blest are those who hunger and thirst to see right prevail; they shall be satisfied" (NEB).

The Merciful (5:7)

Like the third beatitude, the fifth finds no direct parallel in Luke (but cf. Luke 6:36). As in the second, fourth, and eighth beatitudes, the verb in the second clause is to be seen as a "divine passive," that is, the unexpressed subject of the action is God: "Blessed are those who show mercy to their fellows, for God will show mercy on them."

The concept of mercy is very important to Matthew. In two important passages he inserts a classic statement from Hos. 6:6, "I desire mercy, and not sacrifice" (Matt. 9:13; 12:7). For this Evangelist, "mercy" is a broad term, including both compassion (e.g., 9:27; 15:22; 17:15; 20:30–31; cf. Luke 10:37) and forgiveness (18:33). As in the Hebrew Scriptures, mercy is less an attitude than an activity. Thus in Matt. 23:23 mercy, like justice and faith, is presented as something to be *done.*

Because of the form of the beatitude, one might think that mercy is motivated by the fear that otherwise God will withhold mercy (see James 2:13). Again we must regard the Old Testament background as constitutive of a correct understanding. The commonest credo of the Hebrew Scriptures appears first at Exod. 34:6 and is repeated (with minor variations) in many subsequent passages: "The LORD, the LORD, a God merciful and gracious, slow to anger, and abounding in steadfast love and faithfulness." The implicit assumption of passages in which human mercy is extolled is that the merciful imitate their God. This theme finds eloquent expression in the parable of Matt. 18:23–35, where the king,

40

representing God, asks the unforgiving servant, "Should not you have had mercy on your fellow servant, as I had mercy on you?" Compare Luke 6:36.

Possibly this beatitude was added as further comment on the condition of the poor, since *eleēmones* ("merciful") is related to *eleēmosynē* ("almsgiving," as in Matt. 6:2) and is often used of those who assist the needy. In this case it could be paraphrased, "Blessed are those who give compassionately to the poor, for they will be recipients of God's compassion."

The Pure in Heart (5:8)

The Greek adjective *katharos* means both clean, as in "a clean linen shroud" (Matt. 27:59), and pure, that is, unadulterated or unalloyed, as in "pure gold" (Rev. 21:21). Since "pure in heart" seems to reflect Ps. 24:4, our choice between "pure" and "clean" may be guided by our understanding of that passage. Since "pure heart" is there in parallel with "clean hands," one is inclined to regard the pure in heart as those who are innocent not only of moral failures ("clean hands") but also of evil intentions (the heart being understood as the seat of the will). Here would be included both the "adultery of the eyes" of Matt. 5:28 and other evil thoughts (15:19).

If such is the meaning, however, there are none who qualify for the blessing. As Paul reminds us, all have sinned and fallen short of the glory of God (Rom. 3:23). Either the psalmist is unduly optimistic about the perfectibility of the saints or he is using the term to designate something other than absolute moral perfection. Perhaps he means those who are innocent regarding the grosser sins (murder, adultery, theft). On the other hand, perhaps he is using the adjective in its other sense, "unalloyed." The same Hebrew root occurs in this sense in II Sam. 22:27: "With the pure thou dost show thyself pure," where there is no question of God being immoral when dealing with the immoral. Taken in this way, the pure in heart are those whose devotion to God is unalloyed. They are not double-minded (James 1:8); they do not attempt to serve both mammon and God (Matt. 6:24). Such an understanding accords well with the thesis enunciated by Kierkegaard in his book title *Purity of Heart Is to Will One Thing.*

The beatific vision promised to the pure in heart is probably eschatological; in the coming kingdom it will be their pleasure to see God face to face (see I Cor. 13:12).

41

The Peacemakers (5:9)

It is clear that "peacemakers" designates not those who live in peace, enjoying its fruits, but those who devote themselves to the hard work of reconciling hostile individuals, families, groups, and nations.

It is noteworthy that this beatitude was first uttered during the Pax Romana. By dint of military superiority the Romans had put an end to small wars between competing client states, had rid the Mediterranean Sea of pirates, and had greatly diminished brigandage on land. There was an absence of war except on the empire's frontiers. But peace in the Hebrew sense, *shalom*, harmonious cooperation aimed at the welfare of all, could not be established by the Roman legions.

The creators of *shalom* will deserve to be called the sons and daughters of God, because they have chosen to imitate his magnanimity. Remembering that he makes his sun rise on the evil and on the good, and sends rain on the just and on the unjust (Matt. 5:45), they strive to return good for evil and to love those they do not like. Where others build walls, they painstakingly construct bridges.

The efforts of peacemakers often seem utterly futile, but their work is never unsuccessful. Their living testimony to God's intended *shalom* keeps the vision alive.

Persecuted for Righteousness' Sake (5:10)

In Greek as in English the phrase "for righteousness' sake" is ambiguous. "For the sake of" can point either to the *cause* or to the *occasion* of persecution. Put in other words, it can refer to the motivation of the persecuted or of the persecutors. A similar ambiguity is presented by I Peter 4:16: "Yet if one suffers as a Christian." Here it is not clear whether the adversaries are hostile to the Christians' religion or simply resentful of their restrained behavior (see I Peter 3:14; 4:4). Christians would insist that their conduct was the direct product of their faith and would therefore regard the persecution as caused by their commitment to Christ, but their enemies in that polytheistic environment may have cared very little about their strange religious beliefs.

42

In Matthew's understanding, therefore, the beatitude may declare blessed either those who are maligned simply because of their good behavior as in I Peter or those whose faith in

Christ (for whose sake they are righteous) arouses antipathy. The latter seems the more likely. In this case the eighth beatitude anticipates the "on my account" of the ninth.

Persecuted Prophets (5:11–12)

The final beatitude differs in form from the first eight, employing the second person plural, as do all four Lukan beatitudes (Luke 6:20–23). The two versions probably do not represent varying translations of a common Aramaic saying but editorial activity on the part of the Evangelists or previous transmitters of the tradition. When such alterations are subtracted, the earlier version emerges as follows: "Blessed are you when they revile you and slander you because of me. Rejoice and exult, because your reward is great in heaven, for so they did to the prophets."

If this hypothetical reconstruction is correct, Matthew has introduced two interesting changes. First, the verb "persecute," already employed in verse 10, is introduced at two different points (it is absent from Luke's version). Second, the phrase "the ones before you" is appended to "the prophets." Matthew's intention can be glimpsed by comparing his revised beatitude with 23:34: "Therefore I send you prophets and wise men and scribes, some of whom you will . . . persecute from town to town" (see also 10:23). The Evangelist apparently regarded Christian missionaries who proclaimed the gospel to fellow Jews as standing within the prophetic tradition. A frequently hostile response was to be expected, in view of the tradition that Israel always persecutes its prophets (see II Chron. 36:15–16; Neh. 9:26; Acts 7:52). Matthew's version of the beatitude was probably prompted by the unhappy experience of Jewish-Christian missionaries. Christians who take their faith seriously and consequently are impelled to take a stand on moral issues and to support controversial or unpopular causes must expect to be ridiculed and maligned. Such hostility is unpleasant but not crushing to those who are convinced that God's approbation is more important by far than fleeting popularity. The solitary crusader finds solace in the dictum, "One with God constitutes a majority."

Let Your Light Shine (5:13–16)

Set between the beatitudes and the programmatic statement of verses 17–20, these sayings are best seen as selected and edited for the purpose of effecting a transition between the two weightier passages. The emphatic "you" with which the section opens ties it closely to the final beatitude: "You, who are persecuted for my sake, are precisely the ones who must function as salt." Similarly, the concluding saying of the group, in speaking about good behavior, points forward to the remainder of chapter 5, which will give illustrations of the conduct expected of Jesus' followers.

Three general observations may be made concerning the way in which the twin metaphors of salt and light function in these verses. First, the indicative is made the basis of an imperative. The categorical statements "You are the salt of the earth" and "You are the light of the world" are presented without justification (why?) or interpretation (how?). The implicit imperative is contained in the modifying phrase: "You are salt, yes, but for the earth, not for yourselves. You are light, but for the whole world, not for a closed fellowship." These verses are an anticipation of the missionary imperative with which the Gospel will close (28:18–20).

Second, the "you" is corporate: "You [plural] are the light [singular] of the world." This is seen by comparing the saying with Phil. 2:15, "among whom you shine as *lights* in the world." Each Christian is individually called to be such a light, but in Matt. 5:13–14 the community as a whole is challenged to fulfill its corporate mission of serving as salt and light for the world. Such a task cannot be accomplished by independent individuals. It is one we must work at together.

"The salt of the earth" has been naturalized into the English language as a designation for people we regard as especially good. This makes it all the harder for us to appreciate how strange the phrase must have originally sounded. We can perhaps catch its force better by substituting another seasoning: "You are red hot pepper for the whole earth!" In this way we are reminded that the statement refers not to *status,* as if it said "You are the world's ethical elite," but to *function:* "You must add zest to the life of the whole world."

The attached sayings, which have parallels in Luke 14:

44

34–35 and a more distant echo in Mark 9:50, are probably based on a Palestinian proverb concerning the uselessness of impure salt from which the sodium chloride has been leached. The point is unmistakable, as is also its modern application. Any church that adapts itself so completely to the secular world around it that its distinctive calling is forgotten has rendered itself useless. Its vaunted salt has become tasteless and uninteresting.

In the religion of ancient Israel it was assumed that God was not only the source of light for daily life ("Thy word is a lamp to my feet and a light to my path," Ps. 119:105) but light itself ("In thy light do we see light," Ps. 36:9). This is made more explicit by a New Testament writer: "God is light and in him is no darkness at all" (I John 1:5). Whereas Torah was seen as the primary mediation of God's light by rabbinic Judaism, Christians quickly ascribed this role to Jesus: "I am the light of the world" (John 8:12). Paul declared that he had glimpsed "the light of the knowledge of the glory of God in the face of Christ" (II Cor. 4:6).

In what sense, then, can the church be described as the light of the world? In a derived sense only. It is only as the church genuinely proclaims Christ as Lord, that is, not by mouthing theological platitudes but by manifesting his life in its life, that the church can truly be the light of the world (cf. II Cor. 4:5). The church needs to remember constantly that it is in fact not the light itself but only the window through which the light is to be seen. As Deutero-Isaiah makes clear, to be "a light for the Gentiles" means servanthood (Isa. 49:6).

This understanding seems opposed by the attached saying, "A city set on a hill cannot be hid," which appears to suggest that the church's role is inviolate. The context, however, strongly implies that the saying must be read as an imperative rather than as an indicative: "You must be like a city on a hill, like a lamp in full view." There may be times in dire persecution when the church can survive only by rendering itself invisible. Such occasions aside, it is called to visibility. The wish to be seen is all too human, however; it is fed by our insatiable vanity. Here the motive derives rather from a vivid awareness of the greatness of God. The church's good works are to function in the secular world as indelibly etched pictures of the Father's love.

It is entirely fitting that the first instance of Jesus' favorite

45

name for God, "Father," should occur in this passage. The God who is praised more highly by acts of generosity to the poor and by kindnesses performed for enemies than by the most eloquent prayers is better conceived as a caring parent than as an impersonal force. To call God "Father," rightly understood, is to conceive religious obligation in interpersonal terms. The Christian use of "Father" ought not to preclude the use of feminine images for God as found in the Hebrew Scriptures. The essential contribution of "Father" to our consideration of God is not masculinity but the metaphor of the loving parent.

Not to Destroy but to Fulfill (5:17–20)

This is perhaps the most difficult passage to be found anywhere in the Gospel. The difficulty pertains not only to ambiguity in certain key words such as "destroy" and "fulfill" but also to tensions between different clauses in the passage and between this passage and others in Matthew. Apart from a partial parallel for verse 18 in Luke 16:17, the material is peculiar to Matthew. The editor's hand is strongly suspected at a number of points, but there is little consensus among scholars concerning the origin of the separate parts.

Our starting point for uncovering Matthew's understanding of the passage must be the context in which he has placed it. It serves as a preface to the antitheses (vv. 21–48), which present Jesus as the God-authorized interpreter of the law. It must be assumed, then, that verses 17–20 are concerned with the relationship between Jesus and the law on the one hand and between his followers and the law on the other.

The central issue in the exegesis of verse 17 is the meaning of *plērōsai* ("fulfill"). It has been argued that, since Matthew regularly uses this verb with respect to the fulfillment of Old Testament prophecy (1:22; etc.) and because the verse explicitly includes "the prophets," the verb is used here in a salvation-historical way ("I am the fulfillment of what is prophesied in the law and the prophets"). This proposal, however, ignores the immediate context, which is concerned with the law and its proper observance.

A second solution focuses on the fact that "fulfill" is used by Paul in the sense of "do" or "obey," as, for example, in Gal. 6:2: "Bear one another's burdens, and in this way you will fulfill the law of Christ." This suggestion, however, requires that we take *katalysai* ("destroy") in the rare sense of "break" law, that is, transgress. When used with "law," "commandment," or something similar, this verb more often means "tear down," that is, render null and void, as in II Macc. 2:22, which praises the Maccabeans who "restored the laws which were about to be *abolished.*" It is most improbable that Jesus would have said, or that any early Christian would have thought he had said, "Do not think that I have come to transgress the law or the prophets; I have not come to transgress but to obey." That is, the "I came" sayings speak of Jesus' mission, and it is hardly likely that anyone, whether opponent or antinomian follower, would have conceived of Jesus' mission as intentional disobedience to as many laws as possible.

If *katalysai* means "abrogate," however, it is probable that *plērōsai* means "establish" or "confirm." The corresponding Hebrew word for "fill" is so used in I Kings 1:14, where Nathan says to Bathsheba, "I also will come in after you and *confirm* your words" (the Septuagint uses *plēroō* here). Accordingly, Matt. 5:17 anticipates a misunderstanding of the antitheses (vv. 21–48) as utterances abrogating laws found in the Mosaic code. We can paraphrase verse 17: "Do not suppose that my mission is to abrogate the law or the prophets' interpretation of the law; my mission is not to abrogate but rather to confirm the law and the prophets by interpreting Scripture in terms of God's ultimate will." Because of the inherent ambiguity in "fulfill," however, we cannot exclude the possibility that Matthew wished the verb to be understood in more than one sense.

The following verse (v. 18) appears to many commentators as so conservative that they have difficulty attributing it to Jesus. Since it has a parallel in Luke 16:17, some suggest that it does derive from Jesus but was meant ironically: "It is easier for heaven and earth to pass away than for the scribes to give up the tiniest detail of the Mosaic law." There is, however, little difficulty in ascribing the statement to Jesus once we recognize that it expresses the universal view of first-century Jews. A "high" view of the inspiration of Scripture was held by all, since God was seen as the ultimate author. The Sadducees, the Pharisees, the Essenes, and other sects, including the Jesus movement, disagreed vigorously about how various passages should be interpreted and applied, but there was no disagreement at the theoretical level. The shared assumption of the rabbis and the authors of the New Testament is that "Scripture cannot be

47

set aside" (John 10:36, NEB), because "all scripture is inspired by God" (II Tim. 3:16). This theoretical "fundamentalism" did not inhibit innovations in interpretation that in fact departed radically from the strict letter of the law. Many of the prescriptions of the Mosaic code had become dead letters by the first century, including the majority of death penalty rules. It was thus possible for Matthew to affirm the categorical statement of verse 18 while himself exhibiting remarkable freedom in altering jots and tittles in his scriptural quotations (see comments on 27:9–10).

The final clause of verse 18, "until all is accomplished," is puzzling. If it is correct to say that the function of the saying is to affirm a high view of Scripture, then neither the earlier clause "till heaven and earth pass away" nor this last clause points to a time when Scripture will no longer be valid. It probably looks forward to the complete actualization of God's will (cf. 6:10), not to the revocation of the law.

Verse 19 is still more puzzling. It appears to support a Judaism more stringent than the Essene rigorists of Qumran. It is not impossible that a few Jewish Christians held such a position, but there is no firm evidence in favor of this hypothesis, and it does not explain how Matthew, who supported a nonconservative view of the Sabbath and divorce rules (see comments on 5:31–32 and 12:1–8) could ascribe such a statement to Jesus. It seems better on the whole, therefore, to treat verse 19 as further comment on verse 18. Seen in this light, verse 19 speaks not of the rigor of application of Torah's rules but rather of respect for Scripture. At some point in the history of Jewish Christianity a critical stance toward the Scriptures was adopted by the Ebionites, who dared to propose that in the law of Moses there were false passages that derived not from the Holy Spirit but from human sin. The roots of this movement may have lain in the first century in a rejection of animal sacrifices. While the Jewish observance of Torah tolerated many variations, it is likely that any who abrogated laws forthrightly instead of by interpretation were regarded as threatening to the very existence of Israel. It seems likely, therefore, that verse 19 was aimed by Matthew at radical Christians who challenged the authority of Scripture. If this is the case, however, it is significant that these radicals are not denied a place in the age to come but are simply assigned the lowest rank in the kingdom. Why? Because, for Matthew, the truest test of belonging to

48

Jesus (and thus having a place in the kingdom) is ethical behavior (see 7:21–28). To reject the inspiration of certain passages of Scripture was, for Matthew, a serious theological error but not a mortal sin.

It can be argued that such an understanding of verse 19*a* is invalidated by verse 19*b;* here practice is in view as well as theory. Perhaps verse 19*a* was cherished by conservative Jewish Christians, who added verse 19*b* as commentary in support of their observant life-style. In this case Matthew may have retained the verse as a whole, either because it came to him in this form and he was reluctant to emend it or because he himself was favorably disposed to an orthodox observance on the part of Christian Jews. In any event, such observance was, for him, subordinate to the fulfillment of the love command and "the weightier demands of the law—justice, mercy, and good faith" (23:23, REB).

Verse 20 serves not only as the conclusion to this programmatic statement regarding the authority of the law but as the introduction to the antitheses that follow. The key word is "righteousness." Here there is no question of an allusion to God's saving righteousness or the righteousness based on faith. Attention is focused entirely on human obedience to God's will. The reference to the scribes and Pharisees constitutes a backhanded compliment. The righteousness of Jesus' followers must exceed even that high level attained by the rigorist opponents. As the antitheses and other teaching will demonstrate, however, it is not a question of Christians being required to exceed the righteousness of the scribes and Pharisees *quantitatively.* The difference must be *qualitative.* Their obedience must be to the spirit of the Torah as revealed to them by Jesus, not merely to the letter as strictly construed by their opponents. Not bad theology (v. 19) but bad behavior (including sins of omission) will result in exclusion from the kingdom.

At first glance this passage seems to be so intimately related to first-century Judaism that it has little to say to modern Christians. As children of the Enlightenment we can no longer innocently espouse the high view of Scripture that locates its authority atomistically in its jots and tittles. We do, however, affirm its authority as a whole, and, like Jesus, Matthew, and Paul, we *interpret* its requirements by subordinating many specific injunctions to broader principles such as the love command.

49

A few decades after the writing of the First Gospel, Marcion shocked the church by denouncing the Old Testament as the product of demons, unfit for Christian use. Marcion's view was soundly rejected, but his spirit still haunts the Gentile church. We tend to affirm the Hebrew Scriptures in principle but slight them in practice. The ghost of Marcion can be exorcized only by those who inform themselves concerning the rootedness of the New Testament in the Old. Matthew 5:17–20 reminds us of that rootedness.

Six Antitheses (5:21–48)

Before we examine the six antitheses individually, it is incumbent upon us to consider the role played by the passage as a whole. Although Mark and Luke contain parallels to some of the material, none of these are given in the antithetical form found in Matthew ("You have heard that it was said to those of ancient times. . . . But I say to you . . ."). Matthew intends in this section to present Jesus' interpretation of God's will in a way that contrasts it with previous understandings.

It is much disputed whether the antitheses are intended to place Jesus over against other Jewish interpreters of Torah or over against Torah itself. In favor of the latter is the probability that "it was said" is a divine passive, referring not to Moses or later interpreters but to God's word. From 5:17, however, it is clear that Matthew himself believes that Jesus' teaching is not opposed to the Old Testament but "fulfills" it. The antitheses are therefore to be seen as presenting Jesus' teaching as authentic interpretation of the word of God over against all previous understandings. For Matthew, the authority of the statements introduced by "But I say to you" is not at all comparable with the hermeneutical authority of other Jewish interpreters of Scripture (see 7:29); it is the authority of the Messiah, the Son of the living God. Jesus' teachings are thus not simply interpretations of Torah but supplementary additions. At one level Jesus' teachings thus constitute a messianic Torah which for Christians will take priority over the Mosaic Torah (see 28:20, "teaching them to observe all that I have commanded you"). For Matthew, however, they must be perceived at a deeper level as Jesus' authoritative interpretation of God's will as revealed in the Scriptures.

Underlying the first and fifth antitheses as well as the sixth is the primacy of the love command as the key to the Scriptures. It can be argued that the same is true of the others as well. Although Matthew would insist that Jesus' status authorized him to enact new legislation for the people of God, this does not seem to be his point here. What Jesus teaches brings to articulation the ultimate purpose of God for his people expressed in Torah. For example, while the Mosaic principle of "an eye for an eye" sets limits to legal revenge as a way of setting things right, God's own way with Israel far exceeded such retributive justice and summoned his people to overcome evil with good. In the fifth antithesis Jesus neither abrogates the law of talion nor places another law beside it but speaks in nonlegal terms of the life of the kingdom of God, where behavior must be directed by a higher principle. What is presented in this passage is not a new law but a call to a new way of life.

Anger (5:21–26)

The first two antitheses are related to the Ten Commandments. It is not in the least suggested that these commandments are outdated. In each case it is a matter of probing deeper behind the commandment to the will of God. The prohibition of murder (Exod. 20:13) expresses God's intention that humans do no damage to one another. Its explicit reference is to the extreme case, but the underlying purpose of God condemns the anger that gives birth to physical violence and murder.

If *mōre* ("fool") is not also a transliteration of a Semitic word but is proper Greek, it may simply represent some transmitter's attempt to render *raka* (a term of abuse of uncertain origin) intelligible to Greek-speaking Christians. It is clear in any case that these two clauses condemn abusive language. An insulting remark to a fellow human being is not to be lightly regarded. "I tell you this: every thoughtless word you speak you will have to account for on the day of judgement" (Matt. 12:36, REB).

Although verses 23–24 may originally have had a broader application, in their Matthean setting they surely refer to outbursts of anger, particularly those addressed to another member of the Christian fellowship ("your brother or sister"). The juxtaposition with verse 22 is instructive. While angry outbursts are denounced in verse 22 as punishable by hellfire, in verses 23–24 the forgiving grace of God comes to the fore. While anger is damnable, genuine repentance permits reconciliation with God as well as with the injured sister or brother.

51

These verses are illustrative of the hyperbolic power of Jesus' teaching. The advice is eminently impractical. It was surely not possible to leave unattended even a cereal offering in the busy altar area, let alone a pair of pigeons or a lively goat! The point is dramatically made. Whatever our gift to God, its acceptance is conditional upon honest repentance concerning the ways in which we have injured our neighbors.

The concluding verses of the passage are drawn from Q's parable of the defendant (see Luke 12:58–59). In Luke's setting the parable constitutes an eschatological warning: "You are like a man who is about to be thrown into debtors' prison. While he is free, he can choose to placate his creditor, but soon it will be too late. God's rule is about to come. There is still time for repentance, but you must seize the opportunity before it is too late."

It is frequently argued that Matthew has taken the eschatological parable and converted it into prudential advice. Just as one must be ready to seek reconciliation with a fellow Christian whom one has insulted, so must one be quick to pacify a non-Christian opponent before the chance is lost. This is a possible interpretation, but it may do less than justice to Matthew's context. If anger is really viewed by Matthew as a mortal sin, punishable by the fires of Gehenna, then it is unlikely that he pedestrianizes the parable as suggested. Verses 23–24 are concerned ultimately with reconciliation with God; verses 24–25 simply repeat in parabolic language the point of the preceding verses.

As Jewish commentators are quick to point out, there is nothing particularly novel in this first antithesis. There are numerous parallels in the Jewish wisdom tradition as well as in rabbinic literature. Why, then, the antithetical form? It seems probable that, for Matthew, Jesus' authority lay less in the novelty of his teaching than in its determined focus on interpersonal relationships. Whereas other teachers stressed both ritual and ethical obligations, Jesus was remembered as strongly subordinating the former to the latter. Twice Matthew reminds us of this in his use of Hos. 6:6: "For I desire mercy, and not sacrifice" (Matt. 9:13; 12:7).

Lust (5:27–30)

52

Like the first antithesis, the second is based on one of the Ten Commandments and seeks to go beyond its literal sense to a deeper intention. The commandment (Exod. 20:14) as originally understood referred to a special kind of theft; the adulterer was guilty of depriving a married man of his exclusive rights respecting his wife and so of rendering her "damaged goods." That a wife was viewed as a piece of property is reflected also in the Tenth Commandment (Exod. 20:17), where "house" is the general term covering everything a man owns and "wife" is the first-named possession.

The Hebrew verb for covet apparently means more than simply "idle envy"; it implies intentional planning to obtain something for oneself (see Exod. 34:24; Micah 2:2). This nuance is left behind in the Greek translation of Exod. 20:17, which employs *epithymein* ("desire") as in Matt. 5:28. What is prohibited in the Greek version is not the formulation of a plan for seducing a neighbor's wife but the mental act of lusting after her. Why was this regarded as evil? It is possible that lust was regarded as in some way a violation of a woman's purity, but more probably it was condemned as the ultimate cause of adultery, as frequent allusions in the wisdom literature testify ("Can a man carry fire in his bosom and his clothes not be burned?" Prov. 6:27).

As in the first antithesis, there is nothing novel in the second. Jewish literature was well supplied with warnings that in sexual matters the thought is father to the deed. If there is novelty, it is provided by the context in Jesus' ministry and in the subsequent fellowship of the church, where women were not avoided as seductresses but welcomed as sisters. As Matthew's text makes clear, it is therefore no sin for a man to look at a woman. What is prohibited is looking at a woman "for the purpose of lusting after her" (a more literal translation of v. 28). The new relationship with women among Jesus' followers required of men a new kind of self-discipline. Verses 29–30, drawn from a very different context in Mark 9:43–48, are placed here by Matthew (and the order is inverted so as to present the lustful eye before the incontinent hand) for the purpose of stressing the rigor with which male followers of Jesus must master their sexual desires.

Divorce (5:31–32)

The topic of divorce will be treated more fully at its parallel in 19:3–12. Here it will be sufficient to emphasize that Jesus does not abrogate any Old Testament law in this third antithe-

53

sis. Divorce is not commanded in Deut. 24:1 but acknowledged and regulated. Jesus' teaching proposes to go behind the regulation of divorce to God's intention regarding marriage. The implicit assumption of verse 32 is that God intended monogamy, not seriatim polygamy.

As we shall see in 19:3–12, what is especially interesting in Jesus' treatment of divorce is his concern for the rights of women. Whoever divorces his wife, "except on the ground of unchastity" (see comments on 19:9), deprives her of her right to support and thus renders it probable that she will enter into a second marriage in order to survive.

Interpreters of these verses must be careful not to translate into legal statute what is presented as an evangelic counsel. That is, it ought not to be treated differently than the other antitheses, none of which has been or can be converted into law. While it points to God's ultimate will for men and women, there are numerous instances in which a marriage is no longer real, whether because of infidelity, neglect, abuse, failure to communicate, or simply unresolved tensions regarding reciprocal expectations. While every effort should be made to redeem fractured marriages, some must be acknowledged as beyond repair. In such cases divorce may be not only the lesser of two evils from the point of view of God's ultimate will but also a positive step.

Oaths (5:33–37)

In 23:16–21 Jesus inveighs against a false casuistry that too subtly distinguishes between binding and nonbinding oaths. In 5:33–37 it is the reckless use of oaths that is condemned. The quotations, which appear to be rather free renderings of Lev. 19:12 and Ps. 50:14, do not *require* oaths but insist on truthfulness in oath taking and fidelity to promises made. Again, Jesus does not contradict these requirements but points beyond them. It is God's will that men and women be absolutely truthful in their words and faithful to their commitments. Where such truthfulness and faithfulness are present, they cannot be enhanced by oaths of any sort. Certifying one's word by appeal to heaven, earth, Jerusalem, or one's head (such oaths were in fact current in contemporary Judaism) simply raises suspicion concerning the depth of one's commitment to the truth and to promises. Compare James 5:12.

54

The first-century Jewish philosopher Philo roundly condemned those who unashamedly invoked the name of God in pointless oaths. He would be equally shocked by the constant misuse of "God" by many Christians. If Jesus was distressed by the linguistic habits of those who swore by their own head, he would surely be disgusted by our careless use of holy names.

Nonviolent Resistance (5:38–42)

The fifth antithesis has been of immense importance in the ongoing debate over pacifism and the obligations of Christian politicians. For Matthew, the issue was more circumscribed, since the emperor alone had the right to declare war or conclude a peace with his enemies. The appropriateness of violent resistance to Roman hegemony, however, had been a matter of existential import to Christians of Palestine in the years leading up to the First Jewish Revolt of 66–73 C.E. Indeed, there is good reason to believe that the sayings of this group, in their original Aramaic form, constituted comments by Jesus on the incipient Zealotism that already in his day was fomenting armed rebellion against Rome. Although the sayings are expressed in general terms, they obtain a special force when seen against the background of political unrest.

In its earliest form the law of talion ("an eye for an eye") was intended to set strict limits on the right to revenge: one could not avenge the loss of an eye by violently exacting two eyes from the enemy. By Jesus' day Jewish law further restricted vengefulness by substituting monetary compensation for the removal of the aggressor's eye. Jesus' substitution is far more radical: he challenges his followers to renounce their right to retaliation. They are to suffer loss without seeking recourse in the courts. The verb *anthistēmi,* usually rendered "resist" in verse 39, has no forensic connotation; it is used more often in a military context with the sense "offer armed resistance." In relation to the law of talion, however, it clearly refers to the legal right to sue for compensation from an aggressor. In view of the reference to litigation in verse 40, this is the most natural understanding of "Do not resist an evil person" in verse 39*a.* Such an interpretation is by no means rendered unlikely by verse 39*b:* "But if one strikes you on the right cheek, turn to him the other also." It has been noted that a slap on the right cheek is either the blow of a left-handed person or, as seems more likely, a backhanded insult effected with the right hand. Such an insult was recognized by Jewish law as an injury for

55

which compensation could be sought before a judge. The Gospels contain no narratives in which Jesus' followers are insulted in this way, but there is no reason to doubt that their abandonment of families and vocations attracted insults from some who had no sympathy for such "irresponsible" piety. In any event, in the postresurrection mission to Israel those who proclaimed the crucified Messiah must often have been maligned and insulted (see 5:11–12). This saying challenged the Jewish-Christian missionaries to accept insults without attempting to retaliate.

It is possible, however, that the principle of talion is here attacked in its more common, nonlegal sense of "tit for tat" (as reflected in the bumper sticker, "I don't get mad—I get even"). Did Jesus have in mind the thirst for revenge against Rome? Is the blow to the right cheek a figurative expression, referring to the humiliation administered to the proud Jewish people by Roman procurators and their subordinates?

At first glance verse 40 appears to counsel passivity in litigation. If someone uses legal means to deprive you of your tunic, do not resist him; give him your cloak as well and go naked! According to Luke, it is a matter of robbery: if someone forcibly takes your cloak, give him your tunic as well. Since nudity is the result in both versions, we should regard this as another instance of Jesus' use of figurative language. Matthew's "legal robbery" and Luke's violent theft may refer to the plundering of Jewish Palestine by Rome and its puppets through onerous taxation. In response to the revolutionaries' call for armed resistance, Jesus counsels, "Let the oppressor have his way, and leave vengeance to God."

The political interpretation of these verses is supported by verse 41: "If someone in authority presses you into service for one mile, go with him two" (REB). The verb *aggareuō* is technical. It is a Persian loanword, having reference originally to compulsory service in the postal system. It is found in a number of imperial documents in connection with the commandeering of pack animals and grain boats for the conveyance of military supplies, and it occurs as a loanword in the rabbinic literature with the same meaning. There is ample evidence that soldiers were frequently guilty of abusing their right to impress local civilians and that this was a cause of great resentment. Apart from Matt. 5:41 the only allusion to the practice in the New Testament is found in Mark 15:21 and parallels, where Simon of Cyrene is impressed into carrying Jesus' cross. The word itself is vague in terms of the impressing authority. It is not necessary to assume that the saying has in mind only soldiers of the occupying army. Presumably Herod's soldiers could have exercised this power. It is significant, however, that the unit of distance here specified is the Roman *milion* (from which our English "mile" is derived), not the Greek *stadion* that is used for longer distances everywhere else in the New Testament (e.g., Luke 24:13; John 6:19). Even Josephus, in his many discussions of Rome's war with the Jews, consistently uses *stadion*, never *milion*, despite the fact that he writes in Rome under the patronage of the emperor! Jesus' use of "mile" would have sounded as foreign to his audience as "kilometer" in an American conversation. His hearers undoubtedly perceived therein an allusion to the occupying power.

In the face of widespread resentment against the practice of impressment, Jesus urged not only willing compliance but double service. How radical! How provocative! Freedom fighters in his audience must have regarded him as a traitor. Those who knew him better undoubtedly recognized that his point was well taken. Resistance to Rome was futile, and the nourishing of bitter resentment was self-destructive. By going a second mile, one could demonstrate to the oppressor one's inner freedom from oppression.

The final saying in the group, verse 42, has nothing to do with the theme of nonretaliation. Matthew apparently found it in his source (see Luke 6:30) and retained it despite the fact that it does not fit his context well. It reflects the ancient Israelite tradition of benevolence as reflected, for example, in Deut. 15:7–8. It is in harmony with its setting at one important point: like the preceding sayings, it demands a self-renunciation that suppresses one's natural inclination to defend one's rights and protect one's possessions.

What is the function of the sayings about nonresistance? It is clear that, in their present form at least, they do not contemplate the conversion of the oppressor. Turning the other cheek is not urged as a strategy for altering the enemy's behavior. Jesus' passion amply illustrated the truth that this is seldom an effective strategy. Nor is the practice of nonretaliation prescribed as a technique for spiritual self-improvement, although this may well prove to be an important by-product. In the context of 5:21–48 these sayings purport to interpret God's will

57

for the human community. Although not intended to be taken in their most literal sense, as is most evident in verse 40, neither are they to be domesticated by reduction to "merely figurative language." They are meant to shock the imagination and instill a profounder insight into God's intention. The old ways of retaliation and self-protection must give way to a gentler, more magnanimous approach to those we deem enemies. The rationale is provided by the final antithesis.

Love for Enemies (5:43–48)

In the closing verses of Matthew 5 the costly imperatives of the antitheses reach their climax. We are commanded to regard enemies as neighbors whom we must love. It was hard enough to be told that we must not lose our temper (vv. 21–26) and must renounce the right to retaliate (vv. 38–42); now we are instructed that we must love those who hate and harm us. Why does Jesus expect the impossible of us?

It is not surprising that many commentators have seen the imperatives of verses 21–48 as intended to drive us to despair by proving how incapable we are of satisfying God's righteous demands and thus to force us to recognize our total dependence on God's saving act in Christ. While this is an appropriate response to the passage, it is improbable that Matthew understood it in this way or that Jesus intended his teaching to be so understood. Nor did the early church treat the command to love enemies as impossible. In the centuries of state persecution, Christian writers frequently appealed to the fact that their brothers and sisters loved their persecutors and prayed for them.

A proper understanding of this climactic imperative requires that several issues be addressed: (1) What kind of enemy did Jesus have in mind? (2) What did he mean by love? (3) What is the theological grounding for this command that so cuts against the grain of normal human emotions?

Since these verses belong together with those concerning nonretaliation, it is probable that Jesus did not intend that "enemies" be taken exclusively as either national or personal. Both the Roman soldier who impressed a Galilean into carrying his pack one mile and the persecutor who publicly insulted a disciple with a backhanded slap on the cheek were to be loved, not hated.

What does it mean to love a person whose hostility threatens us and whose behavior we heartily abhor? A first step in understanding is to recognize that Jesus was not referring simply to feelings. This can be seen from another difficult text, Luke 14:26: "If any one comes to me and does not *hate* his own father and mother and wife and children and brothers and sisters, yes, and even his own life, he cannot be my disciple." Clearly, Jesus did not mean by *hate* that every follower nourish intensely hostile feelings toward himself and all his close relatives. The saying uses hyperbolic language to talk about setting priorities. In the same way *love,* while not excluding feelings, was probably intended to refer primarily to *actions.* To love the Roman soldier or the face-slapping persecutor was not to experience "warm, fuzzy feelings" but to act in a positive way. As stressed in the title of a book of sermons by Frederick Speakman, love is something you do. Regarding the soldier and the persecutor, Jesus made concrete suggestions: walk a second mile, turn the other cheek. For the rest he leaves it up to our imagination to discover in each situation what loving personal or national enemies will require of us in reactive behavior. What is absolutely clear from the examples he gives is that the Christian response must be *abnormal;* to *negative* attitudes and acts we must make *positive* responses.

What does it mean to *pray* for one's enemies? Presumably, it means more than simply entreating God to alter their attitudes and behavior, although such prayer is by no means excluded. Praying for enemies involves a serious attempt to see them from God's point of view. We cannot earnestly pray for enemies without acknowledging our common humanity; they too have been created in the image of God, and no behavior, no matter how nefarious, can erase that image. Honest prayer thus compels us to make the distinction every parent must make continually between the child and his or her behavior: "I love you, but I don't like what you are doing." We cannot pray fervently for our enemies without reminding ourselves that the God who is able to love us despite our disobedience is able to love also those who hate and abuse us. Seeing our enemies in the light of God's love is the first step toward surprising them with positive acts.

This clearly broaches the third issue, concerning the theological grounding of love for enemies. Before we examine Matthew's understanding of the issue, however, we must deal with a misconception. It is frequently suggested that the command

59

to love one's enemies is a piece of prudential advice: doing good is an effective way of disarming an enemy and making of him or her a friend. That this was a very early understanding is demonstrated by the comment in *Didache* 1:3: "Thus you will have no enemy." A similar perspective may be reflected in Prov. 25:21–22 (quoted by Paul in Rom. 12:20): "If your enemy is hungry, give him bread to eat; and if he is thirsty, give him water to drink; for you will heap coals of fire on his head, and the LORD will reward you." Whipping an enemy with kindness will humiliate the enemy and produce a positive benefit. Certainly, the conversion of an enemy to a friend is sometimes a happy by-product of a Christian's obedience to the command, but this is by no means a necessary result and does not supply the motive for obedience. The Christ whose enemies nailed him to a cross asks us to love our enemies without expecting any miraculous change of heart. The same, of course, is true if the enemies are not personal but national or "class" (racial, sexist, or economic oppressors). While love for enemies expressed in nonviolent resistance may in some situations prove to be an effective weapon in the struggle for social justice, nothing in 5:43–48 suggests that this hope provides the motivation for obeying the command.

Perhaps this explains why Jesus chose to use the verb "love" in his teaching about the treatment of enemies. Both Jewish and Greco-Roman ethicists advocated nonresistance as an appropriate response with anticipated benefits. Josephus, who reflects both Jewish and Stoic ethics, puts a speech in the mouth of Agrippa on the theme "There is nothing to check blows like submission." Love, however, is not a weapon or tool. Genuine love has no ulterior motive; its purpose is simply to benefit the one loved, regardless of the response.

Matthew's theological grounding of love for enemies is simple and unequivocal: "so that you may be children of your Father who is in heaven." The ultimate sanction appealed to is not the *will* of God ("Do it, no matter how difficult, because God commands it!") but the *nature* of God. It accords with God's nature to treat good and evil magnanimously, as reflected in the natural realm, where the blessings of sunshine and rain are bestowed on good and bad alike (v. 45).

60 In Semitic thought, "son" (or "daughter") is used figuratively to express the idea that a person shares the quality or nature of the source specified. Jesus named James and John

"sons of thunder" (Mark 3:17). Barnabas was known as "son of consolation" (Acts 4:36) and Judas as "son of perdition" (John 17:12). In I Thess. 5:5, Paul writes, "For you are all children of light and children of the day." To become a son or a daughter of God, then, is to participate in the divine nature by reflecting God's unconditional love for all made in God's image.

The reference to sons and daughters of God in verse 45 takes us back to verse 9, the beatitude for the peacemakers, who "shall be called children of God." In Jewish tradition, God is the peacemaker par excellence (Ps. 46:9). To love one's enemies is to share in God's peacemaking and thereby to manifest the glory of God.

This high calling is contrasted in verses 46–47 with the way of the world. Even the despised tax collectors love those who love them, and the Gentiles greet those they hold in affectionate regard. In human society everywhere, it is normal to return love for love and hate for hate. Christians who do no more than this fade into the background; they cannot serve the world as salt and light (v. 16). Their righteousness does not exceed that of the scribes and Pharisees; they do not manifest the life of the kingdom of heaven (v. 20).

If the command to love one's enemies strikes many a Christian as a burden grievous to be born, the imperative with which Matthew 5 ends seems totally unreasonable: *"You, therefore, must be perfect, as your heavenly Father is perfect."* (In the Greek of this verse the *you* is emphatic; it serves to highlight the contrast between those addressed and the tax collectors and Gentiles of the preceding verses.) Is it not presumptuous to suggest that any mortal can be perfect as God is perfect? The English word is defined as meaning "entirely without fault or defect." Christians have made such a claim for Jesus but not for any of his followers, ancient or modern. The form of the imperative (in the Greek it is in fact a future: "You will be perfect") classes it as different in kind from the simpler command "Swear not at all" (v. 34). It is a strong invitation to participate in God's perfection by imitating the divine behavior. It is modeled, perhaps, on the very similar declaration of Lev. 19:2 (cited in I Peter 1:16): "You shall be holy; for I the LORD your God am holy." It is not that the holiness of men and women is identical to God's holiness but that there will be a correspondence. Just as we are made in the divine image, so is it open to us to imitate God's moral earnestness.

61

Luke has interpreted this difficult verse by employing a different adjective: "Be merciful, even as your Father is merciful" (Luke 6:36). A similar statement appears in the Jewish Talmud: "Be compassionate and merciful as He is compassionate and merciful" (*Shabbath* 133b). In view of the context in Matthew's Gospel, it seems likely that "perfect" is intended specifically with reference to love. Matthew's understanding seems to be: "You are to be all-embracing in your love, in imitation of God, whose love embraces all."

Our response to the challenge of verses 43–48 is ambivalent. On the one hand, we acknowledge that love for enemies constitutes a sublime ideal and that as Christians we ought to submit ourselves to its pressure. On the other hand, we are troubled by the suggestion that we should love those who despise and injure their neighbors, whether or not we happen to be their victims. The question of II Chron. 19:2 strikes a very responsive chord in us: "Should you help the wicked and love those who hate the LORD?" Righteous indignation at the misdeeds of others is not only a very natural and powerful human emotion but an important one as well; it is the power behind the struggle for justice. Does Jesus expect us to suppress our indignation and treat only positively those who misuse and abuse their fellows?

The sayings of Matt. 5:43–48 by no means suggest that we should condone evil or appease bullies. Both judgment and mercy are expressive of God's nature. This passage warns us against usurping God's exclusive right to vengeance. Our responsibility is a more modest one; we are to communicate the reality of God to the world by reflecting God's all-inclusive love.

Dietrich Bonhoeffer demonstrated by his behavior that he by no means condoned the evil deeds of the Nazis, yet he treated his prison warders cheerfully, with the respect due them as fellow human beings.

Personal Piety (6:1–18)

If Luke 6:20–49 represents, as many scholars have argued, a short Q sermon, then Matthew 6 has been inserted into the middle of it, that is, between Luke 6:36 ("Be merciful, as your Father is merciful") and Luke 6:37 ("And do not judge, and you will by no means be judged"). The purpose of this added material is to provide further illustrations of what is meant by the

better righteousness of Matt. 5:20. Having presented new interpretations of old laws in the antitheses, Matthew now turns to
three religious practices by means of which the better righteousness can be exhibited: charitable donations, prayer, and
fasting.

The first thing to notice about this section is that the religious practices here discussed are traditional to Judaism and are
presented matter-of-factly. The passage does not exhort readers
to give, pray, and fast but assumes that they will. What is urged
is, rather, a particular manner of fulfilling these traditional obligations.

The three subsections share a common structure. Each begins with a negative example involving the practice of "the
hypocrites" and their reward and concludes with a suggestion
for the proper fulfillment of the obligation, together with a
promise of heavenly reward. To the whole is prefixed a general
introduction (v. 1). The repetitive pattern serves to reinforce
the basic principle enunciated in the opening verse: the *manner* in which religious obligations are fulfilled is more important
than the fulfillment itself. That is, the passage does not intend
to suggest that giving, prayer, and fasting are the most important acts of a proper piety but simply offers these three as
illustrations of the principle, which can then be applied to other
religious practices.

The principle is very simple. True religion consists in acknowledging that God alone is God. True piety, therefore, com-
prises practices that give form and substance to this
acknowledgment. Giving, prayer, or fasting, if undertaken for
the praise it will win from others, is basically irreligious, and the
practitioner who pretends to be seeking to glorify God but in
fact is intent only on seeking self-glory is a hypocrite.

Charitable Donations (6:1–4)

In contrast to the surrounding Greco-Roman society, Jews
regarded giving money to the poor as a religious obligation and
not merely a humanitarian one. This perception was grounded
in the Torah (Deut. 15:11).

In many societies, ancient and modern, the ability to give
away money or possessions in significant amounts is perceived
by all as a sign of power. The "biggest man" (or woman) is the
one who can give away the most. It was only natural that many
in Jesus' day, as in our own, were eager to have others in the

63

community observe their largesse and ascribe to them a social status befitting their benevolence. The times and places of giving were chosen with visibility in mind (v. 2). Using a hyperbolic metaphor, Jesus declared that such persons announced their gifts with a trumpet blast, as when announcing the presence of the king (see II Kings 11:14). They get what they want; their public service is paid for in full by the adulation of the witnesses. It is hypocritical, however, to claim that such giving is a *religious* act. Those who wish to honor God by their giving must exclude this secular reward by striving for secrecy. Again Jesus employs a powerful illustration: "Don't let your left hand know what your right hand is doing."

The promise "Your Father . . . will reward you" troubles some readers, because it seems expressive of salvation by merits. Two considerations count against such an understanding. First, the implicit context of this and other sayings in the Sermon on the Mount is the gospel of the kingdom (4:23). The imperative is based on the indicative, not on the promise of reward. Second, the language of rewards is not to be taken in so literalistic a fashion. It really says no more than the parabolic affirmation, "Well done, good and faithful servant; . . . enter into the joy of your master" (25:21). The one who gives secretly will receive approbation from the God who seeks such acts of worship.

There appears to be a tension between this passage and the verse that sounds the theme for 5:17—7:12: "Let your light so shine before others, that they may see your good works and give glory to your Father who is in heaven" (5:16). The tension disappears when we recognize that 5:16 uses the second person plural, not the second singular as in 6:1–4. Since individuals may be tempted to glorify God by letting their good deeds be visible, it is better to let the community accept responsibility.

Private Prayer (6:5–15)

Despite the reference to the synagogues in verse 5, this passage is concerned not with corporate worship but with private prayers. It was customary for Jews to pause in whatever they were doing about 3 P.M. in order to offer prayers in conjunction with the evening sacrifice in the temple. The structure and the content of such prayers were not prescribed, since they were essentially private. The "hypocrites" are reproached for performing their prayer obligation in the most visible way on a wide street where there will be many passersby. Apparently their private prayers are ostentatious even within the synagogue. In effect, their prayers are directed not to God but to their human audience, and from humans alone will they get their reward.

The allusion to the "inner room" in verse 6 is therefore not at all intended to suggest that Jesus was opposed to corporate worship in the synagogue. Nor should it be taken in a literalistic fashion, since many of his hearers lived in simple homes that lacked such a private room. The point is clear: private prayer must be directed to God alone.

Verses 7 and 8 are probably taken from a different source; they disturb the pattern by adding a second negative example, that of the Gentiles who "pile up empty phrases" or "babble," because they think there is greater effectiveness in wordy prayers. What is here castigated is not length and repetition as such (Jesus is represented as repeating his prayer in Gethsemane, 26:39–44) but a mistaken attitude that regards prayer as a magical means of manipulating God into doing our bidding. Such prayer is truly pagan, unmindful of the nature of God. "Be not rash with your mouth, nor let your heart be hasty to utter a word before God, for God is in heaven, and you upon earth; therefore let your words be few" (Eccles. 5:2; cf. 7:14). Authentic prayer acknowledges that God is concerned about our needs before we ask him (see v. 32).

The Lord's Prayer (6:9–13). The symmetry of the thrice-used pattern of 6:1–18 is marred by the insertion at this point of the Lord's Prayer. In terms of content, however, the insertion is apt. Matthew quite properly regards the Lord's Prayer as a model for private prayer. There is not the slightest suggestion that this prayer was presented by Jesus to his disciples as a *substitute* for the corporate prayers of the synagogue. Eventually the fledgling religion developed its own distinctive liturgy (albeit one heavily dependent on Jewish antecedents), and in this liturgy the Lord's Prayer later had its place, but it was not so in the beginning. When *Didache* 8:3 instructs readers to recite the Lord's Prayer three times a day it undoubtedly reflects the Jewish practice of engaging in private prayer in the early morning, midafternoon, and at sunset (cf. Dan. 6:10).

In Luke's introduction to the Lord's Prayer a disciple asks Jesus, "Lord, teach us to pray, as John taught his disciples" (Luke 11:1). Since it must be assumed that Jesus' disciples were

65

not irreligious renegades, we can take for granted that they had been taught Hebrew and how to read the synagogue prayers. What Luke's introduction suggests, therefore, is that Jesus was asked to provide his followers with a model for private prayer, just as other leading teachers and John had done. The possession of such a prayer would distinguish Jesus' disciples from others.

The most noticeable characteristic of the Lord's Prayer is its Jewishness. Almost every phrase has its parallel in Jewish literature. Conspicuously missing are distinctively Christian elements, such as a prayer for the return of Jesus Messiah or a supplication for his church. There is not even an appended "In Jesus' name we pray." For this reason it has been proposed that the Lord's Prayer can be prayed by both Jews and Christians. Indeed, one rabbi has said that the prayer might well have become a part of the synagogue liturgy had Jesus remained a charismatic Jewish teacher. This is not at all to suggest, however, that the Lord's Prayer is simply a collage of borrowed liturgical phrases. It has its own integrity, reflective of the teaching of Jesus. In this sense it is genuinely Christian.

The prayer divides itself into two main sections, consisting of "you" and "we" petitions respectively. The opening lines establish the context in which the requests of the second part are to be understood. The opening words of Matthew's version of the prayer, "Our Father, the one in the heavens," can be found in formal Jewish prayers. Luke's simple one-word address, "Father," reflects Jesus' characteristic way of addressing God as *abba* (see Mark 14:36; Rom. 8:15; Gal. 4:6). The term was an affectionate one used by small children, but it was also employed occasionally by adults when speaking to a respected older man. It seems not to have been used in prayer. A growing consensus of scholarship maintains that, while Jesus' idiosyncratic use of *abba* cannot be used to demonstrate that he regarded himself as the Father's "Son" in a unique sense, it does bespeak his theology of the gracious Father who had sent him to eat with tax collectors and sinners. If there had been nothing unusual or significant in Jesus' use of *abba*, Mark and Paul would not have bothered to transliterate it for their Gentile Christian readers. Although Matthew here elaborates the address, he by no means intends to obscure Jesus' emphasis on the gracious Father. He uses "Father" for God more frequently than any other New Testament writer.

The opening petition, "Hallowed be thy name," is in some

66

respects the most difficult to understand and appropriate. "Name," of course, is simply a way of referring to God. When Deut. 12:11 alludes to "the place which the LORD your God will choose, to make his name dwell there," the author means that *God* will dwell in Jerusalem. The problem resides rather in the verb. Most English versions, from Wycliffe to the latest translations, employ the subjunctive mood, which is in itself ambiguous. Does the subjunctive express a wish or a hope, just as "Long live the king!" means "I hope the king lives to a ripe old age"? Or is it simply a polite way of expressing an indirect command? Whatever the intentions of the translators, the Greek is clearer than the English. Matthew and Luke employ not the subjunctive but the indirect imperative: "Let your name be sanctified." This indirect command should be taken as a strong entreaty, just like the direct command "Give us this day our daily bread."

Although the petition is addressed to God, the passive voice of the verb leaves it unclear whether God or humans are to sanctify the name. Scholars are probably correct in seeing here an instance of the divine passive, where God is the assumed subject of the action, but this is not made explicit because of a desire to show due reverence (see Matt. 16:21, where "be raised" can only mean "be raised by God," as in Acts 2:24). Support for this position is found in the parallelism between this line and the next, "Let your kingdom come."

It was the theologian Karl Barth who most forcefully insisted that the idea so dear to liberal Christians of building the kingdom of God on earth is an expression of bad theology. The biblical writers make it clear that only God can bring his kingdom; our task is to pray for it and wait. In response to Barth's theology Robert McAfee Brown produced a fine parody of a familiar hymn (*The Bible Speaks to You,* p. 211):

> Sit down, O men of God,
>   His Kingdom he will bring,
> Just as and when and where he will,
>   You cannot do a thing.

Despite the parody, Barth's point remains valid. We cannot build the kingdom of God on earth, because even our best efforts toward peace, justice, and community are compromised by sin. Only God can bring the ultimate transformation that includes the radical annulment of sin.

If the petition "Let your kingdom come" urges *God* to

67

establish his rule on earth, it is probable that "Let your name be sanctified" is aimed in the same direction. It could be restated in more direct language as "Sanctify your name." It entreats God to demonstrate his holiness by compelling all to acknowledge his sovereignty. Since God's holiness is sometimes mentioned in passages that deal with his activity as judge (e.g., Ezek. 38:22–23), it is even possible that in this first petition of the Lord's Prayer, Jesus taught his disciples to implore God the judge to tarry no longer: "Exhibit your holiness by calling the court to session! Let the last judgment begin!"

Like the first two, the third petition is eschatological in its scope. While the prayer "Help us to do your will" is one that every Christian should pray daily, that prayer should not be confused with the entreaty that God act in accordance with his ultimate will for the world.

Because of the eschatological focus of the first half of the Lord's Prayer, some scholars argue that the second half should be seen in the same light: the bread for which petition is offered in verse 11 must be the renewed manna of the end time, or perhaps the bread of the messianic banquet; the forgiveness of verse 12 is acquittal at the last judgment; the testing of which verse 13 speaks is that of the messianic woes which will precede the golden age. This interpretation of the "we" petitions has not won many followers. It seems far more probable that the prayer for bread should be taken in its most literal sense because of its emphasis on today: "Give us today our bread for the morrow." While the first half of the prayer anticipates the grand reversal at God's termination of history, the bread petition addresses the very real need of the poor in the meantime. Ulrich Luz reminds us that this prayer had in mind not all classes of people in Palestine but more especially the day laborers, whose pay, received at the end of each working day, enabled their families to eat on the following day. If they were not hired (see Matt. 20:1–16), their families went hungry. How shall economically secure Western Christians pray such a prayer today? Not by allegorizing the bread and allowing it to stand for all of our material needs. The only authentic way for us to pray this petition, Luz insists, is by identifying with the poor, especially those of the third world, for whom subsistence is a daily concern (Luz, *Matthew 1–7*, p. 383).

Standing behind the supplication for forgiveness is the centuries-old conviction that the God of Israel is a forgiving God

(Exod. 34:7), a conviction that found eloquent expression in the synagogue liturgy of Jesus' day. When the author of Psalm 103 counted up the blessings for which his soul should bless God, forgiveness of iniquity was placed first on the list. Psalm 130:4 observes that God's readiness to forgive is cause for awe. Despite this celebration of God's forgiving nature, however, both the Hebrew Scriptures and later Jewish tradition were fully aware that divine forgiveness is not automatic. God is not indulgently tolerant of moral failure, as when a doting grandfather smiles at the childish pranks of beloved grandchildren. Moreover, forgiveness is not unconditional; it assumes repentance on the part of the recipient. There is no point in a man begging for divine forgiveness for having beaten his daughter in a drunken rage if he has no intention of dealing with his drinking problem. Behind actual forgiveness, however, lies readiness to forgive, an attitude that is constant in God but inconstant in us. Our determination *not* to forgive another is a form of impenitence that blocks the flow of divine forgiveness. The Lord's Prayer and the attached commentary (vv. 14–15) do not suggest that God's pardon is doled out in proportion to the number of times we have forgiven; it is, rather, that we must genuinely repent our hardness of heart before expecting to receive God's mercy (see Eccles. 28:1–6 and Matt. 18:21–35).

In Jesus' eschatological prayer the petition for forgiveness, like the prayer for the poor, concerns "in the meantime." In the interim between Jesus' announcement of the kingdom and its final arrival those who follow him and pray "Thy kingdom come!" must anticipate the full establishment of God's rule by manifesting God's readiness to forgive.

The third of the "we" petitions is likewise for the meantime. It has sometimes been treated as an eschatological entreaty: "Bring us not into the severe testing of the messianic woes" (see Rev. 3:10). This interpretation should be rejected, because the word that means "testing" or "temptation" lacks the definite article. Taken at its most literalistic level, "Lead us not into temptation" is decidedly misleading. As James insists, "Let no one say when he is tempted, 'I am tempted by God'; for God cannot be tempted with evil and he himself tempts no one; but each person is tempted when he is lured and enticed by his own desire" (James 1:13–14). Moreover, it is unrealistic to pray "Let me not be tempted." The Gospels testify that Jesus himself was put to the test at the Jordan and in Gethsemane,

69

and the Epistle to the Hebrews affirms that our Master "in every respect has been tempted as we are, yet without sinning" (Heb. 4:15). To be human is to face temptation daily. Many temptations, having been dealt with, no longer exercise any real power over us, but others remain troublesome throughout our lives. And there are unanticipated temptations that catch us off guard and find us vulnerable. It is probable, therefore, that the way most Christians have understood this petition, while in tension with its surface meaning, is nonetheless correct: "Grant me strength to resist temptation."

The complement to the third "we" petition, "but deliver us from evil," since it is missing from Luke's version, is probably an early attempt to understand the puzzling line "Lead us not into temptation." It can be understood to mean "Rescue us from the evil one," since the same words are used to designate the devil in Matt. 13:19, 38, and the devil is known as the tempter (Matt. 4:3). Another attractive proposal is that reference is here made to the Jewish doctrine of the evil impulse, a power within us all that lures us into doing what we know to be wrong. It is more likely, however, that "evil" is used here in a very general sense. Such seems to be the understanding of *Didache* 10:6: "Remember your church, Lord, to deliver it from all evil."

Nineteen centuries have elapsed since Jesus first gave us this prayer which entreats God to sanctify his name by establishing his kingdom and compelling all to conform to his will, and the prayer remains unanswered. Unless humans are so foolish as to destroy the world by nuclear warfare or unrepentant pollution, it seems likely that human history will continue for centuries to come. Does this render Jesus' kingdom prayer irrelevant? The solution to the puzzle is provided by Matt. 12:28: "But if it is by the Spirit of God that I cast out demons, then the kingdom of God has come upon you." Jesus believed that the full establishment of God's rule lay in the future, but the assurance of that future event lay in the present. In his ministry the kingdom of God had already dawned. Barth was right; we must not be so foolish as to think that we can bring in the kingdom. But we can be signs of the kingdom. Only God can truly and ultimately sanctify his name, but we can anticipate God's action by marching to a different tune than the secular world around us. God's name is hallowed as we witness to his nature by caring for the poor, forgiving those who have trespassed against us,

70

and resisting temptation. Implicit in the direct prayer, "Thy kingdom come!" is the indirect prayer, "Let thy will be done in, through, and by me, that I may become an effective sign of the dawning kingdom."

Fasting (6:16–18)

The third illustration of the correct attitude in religious observances is provided by fasting. Among Jews, fasting had an ancient and honored position as a means of exhibiting humility before God and thus securing his favor. David fasted in the hope that God's anger might be averted and the offspring of his adultery with Bathsheba would be allowed to live (II Sam. 12: 22). Yom Kippur, the Day of Atonement, required fasting of all (Lev. 16:29; see Acts 27:9). It became a general practice for Palestinian Jews to join in regular community fasts when the fall rains did not appear on schedule; the later the rains, the more frequent the fasts.

The teaching of verses 16–18, which assumes that fasting will occur, may refer to the fasts for rain as well as to Yom Kippur. Even in the context of community obligations a religious practice must be engaged in for religious motives and not for the sake of winning the community's approval. The true fast is invisible, because it involves the inner self, in accordance with the advice of Joel 2:13: "Rend your hearts and not your garments."

The Right Use of Money (6:19–34)

Matthew's second large insertion into the sermon consists of individual sayings (vv. 19–24) and one longer section (vv. 25–34), all of which are concerned with a believer's relationship to the workaday world of gaining and spending money. The point seems to be that a believer's attitude toward money is another illustration of the "better righteousness" demanded of Jesus' followers (5:20).

What Do You Treasure Most? (6:19–21)

One of the most noticeable characteristics of the human species is its proclivity to collect things. Apart from a few groups such as the African pygmies, who must carry on their backs whatever they own, humans everywhere collect "treasures" and assign status to one another on the basis of what has been

71

acquired. In some societies one is judged by one's livestock, in others by the possession of precious metals and rare stones. In a money economy the acquisition of financial assets becomes the primary goal for any who aspire to a higher status. Once achieved, this higher status can then be displayed to community view in luxury cars, sumptuous homes, rare jewelry, and fine paintings—to name only a few of our collectibles!

These verses challenge the equation of a person's worth with his or her acquisitions. Treasured clothing (a woman's dowry often consisted, in part, of expensive textiles) is vulnerable to insects. Wooden chests and books are subject to destruction by worms. Treasures that cannot be eaten can be stolen. The list could have been extended: livestock can become diseased, stored grain can spoil, and, in our day, the stock market can plunge. Those who assess their own worth and that of others in terms of acquired treasures render themselves exceedingly vulnerable to the vicissitudes of life. Jesus' followers are instructed to avoid such insecurity by accumulating an invulnerable treasure consisting of kindnesses performed for the glory of God.

The Generous Eye (6:22–23)

The ancients regarded the eye not as a window through which light entered but as a lamp that projected light and thus grasped the external world. The statement "The lamp of the body is the eye" thus constituted a truism. It is used, however, in a parabolic way to tease the mind into apprehending a profounder truth. "If your eye is *haplous,* your whole body will be illuminated." The word *haplous,* meaning literally "single" or "simple," was not normally used with "eye."

Matthew takes his cue from the use of "evil eye" in Jewish literature. In Prov. 23:6; 28:22, "evil eye" refers to an envious, grudging, or miserly spirit, while "good eye" connotes its opposite: a generous, compassionate attitude. Matthew infers that the *haplous* eye is the equivalent of "the good eye" of Prov. 22:9: "He who has a bountiful [lit., good] eye will be blessed, for he shares his bread with the poor." Taken in this way, verses 22–23 seem to mean: "Just as a blind person's life is darkened because of eye malfunction, so the miser's life is darkened by failure to deal generously with others." The person who extinguishes compassion, "the lamp of the body," consigns himself or herself to a twilight existence.

72

God or Money? (6:24)

Mammon is an Aramaic word meaning "money" or "possessions." In itself it is neutral, as is indicated by the fact that in Luke 16:9, 11 it is modified ("mammon of unrighteousness," KJV, and "unrighteous mammon," RSV). Why was it not translated? Apparently it was felt that it could in this way be presented more forcefully as a false god, an idol. A similar rhetorical move is made in English when we capitalize the expression "the Almighty Dollar." There was no pagan god called Mammon.

Our materialistic civilization ought to be well aware of the bewitching power of money and possessions, but acquisitiveness has become so much a part of the air we breathe that we lack the distance necessary for a proper critique. We piously affirm that we have chosen to serve God, not mammon, but in our daily life it is mammon that sets our priorities and determines our choices. We would like to show a more bountiful eye toward the poor, but we cannot, because we need so much for ourselves. We plan to be more charitable in the future, but at the moment there are too many things we have to buy. We work overtime or at a second job rather than spend time with our children, because there is so much that we want to get for them.

Not with our minds but with our lives we have treated Matt. 6:24 as if it were a parallel to 22:21: "Render to mammon the things that are mammon's, and to God the things that are God's." To God belongs one hour on Sunday. Mammon gets the rest!

Don't Be Frantic About Necessities! (6:25–34)

Of all the passages in the Bible about trust in God, this is probably the most beloved. Why does it move us more powerfully than the straightforward advice of Phil. 4:6 ("Have no anxiety about anything, but in everything by prayer and supplication with thanksgiving let your requests be made known before God")? Its power is related to its poetic character. Whether or not the original lines as uttered by Jesus in Aramaic constituted prose or poetry is still debated, but undisputed is the fact that the passage moves in accordance with a poetic logic that is very different from the prosaic logic of our everyday world.

73

Taken at face value, the passage abets irresponsibility and laziness. Indeed, one can well imagine that the religious enthusiasts of Thessalonica who abandoned their vocations in the expectation that the church would provide for them (II Thess. 3:6–13) may have been encouraged to do so by hearing these words of Jesus.

Furthermore, it is not true to say that all birds are adequately fed and that all lilies reach their fullest beauty. Droughts and other catastrophes cut short the lives of both birds and flowers as well as of humans who trust in God. It simply is not the case that those who seek first the kingdom of God find invariably that all things necessary for life are added to them. And how unwise it is to counsel "Do not be concerned about tomorrow" (Matt. 6:34). Careful planning can avoid the worst effect of drought and plague. Compare Prov. 6:6.

We can defend the passage against some of these criticisms by remembering its original context. Jesus' closest disciples abandoned their vocations in order to be with him full-time, to learn from him and to share his work of announcing God's kingdom. They became as dependent on God's providential care as the birds and the flowers. After Easter, the passage was probably treasured and transmitted primarily by missionaries who went from village to village spreading the good news of the resurrection. Their commitment to the gospel rendered them dependent on local hospitality, through which God cared for their needs. Matthew, however, sets the passage not in chapter 10, which deals with itinerant missionaries, but in this section of the Sermon on the Mount that addresses the right use of money. The passage thus serves as commentary on the sayings about treasures, generosity, and mammon and addresses Christians generally, both rich and poor.

The passage can be appropriated by all when it is read as poetry instead of prose. "The birds of the heaven" and "the lilies of the field" become larger than life. They are not models to be imitated but powerful symbols of God's providential care. It is irrelevant that some birds starve and some lilies fail to mature. The rhetorical development of these symbols draws our attention away from our frantic pursuit of the necessities of life to a calmer vision of God's bountiful care in the natural world.

74

The focus on divine providence permits several complementary readings of the text, each of which is legitimate in its own way. An *ecological reading* allows the symbols to direct our gaze at the marvelous interdependence of the myriad life forms on Planet Earth, and invites us to reconsider the relationship that links human beings to other living things. In our frenzy to provide ourselves with so much in excess of basic needs, we have allowed our economics and technology to get out of touch with the needs of the environment. God's care for birds and lilies is interfered with by our pesticides and acid rain. A proper appreciation of divine providence as reflected in the balance of nature can assist us to amend our ways.

A *social justice reading* of the text recognizes the possibility that in its original use by Jesus the passage may have been addressed not only to the disciples who had made themselves poor for the sake of the kingdom of God but also to the involuntarily poor. Like the birds, the poor did not sow or gather into barns but were dependent on uncertain wages as day laborers (see Matt. 20:6–7) and on charity. The passage assures the poor that in God's sight they are of more value than birds and lilies, whose life exhibits God's continuing care. Yet how is God's care for the poor to be experienced? Not by manna from heaven but through human instruments. The affluent, who have no need to be concerned about daily needs, are summoned by the passage to identify with those who must be so concerned and to seek ways of incarnating God's bias in favor of the poor.

A third reading of the text can perhaps be designated *celebrative*. The passage invites us to consider how the lilies of the field reflect the glory of the Creator. Nature does not prove God's existence, but for those to whom the self-disclosing Lord of the universe has been revealed, the wonders of nature are a cause for celebration. Even greater cause of joy is to be found, however, in our relationship to the heavenly Father who knows our needs before we ask (v. 32 looks back to v. 8). To enter into this passage is to rejoice in the power and love of God.

What kind of commentary does this passage offer on the preceding sayings concerning acquisitiveness, miserliness, and our idolatrous devotion to mammon? It helps us to view our money matters from a more distanced perspective. Despite the assurance of verse 33, we know that our money problems will not all be solved by an unquestioning confidence in God. Even Paul, whose confidence in God was unbounded, often went hungry and without shelter (II Cor. 11:27). What Paul learned from his deprivations was that God was greater than his needs

75

(see Phil. 4:11, 13). By "seeking first his kingdom and his righteousness" we do not adopt an otherworldly view of economics and money, but we assess their usefulness in relation to other more serious matters, such as the ecological plight of the planet and the deprivations of the poor.

Judge Not! (7:1–6)

The word "judgmentalism" does not appear in all dictionaries, but it names a phenomenon we know all too well. Judgmentalism is a social sin; it is the habit of constantly finding fault with what others say and do. It is a disease of the spirit. The critic arrogantly assumes a superiority that entitles him or her to assess the failings of others.

In this passage Jesus declares that the higher righteousness of the kingdom of God (5:20) involves the resolute renunciation of our proclivity to judge others more harshly than we judge ourselves. Just as obesity can be cured only by persistent dieting, so the insidious self-indulgence of faultfinding can be mastered only by rigorous discipline.

Having inserted all the material of chapter 6 into the middle of the shorter Q sermon, Matthew now returns to his source. In the earlier collection, the passage about judging others probably occurred immediately after the section on loving enemies, which concluded with a call to imitate God's compassion (Matt. 5:48; Luke 6:36). It is in response to God's overwhelming mercy that we renounce the habit of harshly judging others. Matthew is well aware of this connection, as is indicated by his later inclusion of the parable of the unforgiving debtor (18:23–35). Just as we forgive because we have been forgiven, so we are generous in our judgment of others because God has dealt generously with us. Matthew's new context also implies this, since the section on judging is now preceded by a passage that celebrates the generosity of divine providence.

At first sight the words "Judge not, that you be not judged" seem to constitute an absolute prohibition. Under no conditions can a follower of Jesus presume to pass judgment on the behavior of another. This understanding seems to be reflected in Paul's appropriation of the teaching: "Therefore you have no excuse, whoever you are, when you judge others; for in passing judgment on another you condemn yourself, because you, the judge, are doing the very same things" (Rom. 2:1, NRSV).

From other passages, however, it is clear that Paul not only expected but insisted that Christians pass judgment on one another. The cohabitation of a man with his stepmother was not to be tolerated (I Cor. 5:1–5). Apparently Paul distinguished between sins that threatened the moral health of the Christian community and those that in his opinion were much less serious. A similar distinction is made by Matthew. In 18:15–17 a situation is envisaged in which one Christian has seriously injured another. No clue as to the nature of the trespass is given, but it must be grievous, since, in the absence of repentance and reconciliation, the offender is to be excommunicated. Similarly, in 7:15–20 readers of Matthew's Gospel are warned to be on guard against false prophets, whose identity is revealed in their behavior. Clearly, Christians are to judge such persons and hold themselves aloof from their false prophesying. Indeed, the saying about not giving dogs what is holy or casting pearls before swine (v. 6), whatever its origin, assumes the necessity of making judgments concerning who are to be regarded as "dogs" or "swine" and therefore unworthy of "holy things."

These various passages suggest that we cannot totally abstain from judging one another. What, then, is intended by the prohibition of 7:1? Two misconceptions must be avoided. First, it is not simply a matter of prudential advice: "People will treat you as harshly or as generously as you treat them." While such counsel is sound, it is far more likely that the verb "you will be judged" is a divine passive, referring to God's judgment. Second, it would be erroneous to take the opening statement to mean, "If you tolerate the sins of others, you will escape the last judgment unscathed." No such easy evasion can have been intended either by Jesus or by Matthew! The following verse indicates that it is a matter of severity: If you harshly judge others, you must expect to be judged harshly by the judge of all. What this means, of course, is that those guilty of the sin of judgmentalism must expect to render account for this particular form of self-indulgence as for others. In the context of the gospel, however, this hateful habit takes on a still darker hue, because it is expressive of ingratitude. After God has dealt so graciously with our manifold shortcomings, how can we dare to treat others in such a mean-spirited fashion! (See 18:23–35.)

In Matthew's Gospel the word "hypocrite" usually refers to the Pharisees and their scribes. No such allusion should be seen here (cf. Luke 6:42). The verse reminds us that there is inevita-

77

bly an element of hypocrisy in all hypercriticism; the critic has to pretend that he or she is not guilty of similar (if not identical) faults.

It is neither desirable nor possible to silence all criticisms of others at home, at work, at church, and elsewhere. Being the fallible creatures that we are, we very much need criticism to help us treat others better and to enable us to become more productive members of the team. This passage reminds us that destructive criticism is counterproductive. Harsh and petty faultfinding becomes a corrosive chemical that erodes relationships wherever people have to work together to achieve common goals.

Ask! Seek! Knock! (7:7–11)

On first impression, these verses appear to be exceedingly naive. They seem to promise categorically that we can get anything we pray for as long as we pray with sufficient tenacity and intensity. On the basis of these sayings, radio and television evangelists assure us that we can pray successfully for a million dollars if only we follow their recipe for prayer and "cooperate with the Lord" as we pursue the goal.

The New Testament makes it perfectly clear that prayer is not intended as a means of manipulating God into satisfying our selfish desires. Indeed, even unselfish prayers for healing may go unanswered. Paul informs us that he prayed three times that his "thorn in the flesh," apparently some physical affliction that presumably affected his work, should be removed, but the answer he received was simply "My grace is sufficient for you, for my power is made perfect in weakness" (II Cor. 12:9). In Gethsemane, Jesus prayed earnestly, "My Father, if it be possible, let this cup pass from me," but concluded, "Nevertheless, not as I will, but as thou wilt" (Matt. 26:39).

A first step toward a less naive understanding of the verses can be made when we observe how Matthew has appropriated them. This little section concludes the long string of imperatives that constitute the core of the Sermon on the Mount from 5:21 to 7:6. We have been asked to forgo anger and retaliation, to love our enemies and forgive those who have injured us, and to control our criticism of others. How can we fulfill all these demands and manifest the higher righteousness of the kingdom? These verses remind us that for us this is impossible, but

78

with God all things are possible (see 19:26). That is, only by persistently asking, seeking, and knocking at heaven's door through prayer will we find grace to obey these impossible demands. Solely through tenacious dependence on God's graciousness can we deal graciously with those who provoke a negative reaction in us.

Encouragement is provided by an analogy with human fathers who, despite being evil, nonetheless deal generously with their children. If those whose goodness is mediocre at best are ready to take seriously the requests of their children, how much more will the heavenly Father give good things to those who ask him. Where Matthew has "good things," Luke reads "the Holy Spirit" (Luke 11:13). Because of Luke's special interest in the Holy Spirit it is usually assumed that Matthew's "good things" better represents the earliest form of the saying. In view of his placement of the sayings, however, it is possible that Matthew's understanding is close to Luke's: both perceive the answer to Christian prayer as consisting of Christian graces, not material treasures. It is the Holy Spirit that makes possible a suprahuman love of enemies (cf. Gal. 5:22–23).

When William Carey, the father of the modern missionary movement, was about to leave for India, he preached a sermon that became a clarion call to many: "Expect Great Things from God, Attempt Great Things for God." These two imperatives communicate the essence of verses 7–11. To take seriously the terrifying demands of the Sermon on the Mount is to take still more seriously God's readiness to assist us in fulfilling them.

The Golden Rule (7:12)

Matthew 7:12 deserves special attention, not only because of the important role it has played generally in Christendom (for many outside the church it represents the epitome of Jesus' teaching) but more especially because of the significant location given it by Matthew.

It is now widely acknowledged that the Golden Rule was not original to Jesus. With slight variations it is found in many authors, Jewish and non-Jewish. In the pre-Christian apocryphal book of Tobit we read, "And what you hate, do not do to any one" (Tobit 4:15). Hillel, a contemporary of Jesus, is reported to have said to a Gentile inquirer, "What is hateful to you, do not do to your neighbor: that is the whole Torah, while

79

the rest is commentary thereon; go and learn it" (*Shabbath* 31a). The formulation attributed to Jesus is positive rather than negative, but no great emphasis should be placed on this difference, since each formulation implies the other when applied to specific situations. "If it is hateful for you to starve, do not act in such a way that your neighbor will starve" is not materially different from "If you wish that your neighbor would keep you from starving, you must feed your starving neighbor." In some contexts the positive rule may exhort action, while the negative version simply encourages inaction. In others the negative rule may seem more effective. There is probably little difference in the way the two formulations function in the practical, everyday ethics of the followers of Hillel and the followers of Jesus.

More serious than the question of originality is the challenge that the rule is secular rather than religious, that is, that it is grounded in human wisdom rather than in God's relation to humans. Its detractors claim that it is anthropocentric and based on a "naive egoism"; the individual is allowed to direct his or her ethical behavior on the basis of a private world of feelings. The difficulty can be seen when specific applications are envisioned. If we treat persons of another culture only as we would like to be treated, our behavior may be offensive. Another potential problem arises from a literalistic reading of the maxim: "Don't report illegal behavior if you don't want anyone to report your illegal behavior"; "If you like to attend wild parties, you must give wild parties." As an ethical principle, the Golden Rule is remarkably susceptible to unethical appropriations!

For this reason the Golden Rule is "golden" only when interpreted in the light of its Christian context, not in a secularized abstraction. In Luke it occurs as a kind of summary in the middle of the section on loving enemies and forgoing retaliation (Luke 6:3). This context gives the rule a loftiness it cannot have in isolation. Doing as you would be done by now means far more than calculating one's self-interest, because its meaning is illustrated by love of enemies and nonretaliation. The rule is then immediately contrasted with reactive reciprocity in the following verses, for example, Luke 6:34: "If you lend to those from whom you hope to receive, what credit is that to you? Even sinners lend to sinners, to receive as much again." The ultimate clue for interpreting and applying the Golden Rule is provided by the section's concluding verse: "Be merciful, just as your Father is merciful" (Luke 6:36).

It seems probable that Luke's location of the Golden Rule reflects its setting in the earlier Q sermon more accurately than Matthew's. In the First Gospel, the rule has been moved from the section on love of enemies to 7:12, where it follows the sayings on prayer. It appears to fit this new location poorly, until we notice its place in the overall scheme of the Sermon on the Mount. At this point, we complete the long section on the better righteousness initiated at 5:20 and begin the concluding eschatological section. In its new location, the Golden Rule serves Matthew as a summary not merely of the sayings about love of enemies and nonretaliation but of all the other ethical teaching as well. It becomes for Matthew a shorthand reference to all the intervening material concerning the righteousness that anticipates the kingdom of heaven.

One indicator of this function is Matthew's addition, "for this is the law and the prophets." These words take the reader back to their first use at 5:17 and thus bracket the central core of the sermon. The Golden Rule is to be understood and applied as a *Christian* principle, that is, as a summary of *Jesus'* interpretation of the law and the prophets. To treat it in any other way is, for Matthew, to wrench it from its proper context of meaning.

Also essential to its context of meaning is its relationship to Jesus' proclamation of the good news of the kingdom (4:23). As in the case of the other imperatives of the Sermon on the Mount, the ethic of the Golden Rule is a "therefore" ethic. The ground of obligation is not prudent self-interest but the boundless grace of God, whose magnanimity we are to imitate (see 5:43–48).

Eschatological Epilogue (7:13–27)

With the enunciation of the Golden Rule the basic instruction of the Sermon on the Mount is completed. What remains is a series of eschatological warnings, whose function is to exhort Jesus' followers to take seriously the core teachings of 5:17—7:12. The key word in this hortatory section is *doing* (as in the Golden Rule). This is not as obvious in English translations as in the Greek, where the verb *poieō* ("do" or "make") occurs nine times.

81

In verses 13–14, regarding the narrow gate, this emphasis on doing is implicit only. Indeed, considered out of context, these verses might well be taken in a very different way. The

narrow gate might represent correct theology rather than obedience to Jesus' ethical teaching ("Only orthodox believers will
enter into life"). Or the verses might be understood in terms of
a Gnostic version of election ("A few are destined to be saved
in virtue of their divine origin, but the many, whose souls are
earthbound, will perish with the material universe"). It is perhaps to avoid misunderstanding that Matthew has supplemented the metaphor of the narrow gate (the parallel in Luke
13:24 mentions only a narrow door) by the traditional Jewish
motif of the two ways, the way of the righteous and the way of
the wicked (see Ps. 1:6).

When verses 13–14 receive our attention in preaching or
teaching it will be wise to observe that their intention is practical, not dogmatic. It would be a mistake to insist that we are
here taught that God has destined most people for hell. In the
Lukan parallel Jesus avoids giving a direct response to the question, "Lord, will those who are saved be few?" (Luke 13:23). It
is not necessary for us to know the ratio of damned to saved.
What is essential is that we take with utter seriousness our
responsibility to do what is right.

In verse 14 the word that is translated "hard" is not the
normal Greek word for "difficult" but is one that means "con-
stricted" or "pressed upon." It derives from a verb meaning
"press," which occurs frequently in the New Testament with
the metaphorical sense "oppress," "afflict," or "distress" (as in
II Thess. 1:6–7). Since the Greek word for "narrow" in the same
verse can also be used metaphorically with the meaning "troubled" or "beset with difficulty," it is possible that Matthew's first
readers understood the statement as reminding them that the
Christian way involves misunderstanding, rejection, and persecution. Those who strive to do what is right, instead of adhering
to a lowest-common-denominator morality, must not expect to
receive popular acclaim (see I Peter 4:4).

On first impression the next subsection, verses 15–20, seems
to depart from the central thrust of the section as a whole,
which exhorts doing what is right. At face value it constitutes
a warning against false prophets, comparable to that of I John
4:1: "Beloved, do not believe every spirit, but test the spirits to
see whether they are of God; for many false prophets have gone
out into the world." Whereas the Johannine epistle is concerned primarily with the erroneous Christology of the false
prophets (I John 4:2–3), Matthew makes no reference to their

82

teaching but only to their behavior, which is of special concern to him. In this concluding passage of the Sermon on the Mount, attention is focused steadily on the behavior of rank-and-file members of the church. The false prophets are introduced only because their conduct provides a bad model for ordinary Christians. Their charismatic powers set them apart and render them fascinating. For this reason, their failure to take Jesus' moral teaching seriously can have grave consequences for those who look up to them as "outstanding Christian leaders." These visitors (many of the Christian prophets were itinerants, according to the *Didache*) come "in sheep's clothing," that is, they seem like authentic members of Christ's flock, but the discordance between their profession and their practice reveals that they are really "ravenous wolves"; their conduct threatens to destroy the flock by seducing its members from the narrow way to the broad way leading to destruction. Support for this interpretation is provided by Matt. 24:11–12: "And many false prophets will arise and lead many astray. And because of the increase of lawlessness the love of many will grow cold." Here, as in 7:15–20, the emphasis is on proper living, not on correct belief.

The climax of this eschatological epilogue occurs in verses 21–23. Indeed, these verses are among the most important in Matthew. They repeat the motif of the "surpassing righteousness" of 5:20 and make it more explicit. They set the tone for the Gospel as a whole. Whereas Mark emphasizes the necessity of accepting Jesus as the crucified Christ and following him on the path of self-denial, Matthew's stress is on manifesting one's devotion to Jesus as Lord by obeying his ethical instructions. The righteousness that surpasses that of the scribes and Pharisees (5:20) consists not in possessing the teachings of Jesus but in acting upon them. The Great Commission reaffirms this emphasis. The disciples are challenged to go to the Gentiles and make of them doers of Christ's teachings (28:18–20).

In order to achieve this effect Matthew combines a saying from the earlier Q sermon, which is preserved at Luke 6:46 as the introduction to the parable of the two builders, with a judgment parable found at Luke 13:25–27, also drawn from Q. In Matthew's editing, the parable is transposed into a judgment scene located "on that day," that is, the day of Jesus' return (see 24:36–44).

Several problems attend the interpretation of verses 21–23.

83

First, is Jesus presented as the eschatological judge or merely as the advocate who witnesses for or against his followers at the last judgment, where God is judge? It has been argued that the latter is the more likely, in view of the formula "Depart from me," which, it is claimed, is not the language of a judge. It is true that the words "I never knew you" fit the picture of Jesus as advocate. They constitute a renunciation formula: there has never been an authentic relationship between Jesus and these pseudodisciples (for the use of "know" in this relational sense, see Amos 3:2; I Cor. 8:3; Gal. 4:9). The verb "confess," a technical term that reappears in 10:32 in a similar context, also suits a portrayal of Jesus as witness. This evidence can, however, be seen as pointing in a different direction. The final command, "Depart from me, you evildoers," appears to be a quotation from Ps. 6:8, identified by its superscription as "a psalm of David." To a modern reader this psalm contains nothing that would suggest a messianic prophecy, but to early Christians any psalm of David had potential relevance to David's great successor, the Messiah. If Matthew or his source (compare Luke 13:27) intended that readers see here an allusion to the psalm, it is probable that the words were to be perceived as the utterance of the Son of David. In this case, the alternative "ultimate judge, or advocate before God?" needs to be reconsidered. The Messiah is here represented as excluding from his realm those of his followers who have proved themselves unworthy of participation. Their protesting question implies that they have already been condemned. Here as in 25:41 it is the king who speaks. Whereas in the later passage the king addresses those who have never known him (see the comments on 25:31–46), here he speaks to followers who have boasted of their relationship to the exalted Messiah but have in truth denied him by their conduct. As in 10:32–33, Jesus' future denial of disciples who have denied him may have been conceived by Matthew as taking place "before my Father in heaven." Despite the fact that full authority has been bestowed on the Son (28:18), the Father remains the ultimate judge (see 10:28).

Second, is the Messiahship of Jesus disclosed to the narrative audience by these verses? In accordance with the motif of the messianic secret, none but the demons are supposed to recognize Jesus as Messiah until Peter's divinely inspired confession in 16:16. A similar problem is presented by the confession of the disciples as a group in 14:33: "Truly you are the Son of God."

Apparently Matthew was not as concerned about consistency in this matter as Mark. Nevertheless it must be observed that Matthew does not use "the Christ" in any narrative setting before Peter's confession. While there is thus no formal violation of the secret, its ultimate disclosure is liberally foreshadowed in passages such as this one. The hidden Messiah speaks openly of his eschatological role but does not identify himself by the title.

Third, are the false prophets condemned for failure to observe the law of Moses? In 7:23 the RSV rendering "evildoers" paraphrases a Greek phrase that literally means "those who work lawlessness." It has been proposed that "lawlessness" was employed by Matthew or his Jewish-Christian source as a reference to the non-Jewish life-style of Gentile Christians. This is most unlikely. Circumcision, a central issue in the dispute between Paul and conservative Jewish Christians, is never mentioned in the First Gospel. While the Matthean Jesus himself is loyal to the law, nothing in the completed Gospel suggests that the author sided with the rigorist Jewish Christians over against James, Peter, and John, who agreed with Paul that Gentile Christians need not become Jewish proselytes (see Gal. 2:1–10). It is significant that the Great Commission explicitly emphasizes Jesus' teachings, not the Torah as such (28:18–20).

It is best, therefore, to take "lawlessness" in an ethical rather than a ceremonial sense. The charismatics who invoke Jesus as Lord and prophesy and heal in his name are castigated for their failure to do the will of the Father in heaven, that is, to follow the narrow way and produce the moral fruits of a true commitment to Jesus. They are indeed doers—they point to all they have done as religious leaders—but not even miracles can cover up their moral failures. The same point is made eloquently by Paul: "And if I have prophetic powers, and understand all mysteries and all knowledge, and if I have all faith, so as to remove mountains, but have not love, I am nothing" (I Cor. 13:2).

While the verb "prophesy" connects the charismatics of verses 21–23 with the false prophets of verses 15–20, their literary role has changed. Whereas the earlier passage warns readers not to imitate the behavior of false prophets, in this passage they are held up as a fearful example of what can happen to any Christian. If even such outstanding Christian leaders, who amaze all with their spiritual powers, cannot hide behind their

85

religious accomplishments, how much more exposed are simple Christians who can make no such boast? All will be judged not for their religiousness but for what they have done and left undone (see 16:27).

Like the Q sermon on which both Matthew and Luke seem to depend, the Sermon on the Mount concludes with the parable of the two builders. It is possible that it had become traditional to complete collections of Jesus' eschatological teachings with one or more parables, since this is true of the collection in Mark 13 and of the expanded version of this in Matthew 24–25. Such would not be surprising, since the primary focus of the parables was on the urgency of decision required by the imminent arrival of the kingdom of God.

Luke has rewritten the parable for a non-Palestinian audience. Instead of a violent storm, he employs the image of a suddenly rising river, a phenomenon well known elsewhere but not found in Galilee and Judea. Luke stresses the quality of the workmanship; the first house withstands the river's flood because its builder dug deep and laid a good foundation (Luke 6:48). Matthew's editing in this instance is more conservative. He preserves the original Palestinian setting. The two houses represent not good and bad construction practices but wise and foolish choices of a site. The foolish man builds as well as the wise but makes the incredible mistake of erecting his house on the sands of a wadi, the dry bed of a seasonal river. When the rainy season arrives with its violent storms, a wild torrent rushes down the wadi from the hills and engulfs the house. The stupid man had chosen an easy building site without considering the consequences of his choice.

The parable sharply contrasts two ways of responding to Jesus' teaching. The "outstanding church leaders" mentioned in verses 21–23 have indeed heard Jesus' words over and over again, but they have refused to make those words the rule of life. As a result, their reputation as eminent Christians is built on nothing more solid than shifting sand. On the other hand, there are humble Christians who can claim no special gifts but who listen intently to Jesus' words and strive to live by them. The lives they build upon the rock will be able to withstand the storms of this life and of the final judgment.

The Response to the Sermon (7:28–29)

No audience response is appended to Luke's Sermon on the Plain (see Luke 7:1), but Matthew, who has set the sermon at that point on the story line occupied by Mark's account of an exorcism in the Capernaum synagogue, takes from Mark 1:22 the note that those who heard Jesus' teaching were "astounded" (NRSV). The Greek verb often implies fear, sometimes panic. What prompts apprehensive astonishment in the listeners is not so much the content of the teaching as the *authority* with which Jesus declares God's purpose for their lives.

The motif of Jesus' authority, which appears here for the first time, will recur repeatedly (8:9; 9:6; 10:1; 21:23), until we finally reach the climactic declaration of the Great Commission, "All authority in heaven and on earth has been given to me" (28:18). The awesomeness of that plenipotentiary authority is here anticipated in the consternation of the crowds. In this way Matthew reminds us at the end of the sermon as at its beginning (see comments on 5:1) that the Sermon on the Mount is a *christological* statement. We are meant to hear in it not merely a wise teacher but our Lord and King.

Matthew 8:1—9:38
The Messiah Manifests Divine Power

Jesus was remembered by friends and foes alike as a healer. His enemies attributed his successful cures to the use of magic or collusion with the devil (see 9:34). Matthew's point in presenting a collection of miracle stories in chapters 8–9, therefore, is not to establish that Jesus was a miracle worker but to make clearer for his readers the significance of this activity. Jesus is not to be seen as just another "divine man," comparable to the many magicians and healers who roamed the Greco-Roman world. The one whose miracles are here recounted is God's Son (3:17). Each story thus points to Jesus as the obedient Son of God, the Messiah, in and through whom God's power is manifested for the sake of God's people. If a gospel is a passion narrative with an extended introduction (see the Introduction),

87

then clearly the miracle stories play an important part in defining the man who must die.

Because the healings focus primarily on individuals, allowing the corporate dimension of the Messiah's relationship to his people to be eclipsed, Matthew carefully brackets the miracles collection with allusions to crowds: "When he came down from the mountain, great crowds followed him" (8:1); "And when the demon had been cast out, the dumb man spoke; and the crowds marveled, saying, 'Never was anything like this seen in Israel' " (9:33). Unlike the final story, in the first story the crowds play no role; the command to silence of 8:4 implies that the multitudes do not witness the cleansing. Their presence in verse 1 is thus motivated by the Evangelist's desire to remind us that Jesus' miracles are not to be seen as private contracts between a physician and his patient but as the Messiah's ministry to his people. As we shall see, Matthew reinforces this with a scriptural quotation at the conclusion of the first cycle of three miracle stories (8:17).

The collection is divided by Matthew into three groupings of three stories each (comprising ten miracles, since the seventh story includes two healings), followed by a brief summary and transition. The second and third trios are separated by material concerning discipleship and fasting.

Healing the Excluded (8:1–17)

Matthew's selection of the first three miracles seems to be dictated by the fact that in each case the recipient is excluded from full participation in Israel: the leper is excluded as unclean, the centurion's servant as a Gentile, and Peter's mother-in-law as a woman. Undoubtedly Matthew's readers, whose exciting fellowship embraced Jew and Gentile, slave and free, male and female, felt the symbolic force of these three stories better than we. The Messiah Jesus had healed broken relationships as well as diseased bodies and had brought a new people of God into existence (see comments on 21:43 regarding this new people).

The Leper (8:2–3)

88

The story of the leper seems to have been accorded primacy of place (it occurs at a later point in Mark's collection of miracles, Mark 1:40–45) because it demonstrates the truth of

5:17–20. Jesus does not abrogate the law either in his teaching or in his healing; he insists that the cleansed leper present himself to the priest and fulfill the obligations of Leviticus 13—15.

The suppliant in this very brief story firmly believes that Jesus has been empowered by God to work miracles. The function of the miracle is thus not to awaken faith but to exhibit it. While many of his people refused to accept Jesus, this unclean person, excluded from normal relationships and synagogue worship, acknowledged Jesus' authority. The leper is thus presented at the beginning of the collection as a paradigm for Matthew's readers.

Why does the leper say *"If* you will"? Clearly the doubt attaches not to Jesus' power but to his inclination to heal such a case as this. Leprosy is not included among the afflictions cured by Jesus in the summary of 4:23–24 (but see 10:8; 11:5). In the Old Testament and later Jewish tradition, leprosy was often regarded as a punishment for sin (see Num. 12:9–10; II Kings 5:27). The horror with which it was viewed related less to the physical condition itself and the possibility of contagion (the Hebrew and Greek terms translated "leprosy" comprised many mild skin diseases in addition to those severe infections now so designated) than to the ritual uncleanness that required continuous exclusion from the community. At the narrative level, the petitioner is not certain that the man of God will consider him worthy of divine healing. At the theological level, the Gentile readers of the Gospel, excluded by Gentile uncleanness from Israel, would rejoice that the Messiah did not consider them unworthy but willed to cleanse the unclean and admit them to his kingdom. Many readers would remember that the most famous case of a supernatural cleansing of a leper in Scripture involved a Gentile (II Kings 5; see Luke 4:27).

In yet another respect the leper provided an example for the earliest readers. While his words "If you will" reflect his sense of unworthiness, his behavior is boldly confident. Whereas the law required lepers to remain at a safe distance so as to prevent accidental communication of uncleanness (see Lev. 13:45–46; Luke 17:12), this man kneels close enough to Jesus to be touched by an outstretched hand. Christians must be as bold in their supplications for cleansing and healing.

The command to silence appears ineffectual. After all, the healing will be evident as soon as the former leper rejoins his

89

family and community. For Matthew, the point is christological: Jesus the Messiah does not perform healings for the sake of winning the adulation of the populace but as the humbly obedient servant of the Lord (see 8:17 and 12:15–21). He was not a deceiver *(planos)* who misled the people by a public display of false signs, as his enemies claimed (27:63; cf. 24:24). At a later point Jesus refuses to perform signs to certify his status (12:38–39; 16:1–4).

The Centurion (8:5–13)

Matthew's editing suggests that for him this story had more than one function. Most obviously, it served in the miracles collection as one of ten illustrations of Jesus' miraculous power. In comparison with the other healing stories, it attributes to Jesus a more spectacular power: he is able to heal someone at a distance, whereas he normally heals by touch (8:3, 15) or with an authoritative word addressed directly to the patient (e.g., 9:6). It must be observed, however, that Matthew makes little of this feature of the healing; the miracle is reported matter-of-factly, without special note.

The decision to place the story here rather than at some other point in the Gospel seems to be related to the fact that the centurion and his servant are Gentiles and therefore are excluded, like the leper and Peter's mother-in-law, from full participation in Israel's religion. Jesus is the Messiah by whose power and authority the excluded are included. This story must have been especially dear to Gentile members of Matthew's church. It is important to note, however, that the historical constraints of Jesus' ministry are not ignored by the story. In response to the request of the Canaanite woman for an exorcism Jesus declares, "I was sent only to the lost sheep of the house of Israel" (15:24). As in the later story involving a Gentile, so here the healing of a Gentile is truly exceptional, anticipating the postresurrection mission to the pagan world (28:18–20) but not inaugurating it prematurely. As suggested by John 12:20–24, Jesus can minister properly to Gentiles only by dying for them.

For this reason, verse 7 should be taken as a question: "And he said to him, 'Am *I* to come and heal him?' " (the emphatic *egō* ["I"] is ignored by most translations). Jesus shows the same reluctance here as in 15:23–24. He feels no call from God to minister to those beyond the bounds of God's people. As in

15:28, Jesus is here persuaded to make an exception to his rule because of the remarkable faith exhibited by the Gentile. The officer responds to Jesus' reluctance by insisting that it will not be necessary to contract ritual uncleanness by entering the home of a non-Jew; he is confident that Jesus possesses God-given authority to heal at a distance.

It is sometimes proposed that the expression "under authority" in verse 9 is the mistranslation of an Aramaic phrase meaning "having authority," since the officer speaks only of his subordinates, not of his superiors. The phrase makes perfect sense in the context if we remember that the point of the analogy is that the officer receives his authority to issue commands from his superior. In the same way, he implies, Jesus has received authority from God, an authority that allows him to command unseen spirits (angels) to do his bidding.

For Matthew, the story has a third function as well. This is indicated by his inserting into the story verses 11–12, a saying found in a very different context in Luke 13:28–29. Instead of simply praising the faith of the Gentile, as in 15:28 and in the Lukan parallel to this story (Luke 7:9), Matthew makes this the occasion for a stern warning to Jews, whose birth as Abraham's posterity makes them "sons and daughters of the kingdom" (v. 12) but who nonetheless forfeit their birthright by refusing to accept Jesus as the Lord's Anointed. One suspects that this third use of the miracle story was prompted in part at least by the continuing failure of the Jewish-Christian mission to Israel (see comments on 10:16–25).

Why is the centurion's faith praised so highly? His is not simply a bold confidence in Jesus' ability as a healer. The Gentile attributes to him a special authority, the authority to issue commands on God's behalf. This implicit confession thus foreshadows Peter's declaration, "You are the Messiah, the Son of the living God" (16:16, NRSV).

Jesus' word of praise of the centurion's faith is spoken "to those who followed him" (v. 10). Since "follow" is used technically in many passages as a way of referring to discipleship (e.g., 9:9), it seems probable that Matthew wishes the readers of the Gospel to take to heart both the praise and the warning. Christians must not simply address Jesus as "Lord" but humbly acknowledge his right to rule their lives day by day. As sons and daughters of the kingdom, they must not take their birthright for granted. Many will come from east and west, yes, from

91

Africa and Asia, and sit in judgment on the nominal Christians of America and Europe, who too glibly call Jesus "Lord, Lord" and do not do what he says (7:21–27).

Peter's Mother-in-law (8:14–17)

As usual, Matthew abbreviates the Markan story about Peter's mother-in-law (Mark 1:29–31). Since no other persons now appear, we receive the impression that Jesus is alone with the woman. Whereas Mark's story ends with her serving *them*, Matthew has, "She arose and served *him.*"

One must be wary of making too much of such a detail, which, after all, may simply be the result of shortening the narrative. Since Matthew is intent on interpreting the stories about Jesus for his contemporaries, however, it is possible that he wants his readers to find a paradigm here. If Peter's mother-in-law is placed in this triptych with the leper and the centurion because all three are denied full participation in Israel's religion, then women in Matthew's church were perhaps encouraged to see here a statement about their empowerment. Jesus had freed them from marginality so that, like Euodia and Syntyche, whom Paul calls fellow workers in the gospel (Phil. 4:3), they might rise and serve him. (For the motif of "serving" Jesus, see John 12:26.)

Mark's accompanying narrative concerning the crowd gathered outside Peter's house in expectation of exorcisms and healings (Mark 1:32–34) is reduced by Matthew to a single verse, which functions not so much as a story as a summary. Matthew is careful to correct the impression that Jesus was not able to heal everyone. Whereas Mark states that they brought *all* who were sick or demon-possessed and Jesus healed *many,* Matthew relates that they brought *many* and he healed *all* (v. 16).

To the summary Matthew attaches one of his "fulfillment quotations" (see comments on 2:13–23). Verse 17 is not a separate sentence, as suggested by most English translations, but a continuation: ". . . and healed all that were sick, so that what was said by Isaiah the prophet might be fulfilled, namely, 'He himself took our sicknesses and carried our diseases.' "

Although Matthew's rendering of Isa. 53:4 does not correspond closely with what we normally read in our English versions, it is actually a good, literal translation of the Hebrew text, apart from the omission of the first word ("Surely"). He refuses

92

to spiritualize the text, as does the Septuagint, which renders the Hebrew word for "sicknesses" as "sins" ("This man bears our sins and suffers for us"). To Matthew, it is important that Isaiah prophesied that the Messiah would deal with the people's bodily ills.

Modern scholarship distinguishes carefully between the Suffering Servant of Isaiah 40–55 and the Messiah. Indeed, it has often been proposed that Jesus was the first to combine these two conceptions, applying them both to his own person. There was, however, no unified, authoritative doctrine of the Messiah in the first century, and therefore it is erroneous to assume that Jews would have regarded it as ludicrous to take statements concerning the Servant of the Lord as messianic prophecies. This was in fact done by the later targum, despite Christian appropriation of Isaiah 53 as a prophecy of the crucifixion.

It is frequently claimed that Jesus' contemporaries would not have regarded his healing activity as a sign of his messianic dignity, since everyone expected the Messiah to function as a king, not as a healer. This oversimplifies. Certainly the most popular notions expected the Messiah to "restore the kingdom to Israel" (see Acts 1:6), but there was wide divergence of opinion concerning how the Messiah would manifest himself prior to accomplishing this task. Apparently Jesus' conviction that the power of God was at work in his healing activity caused people to wonder, "Can this be the Son of David?" (Matt. 12:23). While no one expected the Lord's Anointed to be a physician, he was expected to shepherd his people and improve their physical condition. It was evidently possible to interpret his healings as indications of his messianic vocation.

Matthew's approach, as evidenced by his use of Isa. 53:4, is to treat the miracles as proof not so much of Jesus' Messiahship as of his *obedience.* It had been prophesied that the Lord's Servant (Isa. 52:12) would deal with the physical ills of his people. Obediently, Jesus fulfills this role. For this reason, there can be no self-glorification on Jesus' part. He performs miracles not to astound an audience and win a popular following (see 8:4) but solely to give expression to God's care for his sick and suffering people. He heals because it is God's will that he heal.

The Second Trio (8:18—9:8)

By placing the explanatory fulfillment quotation at the end of the first trio, Matthew suggests that the theme of the second group will be different. We will find that the underlying emphasis in this next section is on discipleship. The miracles speak of Jesus' power and authority; discipleship means submitting oneself to that power and authority.

Authority Over the Powers of Chaos (8:18–27)

By skillful editorial work Matthew combines discipleship sayings with the story about Jesus calming a storm by inserting the discipleship sayings into the sea narrative after the opening sentence, "Now when Jesus saw great crowds around him, he gave orders to go over to the other side." That is, the journey has in principle already begun when the question of what it means to follow Jesus is raised. This impression is reinforced when the miracle story is resumed in verse 23: "And when he got into the boat, his disciples *followed* him" (see 4:19; 9:9). In this way the storm narrative becomes an acted parable about what it means to follow Jesus.

In his response to the scribe's offer to follow him Jesus refers to himself by the mysterious name "the Son of man." Wherever the phrase occurs in Matthew it serves as Jesus' peculiar self-designation. The Evangelist never reveals what meaning the expression has for him. Because Jesus' use of the term never arouses any response from the narrative audience, we should probably conclude that it has no revelatory power for Matthew, that is, it says nothing specific about Jesus' nature and destiny. It is not used trivially, however. It occurs in passages where Jesus is speaking about his earthly vocation and heavenly glory. In this first Son of man saying, Jesus refers to the shame of rejection by his people. The saying must not be taken literally, especially in this context, where Jesus has a boat to sleep in! This response to the scribe implies that those who commit themselves to be Jesus' followers must be prepared to be rejected by family and friends. (For further comments on "the Son of man," see Introduction.)

94

Another disciple begs for time off to bury his father (v. 21). The burial of a parent was one of the highest duties in Jewish society, taking precedence over many other obligations dictated by the Mosaic law. It is axiomatic to the disciple that his apprenticeship to Jesus will have to wait until this obligation has been fulfilled. Presumably the father has just died, so the delay will not be long. Jesus' response is so harsh that few scholars doubt its authenticity: "Follow me, and leave the dead to bury their own dead" (v. 22). No one in the early church, surely, would have created such a saying and attributed it to Jesus. It is not clear whether "the dead" who are to bury the disciple's father are spiritually dead or whether the expression is simply a hyperbolic way of saying "Let others fulfill this obligation." In any event, Jesus insists that following him must take precedence over even the highest of family responsibilities. The saying is thus intensely self-revealing. Despite the modesty he shows in calling himself "the Son of man" in the previous saying, in this second word he manifests a very high view of his calling. For the sake of his ministry to Israel his followers must be willing to alienate even close relatives (see comments on 10:34–39).

Both sayings, accordingly, prepare disciples for hardship, ostracism, and alienation. This was indeed to be the experience of Jewish-Christian missionaries at the time the Gospel was written (see comments on 10:16–25). It has been the experience of new Christians wherever the gospel has been proclaimed in a non-Christian culture. It is true also for many in the Christian West. Taking a stand on controversial social issues in Jesus' name can draw the wrath of family and community. Many who feel a call to the ordained ministry or missionary service are treated with contempt by those who should be supportive.

These discipleship sayings thus prepare for the storm narrative that follows. It is fruitless to speculate concerning the historicity of the event. What is important is to establish what the story meant to Matthew and his readers. The church fathers who interpreted this passage as referring to the vulnerable little ship of the church were probably correct. The disciples here represent the church whose faith is buffeted by the storms of persecution, rejection, and poverty. Survival amid the crashing waves is possible only by calling on the master, "Lord, save! We are perishing!" (v. 25).

In his response to this prayer, the Matthean Jesus uses one of Matthew's favorite words, which must be rendered in English by an entire phrase: "you of little faith" (see also 6:30; 14:31; 16:8). This word is used in the First Gospel only with

95

reference to the disciples, that is, the church. It points to a situation in which faith is present but weak and inadequate. A mixture of faith and doubt inhibits confident trust in God.

The story ends with the witnesses asking, "What sort of man is this, that even winds and sea obey him?" (v. 27). The answer, of course, is "the Messiah," who was expected to be supernaturally endowed and thus able to work miracles (Isa. 11:4; *Pss. Sol.* 17:27; *IV Ezra* 13:10). The sea miracle raises the question, but the answer must await Peter's confession in 16:16.

What are modern Christians to do with this strange story that so offends our scientific worldview? Matthew does not make it any easier for us by writing, "And behold a great *seismos* occurred in the sea" (v. 24). *Seismos* literally means "shaking" and elsewhere in Matthew is translated "earthquake" (24:7; 27:54; 28:2). Perhaps Matthew wants his readers to feel that here the disciples are confronted by the powers of chaos and that only Jesus has the divine power to rescue them. Nothing is gained by domesticating the narrative ("The storm accidentally subsided when Jesus woke up"). The story is meant to awe us. Our scientific pragmatism cannot comprehend the mystery of Emmanuel (1:23). We have been summoned into a discipleship in which we begin by calling Jesus "Teacher." In the end, however, we must acknowledge him as "God-with-us," through whom the chaos that threatens us individually and corporately can be subdued.

Authority Over Demonic Forces (8:28–34)

This story is one of the most baffling in the Gospels. The idea of demon possession has little in common with our understanding of mental illness. Stranger still to us is the idea that demons could be transferred from humans to animals by the command of the exorcist. Was it not thought that demons could choose their own victim after being exorcised (see 12:45)? Why would the demons request a transfer to a herd of swine? And since the pigs represented the livelihood of many people, was it not financially irresponsible on Jesus' part to permit their destruction? The presence of the pigs makes it clear that the story concerns Gentile territory on the eastern side of the lake. For Mark, the account perhaps symbolizes the post-Easter mission to the Gentiles; in Mark's version of the story, the healed man proclaims "in the Decapolis" what Jesus has done for him (Mark 5:20). Matthew, however, who elsewhere reminds us that Jesus was sent "only to the lost sheep of the house of Israel" (15:24), downplays this function of the story. Indeed, he is not even interested in the healing as such; all details concerning the state of the patients after the double exorcism are omitted (contrast Mark 5:15). In Matthew's greatly abbreviated narrative, the emphasis rests entirely on the dialogue between Jesus and the demons and on the authority exhibited by Jesus.

The story about the pigs follows immediately upon the storm narrative. While it was natural to associate two such stories about Jesus being in a boat on the lake, the juxtaposition may also have had theological significance for the Evangelists. Both stories present Jesus' authority over antidivine forces. The violent sea quake represents the power of chaos to threaten human life externally. The demons symbolize the mysterious evil forces that internally disrupt right thinking and right behavior. Jesus is presented as God's supreme agent, whose power far exceeds the power of evil.

Exorcists in the Greco-Roman world usually employed complicated formulas as a means of subduing a demon. Early readers would have been greatly impressed by the fact that in this story Jesus is able to exorcize a multitude of particularly fierce demons with a single word of command, "Go!" (See also 8:16.) The power channeled through him is not the power of magic but the power of the living God.

An important element of the story is the demons' recognition of Jesus: "What have you to do with us, O Son of God? Have you come here to torment us before the time?" (v. 29). This motif of the supernatural knowledge of demons is familiar to readers of the New Testament (see Mark 1:24; 3:11; 5:7; Acts 19:15; James 2:19). The demons thus acknowledge that their time is limited; at the consummation of the age they will be punished for having opposed God (see Matt. 25:41; Rev. 20:10). Their objection is that the time of the last judgment has not yet come. Why are they being subdued "before the time"? They entreat the Messiah, the one destined to judge them on God's behalf at the final reckoning, not to condemn them to torment in hell prematurely but to allow them in the interim to inhabit unclean animals—surely the Jewish Messiah will not deny them so modest a request! Jewish readers of the story, for whom pork was a forbidden food, will have found the outcome highly entertaining. The joke is on the demons! The evil spirits do not foresee that the quiet herd of pigs will be panicked by this

97

invasion. Both pigs and demons are destroyed in the waters of the lake. The destruction of the unclean pigs and the unclean spirits thus serves as an anticipation of God's eventual victory over all forms of evil.

The local inhabitants who come to meet Jesus are overawed by the event. They are neither joyful at the healing as they should be (they can now travel freely along the path to the cemetery and the lake—see v. 28) nor angry at the loss of their pigs, but frightened by the presence of so powerful an exorcist. He is not only a foreigner but a dangerous one. They beg him to leave them and go back where he came from. They have no inkling that the king of kings has touched their soil.

Although it is difficult for modern Christians to enter the world of thought of this narrative, it can nonetheless have powerful symbolic value for us. First, it illustrates the truth of 8:20. Those who are called by Jesus to be his followers, today as in the first century, must expect to be unwelcome among those whose religious or economic security is threatened. To name the demons in modern society is to incur disfavor.

Second, Jesus' appearance in our midst means gain and loss. To be liberated by him from the demon of materialism, for example, is gain indeed, but the accompanying loss is real. While Jewish Christians may have laughed at the destruction of the Gentile pigs, Gentile Christians may well have seen in this detail a symbolic reference to their loss of economic security through alienation from their pagan families. At all times in the history of the church, becoming a disciple of Jesus has meant for some the voluntary renunciation of wealth.

Authority to Forgive Sins (9:1–8)

Endemic to the human situation are feelings of guilt. We often feel excessively guilty for trivial offenses that have more to do with manners than morals, while failing to experience pangs of conscience over more serious trespasses against our neighbors. Nevertheless, except for sociopathic individuals whose consciences have failed to develop normally, all human beings know the guilt that results from failing to obey accepted standards of right and wrong. And wherever God is conceived as moral sovereign of the universe, offenses against other people are correctly seen as violations of God's will, that is, as sins committed against God. Just as a child shrinks from facing a parent whose command has been disobeyed, so believers fear

God's righteous anger. A bad conscience makes it difficult to worship God with joy and to delight in God's ways.

From the earliest stages of Israel's religious experience the God of Abraham was known as a forgiving God. A theme that recurs with great frequency in the Hebrew Scriptures is sounded at Exod. 34:6–7: "The LORD, the LORD, a God merciful and gracious, slow to anger, and abounding in steadfast love and faithfulness, . . . forgiving iniquity and transgression and sin." Prophets and psalmists reiterate this experience-based confidence in God's readiness to forgive. Regular synagogue services as well as the annual observance of Yom Kippur institutionalized this conviction by scheduling public confessions and prayers for forgiveness.

Because of his religious background, then, the paralyzed Jew who was brought to Jesus undoubtedly believed in the forgiveness of sins. A great gulf is fixed, however, between theoretical belief and existential experience. With his head he knew about God's readiness to forgive, but his tormented conscience could not appropriate that pardon.

This third narrative in the second trio of miracle stories continues the emphasis on Jesus' authority over evil. Just as the storm narrative stressed Jesus' authority over the powers of chaos and the story about the pigs focused on his authority over internalized powers of evil, so this third story presents Jesus as the one who has power over the evil of guilt. The narrative is not intended to teach that all sickness is due to sin, but clearly in this instance the man's paralysis strongly symbolizes the fact that guilt is paralyzing. We cannot serve God as we ought when we are crippled by feelings of guilt.

Jesus deals first with the man's primary problem, namely, his inability to appropriate God's forgiveness. The narrative suggests that it is the faith of his friends, not his own, that has brought him to Jesus. Responding to their faith, Jesus says to the paralyzed man, "Have confidence, child!" What basis does he have for confidence? The faith of his friends! Often when our own faith is faltering, we must allow ourselves to be carried by the faith of others. What makes this valid is the fact that faith is a corporate activity, not simply a private exercise. When we cannot feel God's reality, we must lean on the perception of others.

99

The man who has lost all confidence in God's readiness to deal positively with him is addressed affectionately as "Child."

It is to be seen not as a demeaning epithet, accusing the man of immaturity, but rather as a firm reminder that he is a person of worth for whom God cares.

The narrative shows no interest in the paralytic's response to Jesus' saving declaration, "Your sins are forgiven." Instead, it turns to the christological question: What gives Jesus the right to make such a statement? Opponents conclude, "This man is blaspheming," that is, he is usurping God's role (cf. Mark 2:7). In Matthew's version, Jesus responds by attacking not the logic but the motives of his critics' reasoning: "To what end do you conceive immoral thoughts in your hearts?" (v. 4). Instead of rejoicing in the fact that the man of God in their midst is able to communicate God's forgiveness to a sin-sick soul, they intend to use Jesus' words against him. Jesus foils their stratagem by a positive demonstration that he is God's authorized representative.

The narrative does not identify who Jesus is. The self-designation "the Son of man" does not relieve the mystery for the audience but only heightens it. The story by no means implies that the critics are right, that is, that Jesus claims to be God. In the Hebrew Scriptures, prophets function as messengers of God's forgiveness (II Sam. 12:13; Isa. 40:2). Christian readers know, however, that the one who here demonstrates his authority to communicate God's pardon is the one whose life will be poured out for many for the forgiveness of sins (26:28).

The awestruck audience glorifies God for giving such authority to *human beings* (v. 8). Matthew, by his use of the plural, reminds his readers that Jesus' authority to forgive sins did not leave earth when he was exalted to heaven. As we shall see in 16:19 and 18:18, Matthew's church claimed this authority in Jesus' name.

Can modern Christians also claim such an authority? Yes. This is done formally in the liturgical declaration of pardon, but, like the paralytic, many modern sinners cannot appropriate the promise in a formal setting. As Christ's representatives we can assure the conscience-stricken that forgiveness is available to them just as it has been to us, in the same way that a recovering alcoholic testifies to one not yet recovering that the power to change is available.

Two Additional Disputes (9:9–17)

The preceding passage is what form critics call a mixed form: it is both a miracle story and a controversy narrative. Since the theme of opposition has been introduced into the miracles collection, Matthew is content to follow Mark (2:13–22) in adding two more controversy narratives.

The Right to Associate with Sinners (9:9–13)

The most shocking element in the preceding story is that Jesus offers divine forgiveness prior to repentance, confession, and a request for forgiveness on the part of the paralytic. That shocking theme is developed further in the story about the call of Matthew and the subsequent banquet at which Jesus and sinners recline side by side. To good religious people it was scandalous that Jesus kept such bad company. His enemies ridiculed him as "a glutton and a drunkard, a friend of tax collectors and sinners" (11:19).

How bad was the company Jesus kept? Customs officials like Matthew were greatly despised because they were suspected of collecting more than was due. They were shunned as little better than swindlers and murderers. Who were the other "sinners" with whom Jesus dined? It is not clear whether these were people who were thought guilty of flagrant moral offenses or people whose sin consisted primarily in laxity in observance of the food laws, tithes, and ritual baths. Recently it has been proposed that the "sinners" were people whose very profession constituted a violation of Torah, such as the bankers, whose business involved lending at interest (see Exod. 22:25; see Matt. 25:27).

Why does Jesus recline festally with those shunned by the religious community? Luke explains this curious behavior by recounting the parables of the lost sheep, the lost coin, and the prodigal (Luke 15). Here in Matthew it is explained by a proverb: "It is not the well who need a physician but the sick." Jesus is not merely the friend of tax collectors and sinners but their physician, whether they are able to recognize their illness or not. The explanation continues with Jesus saying, "I came not to call righteous persons but sinners." The Greek verb here translated "call" can also mean "invite," as in the parable of the wedding feast (22:1–10). A significant part of Jesus' vocation is

101

to invite sinners to the messianic banquet. They are invited not because they are worthy but because God in his graciousness wants them to be included.

Jesus felt a special sense of mission to "the lost sheep of the house of Israel" (15:24; see also 10:6) and spoke in a parable about their importance to God (18:10–14). Apparently Jesus had in mind persons whose faith in God had become peripheral instead of the directing core of their existence and who lived as if God did not matter. But why was he so intensely concerned for the lost sheep? Primarily because he was obsessed by the conviction that the Creator, who makes his sun to shine and rain to fall on the evil as well as on the good, is a God whose love encompasses all (5:43–48). There may have been a secondary reason. If Jesus did indeed believe that God had raised him up as Israel's promised Messiah, he must have long pondered those texts which speak of the king as shepherd of God's people. One such text is Zech. 11:15–17. It describes a worthless shepherd who "does not care for the perishing, or seek the wandering, or heal the maimed, or nourish the sound." The authentic shepherd must care for the whole flock, not just for the loyal remnant. In any event, whatever Jesus may have thought, the First Evangelist must have conceived of Jesus' association with sinners as reflecting the authority vested in him as the Lord's Anointed. The one who had authority on earth to forgive sins had also the right to demonstrate to sinners God's readiness to forgive by joining them in a banquet symbolizing the coming feast of the kingdom of God (see 8:11).

Matthew takes the defense of Jesus' right to eat with sinners one step beyond Mark and Luke by adding a scriptural text, Hos. 6:6: "I desire mercy, and not sacrifice." Its function in this context is not to elevate the moral law over the ceremonial law, nor to denounce Jesus' critics for neglecting the former in favor of the latter, but simply to remind all that it is God's nature to be merciful and that Jesus is acting out God's mercy by associating with sinners.

It is characteristic of human communities everywhere to shun members who disregard accepted standards of behavior. In some small societies the limits of toleration are extremely narrow. History reminds us of certain American towns where men were persecuted for defying convention by growing beards. If mainline churches are at the moment diminishing, it may be in part because they have grown too comfortable with

102

a fellowship of like-minded and like-mannered people. The explosion of Methodism in eighteenth-century Britain resulted to no small degree from the fact that cultured women opened their homes to the "riffraff" of the lower classes. In every generation the "tax collectors and sinners" will assume a different appearance, but those who claim to be disciples of the Good Shepherd must diligently seek ways of reaching out and drawing them into the banquet of God's people.

The Right to Be Joyful (9:14–17)

This pericope fits closely with the two preceding passages; all three implicitly stress God's prevenient grace. Just as Jesus declared forgiveness to the paralytic before he asked, so now Jesus defends his disciples' right to celebrate what God is doing in their midst.

From ancient times, Jews had practiced fasting as a means of exhibiting sorrow for sin and thereby averting divine judgment (see II Sam. 12:16–23). Apparently the Baptist practiced fasting and taught his disciples to do the same (11:18). Perhaps through vicarious self-affliction he sought to diminish God's displeasure with Israel. It seems probable that Pharisees and other pious folk also fasted vicariously for Israel (see Luke 2:37; 18:12).

By his nonparticipation in this voluntary fasting program Jesus pointed to its theological weakness. Such fasting ritualizes the absence of God! It emphasizes not what God is doing but what humans must do in order to humor God into behaving favorably. "The Son of man came eating and drinking" (11:19) because Jesus was convinced that God was present and active, initiating his final rule despite Israel's unworthiness. The paralytic of 9:1–8 thus symbolizes Israel, to whom the good news of God's grace was announced *before* the healing of its paralysis.

Jesus' response is couched in metaphor: "The wedding guests cannot mourn as long as the bridegroom is with them, can they?" (v. 15). In Jesus' ministry of healing and association with outcasts and sinners, the arrival of God's rule is being anticipated (see 12:28). God is not absent and morose but present and gracious! What greater reason could there be for celebration?

Did Jesus intimate more than this? The question concerns the symbolic value of "bridegroom" in this little parable. Scholars remind us that there is no evidence that "the Bridegroom" had become an established way of referring to the Messiah,

103

although this symbolism seems to have become part of the early Christian repertoire (see 25:1–13; II Cor. 11:2; Rev. 22:17). The possibility of this development, however, lay ready to hand to any interpreter of Isaiah 61 who regarded the speaker of verse 1 as the Messiah, since this voice continues in verse 10: "I will greatly rejoice in the LORD, . . . for he has clothed me with the garments of salvation, he has covered me with the robe of righteousness, as a bridegroom decks himself with a garland." If Jesus was in fact the one who initiated the use of "bridegroom" as a symbol for the Messiah, however, it was surely a veiled reference only. The Gospel writers do not regard this passage as violating the messianic secret. Whatever the symbolism, the metaphor focuses not so much on the wedding itself as on the central figure (in contrast to the wedding feast of 22:1–10, where the bridegroom plays no role whatsoever). If Jesus was, as the Gospels claim, the author of this parable in 9:15, he was pointing to himself as the one in and through whom God's kingdom was dawning. Although verse 15*b* interrupts the joy with a reminder that the wedding celebration will be curtailed by the forcible removal of the bridegroom, there is no need to assume that this comment originated as an attempt on the part of the post-Easter church to justify its habit of fasting. It is probable that Jesus anticipated a violent death (see comments on 16:21; 26:28). His followers would mourn while awaiting his vindication.

The twin parables of verses 16–17 serve in the first instance as interpretations of the fasting dispute. In a different context the sayings may have assumed the superiority of the old ("No one puts a rag of raw, untreated cloth on a fine old garment— this would not mend it but ruin it! No one puts raw wine in fine, well-seasoned wineskins—it would destroy them!"). In their present setting the twin sayings speak merely of the incompatibility of the new and the old. Fasting represents an old way of responding to God; it is incompatible with the joy with which people should react to what God is doing in Jesus' ministry.

Further reflection suggests, however, that these sayings may offer comment on all three disputes. Various religious groups (scribes, Pharisees, and the disciples of John) have criticized Jesus or his disciples for declaring the forgiveness of sins, associating with sinners, and celebrating when others were fasting. In all three situations Jesus stands for the new over against the old. God is doing a new thing, and it is time to leave behind old habits and find new ways of responding to God's grace.

104

John the Baptist has many followers among modern Christians. We often brood gloomily over the evils of the world instead of searching out and celebrating what God is doing in our midst. We must be alert for signs of grace, and in them we will find cause for authentic celebration.

The Third Trio of Miracle Stories (9:18–34)

The final trio of miracle stories rounds out the collection by adding three miracles that will be assumed by the summary of 11:5 ("The blind receive their sight . . . and the deaf hear and the dead are raised up"). All three stories are "double miracles." The first combines the raising of a dead girl with the healing of a hemorrhaging woman, the second reports the restoration of sight to *two* blind men, and the third tells of a patient with a double affliction, a deaf-mute who is demon-possessed. The theme that unites the three stories is faith. In the first, the faith of the ruler and that of the woman are compared and contrasted. The blind men are explicitly interrogated about their faith. In the third narrative, which completes the entire collection, it is the faith response of the audience that is of importance. Another proposal suggests that these three stories are brought together by Matthew in order to remind his fellow Christians that they possess new life, new insight, and new speech.

The Woman and the Girl (9:18–26)

The intertwined stories of the hemorrhaging woman and the resurrected girl came to Matthew from Mark as a single narrative. In Mark the insertion of the healing of the woman allows the sick child of Mark 5:23 to die before Jesus reaches her. Matthew drastically alters the situation by reporting that the girl is already dead when the father comes to Jesus. The father's request, therefore, is not for the healing of an illness but for a resurrection from the dead. As a result, the intervening event involving the woman has in Matthew a different narrative function. It compares and contrasts the situation of a Jewish woman who is handicapped by a permanent state of uncleanness with that of a male Jew who can approach Jesus directly.

The man manifests remarkable faith: with his hand Jesus will be able to bring the deceased back from the dead (v. 18). Thus, in Matthew's version there is no occasion for Jesus' word of encouragement: "Fear not, only believe!" (Mark 5:36). This command is in effect transferred to the hemorrhaging woman:

105

"Be confident!" (v. 22; cf. v. 2). The confidence exhorted is in the first instance, of course, not self-confidence but confidence in God's readiness to save. From such trust, however, arises authentic confidence in self as the object of God's loving care.

Why is the woman so much more timid than the man? Because she is a woman and because of the nature of her illness. Her medical problem renders her continually unclean according to Lev. 15:25. Anyone who touches her will contract her uncleanness and be disqualified from various religious activities. It is only partly because of this condition, however, that she shrinks from approaching Jesus directly. After all, the bold leper came right up to Jesus the man of God, despite the fact that his state of uncleanness was far more serious than hers (8:2). Nor is it a matter of faith; she is as convinced as the leper that she can obtain healing from Jesus. It seems probable that her timidity is due to her sex. In Jewish society, women ranked little ahead of children and slaves. Her inferior status prevents her from approaching Jesus with the confidence that he will treat her as a human being of equal dignity. Jesus' word to her, "Be confident, daughter," is not paternalistic but affectionate. It assures her that he does indeed regard her as a person worthy of respect.

It is difficult to see why these two stories have become entwined except that both involve females. The Hebrew Scriptures contain two stories about men being translated directly to heaven (Enoch, Gen. 5:24; Elijah, II Kings 2:11) and three stories about two boys and a man being raised from the dead (I Kings 17:17–24; II Kings 4:18–37; 13:20–21). No woman, young or old, is accorded special treatment of this kind! The fact that Jesus troubles himself to restore a *girl* to life may have been significant to early Christians. Girls were generally not highly prized by Jewish fathers, and among pagans female babies were more likely than their brothers to be "exposed," that is, abandoned after birth, either to die or to be raised for slavery by a passerby. If Christians declared proudly to their neighbors, "We do not expose our girl babies!" it was surely due in part to the fact that they had learned from Jesus to regard female believers as equal inheritors of the kingdom of God (see I Peter 3:7).

Early readers undoubtedly found in this story a foreshadowing of their own resurrection. Jesus' word to the mourners, "The girl is not dead but sleeping," would have reminded them of believers who had passed from this life but were not really dead but merely sleeping as they waited for the risen Lord to raise them from their graves to the life of the age to come (see I Cor. 11:30; 15:51; I Thess. 4:14).

Two Blind Men (9:27–31)

In order to illustrate the claim of 11:5 that the works of the Christ included the restoration of sight to the blind, Matthew places here an anticipation of the story of two blind men that will be recounted in 20:29–34. The entreaty is the same here as in the later account: "Have mercy on us, Son of David!" Whereas the later story, which occurs immediately prior to the triumphal entry into Jerusalem, presents the miracle as public, in 9:27–31 it takes place privately "in the house" (v. 28).

Since the request of the two blind men is ambiguous (are they begging for alms?), Jesus asks in 20:32, "What do you want me to do for you?" In 9:28 it is assumed that Jesus knows that their request is for healing. His question concerns instead the level of their faith: "Do you believe that I am able to do this?" In response to their reply "Yes, Lord," Jesus assures them, "According to your faith let it be done to you." This is essentially a reprise of the word to the officer in 8:13, and at the same time it is an anticipation of the word to the Canaanite woman in 15:28. In none of the three instances is human faith treated as a magical power that compels healing. In each case it is to be seen rather as firm confidence that Jesus is the channel of God's power. Whereas the earlier and the later instances both concern Gentiles, here it is Jews whose faith is praised by Jesus. It is perhaps significant, therefore, that these Jews address Jesus as Son of David. In its vocative use, lacking the definite article, the term is not exactly a title—even Joseph is so addressed in Matt. 1:20— yet it strongly suggests that these blind men recognize Jesus as the promised Messiah, while sighted people are unable to do so. Perhaps Matthew assumes that his readers will remember that in Isa. 35:5 it is promised that in the golden age to come the eyes of the blind will be opened. By requesting healing, the blind men are giving voice to the faith that in Jesus' presence the golden age has dawned. This glorious truth must not be prematurely divulged, however. Jesus commands silence. But it is to no avail. The good news cannot be confined (v. 31).

A Demon-possessed Deaf-Mute (9:32–34)

The function of the final miracle story is not merely to fill out the number of miracles (ten) or the number of stories (three

107

trios) but to dramatize the dual response to "the Messiah of Deed." The miracle itself is reported with the greatest brevity. All emphasis lies on the divergent responses of "the crowds" and "the Pharisees." We are probably intended to see these as reactions not to this miracle only but to the series as a whole.

The polarization of responses to Jesus' miracles prepares for the negative reaction to the Christian mission, which will be graphically portrayed in chapter 10. It also anticipates the theme of opposition to Jesus that will appear with increasing frequency beginning with chapter 12, where the intention to destroy Jesus is first introduced (12:14).

The motif of divergent responses to Jesus fascinated the Fourth Evangelist too. In this connection, John employs the Greek word *schisma* (from which our word "schism" derives), which itself comes from the verb "to split." Wherever Jesus goes, he "splits" his audience, creating a sharp division between those who see God at work in him and those who regard him as a manifestation of evil (John 7:43; 9:16; 10:19).

Such a cleaving of the community is still frequently the result wherever Christ is proclaimed in a non-Christian context. By many Christians, however, the *schisma* is experienced internally: one part of our inner being acclaims him as Lord, while another rebels against such abject subservience.

Summary and Transition (9:35–38)

By means of an almost verbatim repetition of 4:23, 9:35 brings to a satisfying conclusion the great complex consisting of the Sermon on the Mount (chaps. 5—7) and the miracles collection (chaps. 8—9). It reiterates the priority of teaching and preaching over healing (see comments on 4:23).

To this summary Matthew appends material whose purpose is to introduce the second great compendium of Jesus' teachings, the mission discourse of chapter 10. The statement of verse 36 about Jesus' compassion seems to have been taken from Mark 6:34, but the compassion is here actualized not in Jesus' own activity but in the suggestion that others must become involved. Mark's picture of the crowds as being "like sheep without a shepherd" is intensified by the addition of "harassed and helpless," or, perhaps, "wounded and lying exhausted." In any event, the phrase is reminiscent of several Old Testament passages that portray God's people as a flock neglected by its shepherds (I Kings 22:17; Jer. 23:1–6; Ezek. 34:1–10; Micah 5:2–4). Of particular significance is the fact that both Jeremiah and Ezekiel present "David" as the future good shepherd of Israel (Jer. 23:5; Ezek. 34:23) who will replace the worthless shepherds. By manifesting compassion for the distressed flock and the lost sheep (see Matt. 10:6; 15:24; 18:10–14), Jesus is presenting himself as the promised "David." This messianic motif, while lying just below the surface, is not exploited in the context. Instead, the need of the sheep prompts a saying about harvesters.

Although Matthew elsewhere uses the harvest as a metaphor for the last judgment (13:24–34, 36–43; see also Rev. 14: 14–20), it must here refer to missionary outreach, as in the earlier source from which he draws the saying (see Luke 10:2; cf. also Rom. 1:13; I Cor. 3:6). The two uses overlap, however. Those who gather fruit now do so in anticipation of the final harvest. This is explicit in John's use of the image (John 4:35–38).

Up to this point Jesus has been the sole missionary. In the next chapter he makes his disciples partners in the work of preaching the gospel and healing. In the present context the command to pray for more laborers seems a little out of place, since Jesus himself is about to send out the Twelve. In placing the saying here, Matthew is concerned primarily not for its narrative context but for its significance for his readers. They— and we—are challenged to pray that the work delegated by Jesus to his followers may involve more and more of those who acknowledge him as Lord.

Ministry Through Disciples and Growing Opposition

MATTHEW 10:1—16:12

Matthew 10:1–42
The Disciples' Ministry and Its Cost

Mainline denominations, whose memberships have been shrinking dramatically for the past quarter century, are challenged to take mission at home far more seriously than they have in the recent past. The discourse of Matthew 10 reminds us, however, that evangelistic activity among those who know us is in some respects more difficult than preaching the gospel in faraway places.

The missionary discourse is occasioned by Mark's narrative about the sending out of the Twelve (Mark 6:7-13). Instead of waiting to present this story after the rejection at Nazareth as Mark does, however, Matthew moves it to this earlier point on the story line, perhaps to suggest that the church's mission is an extension of Jesus' own ministry as Messiah of Word and Messiah of Deed. In 10:1 Jesus gives his twelve disciples authority to *heal every disease and every infirmity,* just as he himself had done according to 9:35. At 10:7 the disciples are instructed to preach exactly what Jesus had preached at 4:17: "The kingdom of heaven has come near." As the sequel to the statement about Jesus' compassion in 9:36, the mission of the Twelve apparently represents for Matthew the post-Easter mission of the church seen as the continuation of Jesus' own ministry.

Travel Instructions (10:1–15)

The first mention of the Twelve at 10:1 seems abrupt, since Matthew has passed over Mark's story of their appointment

(Mark 3:13–19). Although Matthew can assume that his readers have heard of this group, he does not wish "the Twelve" to remain a shadowy concept. He provides their names, and pairs them, reflecting perhaps the Markan tradition that they were sent out two by two (Mark 6:7). Although the New Testament lists of the apostles' names do not fully agree, there is no good reason to doubt that Jesus, in anticipation of the eschatological restoration of God's people, selected twelve of his followers to form a special group symbolizing the twelve tribes of Israel (see 19:28).

If Matthew wants us to see the church's mission prefigured in the sending out of the Twelve, why has he prefaced Mark's account with a saying that rigorously restricts the mission to "the lost sheep of the house of Israel" (vv. 5–6)? Since the Evangelist clearly believes in the worldwide mission ("Go, enlist all the Gentiles as disciples," 28:19), his insertion of this particular saying is baffling. The best explanation seems to be that for Matthew the narrative concerning the Galilean mission must be appropriated at two levels. At the historical level, it is a statement about the activity of Jesus' disciples during his earthly ministry. Since Jesus' own commission at this stage was to Israel alone (15:24), his disciples were bound by the same restriction. At a second level, the narrative symbolizes the mission of the post-Easter church, for which the earlier limitation has been annulled by the risen Christ (28:16–20). Matthew thus gives expression to the principle enunciated so firmly by Paul: "To the Jew first and also to the Greek" (Rom. 1:16). To Matthew the priority of Israel is important both historically and theologically.

The intent of verses 7–8 is summarized in the two imperatives "preach" and "heal." As in the ministry of Jesus, the disciples' proclamation of the good news of the kingdom must be corroborated by signs of the kingdom. Although the miracles they are empowered to effect are not insignificant (the list of v. 8 includes cleansing lepers and raising the dead!), the emphasis clearly lies less on producing spectacular displays of supernatural power than on manifesting concern for God's hurting people. The message about the coming of God's rule must be rendered believable through concrete demonstrations of God's caring. The modern church understands this principle and tries to be faithful to it. Mission boards send out not only evangelists but medical personnel, educators, agricultural missionaries, and others who will communicate the living gospel through visible acts of compassion. Likewise churches reach out to their neighborhoods in effective evangelism when concern for souls is accompanied by genuine concern for bodily existence. "Jesus loves me" becomes more credible to a distraught mother when a church food pantry rescues her children from starvation. There must be no divorce between "preach" and "heal."

There seem to have been two versions of the travel rules. Matthew 10:9–10 differs from Mark 6:8–9 in two significant details: whereas Matthew appears to deny missionaries the use of sandals and a staff, Mark explicitly requires these items. Although Matthew's version can be read as meaning "While on your journey do not acquire for yourselves a second pair of sandals or a second staff," it seems more likely that we are to take these two details as calling for a barefoot, defenseless posture. Apparently two philosophies of mission were in conflict. All agreed that it was best that missionaries demonstrate their faith in God by refusing to take along money and provisions and extra clothes. There was a difference of opinion, however, concerning whether the ascetic stance of denying oneself sandals and a staff would win the admiration of prospective converts or their contempt. Did Matthew believe that Christian travelers should be distinguishable from ordinary people on a journey? Were these visible signs of self-denial intended to communicate the fact that following Jesus inevitably involves self-denial of some kind (see 16:24)?

In any event, the central message of verses 9–10 is "Travel light." When transposed into a modern key, this suggests that Christian missionaries should live simply, free of the excesses of materialism. This will be true both for those who leave home and country to proclaim the gospel in faraway places and for those who want to share their faith with neighbors at home. We must not let our excess baggage get in the way of the gospel. Paul's advice to Christians in Rome is pertinent: "Show the same attitude toward one another, not treating yourselves as superior but associating with humble folk" (Rom. 12:16).

A proper appreciation of verses 11–15 is difficult for us, because we lack an adequate knowledge of the hospitality rules of Jewish Galilee in the first century. Verse 11, for example, seems to assume that these holy travelers can approach the home of their choice and expect to be fed and sheltered there. Any home that extends hospitality but then refuses their message will reveal that it is not in fact "worthy" as previously

112

proposed by their neighbors (v. 11), that is, they are not deserving of a share in the Messiah's kingdom (see vv. 37–38). A community that altogether resists the gospel will be judged more harshly than the notorious cities of the plain of Genesis 19, on the principle that to whom much is offered, of them much will be required (see Luke 12:48). Shaking dust from one's garments ("dust of your feet" apparently meant the dust raised by walking) was a Jewish sign of rejection (see Neh. 5:13; Acts 13:51; 18:6).

Enduring Hostility for Jesus' Sake (10:16–25)

Matthew shows no interest in this missionary journey as a historical happening. As a matter of fact, he neglects to report the event itself; he writes nothing about the disciples' departure and return (contrast Mark 6:12, 30; Luke 9:6, 10). At the conclusion of the discourse it is *Jesus* who goes out teaching and preaching (11:1). What makes the story interesting to Matthew is that it represents for him the post-Easter mission to Israel.

This is indicated by the addition of sayings about persecution. In Mark's story about the mission of the Twelve, there is no hint of violent hostility. The same is true of the parallel account in Luke 10:1–20. These traditions speak only of a refusal to grant hospitality and to receive the gospel. There is no evidence that the disciples experienced violent persecution during Jesus' life. There is ample proof, however, that angry reactions to the post-Easter message did occur among Jews at various times and places. From Acts we learn that there was sporadic persecution in Palestine and that Paul was frequently attacked in diaspora Jewish communities.

Matthew reflects the unhappy experience of Jewish-Christian evangelists by attaching to Mark's travel instructions this paragraph about persecution which he takes largely from Mark's eschatological discourse (see Mark 13:9–13). By transferring this material from its Markan setting to the mission discourse, Matthew alters its meaning: it no longer refers to the sufferings of ordinary Christian believers just prior to Jesus' return in glory but to the persecution of missionaries who go from synagogue to synagogue during the ongoing time of the church.

In his careful editing of the transferred material Matthew gives evidence that for him the decisive break between Christian and non-Christian Jews has already taken place. Where Mark writes "You will be beaten in synagogues" (Mark 13:9), Matthew substitutes "You will be flogged in *their* synagogues." Matthew uses "synagogue" more frequently than any other Gospel writer but always in a negative way. The word is always modified by "their" (4:23; 9:35; 10:17; 12:9; 13:54), except when the context indicates that the synagogue belongs to "the hypocrites" (6:2; 23:6, 34). For Matthew the Jew, the synagogue has become an alien institution in which he no longer belongs.

Verse 17 suggests that some Jewish-Christian missionaries have been haled before Jewish courts. In many diaspora communities, such "councils" probably consisted of the synagogue elders. Charged with breach of peace, they were sentenced to flogging, perhaps the thirty-nine lashes, perhaps a lesser beating with rods (see II Cor. 11:24-25). From Paul's proud boast, "Five times I have received from Jews the forty lashes less one" (II Cor. 11:24), we realize that not all Christian Jews evoked this response from synagogue authorities. Even Paul himself received this punishment relatively seldom—in this passage he is looking back on approximately fifteen years of missionary work. Nevertheless the tension between Christian and non-Christian Jews must sometimes have been very intense. It is not surprising that sharp divisions arose within families, reminding people of such prophecies as Micah 7:6, which is alluded to in Matt. 10:21, 34-35. It must be remembered, however, that verse 21 is prophecy, not a statement of accomplished fact; we need not assume that many Christians suffered martyrdom. Nor is it likely that many were brought before governors and kings (v. 18); there is no evidence that the profession of Christianity was defined by either Jewish or Roman law as a punishable crime at this early date. Only a few outspoken leaders, such as Paul, Peter, and James son of Zebedee, attracted such attention, probably because they aroused widespread anger in Jewish communities.

Two words of assurance are uttered for the benefit of persecuted missionaries. First, they must not be anxious about defending themselves, because the right words will be given them by the Spirit. The phrase "the Spirit of your Father" (v. 20) is unique to Matthew. It may be intended to suggest that the gift of inspired speech is not to be regarded as impersonal but as evidence of the Father's care.

The second word of assurance is that missionaries who en-

114

dure to the end will be saved (v. 22). If taken too literally, this could become a statement in support of salvation by works. The Greek word here translated "saved" can also mean "delivered." Probably what is meant here is simply that those who remain faithful to Jesus, refusing to respond in kind to the hatred of their persecutors, will be delivered unscathed in spirit.

Matthew brackets the persecution material of verses 17–23 with an introduction and a conclusion that serve to interpret the missionaries' experience and that help us to appropriate the passage for our day. According to verse 16, Jesus declares, "Behold, *I* send you out as sheep in the midst of wolves" (note the emphatic *egō*). Sheep surrounded by wolves are extremely vulnerable; survival is little short of miraculous. The conviction that it is Jesus who sends them gives the missionaries the assurance that he will be their sure defense and help them survive spiritually whatever hostility they must encounter. Loving one's religious enemies is possible with the help that Jesus gives.

Further theological undergirding for the missionaries' vulnerability is provided by the conclusion, verses 24–25. Those who proclaim the gospel are reminded that they are called to share Jesus' experience of hostility and rejection. The reference to Beelzebul ties this passage to 9:34 and its statement of the negative response to Jesus' mighty works, and it looks forward to 12:22–32, where the theme is more fully explored.

It has often been remarked that persecution is good for the church. When not beleaguered by outside pressure, the church tends to slip into a comfortable religiosity that takes all too lightly its commitment to God and God's purposes for this planet. With the continuing increase of secularism in "Christendom," the day may come when Western Christians will experience the hostility that is now the common lot of Christians in many parts of Africa and Asia. As we prepare for such an eventuality we must remind ourselves that it is our risen Lord who sends us into the encounter with hostility. He himself suffered and left us an example that we should follow in his steps (I Peter 2:21).

Encouragement to Fearless Confession (10:26–42)

To these warnings about coming persecution are appended sayings that encourage fearless confession. The connection with verses 24–25 is made by means of a "therefore": 115

"Therefore do not fear them" (v. 26). Since Jesus is the one who is sending them out, and since disciples cannot expect to be treated better than their teacher, *therefore* they must rise above their natural fear of their opponents and be faithful to their calling as evangelists.

The first saying in the group, which is closely paralleled in Luke 12:2, assures timid missionaries that there is nothing hidden that will not eventually be made public. Luke takes this to refer to human behavior: "Whatever you have said in the dark shall be heard in the light" (Luke 12:3; cf. Num. 32:23: "Be sure your sin will find you out"). Matthew, however, seems to understand it as referring to the mystery of Jesus' Messiahship and therefore turns the indicative statement into an imperative: "What I tell you in the dark, utter in the light." What had to be kept secret during Jesus' earthly ministry must after Easter be proclaimed from the housetops. This is another illustration of Matthew's skill in interpreting an old saying for a new situation.

Negative and positive sanctions are now provided for faithfulness in proclaiming the gospel. The first is negative: It is not persecutors who should be feared but God, for God is able to condemn to eternal death. Closely attached to this is the positive sanction: Your Father, who cares even for sparrows, cares so much for you that even the hairs of your head are numbered. The hyperbole is effective. God will not protect the evangelists from suffering, since even Jesus had to suffer, but the one whom they call Father will bring his children through suffering to eternal life.

The saying concerning confessing and denying Jesus (vv. 32–33) combines the positive and negative sanctions. There is good reason to believe that this is an authentic saying of Jesus. It has sometimes been regarded as inauthentic because it allegedly refers to confession and denial in a court of law, thus reflecting a post-Easter situation. This is erroneous. The words "confess" and "deny" are frequently used of nonlegal situations, most notably of Peter's denial (see 26:69–75; the verbs are also used of John the Baptist's testimony at John 1:20). Anyone who declared to a would-be disciple, "Follow me, and let the dead bury their own dead" (8:22), must have required unwavering loyalty from his followers. There is no reason to doubt that Jesus expected to be able to testify for or against his followers at the last judgment, since he attributes such a role to the queen of the south and the people of Nineveh (12:41–42). This saying is not

116

the idle threat of a megalomaniac; it is the word of one who was utterly convinced that God had called him to a central role in the world's final drama (see 12:28).

The next paragraph introduces a still more traumatic result of preaching the gospel. Flogging, verbal abuse, and shunning are far easier to bear than alienation from one's nearest kin. Here Matthew presents a group of sayings that appears in slightly longer form in Luke 12:49–53. The opening word about hurling peace onto the earth probably combines two sayings: "I came to hurl fire onto the earth" (Luke 12:49) and "Do you think that I have come to give peace on earth?" (Luke 12:51). Whereas Luke completes the second saying with a reference to division, Matthew uses "sword," a powerful metaphor for the way a community can be split by the preaching of the gospel. The community here in question is the family. Acceptance of the gospel pits children against parents in the bitterest of quarrels, as in Micah 7:6.

This point is reinforced by two sayings. Matthew correctly interprets the hyperbole "hate" found in the Lukan parallel of the first saying (Luke 14:26): "Whoever loves father or mother more than me is not worthy of me." This saying, which seems to be in such tension with the Fifth Commandment, "Honor your father and mother," must be understood in relation to Matt. 8:22, which claims that following Jesus takes priority even over the filial responsibility of burying one's father.

The cross saying (v. 38) puzzles many commentators, who find it difficult to believe that Jesus anticipated Roman crucifixion for his followers in Palestine and who conclude therefore that this must be a postresurrection saying. To this extent they are correct: there is no evidence whatsoever that any of Jesus' disciples were ever crucified in Palestine. It seems best, therefore, to regard verse 38 as an authentic saying but one intended more figuratively than literally. It is probable that the two men crucified beside Jesus were not common thieves but revolutionaries (see comments on 27:38). Since so many resisters had been put to death by the Romans (see Luke 13:1), their bravery undoubtedly became proverbial. Jesus may very well have expected of his followers a commitment as serious as the guerrillas' commitment to revolution. In any event, a figurative understanding seems implicit in the coupling of this saying with the preceding one about "hating" one's family. Disciples of Jesus must be willing to be "crucified" by their families.

117

The trauma of being disowned by parents has been experienced by innumerable young Christians in Africa and Asia, who have found the courage to follow Christ despite enormous family pressure. Even in North America and Europe young people in nominally Christian homes must sometimes face such pressure when their faith in Jesus calls them to full-time Christian service, the Peace Corps, or some other form of poorly paid service to others.

The final saying of the group is in some respects the most puzzling, since it is not clear what is meant by the opening phrase, "the one having found his [her] life." Apparently the saying assumes that the action is incomplete; the life has not been permanently acquired (it could not then be lost). It is best, then, to take the participle as implying *attempted* action, as is done by TEV: "whoever tries to gain his own life." So Luke understands the saying: "Whoever seeks to gain his life will lose it" (Luke 17:33; see also John 12:25). Those who give highest priority to the task of protecting themselves will find that there is nothing left to protect. A man who spends his young adulthood in a continuing effort to "find" himself, indulging his appetites and whims and refusing to be locked into any commitments, may discover only too late what he has lost. Conversely, the person who surrenders freedom by acknowledging Jesus Christ as Lord will indeed find herself or himself. A healthy self-esteem, for which all emerging adults long, will in such cases be based not on the fickle opinion of transitory friends but on God's call and God's love. Not even the bitterest of suffering can take away the sense of one's eternal worth that is given to those who take up their cross and follow Jesus.

The concluding paragraph of this discourse returns to the missionary theme with which the chapter began. Nonacceptance was anticipated in verse 14 ("And if any one will not receive you . . ."). Now the same verb is used positively: "Whoever receives you receives me, and whoever receives me receives him who sent me" (v. 40). Underlying this saying is the *shaliach* conception of ancient Jewish law, according to which a man's duly authorized messenger "is as the man himself." This idea is perhaps reflected in Gal. 4:14, where Paul reminds his readers that they had received him "as Christ Jesus" (see also John 13:20).

118

The verb "receive" is, of course, ambiguous. In such a context it can refer either to receiving the gospel or to extending hospitality to the missionary, or perhaps both. In verse 41 it inclines to the second meaning. According to the *Didache,* the prophets were wandering representatives of Christ who should be given hospitality for only short periods of time, so that they would not settle down but continue traveling (*Didache* 11:3–6). Matthew probably assumes that the person who extends hospitality to a prophet is himself or herself a Christian. "In the name of a prophet" probably means "because he is a prophet, and thus Christ's representative." The one receiving a prophet is generously promised a reward equal to that awaiting the prophet.

"A righteous man" in verse 41*b* may mean "a truly good man," as TEV proposes, but surely the prophet of verse 41*a* could also be described as truly good. One can guess that underlying the Greek word was a Hebrew or Aramaic term that was used to designate Christian believers, in much the same way as "saints" is used by Paul. Perhaps it was used to refer to people we would call "outstanding" or "prominent" Christians. In this case, the saying refers to a traveling Christian who is not a prophet, that is, whose reason for traveling is not the same as a prophet's. While all Christians were expected to spread the word, not all felt called to be wandering missionaries. Thus it is possible that verse 41*b* refers to people like Phoebe (Rom. 16:1–2). Such travelers are also to be received in Christ's name, because they too are his representatives.

This chapter's final saying adds a third kind of representative to the list. "The little ones," as we will learn from 18:6, is a phrase used by Matthew with reference to humble Christians who are not church leaders and who may also be poor. Such persons must not be neglected or treated with disdain, because they too represent Christ. The fact that even the trifling gift of a cup of cold water to one of the little ones will be richly rewarded is ample proof of their importance in God's plan.

Matthew 11:1–30
"Are You the Coming One?"

The overall tone of chapters 11 and 12 is negative; they build on the somber mood of chapter 10, where it has been suggested that nonacceptance of the gospel will be the rule, not the exception. In this way they prepare for the judgment parables of chapter 13. The great complex of chapters 5–9, consisting of the Sermon on the Mount and the miracles collection, concluded with a reference to the fact that Jesus' activity evokes diametrically opposite responses: the crowds marvel, "Never was anything like this seen in Israel," while the Pharisees retort, "He casts out demons by the prince of demons" (9:33–34). In these next two chapters (chaps. 11–12), the negative response is explored further. While the possibility of a positive reaction remains open, as seen in the Great Invitation of 11:28–30 (see also 12:23: "Can this be the Son of David?"), the emphasis is clearly on the negative. We are hereby reminded again that the gospel is not the story of a religious hero but of a dying savior; it is indeed "a passion narrative with an extended introduction" (see Introduction).

Chapter 11 contains three sections: verses 2–15, 16–24, and 25–30. Although the paragraph consisting of verses 16–19 adheres to the first section because of the allusion to John the Baptist in verse 18, its subject is really the negative response of "this generation," and it therefore belongs more naturally with the woes on three Galilean towns (vv. 20–24).

Jesus' Response to the Baptist's Question (11:2–15)

John's question, "Are you the coming one, or shall we await another?" poses a problem for many readers. Had John so quickly forgotten what he had said in 3:14 ("I need to be baptized by you, and do you come to me?")? It is idle to speculate what psychological circumstances in his imprisonment might have caused the heroic prophet to doubt his own earlier conviction concerning Jesus. More to the point, yet just as conjectural, is the proposal that this question, not 3:15, is authentic, that is, that only now, upon hearing news of Jesus' miracles, does it occur to John that Jesus may be the Messiah. Early interpreters suggested that John asked the question only for the sake of his disciples, since he himself knew the answer. Matthew is apparently untroubled by such concerns. In this question John speaks not in his prophetic mode (presumably it is as a prophet that he recognizes Jesus in 3:14) but as a representative member of his people (note the "we" of the second clause). The two halves of the question reflect Israel's positive and negative responses to Jesus' activity (see 9:33–34; 12:23–24).

120

The narrative shows no interest in the questioning as a historical event, since it has no sequel; nothing is said about what John's disciples reported or how he responded. This is beside the point for Matthew. All weight lies on *Jesus'* response to the question.

The answer is indirect, dealing not with Jesus' person as such but with his activity: "The blind receive their sight and the lame walk, lepers are cleansed and the deaf hear, and the dead are raised up, and the poor have good news preached to them" (v. 5). This is clearly not a very satisfactory answer for those who demand the security of certainty. Other prophets in Israel had performed such miracles. Elisha had both cleansed a leper and raised a dead boy to life (II Kings 4–5). As far as we can tell from the surviving writings of the time, nobody in first-century Judaism expected the Messiah to appear as a healer. Of what evidential value, then, can these miracles be as a response to John's question?

It may even be said that Matthew intensifies the problem by the order in which he places the verbs in verse 4. Whereas the Lukan parallel reads, "Go and tell John what you have *seen* and *heard*" (Luke 7:22), Matthew has "what you *hear* and *see.*" By thus giving priority to hearing, Matthew reminds us again that Jesus must be perceived first as Messiah of Word before he can be properly appreciated as Messiah of Deed. This order also gives special emphasis to the fact that Jesus brought joyful news to the poor.

What does the conjunction of healing miracles and good news for the poor signify? That God has inaugurated the kingdom in the public ministry of Jesus. It is generally agreed that verse 5 contains verbal echoes of Isa. 61:1 and 35:5–6. In effect, Jesus' words announce, "This is the time of fulfillment prophesied by Isaiah." The ambiguity remains, however, for not even Isa. 61:1 speaks explicitly of the Messiah. The implicit claim of verse 5 is that Jesus, in and through whom God is inaugurating the kingdom, is in fact the promised Messiah, even though he does not conform to general expectations concerning this figure. As we saw at 8:17, Matthew regards the healing miracles as acts of messianic obedience.

The ambiguity remains, but, as verse 6 emphasizes, ambiguity does not relieve one of the necessity for decision. It is not a theoretical decision (What category does Jesus fit?) but an existential one: What does it mean *for me* that God is opening a new age in and through Jesus? Significantly, verse 6 is ex-

121

pressed not as a condemning woe (contrast v. 21) but as a beatitude: "Blessed is anyone who does not stumble over me" (see 13:57).

John's question concerns the identity of Jesus. In the next paragraph Jesus counters with a question to the crowds about John's identity. It has been proposed that verses 7–8 make ironic references to Herod Antipas, who possessed a fortress (a "king's house") at Machaerus, east of the Dead Sea, and whose symbol on certain coins was a reed found in the Jordan Valley. It was not a powerful political leader (ultimately a "weak reed") such as Herod whom the people had sought at the Jordan but a prophet. But what kind of prophet? "More than a prophet," because of his location in salvation history; he is the end-time messenger who fulfills the prophecy of Mal. 3:1.

Modern Christians are sometimes disturbed to discover that scriptural quotations in the New Testament often depart radically from what appears in the Old Testament. While first-century Jews were very careful to preserve accurately the Hebrew text (even misspellings were carefully retained), they showed no such reserve when translating Scripture into Aramaic, their everyday language. Such a paraphrase (targum) was intended to communicate the meaning behind the letter. What we have in Matt. 11:10, then, is a Christian "targum" of Mal. 3:1, which brings out what was felt to be its real significance by conflating it with Exod. 23:20. The messenger prepares not for God's coming but for the coming of God's deputy, the Messiah.

Verse 11 seems to exclude from the kingdom the greatest of the prophets (the verb "arise" is often used in reference to the appearance of a prophet, as at Deut. 13:1). This is probably a mistaken perception. The point is surely that in the coming kingdom of God the little ones who believe in Jesus (18:6) will be of equal standing with such important witnesses as John.

The interpretations of verses 12–13 are legion. Matthew's wording (cf. Luke 16:16) suggests that he regarded John the Baptist as belonging with Jesus to the age of fulfillment; violent opponents of the kingdom will "plunder" it by persecuting John, Jesus, and others who announce its arrival. Such violence has been predicted by the prophets, including Moses ("the law," v. 13). For the tradition that Israel constantly persecuted its prophets, see II Chron. 36:15–16 and the comments on Matt. 23:29–39.

122

The central point of the paragraph is reached in verse 15, whose importance is underlined by the attached warning of verse 16. John the Baptist is the returning Elijah of Mal. 4:5, whose task it is to prepare the people for the coming of God, or, as in the "targum" of Matt. 11:10, God's deputy. (See comments on 3:1–6; 17:9–13.) If John is Elijah, then for those who have ears to hear, Jesus is the promised Messiah.

These two paragraphs thus prepare for the condemnation of "this generation" and the Galilean towns who should have been prepared for the Messiah's appearance by John's eschatological preaching but who refused to take either John or Jesus seriously.

The Rejection of Jesus by "This Generation" (11:16–24)

The question of verse 3, "Are you the coming one?" dominates the next two paragraphs as well, but now the emphasis falls on those who respond negatively to the question of Jesus' identity.

"This generation" is a collective designation for the majority of Jesus' contemporaries who refuse to believe that he is the inaugurator of the age of fulfillment (see also 12:41–42, 45; 23:36). Just as he has compared those who hear his words but fail to heed them to a foolish builder (7:26–27), so now Jesus compares his unresponsive contemporaries to querulous children who cannot play together happily.

The parable of the children, according to interpreters familiar with Near Eastern customs, reflects gender roles. The round dance that occurred at weddings, accompanied by flutes, was performed by men, while mourning, often done by professionals, was women's work. Thus the parable may represent the girls as reproaching the boys for being unwilling to play wedding, while the boys counter that the girls refuse to play funeral. Another suggestion is that the children who criticize their friends for not cooperating are the lazy ones: they want to play the easy roles and expect the others to engage in the more strenuous dancing and loud wailing. A third possibility is that some or all of the children are being bossy, claiming the right to "call the shots."

123

In its present context the parable is open to several different interpretations, depending on whether or not it is regarded as an allegory concerning John and Jesus. If it is allegorical, there are two main possibilities. The children who propose "Let's play marriage!" can represent Jesus, who joyfully announces the arrival of the kingdom, while those who say "Let's play funeral!" stand for John and his stern warning of coming judgment. On the other hand, the children who do the speaking can be seen as "this generation," who want the dour John to dance and Jesus the preacher of joy to mourn. If the parable is not allegorized, "this generation" is perhaps being compared to neither group of children (those speaking or those being addressed) but to the interaction: children who cannot respond positively to any suggestion end up playing nothing. Jesus' contemporaries prefer to sit on the sidelines uninvolved rather than take seriously either of God's end-time messengers.

The attached saying about the response to John and Jesus is probably authentic, whether originally connected with the parable or not. It is unlikely that any Christian would have created this saying in which John is not subordinated to Jesus and in which Jesus himself is insulted. In the original Aramaic version of the saying, Jesus referred to himself by the humble self-designation *bar enasha* ("a son of man"). In Matthew's Greek the phrase has the appearance of a title but does not in fact function as such. Here as everywhere in Matthew "the Son of man" does nothing to inform the hearers or readers who Jesus is (see Introduction). The point of the saying is clear: this generation is able to "write off" John because of his abstention from normal social intercourse and Jesus for exactly the opposite reason, because of his banqueting with sinners. In this way, both are dismissed as irrelevant.

Many of our contemporaries ("this generation" updated) would probably concur in regarding John as mentally unbalanced (the twentieth-century equivalent of "he has a demon") but would abstain from using insulting language about Jesus. His irrelevance is to them so obvious that he is not often attacked, only ignored.

The final line of the paragraph, "Yet wisdom is justified by her deeds," is difficult to assess. Some scholars urge that reference is here made to the heavenly Wisdom (*Sophia* in Greek), regarded as God's consort at the creation of the world (see Wisd. Sol. 7:22; Sirach 24); because "deeds" here echoes "the deeds of the Christ" of verse 2, Matthew implies that Jesus is the

124

incarnation of Sophia. Several considerations argue against this proposal, however. Elsewhere Matthew employs *sophia* in a nonmythical way (12:42; 13:54), and nowhere in the Gospel is there any suggestion that Jesus is the incarnation of a mythical figure. Indeed, Matthew suggests that blasphemy against Jesus is forgivable, whereas blasphemy against the Holy Spirit is not (12:32); such a statement would be impossible if Matthew regarded Jesus as Sophia incarnate. It is probable, therefore, that "wisdom" here refers not to the mythical Sophia but to God's wisdom which is manifested (and vindicated) in the deeds of the Christ. Also possible is the view that wisdom is here used in a more general, secular sense: "wisdom is demonstrated by its fruits." No matter how "wise and understanding" (v. 25) Jesus' opponents claim to be, their behavior exhibits their lack of wisdom.

The historical occasion of the woes against three Galilean towns cannot be determined from the present literary context. One might suppose them to have been more appropriate to the time when Jesus turned his back on Galilee in order to make his final trip to Jerusalem. They seem to presuppose that Jesus' work in Chorazin, Bethsaida, and Capernaum has proved finally unsuccessful. It seems likely that these sayings were treasured especially by Jewish-Christian missionaries whose Easter gospel prompted as little response in Galilee as had their master's healings (there are no allusions to Galilee in Acts).

Several features of these woes are striking. First, Jesus claims only indirect responsibility for the miracles; they are referred to not as wonders he has wrought but as "manifestations of power" *(dynameis)* which "happened" (most of the English translations are misleading in suggesting that Jesus *did* or *performed* miracles in these towns). The miracles are to be seen as manifestations of God's will to save his people, not as certifications of Jesus' supernatural authority. Jesus is not a religious charlatan who puts on a performance in order to win a following.

Second, the woes present Jesus as rebuking the three towns for failing to *repent,* not for refusing to believe in him. Although there is a relationship between these two activities, the distinction ought not to be collapsed. According to 4:17, the sum and substance of Jesus' message was "Repent, for the kingdom of heaven is at hand." Nowhere does Matthew expand on the meaning of repentance, but certain implications can be drawn

125

from 11:21. If the manifestations of power that happened in Chorazin and Bethsaida had happened in the pagan towns of Tyre and Sidon, they would have repented long ago. Such powerful evidence of God's loving care would have persuaded even pagans to turn to God in confident faith and obedience. That is, the kind of repentance Jesus called for required his hearers to take God seriously and commit their lives to being part of God's plan. This does not mean, however, that Jesus regarded his own role as insignificant. Implicit in his call to repentance and the accompanying healing activity is the conviction that he is the one in and through whom God's saving reality is being manifested. To reject his call is to ignore his significance.

Third, the unresponsive towns are condemned *corporately*. Capernaum, glorying in its own importance ("exalted to heaven"), is warned: "It will be more tolerable on the day of judgment for the land of Sodom than for thee" (the Greek pronoun is singular). The communities are composed primarily of unresponsive individuals, each of whom must render account at the judgment. Individuals, however, are shaped in part by communities. Each town or village develops its own ethos. Some nurture faith in God, while others discourage it. Perhaps Capernaum so reveled in its commercial significance that spiritual issues were marginalized. Wondrous healings by a local prophet apparently attracted only momentary attention; their revelatory significance was ignored.

Capernaums abound in the modern Christian West. Miracles of love are performed daily in Christ's name by a tiny minority, but their revelatory significance is missed. What really counts is the workaday world where money is earned and spent. Community leaders must remember that they can help shape an ethos that takes human values more seriously than dollars and thus encourages openness to what God is doing in our midst.

The Great Invitation (11:25–30)

This passage has always been cherished because of the Great Invitation issued in verse 28 to the overburdened. Before we can fully appreciate that invitation, however, we must examine it in relation to the passage as a whole and also explore the passage's relationship to its context.

The preceding passage, 11:2–24, has developed the theme

126

of Israel's nonacceptance of its Messiah. Even John the Baptist, when hearing in prison about "the deeds of the Christ" (11:2), was uncertain concerning Jesus' identity. In verses 20–24 Jesus pronounces woes on the Galilean cities that had been privileged to witness his kingdom-revealing miracles and yet had not perceived them as "the deeds of the Christ" and consequently had not repented.

The passage now under consideration, verses 25–30, begins by reflecting on the stark contrast between the many who reject and the few who accept Jesus as the inaugurator of God's kingdom. In verse 25 Jesus declares, "I confess you, Father, Lord of heaven and earth." The Greek verb, which in most English versions is rendered as "praise" or "thank," is more often used in the sense of "acknowledge," that is, confess one's sins (Matt. 3:6), or acknowledge a relationship to a superior, that is, God or Jesus (Rom. 14:11; 15:9; Phil. 2:11). A related verb is used in Matt. 10:32: "Everyone therefore who acknowledges me before others, I also will acknowledge before my Father in heaven." In 11:25 Jesus is represented as acknowledging the sovereignty, wisdom, and grace of the hidden God (Isa. 45:15), whom the wise of this world cannot discover but who makes himself known to infants, that is, those who in response to Jesus turn and become like children (18:3). What is revealed to them ("these things") is the significance of Jesus' miracles; in contrast to the inhabitants of the Galilean cities, they are able to perceive the miracles as evidence that God has initiated the final drama.

Why is the response to Jesus critical? "All things have been handed over to me by my Father." This refers not to the post-resurrection *ruling* authority of Jesus (28:18) but to his *revealing* authority. Both his words and his deeds reveal the Father's nature and will. To him alone has it been granted to know the Father so completely.

At first glance verse 27 presents a very polemical stance. It seems to suggest that only Christians know God as Father. This cannot have been Matthew's understanding; the Fatherhood of God is acknowledged not only in the Hebrew Scriptures (Deut. 32:6) but also in synagogue prayers used in Jesus' day. Similarly, the statement could, mistakenly, be taken to mean that Jesus reveals a previously unknown God who is superior to the God of the Jews, as the heretic Marcion was to claim in the second century. This is even more impossible. What the verse claims

127

is that Jesus alone knows God fully, that is, understands his will as that will is being revealed in the inauguration of the kingdom of God. The Son's knowledge of the Father is eschatological knowledge. We might paraphrase: "No one knows what the Father is up to except the Son, in whom God's eschatological will is being actualized." The second half of the verse reflects a similar thought. No one fully understands Jesus' eschatological role except the Father who sent him. Note that here the hiddenness of God (Isa. 45:15) is paralleled by the hiddenness of the Messiah. No one can determine Jesus' meaning simply by observing him; his significance is a matter of divine revelation (see 16:17).

No audience is specified in this passage. Indeed, verses 25–26 might be understood as solitary prayer and verse 27 as soliloquy. Because of verses 28–30, however, it seems more likely that Matthew assumes the presence of "the crowds" of verse 7. In this case, verse 27 must be regarded as another instance of "foreshadowing" on Matthew's part; it anticipates the later acknowledgment that Jesus is "the Messiah, the Son of the living God" (16:16).

Verse 27 has become known as "the thunderbolt from the Johannine heaven." The reciprocal knowledge of the Father and the Son is clearly a theme more characteristic of John than of the Synoptic Gospels. It is not impossible that this saying, which belonged to the collection on which both Matthew and Luke have drawn, was known to John and served, in part at least, as a point of departure for his distinctive theology. We must carefully distinguish, however, between the divergent appropriations of the saying. Whereas for John it speaks of the incarnation of God's eternal Word, for Matthew its language is messianic, referring not to Jesus' essence but to his function.

If we examine verses 28–30 in context, we see that they anticipate the next two passages concerning Sabbath observance. The invitation is issued neither to the work-burdened nor to the sin-burdened but to the law-burdened, upon whose shoulders "the scribes and the Pharisees" have laid an intolerable load (23:4).

The rest that is promised to the weary is not, however, the rest of inactivity. Jesus did not come to abolish the law of Moses but to fulfill it by providing its ultimate interpretation (5:17). What he offers is not a vacation from the law but a less burdensome way of fulfilling it. At certain points his interpretation will

128

be more lenient (Sabbath observance), at others more stringent (divorce) than that of the Pharisees, but law observance as a whole will be simplified by his emphasis on "the weightier matters of the law: justice and mercy and faithfulness" (23:23) and on the double commandment of love (22:37–40). The "rest" is made possible through the provision of a new yoke.

Jesus' yoke is called "easy." The underlying Greek word means "kind." A good yoke is one that is carefully shaped so that there will be a minimum of chafing. Jesus' yoke will be kind to our shoulders, enabling us to carry the load more easily. In this sense alone his burden will be "light." Jesus does not diminish the weight of our accountability to God but helps us to bear this responsibility.

It is possible that "learn from me" means more than simply "listen to my teaching." T. W. Manson (*The Teaching of Jesus*, pp. 239–240) proposed that as a designation for his disciples Jesus selected an Aramaic word that meant not "pupils" but "apprentices." From him they were to learn not merely to think but to do. They were to learn not only by listening but by watching. If Manson is correct, the metaphor of the yoke attains a new force. The yoke is not one that Jesus imposes but one he wears! We remember that commonly a yoke was a wooden instrument that yoked two oxen together and made of them a team. In this word Jesus may be saying: "Become my yoke mate, and learn how to pull the load by working beside me and watching how I do it. The heavy labor will seem lighter when you allow me to help you with it."

Learning from Jesus involves paying serious attention to the fact that he is "gentle and humble in heart." At one level these words serve to contrast Jesus with the Pharisaic teachers of 23:4. At a deeper level they remind us that the service of God requires the spirit of gentleness and humility, as exhibited in Jesus. As apprentices we must watch closely how our master crafts his obedience to God.

Some scholars propose that in verses 28–30 Matthew has drawn heavily on the wisdom language of Ecclus. 51:23–27. While a few reminiscences are possible, a much better case can be made for dependence on Jer. 6:16: "Stand at the crossroads, and look, and ask where the good way lies; and walk in it, and find rest for your souls." Jesus is the one who shows us the good way, where the restless can find rest for their souls.

Now we can see why Matthew has placed verses 28–30 with

129

verses 25–27 as a transition between the woes on the Galilean cities and the Sabbath controversies. Verses 25–27 explain both why Jesus has been rejected by the majority of those who witnessed his miracles and why he is qualified to provide a better yoke to those who are struggling to obey God's will. As the hidden Messiah, he exhibits the kingdom in his deeds, his teaching, and his gentleness.

Matthew 12:1–50
Opposition Intensifies

The negative tone of chapter 11 continues in this next chapter, in preparation for the parables of judgment of 13:1–52. Controversies with the Pharisees (vv. 1–14, 22–37, 38–45) dominate the chapter. The significance of these disputes is illuminated by an interlude (vv. 15–21) and an epilogue (vv. 46–50).

Two Sabbath Disputes (12:1–14)

It has become customary to print verses 1–8 and 9–14 as separate paragraphs, since they report different incidents. The two events are carefully coupled in Matthew's presentation, however. They are conceived as occurring on the same Sabbath, and the same opponents are in view. The decision to destroy Jesus (v. 14) thus serves as the conclusion to the unit as a whole.

The Sabbath controversies are anticipated in 11:25–30, where the promise of an "easy yoke" seems to refer to the yoke of the law of Moses. The "wise and understanding" of 11:25 are not only the unrepentant of the Galilean towns but also the Pharisees of 12:1–14, who are confident that they know what God's will is but who refuse to recognize in Jesus the inaugurator of God's kingdom. Finally, there may be an allusion to the ultimate Sabbath of the kingdom in the promise "I will give you *rest.*" Those who come to Jesus are destined to discover what a real Sabbath is like!

130

Harvesting on the Sabbath? (12:1–8)

The presenting issue in the grainfield dispute is whether plucking a few heads of grain by hand to satisfy personal hunger constitutes harvesting, that is, one of the many forms of work prohibited on the Sabbath. Underlying this is the more fundamental issue: Who has the right to interpret God's will as expressed in the Torah, Jesus or his opponents?

In the narrative the Pharisees declare categorically that what the disciples are doing profanes the Sabbath. Modern Jewish scholars point out that there was a wide diversity of opinion on such matters among first-century interpreters. The Mishnah, a collection of received opinions published about 200 C.E., does not list "plucking" among the thirty-nine varieties of prohibited labor. It is suggested that the view expressed by these Pharisees represents not ordinary Jewish opinion but that of extreme sabbatarians, such as those responsible for the Dead Sea Scrolls and the book of *Jubilees,* for whom the Sabbath could not be violated even to save a life (see I Macc. 2:29–41).

The first argument in defense of the disciples' behavior, however, does not directly address the issue of whether or not the law permits plucking. Instead, it appeals to the indirect support of a historical precedent. Once when David was hungry he transgressed the law by eating holy bread (I Sam. 21:1–6). Such an argument would obviously carry little weight with the rigorists. On the surface it sounds as though Jesus is suggesting that hungry people can break any of the ritual laws of the Pentateuch. It is probable that the argument, meant for Jesus' followers and not for the opponents, is more subtle than this. Just as great David was permitted to profane the holy bread of the tabernacle because of his importance in God's plan for Israel, so the Son of David has authority to permit his followers to profane the Sabbath, not simply because they are hungry but because they are associated with him in the urgent work of the kingdom. If David could profane bread intended as a sacrifice to God, how much more can the Messiah's followers be allowed to observe the Sabbath less rigorously than is demanded by the extreme sabbatarians.

Matthew now adds a second argument which is missing from the parallels (Mark 2:23–28; Luke 6:1–5), perhaps because he feels the need for a rationale that will be taken seriously by non-Christian Jews. The law requires priests to perform certain

131

kinds of work on the Sabbath that would be forbidden to ordinary citizens (see Num. 28:9–10); the cult takes precedence over the Sabbath (see John 7:22–23). But how does the faithfulness of priests in the temple justify the action of the disciples who, after all, are not ministering to the cult but to their own hunger? Jesus employs the traditional "light and heavy" argument of Jewish hermeneutics: "Something more important than the temple is here" (v. 6). If the temple takes precedence over the Sabbath, how much more will something greater than the temple outrank the Sabbath.

What is greater than the temple? Three possibilities have been considered by interpreters. (1) Jesus himself is the "something greater." This is not impossible, especially in view of verse 8, but if this had been Matthew's understanding, he would more likely have used the personal form "someone" rather than the neuter "something." The same expression, in the neuter, is employed again twice in 12:41–42. (2) A second proposal is that Jesus is referring to the kingdom of God; if the work of temple priests grants exemption from Sabbath restrictions, how much more the work of the kingdom of God (compare the argument in John 5:17). This is a plausible interpretation when the saying of verse 6 is considered in isolation, but a third is rendered more probable by the context. (3) The quotation of Hos. 6:6 in the next verse, "I desire mercy, and not sacrifice" (quoted also at 9:13), suggests that God's demand for mercy outranks both temple and Sabbath requirements.

How is the "law of mercy" to be applied in this situation? The Pharisees ought to have shown mercy to the disciples in their need, instead of condemning them for what, at the very most, was a minor infraction of the Sabbath law and was probably not regarded as a transgression at all by more lenient interpreters of the law.

The passage concludes with the climactic statement, "For the Son of man is lord of the sabbath" (v. 8). A number of scholars, Jewish and Christian, have proposed that in Jesus' Aramaic saying the meaning was "Man is lord of the sabbath," that is, human need must take precedence over the abstentions required by the Sabbath commandment. Be that as it may, the Synoptic parallels (Mark 2:28; Luke 6:5) agree with Matthew in attributing lordship over the Sabbath to Jesus himself, who refers to himself as "the Son of man." This is not to say that "the Son of man" is a "title of majesty" connoting divine authority.

Here as everywhere in Matthew it is a mysterious self-designation that makes no assertion about Jesus' identity (see Introduction). The daring claim lies in the statement, not in the self-designation. For Matthew, this saying reiterates the fundamental claim of the Sermon on the Mount: Jesus the Messiah is the ultimate interpreter of the law and the prophets. God has bestowed on him authority to interpret God's will for those entering the kingdom of heaven. Not to the Pharisees and their legal experts but to Jesus must one look for direction on how to obey the Torah.

Does Healing Violate the Sabbath? (12:9–14)

The second scene parallels the first in that there is little basis for the contention that the Sabbath law is being transgressed. Jesus effects a healing by a miraculous word, not by performing any work (such as mixing a medicine or applying a poultice). Nor does Jesus ask the healed person to transgress (contrast John 5:8–10). Indeed, there is evidence that moderate interpreters of the law in Jesus' day permitted certain kinds of medical help on the Sabbath, including treatment of a sore throat and midwifery.

The challenge presented to Jesus by the rigorist sabbatarians is that healing (by whatever means) is a profane activity which should be reserved for ordinary days; the sanctity of the Sabbath should not be violated in this way (see Luke 13:14). Again Jesus appeals to a higher principle: "It is permitted to do good on the sabbath" (v. 12*b*). This principle is supported by another "light and heavy" argument. Jesus presents a hypothetical case: Suppose one of you is so poor that he possesses only one sheep; can you really believe that he will not rescue that sheep from a pit on the Sabbath? The people at Qumran specifically forbade such an act, and presumably the rigorists pictured in this scene would have concurred with the Qumranites, but Jesus is appealing to their conscience: Would you condemn a man who violated your stringent Sabbath rule to save his only sheep? If they yield on this point, the conclusion follows inexorably: a human being is far more precious than a poor man's only sheep!

The conclusion to the two Sabbath controversies is provided by verse 14: the Pharisees plot to destroy Jesus. This is the first explicit indication that the hostility directed toward him will culminate in a violent death. It belongs to the gospel

133

genre to prepare for the passion narrative in this way (see Introduction).

It is sometimes mistakenly proposed that Jesus' death was the direct result of his opposition to Sabbath observance. This is most improbable. There is not a scrap of evidence that Jesus taught his followers to treat the Sabbath like any other day. As far as we can tell, the Sabbath continued to be observed by Jewish Christians and, for a time, by many Gentile Christians as well (although probably with less rigor). There was great diversity among Jews concerning the finer points of the Sabbath law, and as far as we know, no other teacher was persecuted for expressing a divergent opinion on such minor issues as are raised in these two stories. The people of Qumran would have denounced Jesus' lenient attitude, but their opposition would have been verbal, not physical. Despite the murderous hostility attributed to the Pharisees here, they play no role in the plot to execute Jesus (26:3).

In any event, it is evident that *Matthew* does not believe that Jesus disregarded the Fourth Commandment. To the Markan injunction concerning the eschatological flight, "Pray that it may not be in winter" (Mark 13:18), Matthew adds "or on a sabbath" (24:20). The First Evangelist is convinced that Jesus did not come to destroy the law but to fulfill it (5:17), and he understands this to mean that Jesus explains what true obedience to the law involves. The Sabbath is not revoked, but its observance must sometimes yield to a higher principle.

At the beginning of the twentieth century, when the Puritan "Sabbath" possessed many of the constraints of the Sabbath of Jesus' opponents, these passages played an important role in helping to free Sunday from being a day of "frozen activity." Unfortunately, the pendulum has swung far to the other extreme, and Sunday has for many become just another workday. Although it is a mistake to construe Sunday as "the Sabbath" instead of as "the Lord's Day," there is surely communal as well as individual benefit to be gained by preserving the tradition that Sunday is a special day, to be honored not only by corporate worship but also by family activities and by departures from the workaday routine (a long walk, a visit to a nursing home, inviting a lonely person or an overseas student to a good meal). In an increasingly secularized society, Christians must seek their own ways of sanctifying the Day of the Resurrection.

134

Interpretive Interlude (12:15–21)

To the brief report about withdrawal and healing, Matthew attaches his longest quotation from the Old Testament. Although it is introduced with his customary formula, "This was to fulfil what was spoken by the prophet" (see comments on 2:13–23), the quotation is only loosely connected with the preceding command not to make him known; in the quotation it is the servant himself who does not cry aloud. Perhaps the fulfillment refers rather to the withdrawal of Jesus mentioned in verse 15; aware of the Pharisees' plot to entrap him by public debate over political issues (see 22:15), Jesus refuses to wrangle or cry aloud in a public place ("nor will any one hear his voice in the streets," v. 19). In any event, the vagueness of the connection suggests that the quotation is more important to Matthew than its immediate context would suggest. This is shown also by its extent. If Matthew's intention was merely to show how Jesus' command to silence or his own withdrawal fulfilled Scripture, he need have cited only verse 19 (Isa. 42:2). His practice is to quote only as much as he needs (see 8:17, where he quotes only two lines of Isaiah 53). Matthew apparently intends his readers to pause in the midst of the controversy narratives and reflect on the meaning of Jesus' ministry as a whole vis-à-vis his rejection by his own people. He wants us to have a "God's-eye view" of what is happening in the gospel story by way of a scriptural prophecy.

For Christians, Isa. 42:1–4 was a messianic prophecy. It seems likely that it was so regarded by non-Christian Jews as well, since the Aramaic targum of Isa. 42:1 specifically refers to the Messiah ("Behold, my servant the Messiah"). The careful reader of Matthew's translation is reminded of God's utterance at the baptism of Jesus: "This is my Son, the Beloved, with whom I am well pleased" (3:17). This divine confirmation of Jesus' Messiahship will be repeated at the transfiguration (17:5). Matthew's quotation, standing midway between the baptism and the transfiguration, reminds the readers that it is God who has created Jesus to serve as Messiah.

It is probable that "my servant" also had messianic associations for first-century Jews. In the Hebrew Scriptures the term is frequently used of David, whom God refers to as "my servant David." The phrase is especially prominent in II Samuel 7 (vv.

135

5, 8; "thy servant David," v. 26), which also contains one of the most important messianic prophecies ("I will be his father, and he shall be my son," v. 14, quoted in Heb. 1:5). The motif becomes more explicitly messianic in Ezek. 34:23–24 because of the passage's future reference: "I will set up over them one shepherd, my servant David, . . . and my servant David shall be prince among them."

In his rendering of Isa. 42:1, Matthew chooses to translate the Hebrew word for servant by *pais*, not *doulos* or *diakonos*, the words normally used in the New Testament for "servant." Although *pais* was sometimes used in this way, in secular Greek as well as in the New Testament it usually means "child" or "son." While most English translations honor the underlying Hebrew by translating Matt. 12:18 as "Behold, my servant," Matthew's readers undoubtedly understood it as properly ambiguous, "Behold my servant/Son."

Thus understood, the quotation illuminates the remainder of the chapter with its sad tale of the rejection of Jesus the Messiah, the Son of God, by the Pharisees and "this generation." The first affirmation is that God will endow the Messiah with the Spirit. This, as we shall see, becomes the major issue in the Beelzebul controversy. The quotation thus confirms in advance Jesus' claim to exorcize by means of God's Spirit (12:28).

The next line, "and he shall proclaim judgment to the Gentiles," should be taken with the last line, "and in his name will the Gentiles hope." Here, as generally in Matthew, *krisis* should be translated "judgment," not "justice" (23:23 is an exception); it regularly refers to the last judgment, at which Jesus will function as judge. Some Jews may well have understood Isa. 42:1 as promising a destructive judgment of the Gentiles, but for Matthew, whose Gospel ends with the commission, "Go, enlist all the Gentiles as my disciples" (28:19), the text must have held a positive meaning. Later in the chapter (v. 41) we are reminded that the Ninevites repented (and were saved) at the preaching of Jonah, which was a proclamation of judgment ("Yet forty days, and Nineveh shall be overthrown," Jonah 3:4). Early Christian missionaries to the Gentiles proclaimed Jesus as judge as well as Savior (see Acts 10:42; 17:31). Since Jesus himself seems not to have announced judgment to any Gentile audience, we can assume that Matthew sees this prophecy as having its fulfillment after Easter, when the risen Christ will be present among his missionaries (28:20). The function of these

136

lines in the midst of the controversies apparently is to emphasize that God's intention is not foiled by the Pharisees' rejection of Jesus, because from ancient times God foretold that the good news about the Messiah would be for the Gentiles as well as for Israel.

Verse 19 seems to be contradicted by the context; Jesus immediately enters into vigorous debate with the Pharisees. Evidently Matthew understood the verse less literally. Two main possibilities have been considered. One proposal is that the emphasis should fall on "nor will any one *hear* his voice," taking the verb in the sense of "hearken to," that is, respond positively in faith and obedience (see 17:5; Acts 3:22–23). Taken in this way, the line predicts the rejection of Jesus by his own people. Others suggest that the lines are to be taken rather as meaning that Jesus refuses to harangue the crowds to whip up support for a political revolution; he is a humble, gentle Messiah (see 11:29). Thus understood, the verse anticipates the passion narrative, in which Jesus refuses to defend himself by political rhetoric.

The application of verse 20 is not clarified by the context, and consequently any proposal is conjectural. A traditional Christian interpretation that understands "bruised reed" and "smoldering wick" as references to sinners is probably as good a guess as any. The humble Messiah will deal gently with sinners up until the time when he victoriously judges the world. Like the Ninevites, they will be given ample opportunity to repent.

The Beelzebul Controversy (12:22–37)

There can be little doubt that Jesus' public ministry provoked controversy, not because of his exorcisms and other healings as such, but because of the radical claims that were implicit in his teaching. Other contemporary religious teachers, such as Hillel and Shammai, had disciples, but none made such imperious demands of followers ("Follow me, and let the dead bury their own dead," 8:22). Since other Jews were practicing exorcism, it was not this activity itself that provoked the Beelzebul charge but Jesus' demeanor as a whole.

In Luke 11:15 the opponents are identified simply as "some of them," that is, members of the crowd. Mark 3:22 refers to them as "the scribes who came down from Jerusalem." In Matthew, "the Pharisees" are specified in order to suggest that this

137

controversy is merely a continuation of the Sabbath disputes that issued in the plot to destroy Jesus (12:14). The wickedness of the plotters is now to be exhibited in blasphemy against the God they claim to be serving.

In Mark the dispute is not occasioned by a specific exorcism, but in Luke we are told that it is the curing of a mute that prompts the amazement of the crowd and the countering charge, "By Beelzebul the ruler of demons he casts out demons" (Luke 11:14–15). Several subtle differences appear in Matthew's account. First, the demoniac is blind as well as mute, that is, the exorcism is still more impressive. (Is it also symbolic for Matthew? Jesus opens the eyes of his followers, so that their tongues are loosed to tell God's good news.) Second, *all the crowds* (an extraordinary phrase not found elsewhere in the Gospels) are "overcome with astonishment"; the verb is a strong one, often meaning "to be out of one's mind," as in Mark 3:21. Perhaps a legitimate colloquial rendering would be "The crowds were going crazy over Jesus!" Third, the spectacular exorcism occasions the most explicit anticipation of Peter's confession of 16:16: "Is this perhaps the Son of David?" (The crowds have thus moved beyond their position of 9:33: "Never has anything like this been seen in Israel.") Thus in Matthew it is fear that the masses will accept Jesus as their Messiah that provokes the blasphemous charge (anticipated in 9:34).

Jesus' responses to the charge are of very different kinds. The first two are rational in their appeal. It is foolish to suggest that he is in league with Beelzebul, who is to be identified with Satan (the origin and meaning of "Beelzebul" are unknown), since this implies the impossible, namely, that Satan is busy undermining his own kingdom. Moreover, what marks Jesus' exorcisms as different in kind from other Jewish exorcisms? Are those others also made possible by Satan? The charge is frivolous. These two arguments together suggest that Jesus' exorcisms are not unique; other exorcists oppose Satan's rule and are thus to be seen as working on God's side, as is Jesus.

The next argument is of a very different order. Jesus claims that his exorcisms are effected through empowerment by God's Spirit (v. 28). "The Spirit of God" is especially important to Matthew in this context; it reappears in the blasphemy saying (vv. 31–32). In this saying Jesus does not deny the fact of other exorcisms but claims a special significance for his own.

The Gospel exorcism stories represent Jesus as effecting his

138

cures without incantations or material objects. We may contrast these with Josephus' account of a Jewish exorcism involving a ring and a plant root, plus a basin of water that was overturned by the demon to signal its departure. No such technique is employed by Jesus. Directly empowered by God, he commands, and the cure is effected.

What kind of argument is this? It appeals not to the reason but to the heart. Jesus challenges his opponents to see in his ministry evidence in support of his unverifiable claim that God is doing something unprecedented in and through him. The results may be the same as in other exorcisms, but for those having eyes to see, it will be clear that Jesus' activity is a manifestation of the Spirit of God.

Let us briefly review what Matthew has told us about the Spirit up to this point. It is the power of God by means of which the Messiah is conceived (1:18). It descends upon him at his baptism (3:16) and leads him into the wilderness to be tested (4:1). John prophesies that the mightier one coming after him will baptize with the Holy Spirit and with fire (3:11), and Jesus promises that his followers will be inspired by the Spirit when persecuted (10:20). Finally, Matthew prepares for the Beelzebul controversy by quoting Isa. 42:1–4, where God promises to put his Spirit on the Messiah (12:18). What we see from these passages is that for Matthew, as for early Christians generally, the Holy Spirit had *eschatological* significance: the appearance of the Spirit in Jesus and his followers was evidence that God was initiating the last act of the drama of salvation. Although it has yet to be consummated, the kingdom of God has been inaugurated in the Spirit-empowered ministry of Jesus.

Many scholars interpret the second half of verse 28 as if it were roughly equivalent to 4:17: "The kingdom of heaven has come near"; Jesus' exorcisms are evidence of the truth of his initial announcement. The phrase "upon you" in 12:28, however, deserves attention. Does "you" refer to the wider audience or to the opponents whom Jesus is directly addressing? What would it mean to say that the kingdom of God has come upon the Pharisees? The Greek verb *ephthasen,* here translated "has come," is occasionally used of the arrival of some *evil* upon someone, as in I Thess. 2:16: "God's wrath has come upon them" (the same idiom occurs in the Septuagint of Judg. 20:34, 42). It is at least possible, therefore, that verse 28 is understood by Matthew as a warning directed to the opponents: "If I am right in my claim of manifesting God's end-time gift of the Spirit, then be assured that God's judgment is already determined against you who deny the Spirit's presence."

The fourth argument, expressed in parabolic form, perhaps depends partly on Isa. 49:24–25: "Can prey be taken from the mighty or the captives of a tyrant be rescued? But thus says the LORD, Even the captives of the mighty shall be taken, and the prey of the tyrant be rescued; for I will contend with those who contend with you, and I will save your children." Satan, the strong man, finds himself powerless to defend his property, the enslaved demoniacs, against the overwhelming power of the Spirit manifested in Jesus. Jesus' victory over Satan ought to be sufficient evidence of whose side he is on.

The attached saying of verse 30 calls for a decision for or against Jesus, insisting that neutrality is ruled out. Those who do not join Jesus in gathering God's eschatological flock are in fact inhibiting this process or scattering the sheep.

The saying about blasphemy against the Holy Spirit is found in a very different context in Luke (12:10). Matthew follows Mark in attaching it to the Beelzebul controversy, where it obtains a far more polemical force. The first half of the double saying constitutes a truism for Jews; it hardly needs to be stated that slanderous words concerning other human beings can be forgiven when true repentance is shown, but blasphemy against God puts one beyond the pale (this half finds no parallel at Luke 12:10). It is the second half (which has no parallel in Mark) that is new. Jesus declares to his critics that forgiveness is possible for those who slander him as a person (as in 11:19, "Behold, a glutton and a drunkard!"), but those who call his miracles "the devil's work" are slandering not him but God. It is not Jesus but his opponents who are working for Beelzebul!

The idea of an unforgivable sin, axiomatic to first-century Jews and Christians (see I John 5:16–17), is problematic to modern Christians, because it seems to set limits on God's ability to deal with even the worst sinners. It is probable that Jesus and others who espoused the idea of an unforgivable sin did not by any means intend thereby to restrict God but wanted instead to emphasize as strongly as possible that human resistance to God is ultimately futile. God's patience with those who insist on calling good evil and evil good will come to an end. Innumerable Christians have tormented themselves unnecessarily by the thought that they are guilty of the unforgivable sin. As wise interpreters have frequently reminded us, those who worry about the unforgivable sin cannot be guilty of it!

In verse 33 Matthew repeats the tree-fruit analogy of 7:16–20 in order to make the point that the Pharisees' words reflect their nature; they speak evil because they are evil (vv. 34–35).

The passage concludes with a curious saying about accountability for "idle" words (vv. 36–37). Modern translations variously render the adjective as "careless," "thoughtless," or "useless." The KJV may best retain the original meaning by being the most literal. The adjective literally means "not working," as in Matt. 20:6: "Why are you standing here *idle* all day?" Words are meant to be effective tools; they should accomplish some useful purpose, as does God's word, which does not return "empty" (Isa. 55:11). In the context of the Beelzebul dispute the reference seems to be to the words of confession. Those who, unlike the Pharisees, confess their faith that God's Spirit is active in Jesus' ministry must make sure that this confession is translated into life. Their deeds must reflect their faith. Ulrich Luz makes this even more explicit: "idle" words are those which do not bring forth works of love. The Pharisees, whose words oppose love, are presented by Matthew as a negative example. (See Luz, *Matthew 8–17,* at 8:36–37.)

The Demand for a Sign (12:38–45)

The final controversy of chapter 12 consists of a demand by Jesus' enemies and three responses from him. Matthew connects this series of sayings with the preceding narrative by identifying those demanding a sign as "some of the scribes and Pharisees" and by using the verb "answered" in verse 38. That is, the demand for a sign is presented by Matthew as the opponents' response to verses 25–37.

From the beginning of chapter 12 it has been the Pharisees who have disputed with Jesus. Now for the first time scribes are associated with them. Although the exact nature of the Pharisees is still disputed because of inadequate and conflicting sources, it is clear that they constituted a party of laymen who were especially rigorous in their observance of the ceremonial law. They were not religious experts or teachers of the law. Included in their movement, however, were teachers, referred to in the Gospels as "scribes," who interpreted Scripture and

141

tradition in accordance with the Pharisaic perspective. (It should be remembered that there were also non-Pharisaic scribes; the scribes associated with the elders and the chief priests in the passion narrative are perhaps such.) Matthew's decision to make specific reference to the Pharisees' scribes in verse 38 may suggest that he regards their question as an exegetical one: "Give us a sign verifying your claims that we can interpret by reference to Scripture; the exorcism you have just performed doesn't qualify."

For Matthew, there is powerful irony in the fact that the demand for a sign follows so closely on verse 28, where Jesus declares that his exorcisms reveal that he is the one empowered by the eschatological gift of the Spirit. Historically, however, the situation must have seemed far more ambiguous to responsible teachers of the law. In the first century, there were many "prophets" who made messianic claims of one sort or another and promised to authenticate those claims by means of notable signs (which they were subsequently unable to accomplish). Such confirmatory miracles had to be predicted in advance of performance. It is entirely possible that wary religious leaders challenged Jesus to defend his unspoken claim in this way. "If you really are the Son of David, as some common people believe, prove it by doing the sort of thing that Scripture predicts the Messiah will do." Healing the sick evidently did not count as a messianic activity for most of Jesus' contemporaries.

Perhaps Jesus' original response is reported in Mark 8:12: "Why does this generation seek a sign? Truly, I say to you, no sign shall be given to this generation." We are reminded of the temptation narrative, where Satan tempts Jesus to demonstrate that he is the Son of God by turning stones into bread or by leaping from the pinnacle of the temple (4:3, 5). Underlying the temptation narrative is the conviction that the Messiah, the Lord's humble anointed one, cannot in any way demonstrate his status, because to do so is to falsify it. Only God can certify the Messiah.

This conviction is likewise reflected in Matthew's version of the saying: No sign except the sign of Jonah. The enigma of "the sign of Jonah" is then elucidated in verse 40: Jonah's three-day sojourn in the sea monster was a foreshadowing of Jesus' brief visit to the realm of the dead. All emphasis is on the brevity of Jesus' stay in Sheol; his removal from that realm by God will be the spectacular eschatological event confirming his Messiah-

142

ship. (Matthew is untroubled by what appears to us to be a discrepancy between *after three days* and *on the third day* found in 16:21. "Three days and three nights" was the ancient way of referring to three calendar days; with an inclusive counting of Friday, Saturday, and Sunday, the two expressions are identical.)

Thus interpreted, verse 40 constitutes this Gospel's first announcement of the death and resurrection of Jesus and is heard as such by the narrative audience (see the sequel in 27:63). When the predicted sign, "the sign of Jonah," is finally enacted by God on Easter morning, its truth is converted into a lie by Jesus' enemies (see comments on 28:11–15).

Jesus responds to the request for a sign with a stern observation: "An evil and adulterous generation seeks for a sign" (v. 39). In this context "adulterous" is metaphorical, recalling the language of the prophets about Israel's unfaithfulness to God (e.g., Hos. 2:2; Jer. 3:8–9; Ezek. 23:37). Whereas the prophets used the analogy with respect to participation in foreign cults, here it seems to refer to a fundamental lack of faith in the living God. The wickedness of the demand for a sign consists in unwillingness to believe that God is present and active in Jesus' ministry.

The second response to the demand for a sign is composed of twin sayings about the last judgment, both involving Gentiles. Many prophetic oracles predict that God will punish Israel's unfaithfulness by means of other nations (see, e.g., Isa. 10:5: "Assyria, rod of my anger"). Since judgment has been transferred theologically from history to the last judgment, the function of the Gentiles changes accordingly. The Ninevites and the queen of the south (i.e., the queen of Sheba of I Kings 10) will condemn "this generation" at the judgment, because they responded positively to a prophet and a wise king, whereas this generation refuses to be moved by something far greater than Jonah and Solomon.

The "something greater" is vague; as in the earlier appearance of the expression in 12:6, the sayings of verses 41–42 do not speak of someone greater. One could suppose that this is simply a modest way of saying the same thing. Although he knows himself to be the Messiah, Jesus refrains from saying forthrightly, "I am greater than Jonah and Solomon." It is possible, however, that the sayings do not have in mind the *person* of Jesus but the *activity* of Jesus and his disciples, in and through which God is working out his purpose for the world.

143

The third and final response to the demand of the scribes and the Pharisees is the parable of the demoniac who ends up in a worse state than before his demon was exorcized. The point of the parable rests in the description of the demon's former "house"; it is found "empty, swept, and put in order." The word here translated "empty" is not the ordinary Greek word with this meaning but a most unusual one; it is not an adjective but a participle meaning "having leisure," that is, not occupied with work. Perhaps our English word "unoccupied" should be used to preserve the wordplay. The house is carefully cleaned and decorated in preparation for a special visitor or new tenant, the Messiah perhaps, but it remains unoccupied. It is "at leisure," that is, uninvolved and unresponsive, unwilling to take the risk of a commitment. Taken in this way, the parable can be regarded as a companion piece to the parable of the children (11:16–17).

In a different context Jesus may have used the parable of the unoccupied house in response to the revolutionary movement that fomented armed resistance to Rome. Jesus had preached love of enemies, going the second mile, and turning the other cheek, but a generation unwilling to take his warnings seriously would have to suffer the fearful punishment of war's ravages in 66–70 C.E. The last state would prove much worse than the first.

In Matthew's context, however, the parable is not ethical but christological in its import. Coming at the end of the long series of disputes that have dominated the chapter, this parable administers the final blow to the opponents for their rejection of Jesus. Their last state will be far worse than their first, because they refuse to acknowledge what God is doing in Jesus.

The modern interpreter must be very careful when preaching or teaching from these controversy narratives. Because Jesus so vehemently attacks the Pharisees and "this generation," the passages have frequently been used in support of a Christian anti-Semitism that Jesus himself would by no means have condoned. Standing in Israel's prophetic tradition, Jesus castigated God's people just as Amos and others had done before him, without thereby condemning Israel to eternal damnation.

144 Christians can best appropriate these passages by applying them not to the Jews but to themselves. Instead of externalizing the dualism of good and evil, faith and unfaith by dividing humanity into "disciples" and "Pharisees," we must emphasize

that the dualism is internal. Inside each Christian is a "disciple" and a "Pharisee." The resistance to Jesus' ministry that brought him to the cross is a resistance each of us knows within.

Jesus' True Family (12:46–50)

That this passage was widely quoted in early Christian literature is readily understandable. Wherever the gospel was received, families were divided, and those cut off from their blood relatives found great comfort in the thought that they belonged to Jesus' true family. The same, of course, is true today, not only in non-Christian cultures where baptism may be accompanied by disownment but also in secularized families of "Christendom," where commitment to Christian service may result in alienation from family members who cannot comprehend or tolerate such a waste of time and talent. The passage is also particularly meaningful to those who have been liberated from an emotional slavery to dysfunctional families and who find a substitute family in the church.

Coming at the conclusion of a series of intense disputes in which the gulf between Jesus and "this generation" becomes ever greater, this little narrative about Jesus' true family sounds a contrasting note. In this respect it functions as a parallel to 11:25–30, which likewise concludes a chapter stressing the non-acceptance of Jesus on the part of most of his contemporaries. Over against the majority is set the small band of men and women who hear Jesus' voice calling "Come unto me. . . . Take my yoke" and respond in faith and obedience.

Concerning the narrative itself, many questions have been raised. Why did Jesus' mother and brothers come to talk to him? Did they think him crazy and want to take him out of the public spotlight so that he could recover (see Mark 3:20–21)? Had they heard of the fury of his opponents and had come to remove him from danger? Or were they disturbed by the immense stress placed on him by constant contact with crowds (see Mark 6:31)? While such questions may fascinate modern readers, they were evidently of little interest to Matthew, who provides no hint of an answer. It is similarly inappropriate to suggest that Jesus here shows a callous disregard for the feelings of his loved ones, because the story does not tell us what happened after the "punch line." We cannot say that Jesus rejects his family because of their lack of faith in him; Matthew does not say that

145

Mary and the brothers are relegated to "this generation." The single point of the story is that, for Jesus, a new spiritual family takes priority over his natural family.

How is the new family defined? "Whoever does the will of my Father in heaven is my brother, and sister, and mother" (v. 50). It is noteworthy that at the end of this chapter, which emphasizes Jesus and his significance as the focal point of God's eschatological activity, the definition of Jesus' true family is not christological but ethical. This is not to say that faith in Jesus is unimportant. In verse 49 Matthew specifically stresses that those to whom Jesus gestures with his hand are *disciples* (the Markan parallel says nothing about disciples), that is, persons who would not have become followers in this sense had they not believed in him. For Matthew, however, it is primarily ethics that distinguishes true from false believers (compare v. 50 with 7:21). Jesus' new family has its own life-style. To be Jesus' sister or brother, one must live the life of the kingdom.

Matthew 13:1–52
Parables of the Kingdom

From the opening verses of chapter 13 one would not suspect that a very different use of language will here be attributed to Jesus. The innocent reader is led to believe that Jesus, having gotten rid of his opponents, now resumes his teaching ministry, making his point by means of a story.

In every culture figurative language, ranging from simple analogies to complex stories and myths, is employed as an effective tool for communicating ideas. In Matthew's Gospel, Jesus has already used such language on numerous occasions (e.g., 7:3–5; 7:24–27; 9:15; 12:29). None of these, however, has Matthew identified as a *parabolē* ("parable"). The Greek word derives from a verb meaning "set side by side," that is, compare. For uninstructed Greek readers the word could designate any kind of comparison. Behind Matthew's Greek, however, stand the Hebrew Scriptures, where the word *mashal*, while likewise representing many kinds of figurative language, was also used for enigmatic speech; it often designated a statement whose meaning was not immediately apparent. In Ezek. 17:2

the prophet is instructed by God, "Son of man, propound a riddle, and speak a *mashal* to the house of Israel." What follows is an allegory, which has to be explained to the audience. It is clear in this instance that a *mashal* is like a riddle, intended to tease the mind into insight rather than to communicate a simple idea by means of an illustration.

It is apparent that Matthew wishes "parables" in verse 3 to recall to the readers this special use of the word. Although he does not define it until verses 34–35, where a quotation of Ps. 78:2 equates "parables" with "things hidden," a special meaning is implied by the disciples' question in verse 10, "Why do you speak to them in parables?" It is not Jesus' customary use of illustrations that prompts this question but his resort to enigmatic language that both conceals and reveals.

In chapter 13 Matthew has collected seven or eight parables (depending on whether v. 52 is counted as a parable), combining Mark's smaller collection (Mark 4:1–34) with parables from his other sources. This is not the only collection of parables in Matthew; three are grouped together in 21:28—22: 14, and another three in 24:45—25:30. We must ask, therefore, what is the function of this particular collection and what sort of parables are here brought together. We can be certain that it is not a haphazard assembly intended merely to illustrate Jesus' skill as a parable maker.

The location provides an initial clue. The parables of chapter 13 constitute Jesus' response to the rejection he has experienced from "this generation" in the preceding two chapters. They provide an explanation for the unresponsiveness of his contemporaries, who are here represented by the crowds (despite the positive depiction of the crowds in 12:23). The parables also contribute to the further development of the dichotomy that divides the audience into those who are for and those who are against Jesus. In this respect they reiterate in stronger terms the contrast enunciated in the final passage of each of the two prior chapters (11:25–30; 12:46–50), where those who accept Jesus' yoke and become his true family are contrasted with the many who reject him.

This emphasis on *contrast* and *separation* dictates both the substance and the structure of the discourse. None of the parables included in this collection is concerned directly with how to live, as, for example, is the parable of the unforgiving debtor (18:23–35). All are "kingdom" parables; all but the first begin

147

with the phrase "The kingdom of heaven is similar to . . . ." Although the parable of the sower lacks the formula, its association with the others suggests that it too should be understood as a parable of the kingdom.

It must be noted that Jesus' kingdom parables do not tell us what the kingdom will be like in its final consummation. Unlike contemporary Jewish apocalyptic writers, Jesus spent no time describing the golden age on a transformed earth or the golden streets of the heavenly Jerusalem. He was less interested in the future than in the present dimension of God's rule. He spoke often of the imminent judgment, but this was in large part because of its meaning for the present. At the heart of all his activity was the conviction that in and through him God's end-time kingdom was invading the world, confronting men and women with the necessity of decision. The kingdom parables are thus concerned primarily with God's action in the present and people's response. Because the reaction to Jesus' message divides people sharply into the receptive and the unreceptive, the kingdom parables also speak of separation and judgment.

The structure of the collection is likewise dictated by this strong emphasis on contrast and separation. This third major discourse differs from the preceding two (the Sermon on the Mount, chaps. 5–7, and the discourse on discipleship and mission, chap. 10) in having two distinct parts, with the second sharply distinguished from the first by a change of setting and audience. While the first half (13:1–33) has a public setting, in the second half (13:36–52) Jesus leaves the crowds and retires to the privacy of a house where he addresses his disciples alone. Between the two parts, Matthew places one of his fulfillment quotations as a further comment on Jesus' use of parables (13: 34–35). This simple structure is slightly complicated by the fact that Jesus speaks to the disciples privately in the first half also (vv. 10–23). Evidently it was regarded as important to instruct the readers immediately after the first parable that these kingdom parables are not just simple illustrations but "riddles" that both conceal and reveal.

Because our primary purpose in this commentary is to assist modern interpreters of the Gospel, it seems advisable to depart from the custom of treating the passages in order. We will begin instead with verses 10–17, which are concerned with the purpose of the parables, and then deal with the sower and its interpretation (vv. 3–9, 18–23), the tares and its interpretation

(vv. 24–30, 36–43) together with the net (vv. 47–50), and finally deal with the two sets of twin parables (the mustard seed and leaven, the treasure and the pearl, vv. 31–33, 44–46), and the parabolic conclusion (vv. 51–52). In most instances we will look at the material at three levels: What was intended by Jesus? How did Matthew reapply the parable? What meaning can it have for us today?

The Purpose of the Parables (13:10–17)

The disciples' question, "Why do you speak to them in parables?" alerts the reader that the sower and the parables to follow are not simple comparisons but enigmatic communications.

While the *life* of the kingdom of heaven can be spoken of openly, there is a *mystery* about the kingdom that requires greater reserve because of the very different response it demands. Divorce, love of enemies, and other matters concerning human relationships can be discussed rationally in relation to what the Scriptures reveal about God's will, but the question of what God is doing in our midst is not of the same order. If someone shouts "Fire!" in a crowded theater, the truth claim can be evaluated in due course—after the building has been evacuated! If Jesus declares that the presence of the Spirit of God in his exorcisms indicates that the last judgment is imminent, an immediate decision is called for as in the theater, but the truth claim cannot be assessed on the basis of empirical data. God does not make himself available for our inspection.

"The secrets of the kingdom," accordingly, are not *taught* but *revealed.* They are presented in the veiled speech of parables to the crowds who are unable to appropriate them and are explained to the disciples who, because of their commitment to following Jesus, are capable of comprehension.

The authenticity of verses 10–17 is challenged by many scholars, who find incredible Mark's suggestion that Jesus taught in parables *in order that* those outside might not perceive, understand, and repent (Mark 4:11–12). This is so out of character for Jesus, they insist, that the whole passage must be questioned. For this reason, many prefer Matthew's version, in which Mark's "in order that" has been replaced by "because," and the last line of Mark's allusion to Isa. 6:9–10 ("lest they should turn again, and be forgiven") has been dropped. There

149

is no "softening" of Mark's theory of the parables in Matthew, however. As Joachim Jeremias has pointed out, Mark's "in order that" refers not to Jesus' purpose but to God's, since it is followed by an indirect quotation of God's word to Isaiah; it is a shorthand way of referring to the fulfillment of God's prediction concerning Israel (*The Parables of Jesus*, p. 17). The substitution of "because," therefore, does not alter the statement significantly, which in Matthew's version can be paraphrased: "I speak to them in veiled speech, because they behave in accordance with God's decree as declared to Isaiah: they see and do not *see*, they hear and do not *hear*, nor do they understand." In Isa. 6:10 the prophet is instructed, "Make the heart of this people fat, and their ears heavy, and shut their eyes" *because* God has already determined to punish his people (Isa. 6:11–13).

It is this somber thought that underlies Matt. 13:10–17. Verse 11 is central: "To you it has been given to know the secrets of the kingdom of heaven, but to them it has not been given." The verbs in the passive voice are properly perceived as "divine passives"; it is not a matter of human intellect and natural insight but of divine revelation (cf. 16:17). God has decreed that there will be a sharp separation between those selected for participation in the kingdom and those who are not. Like Isaiah, Jesus must be obedient to the divine decree and honor it by his use of veiled speech. To those chosen, his parables will serve as a means of revelation. To those not chosen, they will remain enigmas.

The thought of judgment also underlies the paradoxical saying of verse 12, which occurs at a later point in the Markan discussion (Mark 4:25) and is placed here by Matthew as a commentary on verse 11. "Whoever has" refers to the elect, who will participate in all the joys of the kingdom of heaven. "The one who has not" denotes the nonelect, who, claiming to be members of God's people by virtue of descent from Abraham, will lose that status (see 3:9).

What are the secrets of the kingdom of heaven (v. 11)? In view of the way the corresponding Semitic words are used in the apocalyptic literature and at Qumran, it is probable that "secrets" refers to God's plan for the consummation of the age (see also vv. 34–35). God has graciously granted the disciples the privilege of recognizing that in Jesus' activity God is initiating his final rule. By listening to Jesus, they will acquire more knowledge concerning what this means. One of the "secrets" may concern the theological motif that is imparted in these verses, namely, that God has determined to harden Israel (see Rom. 11:25, where Paul uses the same Greek word, *mystērion*, to speak of the hardening of Israel). Jack Kingsbury urges that "secrets" includes ethics as well as eschatology; since the disciples are not simply waiting for the kingdom but already living in it because of Jesus' presence, their behavior must reflect the life of the age to come (*The Parables of Jesus in Matthew 13*, p. 45).

Verses 16–17, "Blessed are your eyes . . . ," are, in Luke, found directly after Jesus' cry of jubilation: "I thank you, Father, . . . that you have hid these things from the wise and understanding, and have revealed them to babes . . ." (Luke 10:21–24). Although separated from the corresponding passage in Matt. 11:25–30 by more than a chapter, these verses are, as in Luke, the natural sequel; "these things" refers most probably to what God is doing in Jesus' ministry (see comments on 11:25–30). Apocalyptic writers wrote enthusiastically of the blessedness of those who would witness the messianic era. *Psalms of Solomon* 18:6 declares, "Blessed shall they be in those days, in that they shall see the good of the Lord which he shall perform for the generation that is to come." In these verses Jesus triumphantly announces: The waiting is over! Blessed are your eyes, for you are witnessing what the prophets anticipated and the righteous of every generation have longed to see!

While verses 10–17 in their present Greek form may not present verbatim what Jesus said on a specific occasion, there is no need to deny that their substance derives from the same mind that pronounced woes against Chorazin, Bethsaida, and Capernaum because they had not repented in response to what God had wrought in their midst (11:20–24). The pessimism of 13:10–17 is pronounced, and, like the woes, this passage may reflect a stage late in Jesus' ministry when it had become evident to him that the majority of the people were not going to respond positively to his message.

Be that as it may, Matthew undoubtedly found these sayings relevant to the failure of the post-Easter mission to Israel (see comments on chap. 10, esp. vv. 16–25). The Evangelist probably viewed this passage as applicable to Christians as well. He was deeply distressed about the mixed state of the church, as we shall see in his treatment of several parables (the tares and the

151

net, 13:24–30, 36–43, 47–50; the wedding garment, 22:11–14). Christians too needed to be warned not to regard their status as church members as a guarantee of future salvation. There were many who appeared to see and hear, whose behavior betrayed the fact that they had not really *understood* (v. 13; see 7:21).

Modern interpreters can likewise appropriate the passage as a warning for complacent Christians. Care must be taken not to exaggerate the predestination idea of verse 11. Matthew here and elsewhere correctly stresses the sovereignty of God, but he by no means intends thereby to diminish human responsibility. Nor should the contrast between the selected and the nonselected be taken by believers as cause for gloating, since those who think they are "in" may in the end be "out," and those who at the moment are unresponsive and thus apparently not elect may yet respond with faith (see Rom. 11:23).

The Sower and Its Interpretation (13:3–9, 18–23)

Modern study of Jesus' parables has produced two important conclusions: (1) Many of the parables have been reinterpreted for the post-Easter situation of the church. (2) Originally the parables were not allegorical but were intended to make one point only. To discover Jesus' intention, therefore, it is necessary to remove allegorical interpretations that have been created to reapply the parables to a later context.

Scholars who have attempted to do this with the parable of the sower argue that the allegorical interpretation of verses 18–23 contains a number of signs of later composition. Originally, it is proposed, Jesus created this parable to strengthen his followers against discouragement in the face of unresponsiveness. The farmer scatters his seed liberally before plowing, knowing that a good many seeds will not reach maturity but confident nonetheless that there will be a good harvest. In this interpretation the three reasons for failure are not to be pressed allegorically; they are simply illustrations of the frustrations a farmer must face.

This rather bland understanding has been improved upon by Jeremias, who emphasizes that the closing detail of the parable is by no means a reflection of a farmer's usual experience. A good harvest would have provided a first-century Galilean farmer with ten bushels for every bushel of seed; a normal return would have been seven and a half. Thus Jesus is not speaking of everyday experience but of God's supernatural activity at the dawning of the kingdom (*The Parables of Jesus*, p. 150). Despite the meager response to Jesus' ministry, God will provide a spectacular harvest! It is this final detail that transforms the parable from being a simple illustration to being enigmatic speech that reveals and conceals the secret of the kingdom.

Other scholars, not content to dismiss verses 18–23 as completely foreign to Jesus' intention, propose a middle way. Although the allegorical interpretation does not accompany the parable in the *Gospel of Thomas*, it may nonetheless transmit faithfully the tradition that Jesus intended the parable to be understood allegorically. Since allegory was employed by Israel's prophets (see, e.g., Ezekiel 17), it is foolish to deny that Jesus could have employed this genre. Accordingly, the sower's three unsuccessful areas may have been meant by Jesus to refer to many of the wider circle of his supporters whose enthusiasm had waned or disappeared (compare John 6:66). Despite these defections, God's purpose for the kingdom would not be thwarted!

One of the problems concerning the reinterpretation of the parable as we have it in verses 18–23 is the confusion it manifests regarding the allegorical significance of the seed. In verse 19 the seed refers unambiguously to "the word of the kingdom" which is sown in human hearts; here people who do not "understand" the word are represented by the soil beside the path. This inclines readers to treat the parable as an allegory about four different soils, only one of which is truly receptive of the implanted seed. In the succeeding verses, however, "that which is sown" refers to different kinds of people, and the various soils now signify the trying situations in which these people find themselves and which prevent them from becoming fruitful. This allegorical understanding is dissatisfying, because it suggests that those who are sown in the good soil are simply lucky; they produce fruit because they have not had to struggle with the temptations of this world or face tribulation and persecution. This is surely not what either Jesus or Matthew intended. Apparently the details of the allegory are not to be pressed to this logical conclusion. The general tenor of the message is clear: those who receive the word of the kingdom and *understand* it, that is, appropriate it not merely intellectually but

153

with a commitment at the depths of their being, will be able to withstand the onslaught of temptation and tribulation and produce a bountiful harvest in terms of the good fruits of obedience to God's will.

Matthew's perception of the contrast between those who receive and "understand" the word and those who simply receive it, drawing as it does on Isa. 6:9–10, must be interpreted from the Old Testament background, where "understand" implies acknowledgment of God's sovereignty. In Ps. 119:34 we read, "Give me understanding, that I may keep thy law and observe it with my whole heart." Here "understanding" refers not to intellectual awareness but to a moral commitment involving one's inmost self. Such an understanding is so far beyond intellectual competence that it is regarded as God's gift. Accordingly, for Matthew the people who hear the word and understand it (v. 23) are those "to whom it has been given" (v. 11). By grace, not by human effort, are they able to incorporate the word into their very being.

How shall we appropriate the parable and its interpretation by the earliest church? Modern interpreters should feel free to take as their point of departure either Jesus' situation or Matthew's. If the suggestion is correct that the parable originally spoke of the great harvest that God would produce despite temporary setbacks, today's preachers and teachers can use it in the same way. Evangelism must be pursued enthusiastically in spite of what appear to be meager results. Our responsibility is to sow the seed; only God can give the increase (cf. I Cor. 3:6).

On the other hand, Matthew's reinterpretation of the parable to fit the situation of his church encourages us to do the same for our time. Our contemporaries also need to be warned of the difference between simply "hearing" the word and "understanding" it. The commitment of today's Christians is threatened less by persecution than by secular scorn ("You don't really believe all that stuff, do you?"), but otherwise little has changed. The cares of the world and the deceitfulness of riches are still able to choke the word. Christians must pray for the gift of understanding, so that what they believe with their minds may be acted out in their daily behavior.

The Tares and the Net (13:24–30, 36–43, 47–50)

These two parables and their interpretations can be looked at together because both are treated as judgment parables.

A certain tension can be observed between the parable of the tares and its interpretation. In the parable itself emphasis is placed on the farmer's patience: "Let both grow together until the harvest" (v. 30*a*). Perhaps Jesus used this parable to point out that human beings are not competent to make the kind of judgments implied in separating wheat from tares; in plucking out what they think are tares, they may very well be pulling up wheat. Only God can make such judgments, and in due course this will be done. In the meantime we must be more patient with one another. Taken in this way, the story becomes a parable of grace. In the strange world of the parable where separation is graciously postponed, it may even be possible for weeds to become wheat!

The interpretation of the parable found in verses 36–43 applies the parable to the time of the church. The risen Christ sows good seed in the world and thus creates the church. Into the midst of this church the devil sows people who do not belong in the kingdom, "children of the evil one" (v. 38). Matthew is greatly disturbed by the mixed state of the church, which contains many who enthusiastically call Jesus "Lord, Lord" but refuse to follow his ethical teaching (7:21–27; see also 13:47–50 and 22:11–14). By means of this interpretation Matthew assures himself and others that a day of reckoning will come to these pseudodisciples; the glorified Christ will send forth his angels to purify the church of all who disregard the moral law.

Remarkable in this interpretation is the absence of any reference to the householder's patience. What was central to the parable is ignored in the allegorical interpretation. Perhaps Matthew was less pleased than Jesus with God's long-suffering!

Concerning the parable of the net (vv. 47–50), scholars debate whether Matthew regards the parable as an allegory about the world or about the church. The latter is the more probable. The net clearly parallels the tares, where the bad seed is an addition to a field sowed with good seed; if the world, not the church, were here in mind, the reverse would be more appropriate. So here it is the "rotten" fish that are removed from the

155

presence of the good ones, according to verse 49. As in the earlier parable, Matthew is here expressing his concern about the mixed state of the church, which contains "rotten" as well as good Christians. The intention of these verses is not to assure good Christians of their predestined salvation as good fish but to warn them that they must persevere in doing what Jesus teaches. Not lip service but lived faith is required of Jesus' followers.

Mustard Seed, Leaven, Treasure, Pearl (13:31–33, 44–46)

In Matthew's collection these parables are found as two pairs with different audiences; the first two are addressed to the crowds, the second two to disciples. Correspondingly, the first set emphasizes God's action, the second stresses the human response.

The mustard seed and leaven are sometimes treated as parables of growth. They do indeed speak of growth, but the emphasis appears to lie rather on the sharp contrast between the initial and final states in each case. That is, neither parable is intended to encourage the church to regard itself as gradually growing and becoming more powerful within the world, or as "leavening" the world. Both proclaim that God's action in the world, while almost imperceptible (the mustard seed was proverbial as the smallest thing that an eye could see) or hidden (as leaven in dough), is nonetheless real and will in God's own time come to full fruition. Both assume that the kingdom of God is not a strictly future reality that will suddenly appear full-blown without any prior activity. In Jesus' ministry the kingdom has been mysteriously inaugurated. Both thus give expression to the "secrets of the kingdom" (v. 11).

Taken in this way, the two parables are not "teaching" but "preaching"; they do not give instruction about what the kingdom is like but call for faith in the God who is active in the tiny movement initiated by Jesus. In this sense they are not simple illustrations but *mashalim*, enigmatic utterances teasing the mind into reflection and response. The twin parables challenge the hearer to leave behind the pedestrian, pragmatic everyday world that treats God as irrelevant and enter a new world where God is the primary reality.

Did Matthew regard these two parables as allegories as he does the prior parables of the sower and the tares? Although no allegorical interpretation is attached, there are details that invite such a view. Whereas Mark 4:32 is content to say that the minuscule mustard seed becomes "the greatest of all shrubs" or "a great plant," Matthew (like Luke) describes it as becoming a *tree*. This hyperbole is justified to some extent, since the bush attains a height of eight to ten feet, and birds are naturally attracted to its shade and seed, but the words "and the birds of heaven dwell in its branches" are strongly reminiscent of Dan. 4:21, which speaks allegorically of a kingdom whose dominion extends to the ends of the earth and incorporates all peoples. Another possible influence is Ezek. 17:23; 31:6. "Birds of heaven" was a common metaphor for Gentiles (see *I Enoch* 90:30, 33, 37). It seems probable, therefore, that either Matthew or his source regarded this parable as an allegory of the expansion of Jesus' movement into the Gentile world. And whereas Mark and the *Gospel of Thomas* declare that the kingdom is like a mustard seed, Matthew's version adds the detail "which a man took and sowed in his field." Since the idea of a farmer taking the trouble to sow a single mustard seed seems farfetched, we are probably to regard this as an allegorical reference to God's action in the world.

Similarly, Matthew's version of the parable of the leaven contains (as does Luke 13:20) the surprising note that the woman hid the leaven in *three measures* of wheat flour, that is, a huge batch of dough made from approximately fifty pounds of flour! It has been estimated that bread sufficient for over one hundred people would come from her oven. We are probably to see here an allusion to Gen. 18:6, where Abraham instructs Sarah to prepare cakes from three measures of flour for his heavenly visitors. In both passages the quantity of flour suggests a festive occasion. This detail perhaps suggests that the final outcome of God's hidden activity will be the messianic banquet at which the heavenly Lord Jesus will dine with his people.

While these allegorical details must be treated with caution, the main point remains secure. God is at work, even though human eyes may fail to perceive what is happening.

The second pair of parables, the treasure and the pearl, stresses the human response to what God is doing. Like buried treasure, God's activity is hidden and must be discovered. Like a pearl of immense value, it must be sought in order to be found.

157

The emphasis, however, falls not on the finding, whether accidental as in the first parable or the result of long diligence as in the second, but on the overwhelming response made to the discovery. In each case the finder sells all he possesses in order to take possession of what he has found.

It is possible to take both as exemplary parables like the Good Samaritan, which concludes with the injunction "Go and do likewise" (Luke 10:37). Perhaps they were so understood by those Palestinian disciples who established communes in Jerusalem after the resurrection (Acts 2:44–46). Although modern Christians also need to be warned against the deceitfulness of affluence (13:22), these parables should not be employed so literally. Understood in this way, the parables can all too easily be misconstrued as teaching that "the kingdom of heaven" is an individual possession that must be earned through the renunciation of material things. Despite all the ethical injunctions of the Gospels, the central thought is that "the kingdom" is something God is doing, that is, it is to be received as a *gift*. The kingdom of heaven is not something that can be *acquired* and henceforth held as a legal and permanent possession; it is a sphere into which one enters (18:3). The parables instruct us that our response to the gracious gift of participation in God's rule must be total. Those whose eyes have been opened to see what God is doing in Jesus must commit themselves wholeheartedly in faith and obedience.

Things New and Old (13:51–52)

Matthew furnishes his parables collection with two endings, neither of which is found at the parallels in Mark 4 and Luke 8. The first reaffirms the fundamental statement of 13:11, "To *you* it has been given to know the secrets of the kingdom of heaven." The disciples here represent Christian believers, for whom the parables function as revelations of what God is doing. For them, the parables are windows, not locked doors. They understand.

The second ending has sometimes been described as an eighth parable, because it employs a similitude: a Christian scribe is like a householder who brings forth from his treasure room things new and old. Others contest this identification, insisting that the characterization of the householder's activity is so artificial that it is to be regarded rather as a simple allegory for what the scribe does.

158

"Scribe" is used in Matthew as the designation of a person who is learned in Scripture and tradition. "Things new and old" is taken by some as referring to Matthew's practice of giving new applications to old traditions about Jesus, as is done, for example, in the parable of the lost sheep (18:10–14). It seems more probable that "new" refers to Christian traditions and "old" to the Scriptures of Israel. The Christian scribe is a learned exegete and transmitter of traditions (including the parables), who is able to interpret the Bible to the Christian community.

Matthew's self-portrait has often been seen in verse 52, and such is not impossible, but the Evangelist does not point to himself alone but to every Christian exegete. Why does Matthew conclude a discourse concerned with the understanding of Christians in general with a reference to "scribes," a small group within the church? Clearly it is verse 51, not verse 52, that serves as a fitting climax to the collection as a whole. The Evangelist presents verse 52 as an important appendix. Ordinary Christians have direct access to the mysteries of the kingdom of heaven as mediated through the parables and other teachings of Jesus, but they require the assistance of theologians who can help them appropriate the wisdom of the Hebrew Scriptures for their understanding of what God is doing in the church.

Note that Matthew, reversing what appears to be the natural order "old and new," stresses the new. It is only natural that Christians should give priority to the New Testament and its direct testimony to Jesus. Matthew's scribe, however, is ever mindful of the importance of the Old Testament. The crypto-Marcionites in our midst, who treat the Old Testament as superfluous, need to be reminded that what God was doing in Jesus was merely a continuation of the grand story that began with the creation. To ignore the Old Testament is to truncate the gospel.

Matthew 13:53—16:12
Messianic Signs Misperceived

159

It is difficult to find any organizing principle underlying the diverse narratives that are placed between the parables collection and Peter's confession, the next major turning point in the gospel story. Assuming Matthew's dependence on Mark, we can say that Matthew is simply following the earlier Gospel without questioning the arrangement of the material. He diverges from Mark's outline at two points only: he omits the passage about the sending out of the Twelve, which he has already used in chapter 10, and omits the healing of Mark 7:31–33, substituting for it a summary of Jesus' healing activity, 15:29–31.

Bracketed by the rejection at Nazareth and the demand for a sign from heaven, this loose collection of narratives can be characterized by the rubric "Messianic Signs Misperceived."

Rejection at Nazareth (13:53–58)

The story about Jesus' return to his hometown appeals to us because of our interest in the humanity of Jesus. We are curious to know more about what Jesus was really like. It is disappointing to us that the Gospels tell us nothing about what he looked like, what kind of voice he had, what sense of humor he displayed, and so forth. This story is important to us because it tells us something about his socioeconomic circumstances, his family, and the neighbors among whom he grew up.

In Mark 6:3 the villagers ask, "Is this not the carpenter, the son of Mary?" Matthew transfers the word "son," so that the question reads, "Is this not the son of the carpenter, whose mother is called Mary?" It is probably not Matthew's intention to suggest that Jesus, though a carpenter's son, was no carpenter himself. This is, rather, affirmed by the phrase, since it was normal for a son to be taught his father's trade. The alteration is intended to remove the sting from Mark's phrase "the son of Mary." Whether his father was living or dead, Jesus would have been identified as "Jesus the son of Joseph" (see John 1:45). To identify him as "the son of Mary" in that culture would have cast aspersions on his legitimacy.

The Greek word *tektōn*, here translated "carpenter," is actually ambiguous. In the Greek translation of the Hebrew Scriptures it is used to denote craftsmen who work with stone, iron, or brass as well as woodworkers. It is sometimes suggested that, because of the scarcity of wood in Galilee, it is more likely that Joseph and Jesus were stonemasons. Josephus, however, seems to use *tektōn* primarily for "carpenter," employing a different word for "mason." Was Nazareth too small to provide a livelihood for a carpenter? This is difficult to assess, since the carpenter produced plows, yokes, and other tools needed by farmers, as well as beds, boxes, and coffins.

No stigma would have been attached to the fact that Jesus was a tradesman. It became customary later for prospective rabbis to learn a trade. Paul is proud that he worked with his hands (I Cor. 4:12; 9:12–14). Indeed, skilled craftsmen would have been highly esteemed in Galilee. Although normally not rich, neither were they poor by community standards; they earned a good livelihood, especially in contrast to the day laborers who were dependent on the needs of landowners (see 20:7). It is entirely possible that when Jesus moved from Nazareth to Capernaum he was financially capable of buying or building a house for himself (4:13; see 13:36).

We are informed by this passage (13:53–58) that Jesus came from a large family; he had four brothers and at least two sisters. According to Acts 1:14, his brothers were among his followers after Easter, and later his brother James became head of the church at Jerusalem (Gal. 2:1–11). Earlier interpreters often maintained that these were not full brothers and sisters of Jesus but either children of Joseph by a former marriage or cousins. Since nothing in this passage or elsewhere in the New Testament corroborates either possibility, recent scholarship is inclined to take the words in their normal sense as referring to other children of Joseph and Mary.

Jesus' sisters are not named. Perhaps their names were not known to the Jerusalem tradition. Presumably their family responsibilities would have kept them in Galilee. It is possible, however, that they became members of the church in Galilee, as did certain cousins of Jesus, according to the early church father Hegesippus. We know nothing of Jesus' relationship to his siblings except that he was so confident of God's direction of his life that he felt free to disappoint their expectations and resist their attempts to control him (see 12:46–50).

We learn little about Jesus' neighbors except that they had difficulty conceiving that God might raise up a prophet from their midst. Nazareth was apparently an insignificant village, since it is not mentioned in the Hebrew Scriptures or in the works of Josephus. Perhaps the residents held the same low opinion of their village as did outsiders like Nathaniel ("Can anything good come out of Nazareth?" John 1:46); if God were to raise up another latter-day prophet like John the Baptist, he

161

would surely choose a more prestigious place of origin. And it would most certainly not be the carpenter's son, whom they had watched growing up.

One of the most remarkable features of the narrative is that Jesus' neighbors are indeed *astounded* (v. 54, NRSV) at his teaching in the synagogue (the same verb is used to describe the reaction of the crowds to the Sermon on the Mount, 7:28), and they do not dispute the report that miracles have been wrought through him, but they refuse to draw any inference from these two activities. Twice they ask, "From where?" (vv. 54, 56) and refuse to answer their question by giving credit to the God of Israel, who is ever capable of making significant instruments out of those who appear to be insignificant men and women from humble places like Nazareth.

Most communities, large or small, are happy to bask in reflected glory when one of their own makes a name for herself or himself in the outside world. This would probably have been true of the Nazarenes had Jesus distinguished himself as the number one cabinetmaker in the construction of a new palace for Herod Antipas at nearby Sepphoris. Jesus' claim to fame, however, was of a very different sort, requiring an existential decision. Jesus challenged them to forget his unremarkable past among them and see in him the focal point of God's end-time activity on behalf of his people. They preferred a more predictable God, who would not interrupt their accustomed understanding of the world. The Nazarenes thus illustrate perfectly the point made in the interpretation of the parables: they are able to see and hear, but they cannot *understand* (13:13). It is not in knowledge about Jesus' and his activities that they are deficient; what they lack is life-transforming insight into the reality that God is doing something strange and new in the carpenter's son, whose family they know so well. Note how this passage and the earlier paragraph about Jesus' true family (12: 46–50) bracket the parables discourse: both illustrate the contrast between merely seeing and hearing Jesus and *understanding* him.

The villagers "stumbled" (RSV, "took offense") over Jesus (v. 57). The verb *skandalizō*, which lies behind our English word "scandalize," is used repeatedly in Matthew. When used with respect to Jesus himself, as here and at 11:6 and 26:31–33, it seems to reflect the early Christian conviction that confrontation with Jesus constituted a moment of decision: one had to

162

respond either with faith or with its opposite, unbelief (v. 58). In the passion narrative, Jesus predicts that his arrest and its sequel will prompt unbelief even in his closest followers; they will all stumble over him, that is, their faith in God's presence in Jesus will be crushed by his apparent failure (26:31, 33).

Like the Nazarenes, some modern church members "stumble" over Jesus with less justification than the bewildered disciples in Gethsemane. Jesus' claims and demands appear excessive to secularists in a world come of age. While including God as a necessary principle in their worldview, they are offended by the claim that the Creative Force of the Universe chose to do something unique and unrepeatable in the life and death of one ancient carpenter. Matthew will not countenance this evasion. Those who are confronted by Jesus must make a decision not only about him but also about his heavenly Father.

Herod's Execution of John (14:1–12)

While seldom selected as a sermon text, this passage has fired the imagination of artists in many fields. In recent times it inspired Oscar Wilde's *Salome* and an opera by Richard Strauss based thereon. At the heart of the artistic interest, of course, is the provocative dancer and her ghoulish reward.

Early tradition is probably correct in identifying the unnamed young girl as Salome, daughter of Herodias by her first husband. Since Salome was married soon after this to her aging great-uncle Philip, tetrarch of the area northeast of the Sea of Galilee (Philip died in 34 C.E.), she would probably have been in her teens at the time of John's death. The Philip referred to in verse 3 was not the tetrarch but another son of Herod the Great, who was living a private life in Jerusalem.

The historicity of the event has been questioned by many. The story contains features of a number of Oriental folktales. It is alleged that in that culture it would be most improbable that a princess would perform a solo dance in front of strange men, especially since they were probably drinking heavily. Others retort that, given the morals of the Herodian court, such a departure from accepted standards is not impossible and is probably an essential ingredient of the story; the men would not have been so fascinated if an ordinary harlot had entertained them with her dancing.   163

A more serious objection is presented by the fact that Josephus, who would probably not have been averse to repeating such a tale for his Roman readers' entertainment, attributes the execution of John to purely political motives. Of course, the two accounts are not strictly contradictory. The Gospels agree that Herod Antipas had earlier arrested John (see 4:12). The date of execution may have been advanced at the urging of Herodias with the support of her daughter. It must be remembered that if John had publicly chastised Antipas for transgressing the incest laws of the Pentateuch (Herodias was his niece as well as the wife of a living brother; see Lev. 18:16), this would have been perceived by friend and foe alike as a political challenge. In order to marry Herodias, Antipas had agreed to divorce his first wife, a Nabatean princess. This constituted a serious affront to her father, King Aretas IV, whose territory adjoined Herod's in Perea. In 36 C.E., a war between the two rulers resulted in the destruction of Herod's army. This bitter defeat was regarded by many Jews as an appropriate punishment for Herod's execution of John, according to Josephus. In view of what was undoubtedly a tense political situation between the divorce and the outbreak of hostilities, John's public denunciation *in Perea* of Herod's remarriage could easily be understood as taking the Nabatean side in the dispute and thus as an act of treason.

Why is this story, whatever its historical origins, included in Mark and Matthew? The Gospels contain few narratives that do not focus on Jesus. Perhaps the closest parallel is the account of Herod the Great's slaughter of the innocents in Bethlehem, but there Jesus is at least indirectly involved as the intended victim (2:16–18). Like the earlier story, the account of John's execution spoke to early Christians about the hostility of this world toward God and his true representatives.

Note that this passage does not constitute a martyrdom narrative in the proper sense. John himself plays no role, he makes no stirring speech, there is no report of his steadfast faith in God, and there is no praise of his courage. All emphasis falls on the hostile ruler and his entourage.

The story proper is presented as a flashback. John is already dead. Herod, hearing about Jesus' public activity, proposes that Jesus is John redivivus. This is not to be taken in its most literal sense. Presumably what is meant is that "Jesus is another John." The ancients apparently believed that it was possible for the spirit of a departed person to contribute to the vitality of a successor (see II Kings 2:9, 15). Herod's comment, then, means

164

little more than that Jesus is truly John's successor, and, implicitly, that he is similarly a political threat to his rule (see Luke 13:31). This prepares us to be sensitive to the political ramifications of the following story about Jesus meeting with five thousand adult males—a politically significant force!

Theologically, the story functions as an anticipation of Jesus' passion. Like John, Jesus will incur the displeasure of this world's political leaders and will be executed. The parallel will become the focus of a dialogue of Jesus with three disciples following the transfiguration (17:9–13).

The Feeding of Five Thousand Men (14:13–21)

This story, which is popularly referred to as "The Feeding of the Five Thousand," should perhaps be called "The Feeding of Twenty Thousand," if Matthew's conclusion, "apart from women and children," is intended to suggest that all the married men brought their wives and children to the wilderness meeting. This is the only miracle story recounted in all four Gospels. Its inclusion in John as well as in the Synoptic Gospels suggests that it was of unusual importance.

Because we are children of the Enlightenment, we tend to focus attention on the question, Did it really happen? Various proposals have been made to "explain" the miracle. According to the most popular of these, people were so moved by Jesus' generosity (or, alternatively, by the generosity of the boy in John's version, John 6:9) that they brought forth the food they had hidden in their clothing or travel pouches, and it was discovered that, by sharing, there was sufficient for all. Another suggestion is that the meal was symbolic and spiritual; not physical but spiritual hunger was satisfied when each person received a minuscule fragment of the shared food. These are both edifying retellings of the story, but they hardly do justice to the story in the Gospels, which intends to report a supernatural event. Since it is impossible to determine precisely what experience underlies the story, it is best to bracket out the question of historicity and ask instead what theological meaning the narrative held for Matthew.

It is instructive to compare Matthew's version with Mark's (Mark 6:32–44). The arrangement of the men in companies of fifty and a hundred, reminiscent perhaps of Exod. 18:25 and military organizations, leaves open the possibility that the

165

"shepherd" who organizes them in this way is to be perceived as a military commander. In Matthew there is no reference to "companies," and Jesus' compassion is directed specifically to the sick in the crowd, and the allusion to women and children guards against a political interpretation of the event.

Although Matthew may have regarded the miraculous meal in the wilderness as in some sense an anticipation both of the messianic banquet and of the Eucharist, neither of these possibilities has been exploited in his retelling of the tale. What is consumed is a far cry from the sumptuous fare of the Messiah's victory celebration. Bread and fish constituted the basic ingredients of a peasant's meal in Galilee. Jesus' miracle provides no cooked dishes, no luxurious fruit, no wine! It directs attention, therefore, not to the future and its superabundance but to the present, when God's providential care can be counted on to supply the bare necessities (see 6:25–34). While not a banquet, it is nonetheless, for Matthew, a messianic meal since the Messiah is the host who supplies his people with food because of his compassion. He is the kind of shepherd king who cares for his flock (Ezek. 34:13–14).

Similarly, and probably for the same reason, the parallel with the Lord's Supper is not developed. Although Matthew employs the same four verbs here as in 26:26 (took, blessed, broke, gave), the substitution of fish for wine makes the suggestion of a eucharistic meal precarious (it is the wine that most clearly points to the death of Jesus). Nor is there any hint in Matthew of John's interpretation of the event as presenting Jesus as the Bread of Life, whose *words* are truly nourishing (John 6:35–63). Because of verse 20 (they ate to satiety, and there were leftovers), the emphasis is not on spiritual but physical needs. The miracle story assures Jesus' followers and the readers of the Gospel that God will hear them when they pray, "Give us this day our daily bread." There is thus a parallel with the story of God's provision of manna in the wilderness (Exodus 16; Numbers 11), a parallel that is explicitly developed in John 6:31, 49.

Under the main theme of the Messiah's caring for his people are several subthemes. First, the story parallels in part a miracle credited to Elisha in II Kings 4:42–44, where twenty loaves of barley bread are shared with a hundred men, who eat and have some to spare, in fulfillment of the word of the Lord, "They shall eat and have some left." The God who empowered

166

Elisha in ancient days to provide for God's people is now active in Jesus to supply God's new people.

Second, as Elisha performed this miracle through the agency of his servant, so Jesus involves his disciples in the multiplication of bread and fish. Although this motif is not greatly developed, it undoubtedly reminded early Christians that they had been called to be God's instruments in meeting the needs of others. In Matthew's Greek the command is emphatic: *"You, you give [the food] to them to eat!"* (v. 16). The prayer "Give us this day our daily bread" requires active participation from those who wish to see it answered.

Third, and in the same vein, the story reminds early and modern readers that God uses what we bring, even if all we have to offer consists of five small loaves and two dried fish. Jesus does not here fall prey to the temptation that he had earlier resisted of turning stones into bread (4:3–4); he uses what his disciples bring to him. Many poor Christians have been encouraged by this story to offer their little for the work of God's kingdom, knowing that no offering is too small for God to use.

Finally, the motif of twelve baskets of leftovers warns against waste. It is natural to think of this detail as pointing to the superabundance of God's supply, but in fact a mere twelve basketfuls after many thousands have eaten suggests a very narrow margin (comparable to one package of frankfurters left from a large family reunion!). The story suggests that God will provide with a little to spare, but there must be no greed or waste, or some will go hungry.

Jesus and Peter Walk on the Lake (14:22–33)

Like the feeding story, this narrative concerning walking on water is a stumbling block to modern Christians. The story was probably regarded skeptically by some in the first century as well, but it was then more widely believed than now that the laws of nature can be suspended by supernatural intervention. It would have been axiomatic for Jewish believers that the God of the exodus was fully capable of empowering Jesus to walk on the water. For such an audience, the question would not have been "Is it possible?" but "Did it actually happen in this case?"

In our more skeptical age, there have been attempts to provide a rational explanation. It has been proposed, for example, that what happened was nothing more than an optical

167

illusion. In the dim light of "the fourth watch of the night" (3 to 6 A.M.) the figure of Jesus was seen as if walking on the water when he was actually walking through the surf in the shallows of the northern end of the lake. While this is credible in theory, it is improbable that such an experience would have been transformed into the story as it has been transmitted to us. The disciples would have quickly discovered their error, and the incident would not have been preserved for posterity.

A very different proposal is that this story derives from a resurrection experience that has erroneously been transferred to the days of Jesus' earthly ministry. There are indeed certain parallels to the story of the risen Christ reported in John 21:1–8. The disciples have been in the boat all night. The encounter occurs very early, perhaps before dawn. As in Matthew's story, Peter climbs out of the boat to go to Jesus. While this suggestion is intriguing, it must remain nothing more than a conjecture. The best approach is to set aside the question of the historicity of the event and to focus instead on what the narrative meant to Matthew.

The first point to be made is that the story of Jesus walking on the water must be interpreted from a Jewish, not a Hellenistic, context. Greek mythology contained stories about divine heroes, demigods whose human mothers had been impregnated by one of the gods, who had the power to walk on water by virtue of their divine origin. Although Gentile readers of the gospel story may have been inclined to see Jesus as here placed in the same class with these mythical heroes, it is most improbable that Matthew intended such a comparison.

Some scholars who approach the story on the basis of its Jewish context find evidence in it of a very high Christology. Since there are a number of passages in the Hebrew Scriptures that speak of God walking on the sea (e.g., Job 9:8; Hab. 3:15; Ps. 77:19), it is argued that what we have in this story is a theophany: Jesus reveals himself to his disciples as a divine being or as God. In support of this, it is alleged that in Jesus' statement to the terrified disciples in verse 27, "Take heart, *egō eimi,* have no fear," the words *egō eimi,* translated "It is I" in most English versions, reflect the theophanic formula of Exod. 3:14, "I AM WHO I AM." This seems to be reading into the passage far more than Matthew intended. The phrase is understood here by Peter in its normal sense: "If it is you, Lord . . . ." The words are meant to identify the walker on the sea as Jesus, not God.

Matthew apparently wrote his Gospel before the early church was threatened by the heresy of docetism that denied the real humanity of Jesus (see II John 7). Had he been confronted by this monstrous error, he might have edited the story to guard it against such misunderstanding. The figure striding the waves is, for him, not a divine being but the Messiah whom God has endowed with supernatural power. Jesus has miraculous ability not by nature but by conferral (see 28:16). That walking on the sea is evidence of divine empowerment, not of divinity, is sufficiently demonstrated by the fact that Peter is empowered to do the same. Other Christians soon found the undeveloped Christology of the Synoptic Gospels unsatisfactory and achieved a more sophisticated understanding of Jesus' divinity on the basis of the doctrine of the incarnation. As a result, the story of Jesus walking on the waves has become a "parable" of the mystery of the Christ, whom we affirm as both human and divine. It is a mistake, however, to impose such an understanding on Matthew, for whom the story seems to have had a very different meaning.

Essential to the story in Matthew's telling of it is the fact that at the time of Jesus' appearance on the lake the boat was far from land and being *tortured* by the waves. This detail suggests that, for Matthew, Jesus' miracle of walking on the sea is not just to "show off" who he is but to come to the aid of his threatened disciples. That is to say, while the story is indeed talking about who Jesus is, it emphasizes his *function* rather than his *nature*. As Messiah he is the one charged and empowered by God to shepherd and care for God's people.

This is in a sense a reprise of the earlier story of the stilling of the storm (8:23–27). As there, so here the boat seems to represent the church, buffeted by temptations, trials, and persecutions. In both, Jesus appears as the church's champion, who is strong to save those who call on him in faith. It is perhaps for the sake of his readers that Matthew writes "those in the boat" where we expect him to have "the disciples" (v. 33). Not just the apostles but all believers are in the endangered ship and dependent upon their savior.

While the narrative of Jesus walking on the lake is found also in Mark 6:45–52 and John 6:15–21, only Matthew includes the supplementary story about Peter, which serves as further commentary on the story. It graphically depicts what it means to be a Christian caught midway between faith and doubt. Peter represents all who dare to believe that Jesus is Savior, take

169

their first steps in confidence that he is able to sustain them, and then forget to keep their gaze fixed on him instead of on the towering waves that threaten to engulf them. In the depth of crisis, when all seems lost, they remember to call on the Savior, and find his grace sufficient for their needs, whose power is made perfect in weakness (II Cor. 12:9).

Similarly, Peter represents the risk-taking of faith. Christians learn to live with uncertainties. The knowledge of faith is not as certain as the knowledge of science, yet it speaks of realities that are of more ultimate importance than the things we can see and touch. To believe in the saving power of Jesus is to take a risk.

Jesus asks Peter in verse 31, "O you of little faith, why did you doubt?" Here *oligopistos* ("of little faith") echoes its earlier appearance in the sea storm (8:28) and anticipates its occurrence in the final passage before Peter's confession (16:8). This word is always used by Matthew with respect to believers, never of unbelievers, that is, its purpose is to rebuke those who fail to draw on their faith. A parallel of sorts is provided by the Fourth Gospel, where believing is always a verb, never a noun; faith is not a possession but an activity. It is like a song that disappears when we stop singing. Those of little faith are warned that they must exercise their little faith or it will wither away like an unused muscle.

The verb *distazō*, translated "doubt" in verse 31, is found in the New Testament only in Matthew (see also 28:17). Christian existence is indeed one of faith mixed with doubt. Only by grace can doubt be kept subordinate. Like the epileptic's father in Mark's Gospel, each Christian must pray continually, "I believe; help my unbelief!" (Mark 9:24).

Matthew's conclusion to the story is radically different from Mark's, where the disciples' response to Jesus' walking on the water is one of astonished bewilderment: "For they did not understand about the loaves, but their hearts were hardened" (Mark 6:52). Mark claims that the disciples could not really understand the meaning of Jesus' Messiahship, which had been exhibited to their unperceptive eyes in the miraculous meal and its sequel, because their hardened hearts needed first to experience Calvary and Easter. Only then would their blindness be removed so that they could perceive Jesus as the Messiah who saves by dying.

170

Matthew essentially agrees with Mark on this theological perspective, but Matthew's literary purposes require that the later faith be "foreshadowed" during the earthly ministry. Just as the Gentile Magi "worship" (do obeisance to) Jesus at his birth long before the Gentile mission begins, so "those in the boat" worship Jesus, even though they do not yet know that it will be only through a shameful death and subsequent resurrection that Jesus will enter fully into his Lordship.

The confession, "Indeed, you are God's Son!" foreshadows Peter's confession of 16:16 without preempting it (see comments on 16:13–20). The first word, literally "truly," seems to function here as it does in 26:73, where the bystanders use it as a way of concurring with the prior testimony of the two servant girls. That is, the shipboard confession may here refer to both preceding miracles, so that we could paraphrase it as: "Now we are convinced that the messianic claim implicit in the feeding miracle was indeed justified." A similar confirmation is attributed to the Gentile soldiers responsible for crucifying Jesus (27:54). Here as everywhere in Matthew, "God's Son" seems to be a functional title, designating Jesus as the supernaturally empowered king of the last days (see comments on 3:17).

Healing in Gennesaret (14:34–36)

This narrative reminds the readers that, despite growing opposition and rejection on the part of religious leaders and of the populace of various towns (11:20–24), Jesus the Messiah continues to demonstrate God's concern for his people by healing the sick.

Faith in Jesus' healing power is here exhibited in the conviction that touching the hem of his garment will suffice. This detail suggests that mass healings took place without Jesus' personal attention to the individual sufferers. This massive response in a particularly populous area of Palestine (Gennesaret was a fertile plain lying south of Capernaum) is now to be contrasted with the negative reaction of religious leaders from Jerusalem.

What Defiles? (15:1–20)

At first glance this account of a dispute over ritual hand washing seems to have little to say to modern Christians. A closer look, however, reveals its continuing relevance. It helps us reassess our priorities.

The historicity of the event described has been questioned

171

by some scholars. Not until after the destruction of the temple was pressure put on ordinary Jews to observe the ritual of washing hands before eating, which the Pentateuch required only of priests (Exod. 30:17–21; Lev. 22:4–7). On the other hand, this later practice undoubtedly had its origins in pietist circles at an earlier date. It is not at all incredible that pietists of Jesus' day may have challenged him with the question, "If you and your disciples are so religious, why don't you observe the pious tradition we follow of washing the hands before eating? For the Torah says, 'You shall be to me a kingdom of priests and a holy nation' " (Exod. 19:6; cf. Isa. 61:6). As in the Sabbath disputes, it is to be expected that Jesus challenged his challengers by subordinating ritual observance to ethical behavior.

It is possible, however, that the present form of the story has been influenced by the later situation. We notice, to begin with, that the challengers are not simply anonymous pietists but Pharisees and scribes who come *from Jerusalem* (the phrase is emphatic). Since in the Synoptic Gospels Jesus visits Jerusalem only in order to die there, the reference to the holy city is ominous; it suggests that the opponents in this narrative constitute part of that united front which will eventually conspire to put Jesus to death. Matthew intensifies the polemic against the Pharisees and scribes by adding verses 12–14, probably because Pharisees represent for him the leaders of contemporary Judaism which has rejected the gospel and its missionaries (see comments on 10:16–23).

Mark's treatment of the dispute differs from Matthew's in important ways. The focal saying of Jesus is more sharply formulated: "There is *nothing* outside the person which, entering, can render him or her unclean; but the things that come forth from the person are what render the person unclean" (Mark 7:15). Mark then explains the force of Jesus' word: "Thus he declared all foods clean" (Mark 7:19). The Second Evangelist is apparently writing for a Gentile church that feels under no obligation to observe the Jewish food laws. Like Paul, he is convinced that nothing is unclean in itself (see Rom. 14:14), and he justifies his conviction on the basis of this saying of Jesus. Matthew, on the other hand, treats the saying much more cautiously. He not only omits Mark's comment about all foods being clean but also edits the saying so that its implications are less radical: "It is not that which enters the mouth that renders a person unclean, but that which comes out of the mouth, this renders the person unclean" (Matt. 15:11).

172

Which Evangelist more accurately reflects the spirit of Jesus? That is a hard question to answer, but two points can be made with some confidence. First, Jesus is remembered as a person who challenged the rigorous piety of some of his contemporaries by insisting that they give precedence to God's moral commandments (see 23:23). Second, neither friends nor foes regarded Jesus as abrogating the ritual laws of Judaism. There is no evidence whatsoever that Jesus taught his followers to eat pork, to work on the Sabbath, or to desist from circumcising male babies. While a number of Christian scholars find evidence in this passage that Jesus was a radical critic of the Torah, Jewish scholars tend not to be impressed by their arguments. The saying in verse 11 is compared favorably with a similar saying of Rabbi Jochanan ben Zakkai. It is probable that in its original Aramaic form the saying was less absolutist than appears in its Greek and English translations: "Not this, but that" does not necessarily negate the first in favor of the second item but merely strongly subordinates it (cf. 10:26; 19:6). On the basis of this observation, J. C. O'Neill paraphrases: "Of course what goes into a man defiles him, but what is far more important than that defilement is the defilement which he utters" (*Messiah: Six Lectures on the Ministry of Jesus,* p. 35). Finally, if Jesus had in fact declared all foods clean, as Mark suggests, it is hard to understand why the early church had such great difficulty regarding table fellowship with Gentiles. Paul would surely have employed this saying of Jesus in his dispute with Peter at Antioch had it so unambiguously supported his position (Gal. 2:11–14). We must conclude, therefore, that Jesus' saying, whatever its original form, was not intended to abolish the Pentateuch food laws. Only gradually did its implications become apparent to a church compelled by the Gentile mission to confront the issue of the ceremonial law.

Although writing for a church that was predominantly Gentile, Matthew seems to have been anxious to protect the remaining Jewish Christians from ridicule for adherence to the Jewish life-style. In his editing of this passage he omits any suggestion that the food and purity laws are obsolete. One technique he uses to limit the radicality of verse 11 is to round the discussion off by returning at the end to the initial issue: "but to eat with unwashed hands does not defile the person" (v. 20). That is, a discussion that Mark views as having radical implications is reduced by Matthew to the deliverance of a specific rule concerning the life-style of Jewish Christians. It must be noted,

173

however, that Matthew does not suggest that all Christians must conform with this life-style.

In the narrative the presenting issue is framed by Jesus as a matter of Scripture versus tradition. In response to the charge that his disciples transgress "the tradition of the elders" (cf. Gal. 1:14), Jesus directs attention to the notorious problem of the *Qorban* (a Hebrew term used in the Torah for gifts dedicated to God). An adult son, piqued by his parents, could vent his rage by making a vow, "Qorban is whatever you might have gained from me." Regardless of whether or not any of his property was subsequently donated to the temple, the vow remained intact and could not be revoked even when the son repented of his behavior, because of the law of oaths (Num. 30:2; cf. Deut. 23:21–23). From the point of view of Jesus' adversaries, the Qorban vow, while open to such abuses, was a matter of scriptural law, not of tradition. The law was clear, and a judge was bound to uphold it, even though he deplored its abuse. Moreover, the law of vows took precedence over the command to honor, that is, support one's parents, because an obligation to God takes priority over an obligation to humans.

Jesus' approach to the problem is legally radical. This is a matter of tradition, not law, he insists, because it is tradition alone that establishes priorities when two laws collide. It is, for example, a matter of tradition that the law of circumcision on the eighth day (Gen. 17:12; Lev. 12:3) is given precedence over the Sabbath law (see John 7:22–23). On what basis can tradition permit an immoral vow to take precedence over God's moral law requiring the support of aging parents? (Later rabbis agreed with Jesus' perspective and created a legal way to disallow such vows.) Exalting the merely legal over the truly moral is sheer hypocrisy, Jesus claims, because it professes allegiance to God's law while disregarding God's will.

As in Matthew 13, the enigmatic statement ("parable") of 15:11 can be "understood" (15:10) only with the help of Jesus' instruction (15:17–20). Here again Matthew carefully edits what he finds in his source (Mark 7:18–23). What is presented in Mark is a general list of vices, given apparently in no particular order. Matthew's editing accomplishes two things. Violations of the Ten Commandments are placed at the center of the list and rearranged to conform with the order of the second table of Exod. 20:13–16 (the Fourth Commandment has already been dealt with in 15:4–6). This emphasis on the moral requirements

174

of the Decalogue is characteristic of early Christianity generally (see Matt. 19:17–19; Rom. 13:8–10). The list is made to begin and end with sins of the mouth, in order to reflect the focus of verse 11 on what proceeds from the mouth. The first vice, *dialogismoi ponēroi,* is translated "evil thoughts" in the RSV and "evil intentions" in the NRSV. If these translations are correct, this first item may be seen as reflecting Jesus' insistence that the intention to commit adultery (for example) is as sinful as the act itself (see comments on 5:27–30). The word *dialogismoi* can just as well refer to spoken thoughts, however; it then usually has a negative connotation, "disputes" or "contentious arguments," as in Rom. 14:1; Phil. 2:14; I Tim. 2:8. In view of the focus on the mouth in 15:11, we are justified in taking the phrase as meaning "rancorous disputes."

Why does Matthew highlight rancorous disputes and slander? We may assume that there were tensions in his church over life-style questions just as in the church at Rome, where Gentile Christians were learning to coexist with Christian Jews of various persuasions. In a discussion of the necessity of maintaining fellowship with Christians whose piety includes abstinence from various foods and the observance of special days, Paul urges all to be patient with one another and accept such differences (Rom. 14:1—15:13).

This passage (15:1–20) has much to say to modern Christians. It reminds us, in the first place, that we too can be guilty of placing tradition ahead of God's moral will. Local tradition ("We have always done it *this* way") can impede the work of the kingdom. Ecclesiastical tradition can get in the way of ecumenical cooperation. And, like Jesus' opponents, we too must be warned not to put the merely legal above the truly moral. It is a regrettable habit of many Christians to speak disdainfully of "Jewish legalism." Rabbis sometimes ask ministers, "Why is it 'legalism' when we take our tradition seriously, but when you do, it is merely a matter of carefully observing the mandates of your book of order?" One is reminded of the church school teacher who concluded a rousing discussion of the parable of the Pharisee and the tax collector (Luke 18:10–14) with the prayer, "Lord, we thank thee that we are not like this Pharisee."

Second, while we are no longer troubled by disputes over the food and purity laws of the Pentateuch, and hand washing before meals is for us a matter of hygiene, not of ritual defile-

175

ment, we still find it possible to quarrel with one another over piety issues and to accuse each other of not being properly religious. Blessed is the congregation whose members treat different opinions and different practices with respect and abstain from verbal attacks. We are *defiled,* Jesus tells us, by the unloving words that spring so readily from our mouths.

The Canaanite Woman (15:21–28)

Some find this passage distressing, because it seems to present Jesus as responding in an uncompassionate way to the cry for help of a Gentile woman. His initial response is simply to ignore her. When she persists and he is compelled to react, his word strikes us as unduly harsh and insensitive: "It is not good to take the children's bread and throw it to the dogs" (v. 26). Although it is by no means true that Jews used the epithet "dog" primarily with reference to Gentiles, the context of the saying certainly suggests that the people whom Jesus normally heals are "children" and the Gentiles, represented by this bold woman, are by contrast "dogs," that is, subhuman and undeserving of God's concern.

There are three main ways of interpreting this verse and its context. The first and easiest method is simply to treat it as inauthentic. Accordingly, it is proposed that the saying was credited to Jesus by conservative Jewish Christians who were opposed to the Gentile mission. Their chauvinism found ready expression in this harsh statement, which was then invested with Jesus' authority by being set in a story in which he was represented as refusing to minister to Gentiles. The story, according to this interpretation, was later "corrected" by someone favorable to the Gentile mission, who supplied a happy ending; the woman, instead of being sent away, was able to win Jesus' praise for her response to his statement and was rewarded with the healing of her daughter.

A second approach treats the story as authentic but argues that Jesus' behavior is not so harsh as modern readers think. The saying may have been a proverb that was no more offensive than our old saw "Charity begins at home." The Greek word for "dogs" found here is the diminutive, which was used with reference to household pets and therefore not to be seen as abusive. (Jesus' Aramaic, however, contained no such diminutive.) It is further suggested that Jesus' statement is not to be seen as his

176

final word to the woman but as a test of her faith; if she passes the test, he will accede to her request.

The third interpretation insists on accepting the story as it stands in all its harshness. The anecdote presents Jesus as a Jewish man of his day, chauvinistic toward women and non-Jews. His limited perspective is in part corrected by the clever retort of a desperately bold woman, who convinces him that Gentiles must also share in God's bounty.

Unfortunately, all three proposals are conjectural. We lack the supporting evidence that would permit a firm choice of one over the others. Possibly each contains an element of truth. There is every reason to believe that some of the stories about Jesus were edited to conform with the convictions of the transmitters. It is possible, therefore, that Jesus' behavior toward the Gentile woman was not so insensitive as the transmitters "remembered." On the other hand, Jesus was capable of speaking firmly ("harshly" from our modern perspective) when he felt the situation demanded it (see 8:22, "Follow me, and let the dead bury their own dead"). Jesus was so convinced of the urgency of his work that we can readily believe he may have told his messengers not to indulge in casual conversations with Jewish men they met along the road (Luke 10:4). In view of such restrictions, it is also credible that he himself avoided contacts with Gentiles, for whom he felt no responsibility. Whether or not the saying of verse 24 belonged originally to the story (it is missing from Mark 7:24–30), it probably reflects accurately Jesus' self-understanding: "I was sent only to the lost sheep of the house of Israel" (cf. 10:5–6).

There is no contradiction between such a self-understanding and the statement of 8:11 concerning the place of Gentiles in the kingdom of God. Like other faithful Jews of his day, Jesus undoubtedly accepted as true the scriptural prophecies that in the last days Gentiles would stream to Zion to worship the God of Israel (Isa. 60:1–14). The conversion of such Gentiles would be effected by divine miracle. Prior to that time, however, repentance had to be preached to Israel while the opportunity for repentance remained. There was great urgency, and the energy of the messengers must not be dissipated.

Why, then, did Jesus "withdraw" into the Gentile territory of Tyre and Sidon? It is often argued that this was a strategic withdrawal to escape his enemies. If Jesus had really wanted to evade pursuers, he would have avoided populated areas and hidden himself in the hills. No, if Jesus truly made such a journey, it was undoubtedly to minister to the lost sheep of the house of Israel. A large Jewish population was to be found north of the Galilean border in the political territories of Tyre and Sidon.

Verse 24 reflects historical fact. This story, and the account of the Capernaum centurion and possibly that concerning the Gadarene demoniac, are the only stories in which Jesus ministers to Gentiles. Each is clearly exceptional. Since all the Gospels were written for churches that were predominantly Gentile in membership, we must assume that the Evangelists would have wished to include as much as possible about Jesus' concern for the Gentiles. People like Paul who championed the Gentile mission could find little support in the ministry of the earthly Jesus. Paul was able to make theological sense of this limitation: "For I tell you that Christ became a servant of the circumcised to show God's faithfulness, in order to confirm the promises given to the patriarchs" (Rom. 15:8). Christ's single-minded devotion to his own people was a manifestation of God's faithfulness to his promises.

What does Matthew make of the story? Like Mark, he places it immediately after the dispute about food and purity laws. This suggests that, just as Jesus' subordination of ritual to ethics anticipates the law-free mission to the Gentiles, so the Gentile woman represents the vast numbers of non-Jews who were to become members of the church. Whereas Mark refers to her as "a Greek, a Syrophoenician by birth," Matthew suggests that she belongs culturally not to the Hellenized population of the cities of Tyre and Sidon but to the rural people. She is a Canaanitess, a representative of the despised indigenous population with which Israel was not supposed to fraternize (Ezra 9:1–12). The confession with which she addresses Jesus, "Lord, Son of David," marks her as the vanguard of Gentile believers.

It is this emphasis on faith that most distinguishes Matthew's version of the story from Mark's. In the Nazareth narrative it was stressed that Jesus refused to do many mighty works there because of their lack of faith (13:58). Jesus was no ordinary physician dispensing wonder drugs to any who could pay him; a relationship of faith was essential. Whereas this may well have been implicit in Mark's narrative, Matthew makes it explicit. It is only because of the woman's faith that Jesus heals her daughter.

178

In this respect, the believing Gentile poses a sharp contrast to the unbelieving Pharisees and scribes from Jerusalem of the preceding passage. Whereas Jesus is rejected by fellow Jews, Gentiles are able to recognize him as their Lord, who has mercy on them and exorcizes the demon of paganism so that they can join the children at God's table. There are very possibly eucharistic overtones in the reference to sharing bread, but of course this cannot be pressed, since Matthew himself does nothing to develop the allusion.

What comfort and guidance can modern Christians draw from the story? It reminds us, first, that we are, as Krister Stendahl has suggested, merely "honorary Jews." To us the woman's response sounds servile; she seems to accept the role of "dogs" for Gentile believers. Matthew probably saw her humility as a necessary ingredient of her faith; it was appropriate that she acknowledge the historical (and therefore theological) priority of God's election of Israel. Paul reminds us in Romans 11 that it is by grace alone that we have been admitted to the ranks of God's salvation-historical people. We have no right to demand the help of Israel's Messiah. Like the woman of the story, we humbly beg his mercy.

Second, the story reminds us that members of despised or oppressed groups must be bold in seeking relief of their misery. The woman is not content to be ignored, because she is convinced that her daughter deserves to be given a chance at living a normal, productive life. Her persistence, based on her faith in a God who can change things for the better, is rewarded.

Healing and Feeding on the Mountain (15:29–39)

Readers are apt to pass quickly over this passage because it seems redundant after the previous summary of Jesus' healing in 14:34–36 and the story of the feeding of the multitude in 14:13–21. Apparently this second feeding miracle was not superfluous to Matthew. After all, he could have omitted it, as does Luke. Matthew not only retains the story but invests it with special significance by creating for it a new and weighty introduction in verses 29–31.

It is often noted that Matthew substitutes the healing summary of verses 29–31 for Mark's healing of a deaf man with a speech impediment (Mark 7:31–37). This is a correct but insufficient observation. Instead of vigorously editing the Markan narrative or replacing it with another story, Matthew creates a

179

scene of mass healings, apparently borrowing language from Isaiah: "Then the eyes of the blind shall be opened, and the ears of the deaf unstopped; then shall the lame man leap like a hart, and the tongue of the dumb sing for joy" (Isa. 35:5–6). In this way he reminds us that Jesus is not just another healer but the Messiah who inaugurates the golden age prophesied by Isaiah.

This is the last such summary in the First Gospel. Its significance is enhanced by the fact that Matthew locates the mass healings and the miraculous meal on *the mountain* (v. 29, correctly rendered in the NRSV; the Evangelist uses the plural "mountains" in 18:12 and 24:16 where the word has no theological significance). The parallel with 5:1 is reinforced by the additional note that Jesus seated himself there. It is possible that these two details were derived by Matthew from the oral tradition, since they are also found in John's account of the miraculous meal (John 6:3), but there is good reason to believe that Matthew wants us to remember that earlier occasion in this Gospel when Jesus sat on a mountain with his disciples in the presence of a large multitude. It is not that he wishes us to think of a specific hill in Galilee, say Mount Tabor. His meaning is theological, not geographical. For him, "the mountain" symbolizes the consummation of the age when God's people will be gathered on the mountain of the Lord (Isa. 2:2–3; Micah 4:1–2). Whereas 5:1 introduced the Sermon on the Mount, a revelation of God's *will* through Jesus' *words,* this second scene on the mountain reveals God's *power* through Jesus' *deeds* of healing and feeding. The reference to the mountain is significant in yet another way; it indicates that Matthew regards this passage as forming an inclusio with the Sermon on the Mount, that is, that the two references to Jesus sitting on the mountain bracket the intervening material. In the Sermon on the Mount we have the beginning of Jesus' ministry to his people as represented by large crowds from various parts of Palestine (see 4:25). From Peter's confession onward, the crowds will not completely disappear, but the focus will be on the disciples and the impending passion. This second story about Jesus feeding an immense multitude allows Matthew to bring the earlier phase of Jesus' ministry to a kind of closure, with the responsive crowds glorifying God for what Jesus has done. (Especially helpful comments on this passage will be found in Terence L. Donaldson's *Jesus on the Mountain,* pp. 122–135.)

The fact that there are two feeding miracles in Matthew

and in Mark (Luke and John have only one) has presented a problem to scholars from patristic days to the present. Recent scholarship has dubbed the second story a "doublet" of the first; it is reasoned that one original story was transmitted by two different routes, in which process the details of the story became sufficiently different that Mark thought he had found stories of two events instead of two accounts of the same event.

Patristic interpreters asked a different kind of question. They queried, not why there were two stories, but why there were two events. They concluded that the first multiplication of loaves and fish fed Jews, the second Gentiles. The numbers of the two accounts were seen as supporting this interpretation: *five* thousand alluded to the Pentateuch and thus to Jews, while *four* thousand, referring to the four winds or the four points of the compass, pointed to the nations of the wider world. Similarly, the twelve baskets of the first story were taken as symbolic of the twelve tribes of Israel, while the seven baskets of the second were seen as alluding to the seventy nations or to the seven deacons of Acts 6 who were appointed to minister to the Hellenists. There is some support for such an interpretation in Mark. The second story follows Mark 7:1–23, where Jesus is presented by the Evangelist as abrogating the food and purity laws (thus making it possible for Gentiles to join Jews in table fellowship) and Mark 7:24–30, where a Gentile woman convinces Jesus that Gentiles can share Israel's blessings. Moreover, the geographical note that Mark prefixes to the intervening story of the deaf-mute seems to locate the feeding miracle in Gentile territory on the east side of the Sea of Galilee (Mark 7:31). The feeding story itself contains the note that "some of them are from afar" (Mark 8:3); similar language is used in Eph. 2:13, 17 as a way of referring to Gentiles. It is sometimes argued that Matthew likewise regards the second feeding as ministering to Gentiles, since he has the crowds glorify the God of Israel (as if they were non-Jews), but such evidence is inconclusive, since Jews are often summoned to praise the God of Israel in the psalms. More impressive is the fact that in 15:29 Matthew edits out all references to Gentile territories and the clause about some being from afar. Moreover, his emphasis in 15:24 on Jesus being sent only to the lost sheep of the house of Israel makes it very unlikely that he regarded the recipients of the second feeding as Gentiles. For him, the rule "Go nowhere among the Gentiles" (10:5) remains in force until the risen Christ issues the

181

command, "Go, enlist all the Gentiles as disciples" (28:19). For Matthew, the incidents involving the Capernaum officer and the Canaanitess are precisely the exceptions that prove the rule. At the symbolic level, however, the miraculous meal is undoubtedly, for the Evangelist, a foretaste of the great messianic banquet which will include Gentiles (see 8:5–13; Luke 22:30; Rev. 19:9).

Jesus' compassion, mentioned in verse 32, is a favorite theme for Matthew, who employs the corresponding verb more often than any other Gospel writer (see also 9:36; 14:14; 20:34). Since the same verb is used to describe the attitude of the king in the parable of the unforgiving debtor, where the king clearly stands for God (18:23–35), Matthew may understand Jesus' compassion as a manifestation of God's loving concern for his people. In this sense also, Jesus is Emmanuel, "God with us" (1:23).

Epilogue to the Galilean Ministry (16:1–12)

If the prior narrative is presented by Matthew as the impressive conclusion of Jesus' ministry to the crowds, which is to be followed by a more intensive ministry to the disciples in preparation for the passion in Jerusalem, this intervening passage must be seen as transitional, constituting an epilogue to the first phase and an anticipation of the second phase of Jesus' ministry.

The passage consists of two scenes, but Matthew has carefully combined them into a single unit through the fourfold repetition of the phrase "the Pharisees and Sadducees" (16:1, 6, 11, 12). Historically speaking, this combination appears most unlikely. The two groups disagreed vigorously. It is improbable that the two warring parties would send a joint delegation from Jerusalem to interview Jesus. Probably Matthew wishes to introduce the Sadducees here in anticipation of the role the priestly party will play in Jesus' death. While disagreeing on many other matters, Jesus' opponents make common cause in their rejection of him.

The first scene (vv. 1–4) is a reprise of the earlier request for a sign by "some of the scribes and Pharisees" (12:38). It is by no means a simple repetition, however. The attack is much harsher. Whereas in the earlier instance the opponents politely ask, "Teacher, we wish to see a sign from you," the new group of enemies is represented as trying to "tempt" or "test" Jesus

182

in their request that he display to them a sign "from heaven," that is, from God.

"Test" as used here has a threefold background. The opponents could justify their confrontation with Jesus on the basis of such passages as Deut. 13:1–3; 18:15–22, which require that prophets be tested to see whether they have truly been sent by God. On the other hand, there are passages that denounce Israel for putting God to the test, notably Ps. 95:8–9 (quoted at Heb. 3:7–11). Although Jesus' opponents may think they are obeying Scripture by testing the prophet, they are in fact putting God to the test; despite the fact that they have seen God's work in Jesus' ministry, they have hardened their hearts and have refused to acknowledge that it is by the Spirit of God that Jesus casts out demons (12:28).

A third background for the passage is found in 4:1–11, where Satan "tests" Jesus (the same Greek verb is used). The suggestion that Jesus leap from the pinnacle of the temple can be seen as a request to display a sign from heaven, since the devil, quoting Scripture, proposes that God's angels will rescue him. In response, Jesus cites Deut. 6:16, which reads in full, "You shall not put the LORD your God to the test, as you tested him at Massah." That is, the opponents have now assumed Satan's role. They are not only displaying their lack of faith by failing to acknowledge that God is at work in Jesus but they are also tempting Jesus to put God to the test by seeking a heavenly ratification of his ministry that will render faith unnecessary.

Jesus' response is curt: "An evil and adulterous generation seeks for a sign, but no sign shall be given to it except the sign of Jonah" (v. 4; vv. 2b–3, absent from many ancient manuscripts, are probably a scribal interpolation—they reflect European rather than Near Eastern weather wisdom, in contrast to that of Luke 12:54–56). There is no need to define "the sign of Jonah," since this has been done in the earlier scene (12:38–40). The abruptness of Jesus' response is then underscored by the laconic comment, "And he left them and departed" (v. 4). There is no point in talking further with these opponents. He will wait until his arrival in Judea to debate them further (the Pharisees appear again in 19:3; the two groups reappear together in 22:34).

At first glance the second scene is very confusing. Two themes alternate without having any obvious relationship to each other or to the first scene. Careful examination, however,

183

reveals the subtle logic. The stage is set by the narrator with the note that the disciples, who have crossed the sea once again, have neglected to take along loaves of bread. The first voice is that of Jesus: "Take heed and beware of the leaven of the Pharisees and Sadducees." Instead of asking Jesus what this strange statement means, the disciples discuss among themselves the fact that they are without bread (most translations of v. 7 attempt to force a connection with v. 6 by introducing words not in the text). They are more concerned about their immediate problem than about the abstruse theological issue being raised by their master. Jesus therefore responds to their concern, leaving his own theme for the moment.

Using one of Matthew's favorite words, Jesus reprimands the disciples for being *people of little faith.* By worrying about their next meal, they are exhibiting their lack of trust in the God who provides their daily bread (6:11). They are scolded for not *remembering* the two miraculous meals. Remembering the mighty acts of God constitutes an important ingredient of Israel's faith experience. "One generation shall laud thy works to another, and shall declare thy mighty acts" (Ps. 145:4). If they truly *remembered,* they would be able to listen to Jesus' warning about leaven instead of worrying about their lack of bread.

After this scolding, the dialogue returns to the first theme. The disciples are warned again about the leaven of the Pharisees and Sadducees, but now they understand that the warning concerns not the leavened bread eaten by the religious leaders but their insidious teaching that can spread like yeast in dough. (Paul likewise uses leaven as a negative metaphor in Gal. 5:9.)

Does Matthew intend us to see here a reference to the teaching of the Pharisees and Sadducees considered in its totality? This seems unlikely, especially since the two parties had such different interpretations of Judaism. Moreover, there must have been many points on which Jesus and his followers agreed with the opinion of the majority of the Pharisees (see 23:2). We should probably limit the warning, therefore, to what is relevant to this context. The disciples are warned against the sign-seeking skepticism of Jesus' opponents. And thus the two motifs of the passage are pulled together: both concern lack of faith in God. The opponents' demand for a sign and the disciples' anxiety about bread have unfaith as their common denominator. Both assume the absence of God, like the people at Massah and Meribah, who asked, "Is the LORD among us or not?" (Exod. 17:7).

184

In Jesus' ministry, God is present and active. The disciples have witnessed the evidence. Instead of demanding certainty as did the Pharisees and Sadducees, the disciples must *remember* and let the memory of God's goodness overrule the anxieties of daily life.

PART THREE

The Messiah's Obedient Submission to Death

MATTHEW 16:13—28:20

From Caesarea Philippi to Jerusalem

MATTHEW 16:13—20:34

Remembering that a gospel is a passion narrative with an extended introduction (see Introduction), we should pause at this point and note that there are two basic versions of the gospel story. In Mark's account (which is expanded in Matthew and Luke), Jesus' ministry to his people is effected almost entirely in Galilee. Jesus goes up to Jerusalem once only, and his purpose is not to minister but to die. No Jerusalem miracles are reported by Mark (but see Matt. 21:14). In John's version, on the other hand, Jesus goes often to the holy city; many "signs" (miracles) are performed there early in Jesus' public ministry (John 2:23), and most of the longer discourses are delivered there. In terms of historical probability the Johannine version has much to commend it. As a male Jew, Jesus was obligated to "appear before the Lord GOD" three times each year (Exod. 23:17) and would presumably have proclaimed his message there to the crowds of fellow pilgrims. What we have in Mark, then, is apparently a schematic limitation of Jesus' positive ministry to Galilee, followed by a trip to Jerusalem to die. The major turning point in the story is Peter's confession near Caesarea Philippi, which prompts Jesus' solemn announcement that he must suffer a violent death (Mark 8:31). Although Jesus does not arrive in Jerusalem for several chapters, the journey begins in principle with this first passion prediction.

187

This central section, which separates the Galilean ministry from the passion story, focuses on Jesus' preparation of the disciples for what is to come. It is punctuated by three passion announcements (Mark 8:31; 9:31; 10:33–34), each of which is followed by narrative material that presents the disciples as incapable of understanding what Jesus has announced. In each case, this prompts teaching concerning what it means to follow Jesus: the way of discipleship is the way of the cross. Thus the basic structure of the central section is provided by these triads of material.

Matthew adapts Mark's basic framework for the section and omits nothing of significance (Mark 9:38–41 does not appear as a unit in Matthew). He mars the symmetry, however, by interposing material between the passion prediction and the accompanying narrative in the second triad (17:24–27) and by transmuting the teaching about discipleship in that subsection into a long discourse about church life (chap. 18).

Matthew 16:13—17:27
The Journey Begins

It is slightly misleading to entitle this subsection "The Journey Begins," since the narrative contains no explicit allusion to the forthcoming trip apart from the vague statement of 17:22 that they were "gathering in Galilee." Indeed, the subsection concludes with Jesus still in Capernaum (17:24). The first passion announcement in 16:21 advises us, however, that the movement from ministry in Galilee to crucifixion in Jerusalem has now begun. In this portion of the story, there is no public instruction and only one healing (17:14–20). Attention is focused on the training of the Twelve.

Peter's Confession (16:13–20)

Peter's confession plays as significant a role in Matthew's Gospel as in Mark's, despite the fact that Matthew has presented a "foreshadowing" in the confession of the disciples in 14:33: "Truly you are the Son of God." It is obvious that Matthew does not wish us to view Peter simply as the spokesman

188

who reiterates the earlier confession, because he has supplemented Mark's story with three verses from another source, verses 17–19, which pronounce an individual blessing on Peter and assign him a unique role.

The story as told by Mark and his successors appears a little artificial. Jesus' first question, "Who do people say that I am?" ("the Son of man" in 16:13 functions unambiguously as Jesus' idiosyncratic way of speaking of himself without betraying the secret of his identity), was surely superfluous; Jesus must have been as aware as the disciples of the various attempts to categorize him. It is noteworthy that Matthew does not add "the Son of David" to Mark's list, despite what he has written in 12:23. The function of the first question is not to evoke a full range of opinions but to provide a foil for the second, by means of which the faith of the disciples can come to expression, "You are the Messiah" (Mark 8:29). In Mark's version, Peter probably speaks for his fellow disciples, and there is no explicit insistence that this is the first moment of messianic faith. The confession is presented primarily as the occasion for new teaching concerning the suffering of the Messiah. In its pre-Markan form the account may not have been at odds with the perspective of the Fourth Gospel, where Andrew announces, "We have found the Messiah" before Peter even meets Jesus (John 1:41).

Matthew materially alters the force of the story by attributing breakthrough significance to Peter's confession: "Blessed are you, Simon Bar-Jona!" The messianic confession is not due to idle human speculation (as in 12:23) but to divine disclosure. God has chosen this one man to be the honored recipient of the fundamental revelation of who Jesus is. The God who declared at Jesus' baptism, "This is my beloved Son" (3:17) has put it into Peter's heart to recognize Jesus as "the Messiah, the Son of the living God."

In the tradition behind verse 18 the nicknaming of Simon may have had a very different context. In John's Gospel, Simon receives his nickname from Jesus at their first meeting (1:42). Mark 3:16 seems to suggest that the naming of Peter occurred at the time Jesus selected twelve to be his closest followers. Because the original occasion is uncertain, the significance of the name is also unclear. The Aramaic term transliterated as *Kēphas* in Greek at John 1:42 and elsewhere ("Cephas" in English translations) was itself ambiguous, meaning usually a movable stone but occasionally an immovable rock. This ambiguity

189

persists in our passage, where two different Greek words are used: "You are *petros* [a stone], and on this *petra* [rock] I will build my church" (v. 18). Because *petros* was not used as a name, it is misleading to translate "You are Peter"; it would be more accurate to render the phrase "You are 'Stone.' " The translation "You are 'Rock' " assumes that *petros*, selected as the appropriate Greek equivalent of *kēphas* because it is masculine, has borrowed the meaning of the following feminine noun *petra*.

Whatever the nickname meant in its original context, for Matthew it clearly marks Peter not just as one stone among many, as in Eph. 2:20 where the apostles and prophets constitute collectively the foundation of the church (cf. Rev. 21:14), but as the church's unique and unrepeatable foundation.

For traditional Roman Catholicism, this text was fundamental to the doctrine that the successive popes, as Peter's legitimate successors, constituted the foundation of the church's authority. In reaction the Reformers understood the rock to be Peter's faith, which was subsequently shared by all Christians. Recent scholars, both Catholic and Protestant, are inclined to regard Peter himself as the rock but as functioning in this capacity in an unrepeatable way. In the history of salvation his role is to be seen as foundational in the emergence of the new messianic community. We can compare the role attributed to Peter here with that envisioned in Luke 22:32: "and when you have turned, strengthen your brothers and sisters." Paul likewise attributes a salvation-historical primacy to Peter in I Cor. 15:5 when listing the resurrection witnesses, and it was Peter alone among the apostles whom Paul sought to interview after his conversion and call (Gal. 1:18). Whether or not Matthew is justified in treating the Caesarea Philippi confession as the basis of Peter's primacy, that primacy is well attested. It is not by accident that Peter appears first in all the New Testament lists of the apostles.

It is sometimes argued that Jesus could not have spoken the saying attributed to him in verse 18, because the historical Jesus could not possibly have anticipated the Christian church. The saying may derive from an early Christian prophet speaking in Jesus' name, or perhaps from Matthew himself, but a setting in the life of Jesus is by no means inconceivable. If Jesus anticipated his death and subsequent resurrection (as will be maintained in this commentary), he must surely have given thought to the future of his "movement" between his death and the final resurrection of the dead. We need not presuppose that he foresaw the institutional church in order to support the authenticity of this saying or something like it in his Aramaic tongue. The word *ekklēsia* ("church") is used frequently in the Septuagint to render various Hebrew words for the community of God's people. We find *ekklēsia* used in this way in Acts 7:38, where Moses is spoken of as being "in the *ekklēsia* in the wilderness" (KJV: "the church in the wilderness"). Similar language is used at Qumran concerning the congregation of the new covenant. If Jesus interpreted his forthcoming death by the broken bread and shared wine of the Last Supper, it is also probable that he regarded his death as significant for a future—that is, postmortem—building of *his* congregation of the new covenant. For this reason, Oscar Cullmann argued that the original context for verses 18–19 was the Last Supper, where, according to Luke 22:31–32, special attention was paid to Peter (*Peter: Disciple—Apostle—Martyr,* p. 190).

There is general agreement that the phrase "the gates of Hades" is poetic language for the power of death (see Isa. 38: 10). What is meant is that the congregation of the new covenant will persist into the age to come despite all the efforts of the powers of darkness to destroy it. "The gates of Hades" may here represent a defensive posture: death will strive to hold in its prison house all who have entered its gates, but the Messiah's congregation will triumphantly storm the gates and rescue those destined for the life of the age to come. This latter suggestion receives some support from the parallel in 12:29 regarding the plundering of the strong man's goods (Satan's victims); see also Rev. 1:18. A scholarly consensus, however, still favors the first interpretation.

"The keys of the kingdom of heaven" (v. 19) refers to the right to admit or exclude (hence the popular tradition that regards St. Peter as the doorkeeper at the pearly gates). Revelation 3:7, borrowing from Isa. 22:22, ascribes this function to the risen Jesus. In Matthew's tradition, the Messiah has delegated this task to Peter. While it is perhaps natural for us to seize on the negative side of this responsibility, we must consider the possibility that the positive should be stressed: as chief missionary of the Easter message, it will be Peter's joyful task to lead many into the kingdom. Through his preaching he will open the doors to life. Matthew may even be reminding conservative

191

Jewish Christians that Peter had the right to admit Gentiles to the Messiah's congregation (see Acts 10).

It is not immediately clear what "binding" and "loosing" mean. Because of the preceding reference to the power of the keys, it is sometimes proposed that "binding" and "loosing" refer to excommunication and readmission. A second possibility is that the terms derive from exorcistic practice, in which Satan (or a specific demon) is "bound" and the victim "loosed." Usually, however, the terms are understood to refer to rulings about what can and what cannot be done by members of the church. Because of the use of these terms in rabbinic Judaism, it has been proposed that Matthew here designates Peter as the Chief Rabbi of Christianity. Although the Acts of the Apostles does not portray Peter as functioning in this way (in Acts 15 the role of Chief Rabbi seems to be held rather by James), we must assume that during his lifetime Peter remained the supreme guarantor of the tradition of Jesus' sayings and thus was in a position to make rulings about such matters as divorce and Sabbath observance.

While these verses ascribe a unique primacy to Peter, there is no suggestion that this role can be passed on to a successor after Peter's death. To the extent that Peter's functions must continue, others in the church must assume them. Here it is instructive to compare these verses with two later passages in the Gospel.

The nearest parallel to verse 19 is found in 18:18, which is addressed not to an individual but to a group. Narratively, the power to bind and loose is promised to the disciples, but in the context (vv. 15–17) this power is vested in congregational leaders or perhaps in the local congregation meeting as a whole. That is, while Peter is given supreme authority in the areas of teaching and discipline, in point of fact this authority will have to be exercised locally, and Peter's removal by death will not alter the situation.

The second passage to be considered in this connection is 23:8–10, where Jesus' followers are sternly warned to guard against establishing a hierarchy. No one, not even Peter, is to be honored as "Rabbi," "Father," or "Teacher," because all are to look to Jesus as their one teacher and to regard one another as fellow disciples. Peter's primacy in the history of salvation is assured, but this does not exalt him above his sisters and brothers in Christ. He is the servant of all.

192

Peter appears frequently in Matthew's Gospel. Occasionally, as here, a unique position is assigned to him. Usually, however, he is presented as typical. In his strengths and his weaknesses he represents ordinary Christians who strive, yet often fail, to be loyal followers of Jesus. Even in this passage which so strongly emphasizes his uniqueness he represents later believers who are called upon to make the same confession. And in the sequel, which dramatically portrays the limitations of his confession, he likewise represents ordinary believers who affirm their faith in Jesus but cannot quite understand why the cross was necessary.

Announcement of the Passion (16:21–28)

The second half of the "hinge" passage (16:13–28) is even more important than the first. Peter's confession, while given special emphasis by Matthew's addition of verses 17–19, functions in the gospel story primarily as the occasion for the first solemn announcement that Jesus must suffer a violent death.

In terms of the *narrative,* this first passion prediction is the watershed that divides the Galilean ministry from the passion. From this point to the triumphal entry into Jerusalem the emphasis is placed on Jesus' preparation of the disciples for his death (the announcement is formally repeated at 17:22–23 and 20:17–19 and mentioned in 17:12). In terms of the *theological message,* however, the announcement serves as the occasion for important instruction concerning what Jesus' death means for the life-style of his followers.

In this first announcement the passion is predicted not merely with a future tense, as in the second and third announcements, but with the theologically significant verb *must* (lit., "it is necessary"). This verb occurs frequently in apocalyptic literature when God's secret for the future is being disclosed (see comments on 24:6). The significance of the verb is enhanced by Matthew's substitution of "show" for Mark's "teach" (Mark 8:31), because "show" is likewise used in apocalyptic literature (the two verbs occur together in Rev. 1:1; 4:1; and 22:6).

While the divine *necessity* of Jesus' suffering is stressed, no *reason* is given. Not until the climactic passage following the third announcement do we learn that the Messiah's death will have saving power ("a ransom for many," 20:28). For the pur- 193 poses of the teaching about discipleship that will follow in this passage, it is sufficient to know that God's plan for his Messiah includes suffering.

Peter's vigorously negative reaction to the passion announcement is historically comprehensible. Contemporary Jewish thought found no reference to a suffering Messiah in the Hebrew Scriptures, and the idea is absent from the vast literature of Jewish apocrypha and pseudepigrapha, including the Dead Sea Scrolls. Nothing in their background prepared Jesus' disciples for the notion that Israel's eschatological champion should suffer a shameful death. The Messiah was expected to inflict suffering and death on Israel's enemies and on the wicked within Israel, not to experience it himself. The Christian message about a crucified Messiah, while merely foolishness to Greeks, was a real stumbling block to Jews, as Paul testifies in I Cor. 1:23–24.

It is noteworthy that in each of the three passion announcements Jesus' resurrection on the third day is predicted, but in no case is there any narrative reaction to this positive promise. Matthew seems to be telling us that the disciples were incapable of hearing anything beyond the negative part of the announcement. This too is fully understandable. Jewish writings had much to say about the final resurrection of the dead but nothing about the resurrection of a single martyr. It is proper, then, that the Easter narrative, while containing the angelic declaration "He is risen, *as he said*" (28:6), nevertheless presents the resurrection as a joyful surprise. It had to be experienced to be believed.

In the Greek, Jesus' harsh response to Peter echoes the climax of the temptation narrative: "Go, Satan!" (4:10). Just as Satan tried to persuade Jesus to disobey God as Israel had disobeyed in the wilderness, so now Peter, serving as Satan's spokesman, attempts to convince Jesus that the divine "must" of suffering can be ignored. The response to Peter, however, differs in one important particular from the word to Satan. To his disciple, Jesus says, "Go *behind me*, Satan!" At one level this seems to mean: "Resume your proper role as a disciple; learn from me, don't try to teach me." Figuratively, however, it may refer to the direction of Jesus' forthcoming journey: "Don't stand in my way; follow me to the cross!"

This latter understanding is supported by the addition that Matthew makes to the saying (cf. Mark 8:33): "You are a *skanda-*

194

lon to me." In secular Greek, the word normally meant "trap," but among Greek-speaking Jews whose primary literature consisted of the Scriptures the word meant "stumbling block," that is, a rock along the path that one stumbles against (see Lev. 19:14: "You shall not . . . put a stumbling block before the blind"). Used figuratively, it referred to causes or occasions of sin (see Matt. 13:41; 18:7) or hindrances to faith (I Cor. 1:23 and Gal. 5:11 refer to the cross as a *skandalon*). In this context the word has a particularly ironic significance: Simon the Stone has placed himself in front of Jesus and become a rock to stumble over. Peter's mind is ruled by human thoughts, not God's thoughts. To human thinking, the cross must ever remain a scandal, but it plays an indispensable role in God's salvation history.

The discipleship sayings of verses 24–26 seem to be variants of the very similar ones presented in 10:37–39. To the cross saying of 10:38 has been added the notion of self-denial. Since the expression "deny oneself" is not native to Hebrew and Aramaic, it is proposed that this Markan idiom (Mark 8:34) is a free rendering of the Semitic expression found in Luke 14:26 in association with the cross saying, "hate one's own life." As can be seen at Matt. 10:37, the First Evangelist correctly interprets this idiom as meaning "love less," that is, give a lower priority to. "Deny oneself" thus means to subordinate one's appetites and desires to God's will for us as made known in Jesus. Self-denial does not mean asceticism and self-flagellation, as was often inferred in medieval monasticism. Such self-denial runs the risk of being centered on the self, as is true in many instances of the secular asceticism of anorexia. Self-denial for the sake of self-denial is an expression of the self's need for control, not of submission to God's thinking (v. 23).

Modern study has shown that for many Christians, especially women, verse 24 has had a negative influence, because it reinforces a cultural pressure to subordinate oneself to others in a way that is not self-affirming. We must stress that the saying, properly understood, calls not for self-effacement but for affirmation of oneself as a child of God. Following Jesus means being ultimately subordinate only to God. Among Christians, there is a subordination, but it must be reciprocal (see Eph. 5:21).

195

The cross saying exhorts not martyrdom but fearlessness in following a crucified Lord (see comments on 10:38). In this sense Luke is justified in interpreting the metaphor of bearing the cross with the adverb "daily" (Luke 9:23). We must be careful, however, not to trivialize this strong exhortation by referring to everyday annoyances and family problems as "crosses we have to bear." The cross signifies not just death but a shameful death. To take up one's cross thus means to accept ridicule and hostility from those whose thinking reflects this world, not God's. We must be prepared to be rejected as our master was rejected. Note the parallel between "take up one's cross" and "Take my yoke upon you" (11:29). Bearing one's cross and taking up Jesus' yoke are complementary: we learn from him how to remain obedient to God in a disobedient world.

Verse 25 is substantially a repetition of 10:39 (see comments on 10:34–39). The following verse reinforces the wisdom of "losing" oneself for Christ's sake, by playing on the two meanings of *psychē* employed in verse 25: to lose one's natural *life* for Christ means finding one's *soul*, in the sense that God will bestow on it the gift of eternal life (see 10:28: God can destroy the soul as well as the body). Thus verse 26a can mean either "What folly to strive to become immensely wealthy and then die!" (as in Luke 12:13–21) or "Why forfeit eternal life by focusing all one's energies on this world's goals?" The same ambiguity is found in the second half of the verse, which seems to mean "With what can we approach God in order to ransom ourselves?" (see Ps. 47:7–9). Although neither meaning should be excluded, probably Matthew intends a reference to life in the age to come.

The discipleship sayings are repeated here because of their importance in relationship to Peter's confession and the first passion announcement. It is not enough to confess Jesus as Messiah and Lord. He must be acknowledged as suffering and crucified Lord, and this acknowledgment must not be one of theory but of practice. To confess Jesus truly means to walk the way of the cross in one's daily life.

The importance of a lived confession is now underlined by two judgment sayings. The first, whether an edited form of Mark 8:38 or from a separate source, finds a parallel in Rev. 22:12: "Behold, I am coming soon, bringing my recompense, to repay everyone for what he or she has done." Whereas the author of the Apocalypse prefers to use first-person language (he never employs "the Son of man"), Matthew's version has

Jesus refer to his glorious future destiny in this modest way, using third-person language and the mysterious self-designation "the Son of man." It is perhaps significant that in this judgment saying Matthew employs not "deeds" (plural) but "practice" (singular). In view of the fact that the context emphasizes suffering, *praxis* may here refer not simply to active deeds but also to one's passive suffering, that is, to one's stance, one's bearing vis-à-vis the world. Taken in this way, the saying functions less as a warning than as a consolation: If you affirm the crucified Christ in your life-style, you will be affirmed!

The last verse of the chapter is an edited version of Mark 9:1. Where Mark has "the kingdom of God having come in power," Matthew substitutes "the Son of man coming in his kingdom." Here "kingdom" means not a place but royal rule. Verse 28 thus reiterates the idea of verse 27 that Jesus the Messiah will return in glory, fully empowered to exercise his royal authority on God's behalf. What is added by verse 28 is the thought that his glorious coming will occur within the natural lifetime of some of Jesus' contemporaries (this idea is repeated at 24:34).

Early Christians, including Paul (Rom. 13:11; I Cor. 15:51) and the seer of Rev. 22:7, 20, expected Jesus to return soon. For later generations the promise of Matt. 16:28 and its parallels has posed a problem, because it is apparently an unfulfilled prophecy. Consequently some have proposed that the prediction of verse 28 is to be seen as having been fulfilled either in the immediately following story of the transfiguration, where some of the disciples behold Jesus in heavenly glory, or at the resurrection (see 28:18). Since Matthew has edited verse 28 to bring it into closer relationship to verse 27, these proposals are not convincing. The promise of Jesus' glorious arrival with his angels remains unfulfilled.

When Matthew wrote his Gospel, perhaps fifteen years or so after the destruction of the temple (see Introduction), a few members of the first generation of believers were probably still alive, and consequently it was possible to hold on to the hope of a literal fulfillment of this promise. The early excitement aroused by the expectation of Jesus' imminent return had, however, given place to the vision of an enormous missionary task. Matthew gives firm expression to the conviction that the end, 197 including Jesus' return in glory, cannot take place until the gospel has been proclaimed to all the Gentiles (24:14). If this task has not been completed before the last members of the first generation have died, so be it. God's grand purpose for the Gentiles must take precedence over the provisional promise concerning "some standing here."

The Transfiguration (17:1–13)

For modern readers, the story of the transfiguration of Jesus is one of the most difficult in the New Testament. It has the form of a historical narrative, but its content is so otherworldly that it is hard for us to accept its historicity. Some have tried to find a historical kernel in the account by citing reports that the faces of mystics caught up in an intense experience of the divine are sometimes transformed by a luminous glow. Such an explanation does not take us very far in understanding this remarkable story.

Whether we reject the story as the product of pious imagination or, by the willing suspension of disbelief, accept all its details as historical, the fact remains that the story points us to mystery, a mystery beyond the reach of historical reconstruction or scientific verification. Employing the appropriate canons of historiography, researchers can talk about Jesus of Nazareth as an itinerant prophet and healer who fell afoul of Roman justice and was crucified as a royal pretender. None of this tells us anything of the mystery of Jesus' person as it was experienced by the community that grew up around him. This story attempts to draw us into that suprahistorical mystery.

Matthew refers to what occurred on the mountain as a "vision" (v. 9). By this, of course, he does not mean to collapse the event into an inner "psychological" experience, since four persons are presented as independent witnesses. What is meant is that the "seeing" is not a natural function of ordinary human eyes but is God-given; God grants the disciples the power to see what otherwise would have been invisible to mortal perception (see Acts 7:31, where the same word is used of Moses' "sight" of the burning bush).

The "high mountain" has traditionally been identified as Mount Tabor in southern Galilee, a hill that rises only a few hundred feet above the surrounding plain. The *high* mountain symbolizes the border zone between earth and heaven, between the material and the spiritual.

It is erroneous to interpret the transfiguration of Jesus as a

198

manifestation of his deity. The story was certainly understood in this way by later Christians who had the benefit of the doctrine of the incarnation, but there is no clear evidence in his Gospel that Matthew was aware of this profound doctrine. To use technical terms, this is not a theophany (a manifestation of a god or of God) but a Christophany (a manifestation of Jesus as the Messiah). This is indicated by several features of the story. First, it is reported that Jesus' face "shone like the sun"; but this is precisely the same language that has already been used to describe the righteous who "will shine like the sun in the kingdom of their Father" (13:43). Jesus is presented not as nonhuman but as a transformed human who will be the pioneer and perfecter of those who will share his heavenly existence (cf. Heb. 2:10; 12:2). Second, in the "vision" Jesus is totally passive; he says nothing and does nothing. Such passivity ill suits a theophany. Finally, if Jesus were here presented as God (worse yet, as a "second god"), the appropriate response of the disciples would have been abject terror. This reaction occurs, rather, after the veiled theophany of verse 5. Instead, Peter speaks to Jesus as he would in normal circumstances. His proposal to build three booths, while not necessarily putting Moses and Elijah on the same level as Jesus, suggests that all three are "heavenly" human beings. According to II Kings 2:11, Elijah was carried to heaven before he suffered mortal death. Jewish tradition ascribed a similar fate to Moses. Jesus is represented as belonging with them because God will exalt him to heaven by resurrection (16:21; 17:9).

The significance of the three booths is uncertain. Because the word translated "booth" is also used to describe the wilderness tabernacle where God resided in the midst of Israel, it is possible that the three tabernacles are proposed by Peter as a means of prolonging the heavenly presence of Moses and Elijah with the transfigured Jesus. Perhaps this detail is intended to suggest that Peter wants to rejoice in the "heavenly Jesus" rather than go to Jerusalem to watch his master suffer a painful death.

In any event, the primary function of Peter's statement is to exhibit that humans cannot comprehend the scene without divine help. Peter's voice is silenced by the utterance from the cloud: "This is my beloved Son, with whom I am well pleased; listen to him" (v. 5). Just as the heavenly voice at Jesus' baptism announced that Jesus was God's Son (the Messiah) in advance

199

of his public ministry, so now, following Peter's confession, the voice from the cloud confirms that Jesus is what Peter has declared him to be. Since it also follows the first passion prediction, however, it does far more: it confims that Jesus is what *he* said he is, namely, a suffering Messiah. The clause "with whom I am well pleased," although repeated verbatim from 3:17, now gains additional significance. God is pleased with Jesus' obedient acceptance of his suffering role.

To the statement of the baptismal voice is added another clause: "listen to him." The ultimate significance of Jesus' role as *teacher* is now confirmed from heaven with words reminiscent of Deut. 18:15: "The LORD your God will raise up for you a prophet like me [Moses] from among you, from your brethren—*him shall you heed.*" Here as elsewhere in the First Gospel, Jesus is presented as the one who is like Moses but vastly superior (see comments on 5:1).

It is debated whether the command "Listen to him" refers to the passion announcement or to Jesus' ethical teaching. It would probably not have occurred to Matthew to make such a distinction. Jesus' teaching concerns God's will for him and for his followers. His ethical instruction can thus not be divorced from his understanding of the necessity of suffering. Loving one's enemies despite ill-treatment is a creative use of suffering in obedience to God's will.

What is most significant about the statement of the heavenly voice, and particularly of its addition, is that here as in the Old Testament generally *word* is given priority over *vision.* Mystical experience of heavenly reality in the form of visual images has its place, but a very healthy emphasis is placed upon God's *will* as communicated through *word.* Seeing Jesus transfigured has value only if it leads the disciples to listen obediently to his divinely authorized teaching.

As they descend the mountain Jesus instructs the three disciples not to report the vision until he has been raised from the dead. This reminder of the forthcoming death of the Messiah prompts the disciples to raise an issue that probably became a point of contention between Jewish-Christian missionaries and synagogue leaders. Since Scripture clearly teaches that Elijah will come before the end and "turn the hearts of fathers to their children and the hearts of children to their fathers" (Mal. 4:5–6), how can Jesus be the end-time Messiah, since Elijah has not come to "restore all things"? Verse 11

is best understood not as a promise but simply as a restatement
of what is said in Malachi, in preparation for Jesus' radical reinterpretation: "Yes, Malachi does say that Elijah will come and
restore all things, *but I say to you* . . . ." The New Testament
writers are not squeamish about acknowledging that God must
sometimes adjust promises to circumstances. Human sin may
necessitate a "midcourse adjustment" in God's grand plan. Just
as Mal. 3:1 is radically revised at Matt. 11:10, so now the
prophet's final statement is subjected to drastic revision: Elijah
has indeed come, but he did not restore all things because
human sin did away with him.

The point of this paragraph is not to prepare for Jewish-
Christian polemics but to serve with the passion announcement
of 16:21 as a framework for the transfiguration narrative. The
"heavenly" Jesus is the Messiah whose violent fate has been
prefigured by John the Baptist. (For the earlier equation of John
the Baptist with Elijah, see comments on 11:7–19.)

It may be of symbolic significance to Matthew that the three
apostles—Peter, James, and John—reappear together with
Jesus only in Gethsemane, where their master wrestles with his
fate. Those who witness his heavenly glory must also witness his
earthly agony. If his followers wish to share his future glory,
they must be prepared to participate in his suffering.

The Disciples' Inability to Heal (17:14–20)

Because this story follows the transfiguration narrative,
preachers have come to treat it as a reminder that, like Jesus
and his disciples, we must return from our mountaintop experiences to the valley of human needs to serve our fellows. There
is nothing wrong with this edifying use of the story, but Matthew's own appropriation of it seems to have been rather different. Jesus resumes his healing ministry with one of his
harshest words of protest (v. 17)!

The object of Jesus' annoyance is not as clear as we might
wish. At first glance it might seem that he is frustrated with
the epileptic's father, but this is unlikely, especially since the
imperative is plural ("Bring *ye* him here to me," v. 17). Some
propose that it is the unsuccessful disciples who are the target
of this sharp reproach, but this again is improbable, because
nowhere else in Matthew is "generation" used with respect to
Jesus' followers. We must conclude, therefore, that the harsh

201

saying is addressed to Israel as a whole, as represented by those present.

The protest is best understood in relationship to the preceding story of the transfiguration. In that heavenly scene Jesus and his three companions had a foretaste of the kingdom of God, but now they have returned to the demon-infested world where Satan is able to play his malevolent role because of human sin. The demon-possessed epileptic is symbolic of a world gone awry because of its refusal to acknowledge the sovereignty of God.

The opening address, "O faithless and perverse generation," seems reminiscent of the Song of Moses in Deut. 32:5, 20, where Israel is upbraided for its unfaithfulness to God. The following question, "How long shall I be with you? How long shall I bear with you?" may perhaps echo God's question in Num. 14:27, "How long shall this wicked congregation murmur against me?" Like the wilderness congregation that continually put the Lord to the test (Num. 14:22) instead of confidently trusting in God's protection, Jesus' contemporaries refuse to believe that God is at work in his ministry. Their rejection of Jesus will lead eventually to his rejection of them (see comments on 23:34–39).

The miracle story itself is told in copious detail by Mark. The inability of the disciples to exorcize the demon is explained as due to the fact that "this kind cannot be driven out by anything but prayer" (Mark 9:29). The assumption seems to be that the disciples have been successful in easier cases (Mark 6:13), but this case is unusually difficult and requires a special technique. Matthew finds this conclusion uninteresting. For him, the main point of the story concerns faith. This motif plays an important part in Mark's version of the dialogue between Jesus and the epileptic's father. Matthew deletes this dialogue; since the central thrust of his Gospel from 16:21 to the entry into Jerusalem concerns Jesus' instruction of the Twelve, he transfers the discussion of faith from the dialogue with the father to that with the disciples. He drastically reduces the details about the illness and its cure in order to allow the sayings about faith to become more prominent. In Matthew's treatment the father is no longer a doubter but an exemplary figure, who *kneels* before Jesus, addresses him as "Lord," and uses the early Christian prayer "Lord, have mercy . . ." (vv. 14–15).

As in 6:30; 8:26; 14:31; and 16:8, the disciples are accused of having little faith. As we have seen in its previous appear-

202

ances, this accusation is very different from the charge of un-faith leveled at "this generation." By their response to Jesus, the disciples have demonstrated that they have faith, but over and over again their behavior indicates that this faith, while genuine, is weak. It needs to be strengthened through exercise.

The saying about "faith like a mustard seed" is apparently drawn from the source used also by Luke (see Luke 17:6). Whereas Luke's version speaks of faith uprooting a sycamore tree and planting it in the sea, Matthew, borrowing from the similar saying he will use later at 21:21, substitutes the image of moving a mountain, a common metaphor for doing whatever everyone thought impossible. In both versions the reference to the minute mustard seed is not intended to suggest that a tiny amount of faith will suffice. What is contrasted is the "insignificance" of faith, as seen from the world's perspective, and the greatness of its results. Faith can effect the impossible!

In Matthew's formulation of the saying, there appears to be a tension between a quantitative and a qualitative view of faith. The expression "little faith" suggests that faith can be very small and yet be genuine, but for it to become effective it must grow into a "larger" faith. The comparison of faith with a mustard seed, on the other hand, suggests that for faith to move mountains it need only be authentic, that is, faith that cannot work miracles is not real faith. We need not attempt to resolve this tension, since there is truth in both perspectives, and each serves as a correction of the other.

Modern Christians need to be challenged, not condemned, by this saying. Like the generation that first read the Gospel, we need to be pushed into great reliance on God's saving power. We must not be allowed to be content with a flickering faith that is not sure whether God has anything to contribute to our everyday lives. We can attempt great things for God only when we expect great things from God.

On the other hand, we must not be bullied by this saying into thinking that if we cannot work miracles of healing, our faith is not genuine. Matthew believes in miracles, but he also knows that many people who seem to be producing supernatural cures in Jesus' name are nonetheless unfaithful Christians (7:21–23). As Paul reminds us in I Cor. 13:2, "If I have all faith, so as to remove mountains, but have not love, I am nothing." For both these writers, ethics is a more dependable test of the genuineness of faith than miracles.

203

The Second Passion Announcement (17:22–23)

In Mark, the second passion announcement (Mark 9:31) is followed immediately by the disciples' dispute over who is the greatest (Mark 9:33–34), which prompts instruction about humility (Mark 9:35–37). The juxtaposition is intentional. Mark tells us that the disciples are incapable of understanding the announcement (Mark 9:32) and then proceeds to illustrate this incomprehension by means of the dispute. Had the disciples understood the way of the cross, they would have abandoned such vain ambitions. Because Matthew separates the announcement from the question about greatness (18:1), however, the function of the former as a foil to the latter is lost. The announcement stands instead in startling isolation, unrelated to what precedes or what follows.

The second is the briefest of the three main announcements that Matthew has in common with Mark. (Still briefer is the final announcement that inaugurates the passion in 26:2.) Whereas the first employed the impersonal verb *dei* ("it is necessary") to indicate that Jesus' death will be in accordance with divine necessity, the second uses *paradidōmi* ("give over, deliver up"). Since the verb is in the passive voice ("The Son of man is going *to be delivered up* into the hands of men"), the person who will deliver him up is unspecified. The reference could be to Judas, who is regularly identified as "the one who delivered up," that is, "the betrayer" (see 10:4; 26:48). It could be argued that Satan is implied (see John 13:2, 27). There is a consensus among scholars, however, that this is best understood as a divine passive, that is, the actor is God, but this is left unexpressed out of reverence for the deity. Paul uses the same verb in the active voice in Rom. 8:32: "He who did not spare his own Son but *delivered him up* for us all."

Whereas Mark reports that the disciples are entirely without understanding, Matthew suggests that they did indeed grasp the first part of the announcement; they are deeply distressed by the unambiguous prediction of Jesus' violent death. They fail completely to hear the equally unambiguous prediction of his resurrection on the third day! The resurrection will have to be experienced before it can be understood.

Avoiding Giving Offense (17:24–27)

Did Jesus pay taxes? On first impression this seems to be the point of the story, and at the earliest stage it probably was, but the function of the passage in Matthew seems to be rather different.

Scholars disagree on whether an authentic incident in the life of Jesus underlies the anecdote and, if authentic, whether the concern is over a secular or a religious tax. Since the time of Jerome there have been many interpreters who have assumed that a secular tax is in view because Jesus' response mentions "the kings of the earth" and contains two technical terms used of secular taxation, *telos* (which the RSV renders here as "toll" but as "revenue" at Rom. 13:7), from which *telōnēs* ("tax collector") is derived, and *kēnsos* (a Latin loanword meaning "census," referring to head taxes based on a census). Most modern scholars oppose this interpretation for several reasons. First, the tax specified is the "two drachma" tax. Since the *didrachmon* was equivalent to the half-shekel, it is argued that the tax referred to is the half-shekel offering of Exod. 30:13, which by the first century had become an annual religious tax imposed on male Jews over nineteen years of age for the support of the temple and its sacrifices. Second, Jesus' saying makes little sense if secular taxation is the topic, since his assertion that "the sons are free" would imply that Jesus and his followers are Caesar's "children," that is, persons exempt from taxation because they belong to the household of the taxing authority. Third, in view of the incident concerning tribute to Caesar (22:15–22), it seems most unlikely that Jesus opposed civil taxation on principle.

The temple tax was of comparatively recent origin and not universally accepted. One of the documents found at Qumran indicates that the Essenes, probably in part because of their hostility toward the priestly hierarchy in Jerusalem, understood Exod. 30:13 as requiring only that each male Jew should present the half-shekel offering once during his lifetime. A later rabbi proposed that the destruction of the temple was due in part to a serious lack of compliance with the temple tax. Noncompliance is readily understandable, since it amounted to two days' wages for a day laborer. The tax was not rigidly enforced.

The religious tax collectors ask Peter, "Does your master

205

pay the half-shekels?" (using the plural of *didrachmon*). This suggests that they are asking not simply whether he will pay this year (it was collected in the month before Passover) but whether it has been his habit to pay each year. Their question implies doubt; they do not assume compliance. Perhaps they wonder whether Jesus shares the Qumran perspective. Since the Pharisees were prominent in their support of the annual tax, it is even possible that the questioners are testing Jesus to see whether he sides with the Pharisees on the issue.

What is the basis for Jesus' rejection of the tax? His response does not explicitly challenge the Pharisees' view of Exod. 30:13. It seems, rather, to attack the very concept of religious taxation. Underlying "the kings of the earth" is the Jewish tradition of referring to God parabolically as a king (see 18:23). Jesus argues that he and his followers are children of the great king and therefore cannot be taxed in his name as if they were foreigners.

Does Jesus object to the very concept of religious taxation in the conviction that the support of organized religion should be on the basis of freewill offerings? Or does he here indicate an ambivalent attitude toward the temple and the religious establishment that used it as a power base? Does his response constitute an attack on the system of atonement by sacrifices, since the tax was used to support the daily burnt offerings? All these have been proposed, but the narrative as transmitted to us does not permit us to identify Jesus' motive with any certainty.

Partly because of the miraculous solution with which the story concludes, some have argued that the tradition derives not from Jesus but from the early Palestinian church, which was confronted with the issue of whether or not they should continue to pay the temple tax in view of their conviction that atonement was to be found only in Jesus' death. The conclusion they reached, perhaps on the basis of a "word of the Lord" pronounced by a Christian prophet, was that they should continue to pay the tax, but only in order that "they" might not be offended.

The verb *skandalizō*, here translated "give offense to," is one of Matthew's favorite words, occurring more frequently in this Gospel than in any other New Testament writing. It means "cause to stumble," often in the sense of "cause to sin" (see 5:29–30; 18:8–9) or "cause to lose one's faith" (24:10, perhaps

26:31, 33), but sometimes merely "give offense to," and thus in the passive "become offended" (11:6; 15:12). The meaning of "scandalize" in this passage depends on the identity of the "them" of verse 27. Does it refer to the tax collectors themselves, to the Pharisees who may have sent them, or to the general populace who may be affected by Jesus' example? If the tradition originated in the early Palestinian church, we can guess that the motive for compliance with the tax was either to avoid giving offense to potential converts or to evade persecution as an "unpatriotic" minority opposed to the national sacrifices.

Matthew's Gospel was probably written after the destruction of the temple, at a time when Jews were compelled to pay the half-shekel tax to Rome as a war reparation. The issue of whether to pay the temple tax was no longer relevant. We must assume, therefore, that the anecdote is inserted by Matthew for a different reason. That reason is suggested by the context.

The focus of Matthew 18 is on relationships within the community of believers. A strong warning is issued against giving offense to any of "these little ones who believe in me" (18:6), who are at risk of becoming lost sheep (18:10–14). In the light of this concern, then, Matthew adds the temple tax story as a prelude to the discourse on church discipline precisely because in it Jesus advocates behavior that does not give offense.

There is an essential offense in the gospel, particularly in its focus on the cross of Christ, that must never be diluted or dissolved (see Gal. 5:11). Jesus' followers are advised, however, not to give unnecessary offense on secondary issues where principle is not involved and compromise is possible. "The children are free" (Matt. 17:26), but that freedom is subject to restriction for the sake of the brothers and sisters in the church as well as of those outside. Christians who have no problem with a moderate use of alcoholic beverages often restrain their freedom in this regard for the sake of recovering alcoholics. Some who are not troubled by traditional language adopt the use of inclusive terms not because of personal conviction but because of a desire not to offend others for whom this is a burning issue. The list of parallel situations could be indefinitely extended. The governing principle is love. Our freedom entails obedience to this higher rule.

Matthew 18:1–35
The Fourth Discourse: Life Together in the Church

Chapter 18 constitutes the fourth of Matthew's five great discourses marked by the concluding formula, "When Jesus had finished these sayings" (or something similar). Each of the five is occasioned by an item in the Markan outline. In this instance it is Mark's story about the Twelve disputing over which of them is the greatest (Mark 9:33–37). This narrative prompts Matthew to bring together various materials relevant to the maintenance of the church's fellowship.

Although the chapter is a unified whole, for purposes of teaching and preaching it can be divided into three sections.

Concern for the Little Ones (18:1–14)

Matthew transposes the dispute of Mark 9:33–37 into the less embarrassing question, "Who then is greatest in the kingdom of heaven?" Only the "then" indicates that the question has a prior history. The fact that the issue is raised is sufficient in itself to indicate that the appetite for prominence was a problem for the earliest followers and for Matthew's church. The modern church is by no means immune to the disease.

In the Markan narrative Jesus sets a child in their midst, and declares, "Whoever receives one such child in my name receives me; and whoever receives me, receives not me but him who sent me" (Mark 9:37). Since Matthew has already used a very similar saying in his missionary discourse at 10:40, he omits the last clause, which he apparently regards as more pertinent to the matter of extending hospitality to missionaries. He precedes it, however, with two very important sayings that help to interpret what it means to "receive" a child in Christ's name.

208   The first of these appears to be Matthew's reformulation of Mark 10:15, "Truly, I say to you, whoever does not receive the kingdom of God like a child shall not enter it." Since the mean-

ing of "receive the kingdom" is not self-evident (it probably means "receive the gospel of the kingdom"), Matthew or his source drastically alters this clause to read: "unless you turn and become like children." The importance of this saying is witnessed by the fact that it occurs also in the Fourth Gospel, reformulated in John's own idiom: "Truly, truly, I say to you, unless one is born anew, one cannot see the kingdom of God" (John 3:3). John explains this as meaning that one must be born "from above" by means of baptism and the operation of the Holy Spirit (John 3:5). Matthew's understanding is not so easily determined, but on the basis of the new context into which he places the saying we may conjecture that "turning around" and "becoming like children" are equivalent expressions, both referring to abandonment of the standards and values of the "natural" world and submission to God's values. In a world left to its own devices people are continually trying to lord it over one another: the rich over the poor, the intelligent over the simple, adults over children, man over woman, whites over blacks—on and on goes the list. "But not so with you; rather let the greatest among you become as the youngest, and the leader as one who serves" (Luke 22:26).

Various suggestions have been made concerning what was originally meant by "become like children." Innocence has been proposed, but children beyond infancy can hardly be described as innocent. As parents ruefully testify, each child illustrates the truth of original sin! Children are naturally (and necessarily) self-centered; only gradually do they learn to consider others and obey the rules that make for happy relationships. Since young children are, however, innocent with respect to adult sexuality, some second-century Christians who were horrified by rampant sexual immorality found in this saying support for their prohibition of all sexual activity. Fortunately, their view was never widely received.

A more helpful suggestion is that "become like a child" means to become as teachable as children. In order to participate in God's kingdom, one must be ready to learn God's ways and live accordingly. Still another possibility is that the point in mind is a child's total dependence on its parents for food, shelter, and care. To enter the kingdom one must learn all over again what it means to be helplessly dependent on a Parent who can be trusted to the uttermost as no human parent can be. This dependency should be neither servile nor infantile, but simply

209

a humble acknowledgment that God is sovereign and his rules must be obeyed. A third proposal, which takes its cue from the context, is that Jesus' followers are here told that they must assume the *status* of a child, that is, they must join the lowest rank of a stratified society. Those who are infected with the world's appetite for lording it over others are here informed that this lust must be completely surrendered.

Humility was not a virtue but a vice for many pagan moralists. To them it smacked of a servility appropriate to slaves, women, and children but indecent among free men. Christians turned this view on its head by treating humility as the antonym not of a proud self-confidence but of haughtiness and arrogance. Precisely because Christian churches were countercultural, bringing men and women, slave and free, rich and poor into the same "club," this attitude was essential to the church's existence. Paul warns Roman Christians not to be haughty but to associate with the lowly (Rom. 12:16) and urges the Philippians: "In humility count others better than yourselves" (Phil. 2:3). To Matthew also, this attitude is indispensable to the Christian fellowship. The saying of verse 4 anticipates the fuller statement of 23:12, where it is insisted that hierarchy is to be renounced and all believers treated as equals.

Because of the new context that Matthew has created for the saying of verse 5, "Whoever receives one such child in my name receives me," we are probably to understand "receive" as meaning not "extend hospitality to," as in 10:40, but "accept as infinitely valuable," that is, treat as warmly as if receiving Jesus into one's home. The only ambiguity in Matthew's saying is whether "one such child" refers to an actual child or to an adult who has turned and become like a child. Both understandings are possible, but perhaps the balance of probability lies with the literal interpretation, in view of the way children are treated in 19:13–15. Children have value not because they are potential adults but because they are already persons whom Jesus champions. To "receive" them is to receive him. Conversely, to reject or mistreat them is to treat him with disdain.

Even if we were correct in regarding verse 5 as referring to actual children, the following verse has undoubtedly moved from the literal to the figurative; the little ones are explicitly defined as people who believe in Jesus, and this can best be understood as referring to adults. It is frequently proposed that "these little ones" here and in verses 10 and 14 designates any followers of Jesus, as in 10:40. On the basis of the present context, however, it would appear that the "little ones" are particularly vulnerable to temptation and apostasy. Perhaps Matthew is thinking of new believers, whose initial enthusiasm exceeds their understanding of and commitment to the new way of life taught by Jesus. He may have in mind young Christians, who are susceptible to pressure from their Jewish or pagan families. Perhaps he envisions people who have no special gifts or charm, humble folk who are easily ignored in any group and who always remain on the periphery of the fellowship.

In any event, the "little ones" are believers who are in danger of being "scandalized," that is, fall away from Christ (*skandalizō* is so used in 13:21; 24:10). Those responsible for causing little ones to fall away are threatened with eternal perdition. No hint is given concerning whether the *skandalon* (stumbling block) of verse 7 is laid before the humble believers by an outsider or an insider. Presumably both possibilities are in view; a vulnerable Christian can be drawn away by a non-Christian or driven away by a fellow believer.

Scholars debate whether the hand, foot, and eye of verses 8–9 are to be understood as in 5:29–30, where severe self-discipline is urged as a defense against sexual immorality, or as figurative references to members of the body of Christ, who must be excommunicated ("cut off") because they place stumbling blocks before other Christians. Neither interpretation is completely satisfying. The second is less probable because of the second person singular ("If thy hand or thy foot offend thee"). Probably we should not take the references to the body literally. Believers are here warned to exercise proper self-discipline, since the end result of continually yielding to various temptations may well be turning away from Christ. While each individual sin can be confessed and forgiven, to abandon Christ is to put oneself beyond the sphere of God's forgiving grace. In view of the context, we may see in these verses another dimension of responsibility. Christians who encourage weak believers to join them in various forms of harmful behavior must consider what the end result will be. To use a modern example, church leaders must exercise restraint in the consumption of beverage alcohol not only to guard themselves against the sin of committing murder by automobile but also because of the influence of their example. 211

The parable of the lost sheep has a very different function

in Luke's Gospel, where it serves to justify Jesus' association with tax collectors and sinners (Luke 15:1–7). Because these Jewish outcasts symbolize the Gentiles for Luke, the parable also speaks in a veiled way of the Gentile mission that Jesus' followers will undertake in his name. At both levels it is an evangelism parable. In Matthew's Gospel, however, the parable speaks of the need to keep backsliding Christians in the church's fellowship. This is indicated not only by the context in which he places the parable but also by the introduction and conclusion that frame it (vv. 10, 14); both speak explicitly of "these little ones" and intimate that they have infinite value in the sight of the Father in heaven.

The opening imperative of verse 10 is sharply put and unambiguous: "See that you do not despise one of these little ones." No member of the fellowship, no matter how weak or marginal, is to be treated as inferior, because even the lowliest Christian has a guardian angel of the highest status, that is, an "angel of the presence." Since it was assumed in contemporary Judaism that only a few angels were permitted to be in the immediate presence of God ("see God's face"), this statement attributes the highest importance to the little ones, an importance that is confirmed by the conclusion in verse 14: it is God's will that *not one* of them should perish, that is, be denied entrance to the kingdom of heaven.

Unfortunately, this parable has become so familiar to us that it no longer shocks us. What kind of shepherd would be so utterly foolish that he would abandon his flock to the hazards of the hills in order to search, perhaps unsuccessfully, for a single sheep? And why would a shepherd rejoice *more* over such a wayward sheep than over the more dependable members of the flock? Jesus, the master parable teller, intended to shock his audience into insight. Only such a foolish shepherd can represent God's concern for each of his straying children.

Most modern congregations surely deserve the sharp warning of verses 10–14 as much as Matthew's. How easy it is for the active members of a church to ignore those who play no leadership role and contribute only modestly to the budget! A Brooklyn minister, visiting one of his inactive members, was told, "Those people over at the church make me feel like a nobody." How many thousands of others there are whose experience has been the same! The foolish shepherd must weep at our continuing disdain for the little ones of his flock.

212

Dealing with Destructive Sin (18:15–20)

This paragraph is difficult for modern Christians, because it deals forthrightly with the effect of unrepented sin on a congregation. We are inclined to "forgive" sins in advance of repentance rather than have to confront the guilty parties.

Serious ambiguity is caused by disagreement among the ancient manuscripts. While the majority include the words "against you" in verse 15, some of our most dependable manuscripts omit them. Does the procedure concern personal injury only, encouraging the aggrieved party to confront the culprit? Or is it a question of a disinterested party attempting to intervene? The former understanding is encouraged by the brief parallel in Luke 17:3: "If your brother sins, rebuke him, and if he repents, forgive him." Since forgiveness is personal, presumably the injury also is personal. The second interpretation is entirely possible, however, in view of other New Testament texts that make Christians responsible for correcting sinners (see Gal. 6:1).

Interpretation of the disciplinary procedure must begin with the conclusion. A brother or a sister who refuses to listen to the church, that is, to accept the church's rebuke and acknowledge the sin, must be ostracized; that person no longer belongs to the fellowship. Because the punishment is so severe, we must infer that the transgressions here envisioned are serious offenses that affect the spiritual health of the congregation as a whole. Modern Christians tend to have a very individualistic conception of sin: "What I do with my life is my business; it's no concern of yours!" Early Christians were more aware of the interactive function of behavior. Serious sexual misconduct, for example, was perceived by spiritual leaders as by no means a private matter but as a cancer threatening the body of Christ (I Cor. 5:1–5).

Other sins destructive of the church's fellowship may have been economic in nature. In I Cor. 6:1–8 Paul speaks in horror of the fact that members of the church are suing one another in the civil courts. He demands to know why there has been no attempt to arbitrate such cases within the congregation. In II Thess. 3:6–15 the economic sin is the freeloading of certain persons who refuse to work but are happy to eat what other people buy. Certainly dishonesty, cheating, and failure to fulfill

213

business obligations can seriously erode Christian fellowship until it becomes a hollow shell. Matthew and Paul agree that these and other conflicts must be dealt with and not be allowed to fester.

Although verse 17, with its provision for "shunning" an unrepentant sinner, implies that serious sins are in view, it is possible that a similar procedure, with a less drastic solution, was employed for more tolerable offenses that were nonetheless deemed injurious to the fellowship. In Phil. 4:2 Paul speaks obliquely of a serious falling out between Euodia and Syntyche that is seriously affecting the fellowship of the congregation and urges a third party to arbitrate the dispute.

The "one or two others" who are involved in the second stage of the procedure are presumably not witnesses to the original offense. Their function as witnesses to the confrontation between the accuser and the accused is twofold: they can protect the accused if the accusation is too harsh or based on a misperception or inadequate information; they can protect the accuser and observe how the accused responds to the charge.

The punishment, "Let that person be to you like a Gentile or a tax collector," sounds alien in a Gospel that stresses Jesus' association with tax collectors and urges a worldwide mission to Gentiles. Does this language derive from a conservative Jewish congregation and reflect traditional prejudice? Or does Matthew, by using these two terms, mean to remind his readers that the ostracized brother or sister is now the object of missionary activity? No certainty on this question seems possible.

By including this passage, Matthew shows that he believes firm action must be taken against a serious offense. He is also aware, however, that those who undertake to correct their neighbors are liable to a sin themselves, a sin that can be described as spiritual arrogance in some instances, as judgmentalism in others, and occasionally as simple hypocrisy. He has already given special prominence to Jesus' injunction, "Judge not, that you be not judged" (7:1). He therefore carefully frames this passage with the parables of the lost sheep and the unforgiving debtor, both of which dramatize the conviction that God's desire is that the sinner be saved, not condemned.

Appended to the procedure for dealing with serious offenses are several sayings that Matthew regards as pertinent to the issue. Verse 18 takes the responsibility laid on Peter in 16:19 and extends it to the local church; as Peter "binds" and "looses"

214

for the church as a whole, so the congregation must exercise these functions relative to its own internal affairs. Although binding and loosing may in the broader context refer to declaring what is permitted or not permitted, here it seems to mean disciplinary action. The congregation has the power to punish or exclude. In doing so, it is acting on God's behalf.

Verse 19 appears at first sight to be alien to the present context; it seems to be speaking of the power of shared prayers. This perception is probably mistaken, however. According to J. D. M. Derrett (*Expository Times* 91 [1979]: 83–86), several technical terms in this verse suggest that the saying refers to out-of-court settlements of disputes. It can be paraphrased: "If two of you can come to an agreement regarding any disputed matter, that agreement will be blessed by my Father in heaven." If the transgression of verse 15 is an economic one, the matter, even if "unrepented," need not be subjected to the binding and loosing power of the congregation as a whole; it can be negotiated, with or without the assistance of third parties (v. 16). What is important is that the dispute be resolved so that fellowship can be restored.

The final verse of the paragraph should be understood in the same light. The term "gathered" is superfluous if the coming together is simply for prayer. The two or three are gathered *in Christ's name*, they meet in the knowledge that they belong to the risen Christ and his watchful eye is over what they do. When two alienated Christians, with or without a mediator, come together to work toward a reconciliation despite all the anger and hurt that separate them, they are humbled and strengthened by the awareness that Christ is in their midst. It is for his sake that they search for a solution to their problem.

There is a sense in which verse 20 interprets not only the immediately preceding saying but all the verses of the paragraph. The risen Christ is "in the midst" of each stage of the procedure of verses 15–17, and it is he who has conferred on the congregation the responsibility of binding and loosing. If the Christian fellowship is to survive the strains imposed by human failure, it will be only because the risen Lord sustains it.

Unlimited Forgiveness (18:21–35)

There is nothing particularly Christian about the practice of forgiveness. Whatever our religion or nonreligion, we must request and grant forgiveness almost every day of our lives. Most of the offenses are trivial and unintentional. Forgiveness becomes problematic only when the trespasses are more serious, when they are intentional, and especially when they are repeated.

Behind Peter's question, "Lord, how often . . . ?" are two possible concerns, one focusing on the offended party and the other on the offender. Experience suggests that there must be limits to patience with misbehavior. Peter may be asking, "If my fellow Christian insults me repeatedly, must I go on suffering this indignity just because he always says 'Sorry, old boy!'?" Or he may be proposing, "Is it in the best interests of my brother for me to go on tolerating uncivil behavior when it is clear that his repentance is superficial and he has no intention of changing?"

These are legitimate concerns, but Jesus' answer addresses neither of them. Both have been dealt with in the preceding paragraph, which encourages confrontation for offenses that threaten Christian fellowship. Instead, Jesus' response transposes the problem from the sphere of ordinary human relationships to another realm.

The first part of the response consists of a statement exhorting unlimited forgiveness. It does more than this, however. "Seventy-seven times" is probably an allusion to Gen. 4:24, where Lamech proudly boasts to his wives that he will avenge himself seventy-sevenfold on anyone who dares to attack him. Forgiveness is thus presented as the antonym of revenge. Followers of Jesus must renounce the very human intention of getting even with someone who repeatedly injures them. They are called to be Lamech's polar opposite.

In the second part of his response to Peter's question Jesus provides the theological grounding for unlimited forgiveness by means of a parable. It is important to note that this is not simply a "Go and do likewise" parable, like that concerning the Good Samaritan. It is a *kingdom* parable: "Therefore the kingdom of heaven may be compared to . . . ." Peter's question addresses a human problem from a human perspective. The parable grounds forgiveness in the nature of God.

At the level of story the parable tells of an Oriental sultan who conducts an audit of the operations of his ministers of state and provincial governors ("servant" or "slave" was used of all administrators, whether "free" or not). It is discovered that one,

216

perhaps the satrap of a wealthy province, has embezzled an immense amount of tax revenue (equivalent to a day's wages for 100,000,000 laborers!). Restitution is impossible. Rather than simply executing the scoundrel, the sultan determines to inflict a more degrading and protracted punishment; the man and his wife and children will be put on the block and sold into slavery, which often involved sexual abuse. (This detail would indicate to a Jewish audience that the story is about Gentiles; Jewish law did not countenance the sale of a wife for her husband's debts.) The embezzler pleads for time to make restitution—a desperately illusory proposal. In response the king displays the whimsical eccentricity of a despot: he abruptly reverses his decision and lets the villain off scot free!

In the second scene the central figure changes his role. He is not now a debtor but a creditor. A "fellow slave"—that is, another member of the king's farflung administration—is delinquent on a small loan (equivalent to a laborer's wages for one hundred days). The debtor begs an extension, using the same words as his counterpart in the first scene. The difference, of course, is that in this instance the promise to repay is credible. The pardoned embezzler stands on his rights and tolerates no breach of the original contract. He takes legal action to have the delinquent thrown into debtors' prison.

The third scene is the same as the first. Other administrative officials, appalled by the embezzler's harsh treatment of his debtor, have reported the incident, and the king has summoned the pardoned criminal to stand again at the bar. The cruel creditor is addressed as *"wicked* slave." The adjective *ponēros* may indeed have here its general connotation of "bad" or "unethical," but in 6:23 and 20:15, where it modifies "eye," it connotes an envious, grudging, or miserly spirit. In the parable, therefore, it may signify "mean-spirited." In his anger at the man's inhumane conduct, the despot once again reverses his judgment and turns the criminal over to his torturers with instructions that they continue to inflict physical pain until full restitution has been made, that is, for the rest of his life.

In our appropriation of this vivid story we must be careful to distinguish between parable and allegory. As in many rabbinic parables, the figure of the king serves allegorically as a reference to God, but this does not mean that all the details of the king's behavior can be taken as statements about the nature of God. Just as we do not regard God as an Oriental despot who

217

would sell women into sexual slavery as punishment for their husbands' sins, so we need not take the concluding detail about unending physical torture as indicative of the divine nature.

Although the story focuses on the heartless behavior of the pardoned criminal, the theological center is the astounding magnanimity of the king. So it is with the kingdom of heaven. Those who wish to be part of that kingdom must imitate the incalculable patience and generosity of its sovereign (see 5:45).

It is a mistake, however, to think of unlimited forgiveness simply as a matter of the imitation of God. Who is capable, by the mere exercise of the will, of becoming "perfect, as your heavenly Father is perfect" (5:48)? We are driven back to the beginning of the discourse. Those who wish to enter the kingdom of unlimited forgiveness are without hope unless they turn and become like children. Only utter dependence on our heavenly Parent will enable us to transcend human wisdom concerning how to deal with those who sin against us and to manifest instead something of God's own way of dealing with sinners.

Also to be avoided is the error of treating the concluding statement legalistically. We must not foolishly believe that we can *earn* God's forgiveness by forgiving others or, conversely, conclude that God is incapable of forgiving even so heinous a sin as our unwillingness to forgive someone who has hurt us deeply. Here as elsewhere in our unfaithfulness God does not stoop to dealing with us in a tit for tat fashion. We are to hear the parable's conclusion in accordance with its intent: it solemnly warns us that we must fervently pray for strength to resist the temptation of getting even with those who have hurt us and for grace to reflect the majestic generosity of the kingdom of heaven.

Unlimited forgiveness is not to be confused with sentimental toleration of hurtful behavior. Christians are often guilty of forgiving too much and too quickly. The misbehavior of alcoholics is not to be laughed off. Ministers who fail to control their sexual impulses are not to be lightly excused. Teenagers who betray their parents' trust are not simply to be forgiven; a much more loving course of action is to insist that they amend their behavior so that they can regain that trust. In these and other instances premature forgiveness is an easy way out that does little to help the offender or to heal a damaged relationship.

Because the matter of dealing with such offenders has been

218

treated in verses 15–20, the last section of the chapter cannot be misconstrued as condoning evil. It does, however, serve as a corrective against a too zealous application of the preceding section. Yes, offenses are to be confronted, but only in a spirit of gentleness (Gal. 6:1). Even when dealing with the stubbornly unrepentant, we must forswear vindictiveness and, by God's grace, give evidence that we are ready to extend forgiveness because we ourselves have been humbled by God's forgiving love.

Matthew 19:1—20:34
On the Way to Jerusalem

Matthew completes the fourth discourse with his customary formula ("And when Jesus finished these sayings") and then adds an important geographical note: Jesus departs from Galilee and comes into "the region of Judea beyond the Jordan" (19:1). He is well on his way toward Jerusalem, where he must die (16:21).

Even here he is followed by large crowds. Whereas the Markan parallel (Mark 10:1) suggests that Jesus *taught* these multitudes, Matthew (v. 2) limits Jesus' ministry to *healing*. For Matthew, the phase of Jesus' activity that began with Peter's confession focuses on the Twelve; it is they, not the crowds, whom Jesus teaches in this section of the Gospel.

Marriage and Celibacy (19:3–12)

The Pharisees, who have been absent from the narrative since before Peter's confession, now reappear, again with hostile intent. Just as they *tested* him in 16:1, so now they test him with a question about marriage: Is it permitted under the Torah for a man to divorce his wife for any reason?

The phrase "for any reason," which is not found in the parallel at Mark 10:2, is ambiguous. The question may be understood as asking whether Jesus favors easy divorce: "Can a man divorce his wife at will, whatever his reason?" On the other hand, it may have reference to the grounds for divorce accepted as legal by the interrogators: "Do you accept the

219

Pharisaic rules for divorce?" If the former understanding is correct, they are perhaps hoping to bring Jesus into disfavor with Jewish men (who regarded it as their right to divorce an unwanted wife) by getting him to admit publicly that he was opposed to easy divorce. The intent may have been still more specific; according to 14:3-4, John's death was due to his opposition to Herod's divorce and remarriage. On the other hand, if the second view is to be preferred, the Pharisees wanted to expose the fact that Jesus' divorce rules differed significantly from theirs.

In any event, we must disabuse ourselves of the opinion once popular among commentators that the Pharisees are here trying to expose Jesus as a teacher who annuls the law of Moses. We are indebted to modern Jewish scholars who have shown that Jesus' view, while distinctive, would not have been regarded as a challenge to the Torah. Jesus is represented in this and the parallel passages not as abrogating the Torah's rules on divorce but as interpreting them, just as other Jewish teachers did. His method is the same as theirs: he interprets one passage by reference to other scriptural passages.

Whereas Mark's discussion begins with the divorce provisions of Deut. 24:1, Matthew reverses the argument, so that Jesus first presents the Creator's original will for marriage and only then addresses the significance of the passage in Deuteronomy. Any meaningful treatment of divorce, Matthew suggests, must be preceded by a study of God's intention for marriage. Genesis 2:24, interpreted against the background of the creation of humans as male and female in Gen. 1:27, is understood as implying that it is God who couples a man and a woman in marriage and that what God does is of permanent validity.

The opponents respond by citing Deuteronomy: "Why then did Moses command one to give a certificate of divorce, and to put her away?" (v. 7). This is not a literal quotation; there is no commandment in Deut. 24:1, only an extended description of a common state of affairs: "If it is the case that a man . . . writes a certificate of divorce, puts it in her hand, and sends her out of his house . . . ." The commandment does not occur until Deut. 24:4, where it is ruled that a divorced wife may not be remarried to her original husband after an intervening marriage. Deuteronomy does not command divorce but merely acknowledges its existence and attempts to regulate it. The opponents infer that what the passage assumes it also "commands," that is, that if there is to be a divorce, it must be

220

effected by the proper execution of a legal document that will allow the woman to remarry. Jesus corrects his opponents by pointing out that Moses did not command divorce but merely permitted it, and did this as a concession to the sinful state of affairs resulting from the fall of Adam and Eve from grace. Such was not God's plan for men and women.

Jesus' ruling on divorce has two parts, as presented in the parallel in Luke 16:18. Matthew gives only half the rule in 19:9, because he has already provided the other half in 5:32. In the earlier passage the ruling focuses on the divorced wife and her remarriage. A man who dismisses a faithful wife is charged by Jesus with the grave sin of making an adulteress of her. Here a socioeconomic assumption is made. It is assumed that a divorced woman will be forced by economic necessity to become another man's wife. Since in Jesus' view the divorce is invalid, she will in effect be living in an adulterous relationship with a man who is legally but not morally her husband. And by marrying her, the second man becomes an adulterer, since in God's eyes she belongs not to him but to her first husband.

In 19:9 this is supplemented by a ruling concerning the original husband: whoever dismisses a faithful wife and marries another woman commits adultery. The wide-ranging significance of this half of the rule has been brought to our attention by a Jewish scholar, Phillip Sigal (*The Halakah of Jesus*, pp. 83–118). Three important implications for Jesus' view of the status of women must be drawn from this passage. First, Jesus ruled against polygamy; if a man is not free to marry another woman because, in Jesus' view, he is still bound to his first wife, this means that God permits him only one wife. (According to Sigal, no rabbinic teacher had yet ruled against polygamy.) Second, Jesus took at least one step toward the removal of the double standard by referring to the husband's sexual relationship with the second woman as adulterous. According to contemporary standards, the man would have been guilty at most of fornication, since the second woman is not married. By insisting that the man is committing adultery *against his first wife,* Jesus radically redefined the role of woman in marriage. Third, Jesus' strict construction of Deut. 24:1 protected women from the arbitrary power of their husbands to divorce them at will. The double standard remains, of course, in the focus on the husband; the case of the wife whose husband is unfaithful is not considered.

The major difference between Matthew's presentation of

221

Jesus' teaching on divorce and the versions found in Mark and Luke is that no exception is made in these other Gospels for the case of adultery. Various attempts have been made to resolve the discrepancy. Some argue that Jesus outlawed divorce completely and that Matthew's treatment represents a later attempt to excuse the remarriage of men whose wives have cheated on them. Paul, in his treatment of marriage and divorce, makes no mention of the Matthean exception (I Cor. 7:1ff.). Sigal argues in favor of the originality of Matthew's version, urging that the First Evangelist is merely making explicit what is implicit in the other versions, namely, that adultery renders the continuance of the marriage impossible, since in Jewish law a man was forbidden further sexual contact with an adulterous wife (see comments on 1:19). Even if this were the case, however, the issue of whether or not the injured husband was permitted to remarry is not resolved. The answer to this question depends in part on how we read the following verses.

Verses 10–12, found only in Matthew, are among the most difficult to understand in the Gospel. To begin with, the comment attributed to the disciples is remarkably strange. Peter, at least, was a married man (8:14; I Cor. 9:5). Are we to suppose that the others, despite Peter's example (or because of it!), could not tolerate the idea of marriage without an escape clause? Calvin was appalled by the selfish ingratitude of the disciples respecting God's wonderful gift of marriage; they were giving thought only to the possibility of inconvenience and boredom for themselves, not to the bondage their wives might have to suffer (*A Harmony of the Gospels*, vol. 2, p. 248). It is perhaps best to assume that "the disciples" here give voice to the objections of a few men in Matthew's largely Gentile church, for whom Jesus' rule on divorce seemed hopelessly out of touch with reality.

Commentators disagree regarding the reference of "this word" in verse 11. Does it refer forward to the saying to be given in verse 12, to the comment of the disciples in verse 10, or to Jesus' pronouncement in verse 9? The first and second possibilities can be grouped together, because they lead to the same interpretation. In this view, the disciples' observation is employed positively by Jesus to point to the great value of voluntary celibacy "for the sake of the kingdom of heaven," understood to mean "for the sake of evangelism or ministry." Paul was celibate and commended this status to other Chris-

222

tians, because "the unmarried man is anxious about the affairs of the Lord, how to please the Lord; but the married man is anxious about worldly affairs, how to please his wife, and his interests are divided" (I Cor. 7:32–34). The apostle's reference to celibacy as a *charisma*, a grace gift from God (I Cor. 7:7), can be seen as a parallel to Matthew's phrase "to whom it has been given."

If, on the other hand, verse 11 refers to the divorce rule, it can be understood as alluding to the fact that Christian men who have divorced unfaithful wives can remain unmarried in loyalty to the Creator's intention of lifelong monogamy, but only because the grace of continence has been bestowed on them from above. While both interpretations are possible, it seems more probable that Matthew is concerned here with the anomalous status of married persons who have been deprived of their marriage partner by the spouse's infidelity.

For the greater part of Christian history, Matthew's version of Jesus' teaching on divorce served both as the law of the church and the law of the land wherever Christianity was the dominant religion (except that it was understood as allowing remarriage to the innocent party in cases of adultery). The modern church has largely abandoned the enforcement of this standard. There are few theologians today who would argue that divorced Christians who remarry should be excommunicated as adulterous. This does not mean, however, that Jesus' teaching on divorce has been declared irrelevant. Modern psychology has given us greater sympathy for those caught in the tyranny of a dysfunctional marriage. At the same time, our increased appreciation of the positive values of marriage has given rise to a deeply felt conviction that God must surely not wish to deny all divorced persons the joy of a genuine marriage. With Jesus, we affirm the Creator's intention that marriage remain a lifelong commitment despite its inevitable frustrations. We acknowledge that in a sinful world this ideal, despite our prayers for grace, may often fail of attainment. The ideal remains our lodestar.

What Does It Take to Become a Child of the Kingdom? (19:13–26)

This next segment of the journey to the passion consists of three short scenes, at the center of which is the dialogue between Jesus and an unnamed young man of great wealth. The story about Jesus and the children prepares for this dialogue. A "postmortem" is provided by a discussion with the disciples concerning how hard it is for the wealthy to enter the kingdom.

Jesus and the Children (19:13–15)

This little anecdote has a twofold significance for Matthew. At a literal level it is treasured as evidence of Jesus' attitude toward children. The disciples represent a traditional viewpoint, according to which children are accorded a low status in society and are by no means permitted to participate fully in organized religion. Jesus insists that children are just as valuable to God as adults.

It seems probable that Jesus' saying was understood by Matthew and his church as authorizing the practice of including children and young people in the corporate life of the church. This is suggested also by his inclusion of children with men and women in the great feeding scenes (14:21; 15:28). Regarded from a sociological point of view, this may have been one of the reasons why Christianity spread so rapidly in the Roman world. There were popular religions for men (Mithraism) and for women (the religion of the Bona Dea). Christianity offered a *family* religion in which both sexes and all ages could participate together.

In the present context the symbolic function of the children has a special importance. They are to be allowed to come to Jesus "because of such is the kingdom of heaven." Matthew has already introduced this idea at 18:3: "Truly, I say to you, unless you turn and become like children, you will by no means enter the kingdom of heaven." The child is the paradigm of what it means to be helplessly dependent on the Father in heaven. With this paradigm clearly in mind, we turn to the central scene of the triptych.

Jesus and the Young Plutocrat (19:16–22)

In Luke the rich man is described as a ruler (Luke 18:18). A fascinating parallel is thus provided by the Nicodemus narrative of John 3. Nicodemus is a ruler and a rich man (John 19:39) who comes to Jesus and is told that he must become like a child (be born again) if he is to enter the kingdom of God. John gives the impression that Nicodemus is an older man (John 3:4). In Mark and Luke the man is also presented as older; he declares that he has kept the commandments from his youth (Mark 10:20; Luke 18:21).

Matthew alters this picture of the rich man by describing him as a *neaniskos*. According to Philo, this word designated a man twenty-one to twenty-eight years of age. Despite his economic power, such a man was probably too young to be a ruler in the sense intended by Luke and John. His youthfulness, however, turns out to be no advantage when it becomes a question of changing his life-style. He is already set in his ways!

In response to the rich man's address, "Good teacher," the Markan Jesus retorts, "Why do you call me good? No one is good except one, God" (Mark 10:18). Matthew, apparently fearing that this response would mistakenly call into question Jesus' sinlessness, edits the question and response so that "good" no longer applies to Jesus. The man asks, "What good [deed] should I do so that I may have eternal life?" Jesus' counterquestion, "Why do you ask me about 'the good [deed]'?" challenges the assumption that doing something good can ever earn one a place in the kingdom. The inquirer's question is inappropriate, because the phrase "the Good" can be applied to God only. The intention of verse 17 is to place emphasis on God as the supreme actor in the drama of the kingdom. This emphasis is picked up again in the last verse of the passage, verse 26.

Following this brief repartee concerning "the Good," two answers are given to the original inquiry. "If you wish to enter life, keep the commandments" presents a proper and traditional answer to the question. The response "Which ones?" probably does not mean that some commandments can be completely neglected; rather, it assumes that a few are "weightier" than others (see 23:23). The commandments specified by verses 18–19 are taken from the second table of the Decalogue (Exod. 20:12–16; Deut. 5:16–20). "Honor your father and mother" is placed last, perhaps because it is a positive command. To it

225

Matthew appends Lev. 19:18: "You shall love your neighbor as yourself," which is not included by Mark and Luke. The emphasis on ethics echoes the prophets' insistence that God prefers ethical behavior to religious sacrifices (Hos. 6:6; see Matt. 9:13; 12:7).

Without hesitation the young man replies, "All these I have kept." While this response sounds very presumptuous to us, especially in view of the inclusion of the love command, it is probably presented by Matthew as a realistic statement. The love command was often understood as alluding to public charity. The young man acknowledges that he has contributed to the needs of widows and orphans in his community.

At this point Mark reports, "And Jesus, looking upon him, loved him" (Mark 10:21). Jesus recognizes in the young man before him a fine, religious, good-living, decent citizen—the kind of person who is a credit to any community. Although Matthew omits this detail, the picture of the uprightness of the man remains untarnished. Whereas in Mark it is Jesus who suggests that something is lacking, in Matthew it is the young man himself who raises the issue. It occurs to him that perhaps something more is required of him than the standard morality that is expected of good, solid citizens, but he cannot guess what that something more might be.

Jesus' second response to the original inquiry adds a new motif to the discussion: "If you wish to be perfect . . ." This statement is easily misunderstood as suggesting that, while the man's behavior has been *good,* he will make himself *perfect* if he adds to his record one supremely good deed, that is, if he sells all his property and gives the proceeds to the poor. On the basis of this text the church developed the notion of two classes of Christian discipleship: ordinary Christians who kept their possessions and "the religious" who took a vow of poverty.

The perfection to which the young man is summoned is that which is expected of all disciples of Jesus. The antitheses of Matthew 5, which are introduced with the warning "For I tell you, unless your righteousness exceeds that of the scribes and Pharisees, you will never enter the kingdom of heaven" (5:20), reach their climax in the statement of 5:48: "You, therefore, must be perfect, as your heavenly Father is perfect." In these antitheses Jesus takes three of the commandments cited in 19:18–19 and radicalizes them. A fourth is expounded in 15:4–6. What is implied by "perfect" in 19:21, then, is not a new rule

226

(voluntary poverty) which is added to the old commandments but Jesus' interpretation of the Torah.

The Greek word *teleios,* here translated "perfect," does not mean "without defect, sinless." It is used to render the Hebrew word *shalēm* in the Greek translation of I Kings 11:4: "And his [Solomon's] heart was not *teleia* with the LORD his God, as was the heart of David his father." What is meant is not sinlessness (of that David was hardly an example!) but undivided devotion. If the young man wishes to manifest the devotion characteristic of those who will participate in the kingdom of heaven, he must become a disciple of Jesus. In his case this will require that he rid himself of the impediment of riches. Matthew does not regard the abandonment of wealth as necessary for all who possess it. He refers to Joseph of Arimathea as a rich man who was also a disciple of Jesus (27:57). Nor is the responsibility of wealth moralized here as it is in the version of the story found in the *Gospel of the Hebrews,* where the rich man is sharply rebuked by Jesus for his neglect of the poor. Despite the promise of treasure in heaven (cf. 6:19–21), the emphasis lies squarely on discipleship. Following Jesus will entail learning to love others more nearly as God loves them (5:43–48); without such love his sacrifice will amount to nothing (I Cor. 13:3).

How great the impediment is can be seen from the young man's sorrowful departure. He probably would not have objected if Jesus had reprimanded him as in the *Gospel of the Hebrews.* He could have been shamed into giving a much more substantial portion of his income to the poor. What he minded was giving up all that wealth means: privilege, status, and economic power. He was not ready to surrender his comfortable and secure world for the unknown, frightening world into which Jesus was calling him. He was identified by his wealth; he did not want to find a new identity. He knew what he was "worth" in his world, and by those standards Jesus and his disciples were "worth" nothing.

In this brief encounter two worlds collide. To move from the old world into the new the young man must become like a child, but he is already too old!

The Postmortem (19:23–26)

Jesus responds to the young man's departure with one of his most memorable hyperboles: "It is easier for a camel to go through the eye of a needle than for a rich man to enter the

227

kingdom of God." While this statement may strike us as an exaggeration, it does not astonish us as much as the disciples' response: "Who then can be saved?" Why are they so dumbfounded? None of them were wealthy. Why should they regard the problem of the rich as engulfing them all? Here we must remember that the young man has been presented as a model citizen: decent, law-abiding, charitable, and religious. His wealth signifies to the disciples that he has been blessed by God. If such a person is not acceptable to God, what hope is there for the rest of us?

The Gospel of Matthew often seems to abet the very natural human assumption that we are saved by works. Faith is assumed; judgment is on the basis of performance (see 7:21). At certain critical points, however, Matthew corrects this misperception. By grace, and grace alone, can we be admitted to the kingdom. While the impediment facing the wealthy is particularly serious, it is present to all. Even poor people insist on defining themselves and others by what they possess (or lack). The world is too much with us, and we become "old" too soon. How can we turn and become children of God's world? For us this is impossible, but with God all things are possible (v. 26).

Rewards and Grace (19:27—20:16)

Although there is no change of scene or audience, the appearance of a new topic justifies treating 19:27 as the beginning of a new section. Despite the affirmation of divine grace in verse 26, Peter asks about rewards. Unlike the wealthy youth who declined to follow Jesus, the Twelve have given up everything to be his disciples. What will their reward be?

The concept of the carrot and the stick is basic to human relationships. From infancy we learn that if we behave well we will be rewarded, if badly, we will be punished. As we mature, it becomes obvious to us that the rule does not always apply. Sometimes our good deeds are either ignored or badly repaid. Often our bad behavior eludes punishment. The validity of the rule is rescued by transposing it from earth to heaven; God is a just judge who will reward good behavior and punish evil deeds. It is therefore a very human question that Peter asks: How will God reward our sacrifices?

228

The answer is given in three parts. In the first (v. 28), the apostles are promised a spectacular reward. At the renewal of all things, when Jesus sits on his glorious throne, his twelve closest followers will sit on twelve thrones, judging the twelve tribes of Israel. The promise contains several ambiguities. It is not clear whether the participle *krinontes,* here translated "judging," means "passing judgment on" or "ruling." It is uncertain whether this activity is to take place on a renewed earth or in a heavenly realm. The significance of the "twelve tribes" is not indicated. Does the saying anticipate the restoration of the lost tribes to Palestine, the resurrection of those who in ancient days belonged to these tribes, or is the notion symbolic only, referring to the messianic community, that is, the church? None of these ambiguities can be resolved. All that is certain is that the apostles are promised glorious roles in the age to come.

There is an apparent tension between verse 28 and the affirmation of 23:8–12 that there is to be no hierarchy among Jesus' followers. The tension is partly resolved when we note that the apostles' reward is postponed to the next world. While this age lasts, they must behave more modestly!

The second part of the response, verse 29, generalizes the concept of a reward for Jesus' followers. Not only the apostles but *all* who sacrifice family relationships or property for Jesus' sake will be rewarded a hundredfold and inherit eternal life (an echo of the young man's question, 19:16). In the Markan parallel the reward of a hundredfold replacement of what has been sacrificed is promised for *this* life; lost loved ones will be replaced by a greatly enlarged family of Christian brothers and sisters, and the use of their homes and lands will make up for lost property (Mark 10:30). It is not clear in Matthew whether he understands the hundredfold reward as pertaining to this life or to the age to come; perhaps he prefers to leave the matter ambiguous. In any event, the effect of verse 29 is to diminish the significance of the *apostles'* (church leaders?) sacrifice by reminding them of the sacrifices made by other followers. The apostles are not to overestimate what they have done!

The saying of verse 30, "But many who are first will be last, and the last will be first," seems to speak of the Grand Reversal, when the poor will become rich and the rich poor (cf. Luke 2:34; 6:20–25). In Mark's context it appears to suggest that Jesus' followers, who have become voluntarily poor by renouncing family and possessions, will become rich, while their persecutors and those who have profited from their sacrifices will become poor. Matthew, however, redirects the saying, giving it

229

a new application by attaching to it the parable of the vineyard workers (20:1–15).

This third part of the response is of special importance to Matthew; it serves as a corrective to the concept of rewards that governs the preceding verses. The parable is offensive to us; it challenges our sense of justice. We empathize with the grumbling workers of verse 12; we too have known capricious employers who rewarded lazy workers more generously than faithful, hardworking employees. But can *God* be so unfair?

Implicit in the parable is the issue of bargaining with God. From the earliest dawn of religion it has been assumed that humans can bargain with the gods to obtain what they want. Three words were often inscribed on ancient Roman shrines: *Do ut des*, "I give in order that you may give." With this declaration the donor made clear that his or her generosity was intended to inspire a like generosity on the part of the god to whom the structure was dedicated. According to Gen. 28:18–22, Jacob attempted to bargain with God for protection and sustenance, promising to reward God with a tithe of his income. The book of Job addresses the issue, "Will someone serve God for nothing?" (see Job 1:9), and concludes with Job's acknowledgment of the greatness of God which humbles all human attempts to lay a claim against the Almighty for services rendered (Job 42:1–6).

The climax of the parable occurs in verse 15: "Am I not allowed to do what I choose with what belongs to me? Or do you begrudge my generosity?" The vineyard owner claims the right to pay his workers not on the basis of their merits but on the basis of his own compassion. Why should such generosity be condemned as injustice? Underlying the parable is the Old Testament conception of God as the Creator who is *good*, that is, generous to all (see, e.g., Ps. 145:9). Jesus reveled in the incredible magnanimity of God (see 5:45). Of course Jesus believed in the God of justice, but in his vision of God the divine compassion greatly outshone the divine justice. Those who worship such a God must imitate his generosity, not begrudge it.

The parable may have served Jesus as a defense of his association with tax collectors and sinners; such persons, even though their service to God came late in life, would be accepted. In this case the parable parallels that of the prodigal; the grumbling of the full-day workers corresponds to the bitter complaint of the elder brother (Luke 15:29). By placing it in this context, Matthew reinterprets the parable. It subordinates rewards to grace. Yes, the sacrifices of the apostles and other followers of Jesus will be honored by God, but the reward will so far outstrip the sacrifice that it must be seen as sheer grace. Although some may feel that their long and costly service qualifies them for a higher rate of pay in the kingdom, all must humbly acknowledge that in fact they are like eleventh-hour workers. None deserves the glorious future that God has prepared for them.

Are any persons especially targeted by the parable? Matthew may have in mind the seniority claims of the original apostles, who claim hierarchical authority (see 23:8–12). Perhaps he is thinking of Jewish Christians in his congregation who resent the leadership now being exercised by former pagans. Perhaps older members begrudge the spiritual gifts manifested in the youth. We understand such tensions. How easy it is for us to grumble to ourselves or to others when newcomers to the church (or recovering alcoholics, or ex-convicts, or "people of a different background") receive more recognition than we who have worked so long and so hard! Such resentment can be overcome only by fixing our gaze on the goodness of God who is generous to all.

The Passion Anticipated and Interpreted (20:17–28)

A gospel is best defined as "a passion narrative with an extended introduction" (see Introduction). In all four Gospels the passion narrative, in the broader sense, begins with Jesus' triumphal entry into Jerusalem. In the First Gospel this occurs at 21:1–11. Matthew 20:17–28 is thus separated from the goal of the gospel story by only a few verses (20:29–34) and can properly be viewed as the climax of the "extended introduction."

Beginning with Peter's confession, the story has focused on the preparation of the disciples for Jesus' death. In this passage we come to the third and climactic passion announcement (in addition to 16:21 and 17:22–23, supplementary predictions are found also at 17:9, 12 and 26:2). Much more detailed than the first two, it has been described as "a table of contents" for the forthcoming passion narrative. In all three announcements Mark refers to Jesus' violent end with the verb "kill" (Mark 8:31;

231

9:31; 10:33–34). Since in this third formulation reference is made to the Gentiles, Matthew substitutes "crucify" in order to make explicit the fact that Jesus will suffer an excruciating, non-Jewish form of execution.

While the narrative function of the three passion announcements is to prepare the disciples, their theological purpose is to assure the readers, first, that Jesus' violent death is not a meaningless accident of history but is a part of God's plan, and, second, that Jesus was not a hapless victim but a knowing partner in the divine strategy. Jesus goes obediently to his death in concurrence with God's will. Is this theology based on history? Although the passion announcements, especially the third, seem to have been edited in the light of subsequent events, there is no need to doubt that Jesus anticipated his death. The violent fate of John the Baptist must surely have reminded him of the age-old tradition that Israel constantly persecuted God's prophets (II Chron. 24:19–21; 36:15–16; cf. Matt. 23:29–37; Luke 13:31–34; Acts 7:52). If Jesus did indeed regard himself as the Messiah, as this commentary assumes, and also came to believe that he was going to suffer a fate similar to that of John the Baptist, he must have concluded that it was God's will that the Messiah endure violence.

Why must the Messiah suffer? While all three announcements stress the divine *necessity* of Jesus' death (see comments on 17:22–23), none suggests the *reason*. God's purpose is not revealed until the final verse of this climactic section (v. 28).

As with the first announcement in 16:21, the third is followed by a narrative that discloses how little the disciples understand what Jesus' death means for his followers. In the first instance Peter was the culprit. Now James and John are given the part.

Mark's story about the brothers (Mark 10:35–45) was embarrassing to Matthew and Luke. Luke omits it entirely. Matthew edits the story so that the request for the most important portfolios in the Messiah's cabinet is presented by Zebedee's wife, not by his sons. (An alternative explanation is that in this Gospel such a request, if presented by James and John, would not be credible, since they had witnessed Jesus' conferral of primacy on Peter in 16:17–19.) This alteration does little to exonerate the two, however, since Jesus' response assumes that the request came from the brothers: "You [plural] do not know what you are asking" (v. 22). The other disciples become angry

232

at James and John, not at their mother (v. 24). According to 16:20, Zebedee's wife ought not to be privy to the secret of Jesus' Messiahship!

Does the story preserve an authentic reminiscence? This is entirely possible. Luke is probably correct in his suggestion that Jesus was surrounded by people who genuinely expected him to "restore Israel" (Acts 1:6; cf. Luke 2:34; 24:21). Until their dreams of worldly grandeur were crushed by his execution, it was perfectly natural for Jesus' closest followers to expect that they should play some prominent role in the Messiah's kingdom. It is also not surprising that some of the Twelve should have expected to be more prominent than others.

Jesus' initial response is not to condemn the brothers' ambition but to point to its price. If they wish to share the Messiah's glory, they must be prepared to partake of his suffering. Following a well-established Jewish tradition, Jesus speaks of his anticipated passion as a cup that he must drink. In the prophets we frequently meet the figure of the cup of God's wrath (Isa. 51:17, 22; Jer. 25:15–28; Ezek. 23:31–32), which reappears in Rev. 14:10; 16:19. It does not follow, however, that the cup that Jesus must drink represents God's anger at sin, since James and John are assured that they will drink the same cup. In the *Martyrdom of Isaiah* 5:13 the prophet anticipates his murderous execution with the words, "For me alone the LORD has mixed the cup." To drink the cup means simply to accept one's God-appointed death (see *Testament of Abraham* [Rec. A] 16:11; Matt. 26:39, 42; John 18:11).

In the present form of the story, the brothers quickly respond that they are prepared to die with Jesus; that is, their ambition for worldly glory has been transposed to a postmortem existence. In an earlier version, they may have shared Peter's perspective (16:22) and have anticipated a much less drastic form of testing for Jesus and for themselves. Jesus assures them that they will indeed experience martyrdom ("drink my cup") but that this will not assure them of the choicest seats in the kingdom, because God alone will select the candidates for this honor. Two points may be drawn from this statement. First, James and John must recognize that, despite their sacrifices and their prominence among Jesus' followers, there may be humble servants of God who are more deserving than they. They may be very surprised when they see those whom God has appointed to the places of greatest honor at the Messiah's side.

233

Second, Jesus does not claim equality with God, just as he does not claim to know the day or the hour the Father has determined for the end of history (24:36). Even though the resurrected Christ will declare that he possesses "all authority in heaven and on earth," it will be made very clear that this is his by conferral, not by original possession ("has been given to me," 28:18).

Even though the brothers' attempt to secure a status above that of their fellow apostles is frustrated, this does not spare them the indignation of the others. The ire of the ten provides the occasion for teaching about the new kind of community that Jesus is establishing, where the only valid ambition will be the aspiration to serve as faithfully as possible. Whereas the pagan world lionizes those who successfully lord it over others, in the fellowship of Jesus' followers greatness will be measured in terms of service. In verse 27*b* this exhortation is intensified by the use of the word "slave." This word refers to status. Christians are here reminded that, no matter how distinguished their service to the church or to humanity, they are not to claim a superior status but to manifest the humility of a slave.

This discussion of ambition and humility reaches its climax in verse 28, in which Jesus points to himself as the model to be followed. Instead of using "I," he modestly refers to himself in third-person speech by means of the self-designation "the Son of man." The speaker, as acknowledged in verse 21, is the Messiah. (This does not mean that "the Son man" is a messianic title; see Introduction.) Whereas most kings demand service of their subjects, this king came not to be served but to serve.

Greek has a number of verbs that are roughly equivalent to the English "serve." The one used here, *diakoneō,* can be used in a general sense (see I Tim. 3:10, 13), but it appears more often in the New Testament with the meaning "provide a personal service," especially "serve food or drink," as is done by Martha in Luke 10:40 and John 12:2. Indeed, this is the only way the verb is used elsewhere in Matthew (4:11; 8:15; 25:44; 27:55). We should therefore consider the possibility of a eucharistic allusion in verse 28*a*. Support is provided by the fact that the nearest parallel, Luke 22:27, follows the institution of the Lord's Supper: "For who is greater, the one who reclines [at table] or the one who serves? Is it not the one who reclines? But I am among you as the one who serves." In the Lukan context it is clear that Jesus' service has included the serving of bread and wine in anticipation of his death. In light of the parallel, then, we may

234

paraphrase verse 28*a:* "The Son of man came not to be waited upon at table but to wait on others, providing nourishment through the gift of his own outpoured life."

Matthew has been preparing us for Jesus' death from the beginning of his Gospel (see comments on 2:13–18). In 1:21 he explained Jesus' name as an indication that "he will save his people from their sins," but not until 20:28 are these two motifs brought together. Now, on the very brink of the passion we finally learn that Jesus' death will constitute "a ransom for many" (v. 28*b*).

The scholarly discussion concerning the background of the phrase "to give his life as a ransom for many" continues unabated. Many insist that its origin is to be found in Isa. 53:12, especially in the Greek translation: "because his life was delivered up to death . . . and he bore the sins of many and on account of their sins he was delivered up." It is clear, however, that the verbal parallel is a distant one at best. But there is no need to draw a straight line between Matt. 20:28 and Isaiah 53. The idea of vicarious suffering is not limited to that passage. It is attributed to the Maccabean martyrs in II Macc. 7:37; IV Macc. 6:29; 17:22 and is found in the writings of the Qumran sect (*Manual of Discipline* 5:6; 8:3). What is unique about the saying of Matt. 20:28 is that it proclaims that none other than the Messiah will offer his life as a ransom for his people.

Two misconceptions of this verse must be carefully avoided. First, the phrase "for many" does not point to a limited atonement. The phrase is properly understood as a Semitism, that is, a Greek phrase that too literally renders an underlying Hebrew or Aramaic idiom. At Qumran "the many" encompassed the whole community. The idiom is correctly rendered in I Tim. 2:5–6: "the man Christ Jesus, who gave himself as a ransom for all."

Second, although "ransom" connotes a sum of money paid to a slaveholder or a captor in order to secure someone's release, the metaphor must not be pressed. It is a mistake, for example, to ask, "To whom is the ransom price paid, Satan or God?" The metaphor is used in Jer. 31:11, where the verb "ransom" is paralleled by "redeem" and the actor is God. The saying of Matt. 20:28 does not explain the mystery of the atonement but simply affirms the fact of Christian experience that in and through Jesus Christ our rebellion against our creator has been overcome.

235

With this statement concerning the significance of Jesus'

death, the extended introduction has reached its goal. We are now ready to enter into the long narrative that relates the Messiah's death and resurrection.

The Healing of Two Blind Men (20:29–34)

This passage seems anticlimactic after 20:17–28. It resumes the healing ministry that was such a prominent part of Jesus' Galilean activity. Indeed, it largely duplicates the story of the healing of two blind men in 9:27–31. It is best viewed as a transitional passage connecting 20:17–28 with the passion narrative. It performs this function by reason of its several motifs. The geographical note "And as they went out of Jericho" moves us closer to Jerusalem and the triumphal entry. The cry of the blind men, "Lord, have mercy on us," which is echoed in the Kyrie Eleison of Christian liturgy, may already have been in use in Matthew's church as a prayer for forgiveness of sins (see also 9:27; 15:22). Even though it serves in the narrative as an appeal for healing, the liturgical use of the prayer is probably to be heard as an overtone. In this way the cry builds on the promise of 20:28 that Jesus' death will atone for sins.

Jesus is publicly addressed as "Son of David." Although this vocative use of the phrase omits the article, there can be little doubt that in this context the expression is meant to be a messianic title, "the Son of David" (in contrast to 1:20, where Joseph is similarly addressed). In 11:2–5 the healing of the blind is the first of "the deeds of the Christ" to be mentioned. Probably Matthew regarded the restoration of sight as an indication that the golden age promised in Isaiah was being inaugurated by Jesus (see Isa. 35:5). Whereas the men who receive their sight in 9:27–31 are strictly charged to tell no one, no such prohibition is found in this later story. The king is about to make his royal entry into Jerusalem. The time for silence is past. The blind men's cry anticipates the acclamation of the crowd a few verses later (21:9).

In the earlier version of the story in 9:27–31, as in the Markan story of Bartimaeus (Mark 10:46–52), the focus of the narrative is on faith. In this later telling of the story, Matthew makes a significant change in emphasis. The reference to faith is replaced by a note about Jesus' compassion: "And being compassionate, Jesus touched their eyes" (v. 34). Here we are probably to hear an echo of earlier verses alluding to the Messiah's compassion for his people (9:36; 14:14; 15:32). It is as the compassionate Messiah that Jesus goes on his way to Jerusalem to die for his people.

The last clause of the "extended introduction" is "and they followed him" (v. 34). The symbolic significance of blindness should not be overlooked (see 13:10–17). Jesus is the Savior who opens the eyes of sinners so that they can follow him.

Conflict in Jerusalem

MATTHEW 21:1—25:46

Strictly speaking, "the passion of Jesus" refers to the illtreatment and crucifixion he suffered following his arrest. Closely related are the stories about Judas' conspiracy and the Last Supper, so that the passion narrative proper begins at 26:2. Broadly conceived, however, the passion narrative begins with Jesus' royal entry into Jerusalem and his "cleansing" of the temple. These provocative acts prompt disputes with various opponents, culminating in a long valedictory address (chap. 23). This is followed by the discourse on "the last things" addressed to the disciples alone (chaps. 24–25).

Matthew 21:1–22
The Messiah's Reception in His Capital

The Triumphal Entry (21:1–11)

Jesus will die on the cross as "the King of the Jews" (27:37). The function of the opening passage of the passion narrative is to exhibit Jesus' royal status in a public way.

It is improbable that Jesus' arrival in Jerusalem manifested as open a claim to kingship as Matthew's account suggests. Had a large crowd publicly acclaimed Jesus as their king, the Roman garrison would have promptly cooled the messianic ardor.

237

Moreover, there would have been no difficulty in securing witnesses for a Jewish trial. This does not mean that we must consider the incident as created (rather than interpreted) on the basis of Zech. 9:9. It is probable, however, that the demonstration was on such a small scale that it failed to attract public attention. It may very well have been an "acted parable" in which Jesus consciously acted out the prophecy of Zechariah by riding into the holy city on a donkey. While it was customary for pilgrims to arrive by foot, his action would have seemed only slightly unusual to outsiders. According to John 12:16, not even the disciples perceived the event as the fulfillment of prophecy until after the resurrection.

It seems likely that the incident has been understood and reported in the light of similar stories about triumphal entries (I Kings 1:32–40) and acts of homage to a new king (II Kings 9:13). In Matthew's account the underlying prophecy is not only explicitly quoted but is placed *before* the event to emphasize that Jesus actively fulfills the messianic prophecy.

A number of translations have gone astray in translating the word *praüs* as "humble," apparently out of a desire to bring Matthew's text into greater conformity with the Hebrew of Zech. 9:9. Matthew, however, is here following the Septuagint, which chose to describe the king as *gentle* rather than humble. The quotation thus reinforces the claim of 11:29, "I am *gentle* and humble in heart." Although the notions of gentleness and humility overlap to some extent and occasionally appear side by side, the second ought not to be allowed to eclipse the first. The quotation thus serves to underline the fact that the gentle king arrives in his capital with no sword in his hand, vulnerable to whatever his enemies will choose to do to him. He who taught "Do not resist one who is evil" (5:39) is prepared to live and die by his own word.

According to the rules of Hebrew poetry, the original prophecy mentions only one animal ("on a donkey, on a colt the foal of a donkey"); both halves of the poetic description refer to a *male* animal. Here Matthew prepares a fresh Greek translation (he does not follow the Septuagint), capitalizing on the fact that the Greek word for donkey can be used for either sex. In this way he is able to take the first allusion to a donkey as referring to a she-ass and the second as speaking of her colt. Does Matthew make the prophecy correspond with the event or the event with his perception of the prophecy? Since the

238

Evangelist undoubtedly knew the rules of poetic parallelism, there is perhaps a slight presumption in favor of the former. An unbroken colt usually accompanied its mother. He tells us that the disciples placed garments (their own cloaks, or saddle clothes?) on both animals and that Jesus sat on them. Some interpreters have ridiculed Matthew for suggesting that Jesus was astride two animals simultaneously. Others have suggested that, since it was common to sit on a donkey with both legs on the same side (sidesaddle style), it is possible that the clothes were thrown over both the donkey and the foal at her side, so that Jesus was seen as riding the pair.

The acclamation of the crowd is more explicitly messianic in Matthew than in Mark: "Hosanna to the Son of David." *Hosanna* is the Greek transliteration of a Hebrew imperative phrase meaning "save now," used in Ps. 118:25. Its literal meaning was sometimes forgotten, however; it was used like "Hallelujah," as an ejaculation of praise (as is "salvation" in Rev. 7:10). "The Son of David" connects this passage with the immediately preceding healing of the blind men (20:30–31).

"Blessed is the one who comes in the name of the Lord" is not explicitly messianic. This line from Ps. 118:26 was employed as a greeting by pilgrims attending temple festivals. It was inevitable, however, that Christian imagination would perceive a greater depth of meaning in the cry. Of all the pilgrims attending that Passover festival only Jesus was "the Coming One" (see 11:3), and only he truly came "in the name of the Lord," that is, fully empowered and authorized by God. There would also be levels of meaning in "Lord" for Matthew and his readers. In the psalm the Greek *kyrios* ("Lord") represents the sacred Tetragrammaton, the name "Yahweh." Christians, however, used *kyrios* as a title for their risen Lord.

Matthew further heightens the effect of the Messiah's entry into Jerusalem by reporting that the whole city is shaken as if by an earthquake. The verb *seiō*, which is weakly translated "stirred" by the RSV and the NIV, refers to the action of an earthquake (compare its use in 27:51). The corresponding noun *seismos* is used by Matthew in 8:24; 24:7; 27:54; and 28:2 to indicate a supernatural event. Perhaps Matthew means to suggest that the holy city is shaken to its foundations by the arrival of the Lord's Anointed.

239

In response to the question of the awed populace, "Who is this?" the Messiah's entourage responds, "This is the prophet

Jesus from Nazareth in Galilee" (v. 11). At first glance, this appears to revoke the earlier acclamation of Jesus as Messiah. The titles are not mutually exclusive, however. In 26:68 his enemies challenge him to prophesy while addressing him as "Christ." The prophet Moses was regarded as a kind of king in Jewish tradition, and David as a prophet (Acts 2:30).

What are we to do with this expanded retelling of what was originally an inconspicuous event? Matthew highlights for us the irony implicit in Jesus' last pilgrimage to the holy city. The Son of David enters David's city, but the only throne he finds is a cross. The city that should have welcomed him with its fullest homage refused to accept its gentle king. Shaken as at the news of his birth (2:3), the city sides again with the Herods of this world who maintain the established order. How easy it is for us to think that by celebrating Palm Sunday we acknowledge Jesus as king in a way that Jerusalem failed to do! We need constantly to be humbled by those harsh words that remind us of the superficiality of our Hosannas: "Not everyone who says to me, 'Lord, Lord,' will enter the kingdom of heaven, but only the one who does the will of my Father in heaven" (7:21, NRSV).

The Cleansing of the Temple (21:12–17)

By adding material to the brief narrative concerning Jesus' "cleansing" of the temple, Matthew has redefined its point. Judgment is tempered by grace.

Although this dramatic action is related in all four Gospels (John places it at the beginning of Jesus' ministry, John 2:13–22), it is difficult to reconstruct the historical incident that lies behind the accounts. It is unlikely that Jesus halted the operation of the temple market even for one day. The area was too large for one person to control, and there is no suggestion that his followers assisted him. Moreover, had Jesus interrupted the payment of the temple tax by driving out the money changers, he would have been arrested immediately, not several days later.

Probably Jesus' action in the temple was very limited in extent. It was a symbolic act, comparable to Jeremiah's dramatic parable of breaking the potter's flask (Jer. 19:10). What message did he wish to convey by overturning a few tables and chairs? John suggests that Jesus' anger was prompted simply by the presence of the market in the sacred space of the temple:

240

"Do not make my Father's house a house of trade" (John 2:16; cf. Zech. 14:21). On the basis of rabbinic records it has been proposed that the temple market was a recent innovation introduced by Caiaphas for the purpose of providing ruinous competition to established markets on the Mount of Olives owned by his political enemies. If this were the case, one might guess that the reason why Jesus was not arrested was that the general populace, including many of the temple police, sided with him in his protest against the high priest's market.

In any event, it must be insisted that nothing supports the ever popular interpretation that Jesus, as a champion of the poor, was protesting against dishonesty and price gouging on the part of the vendors and money changers. It is not their business practice but their location that angers Jesus. This is particularly clear in Matthew and Mark, where the *buyers* (the alleged victims!) are ejected along with the sellers. This common misunderstanding usually takes its point of departure from the allusion to the "den of thieves" of Jer. 7:11. This phrase, however, refers not to the site of the thieves' plundering but to the hideout to which they take their booty and where they feel safe: "Will you steal, murder, commit adultery, swear falsely, . . . and then come and stand before me in this house, which is called by my name, and say, 'We are delivered!'—only to go on doing all these abominations? Has this house, which is called by my name, become a den of robbers in your eyes?" (Jer. 7:9–11). The allusion to Jeremiah thus suggests that the market represents to Jesus the secularization of the temple by worshipers (buyers and sellers) whose lives do not conform with their religious profession but who claim nonetheless to find security in their religiosity ("We are delivered!").

On the other hand, the overturning of tables and chairs, like Jeremiah's breaking of the flask, looks very much like a symbol of destruction. It is unlikely that Jesus was attacking the sacrificial system as such, which, after all, was commanded by God according to the Torah. He was intimating, rather, that God's judgment of Israel would include the destruction of the old temple.

Matthew diminishes the force of the temple protest by attaching additional scenes. The Messiah's activity in the temple is positive as well as negative; after publicly objecting to the misuse of the sacred space, he demonstrates God's concern for his people by healing the blind and the lame. It is customary to

241

refer in this connection to II Sam. 5:8, "Therefore it is said, 'The blind and the lame shall not come into the house,' " and to infer that Jesus makes it possible for these excluded persons to participate fully in the temple worship. This is erroneous. Matthew indicates that the blind and the lame are already within the temple when they encounter Jesus. The later rabbinic literature maintains that the blind and the lame were *exempt* from the obligation of attending the festivals but were *permitted.* Jesus' healing serves only to remove the exemption and render them obligated. By locating this healing scene within the temple, however, Matthew suggests that there was value in temple worship; the dramatic action of verses 12–13 did not mean that the temple was so impure that Jesus' followers should boycott its ceremonies (see Acts 3:1; 5:42).

A second scene is indirectly presented in verse 15: children shout in the temple the acclamation that accompanied Jesus into Jerusalem, "Hosanna to the Son of David." Perhaps the young people, like the blind and the lame, represent the marginalized who have a smaller stake in the status quo and who are therefore free to look forward with enthusiasm to the new world that God is bringing into existence. The young people may also symbolize "the little ones" among Jesus' followers (see comments on 18:1–14).

The third scene presents a brief encounter between "the chief priests and the scribes" and Jesus. This unusual combination, which first occurred at the announcement of the Messiah's birth (2:4), reappeared in the third passion announcement (20:18). Though witnesses to the miracles of healing just performed, the opponents are indignant at the public acclamation of the healing Messiah by the young people. Jesus implicitly accepts the acclamation; he refuses to silence the young enthusiasts.

The effect of these additions is to shift the focus from the temple itself to the Lord of the temple (see Mal. 3:1–2). By the introduction of the children's cry the whole passage has become christological. The Messiah condemns the old temple as a den of thieves, and yet by his presence it becomes a place where the blind see again and the lame recover full strength. While it is possible for his followers to continue to worship there, the Messiah far outranks the temple in importance.

242   The narrative of Jesus' action in the temple lends itself all too easily to modern expressions of anti-Judaism and anti-Semitism. Christians must resist this misuse of the passage. We are

best served by taking the passage as challenging us to self-criticism. Does secularism invade our churches? Do we use our religion as a source of security instead of allowing ourselves to be remade by it?

While the judgment theme is prominent in the passage, Matthew has added grace. In the end we must throw ourselves on the mercy of the gentle king who alone can heal our blindness and give us the strength of limb to follow in his steps.

The Miracle of the Fig Tree (21:18–22)

The story of the withering of the fig tree provides the only example of a negative miracle in the Gospels. It is particularly scandalous to modern Christians, because the reported incident appears to be an act of unjustified petulance on Jesus' part. We find it difficult to believe that the Jesus we know from the Sermon on the Mount would be so bad-tempered as to curse a tree that failed to satisfy his hunger.

In Mark the story is divided into two parts so that it brackets—and thus interprets—the cleansing of the temple (Mark 11:12–25). Matthew's location of the entire story after the temple action renders this parabolic function less obvious to the reader. The focus shifts to the teaching on faith and prayer. Because of the wider context, the withered tree *implicitly* represents the judgment of God's unfruitful people, but *explicitly* it symbolizes the power of prayer.

The reference to believing prayer in verse 22 creates a connection between this passage and the preceding (v. 13). The implication seems to be that those frequenting the sanctuary, while doing temple business and engaging in religious activities, were lacking in the vital faith in God that is a prerequisite to effective prayer.

Matthew at 17:20 has already used a saying about faith that can move a mountain (for other teaching on the power of prayer, see 7:7–11). What is distinctive about this version is the introduction of a negative clause as complementary to the positive one: "If you have faith *and do not doubt*" (v. 21). The verb used here is different from the one so translated at 14:31, where Peter is asked, "O man of little faith, why did you doubt?" In that context "doubt" meant "lose confidence in God's power." The special nuance of *diakrinō,* the verb used here, can perhaps be discerned from its appearance in Acts 10:20, where

243

Peter receives divine instruction in a vision: "Rise and go down, and accompany them *without hesitation;* for I have sent them" (see also Rom. 4:20; James 1:6–8).

When interpreting this passage for a modern congregation or class, we must fend off several errors. First, people must not be left with the impression that Jesus teaches that we can get whatever we want by strenuous prayer. Especially to be exorcized is the demonic thought that through prayer we can make a tree or an enemy wither away! Implicit in this teaching because of its location in a Christian Gospel is the conviction that all our prayer requests are subject to the proviso "Not my will but thine be done" (cf. 26:39). Second, people must be relieved of the misperception that only perfect faith is acceptable to God. Certainly we are encouraged to grow in faith, but this is done one step at a time. Third, it is erroneous to believe that only the greatest heroes of the faith can move mountains. Many ordinary Christians, brought to their knees by impossible circumstances, have found through prayer the strength to do what they thought they could never do. Finally, all need to be reminded that faith is not an end in itself. It is not a virtuosity in which to glory: "And if I have all faith, so as to remove mountains, but have not love, I am nothing" (I Cor. 13:2).

Matthew 21:23—22:46
Disputes in the Temple

The next eight units fall naturally into two groups. In the first, Jesus' authority is challenged, and he responds with three parables. In the second, there are three attempts by various antagonists to entrap Jesus, followed by a passage in which Jesus silences them by posing a question they cannot answer. This is followed by the Messiah's valedictory address (chap. 23).

The Authority of Jesus Is Challenged (21:23–27)

Jesus has been challenged to present his credentials at earlier points in the story. The Pharisees, in the company of scribes (12:38) or Sadducees (16:1), demanded that he certify his status by providing a sign from heaven. In the present instance, however, the challenge is much more ominous, since it is posed by those who will constitute the court that will sentence him to death (see 26:3, 47; 27:1).

The opening question, "By what authority?" is ambiguous in the standard English translation. Readers are apt to assume that the questioners are asking, "Do you or do you not have the right to do these things?" The question is not so simple. The Greek interrogative adjective used here means either "Which of several?" (as in 19:18, "Which commandments?") or "Of what kind?" (as in I Cor. 15:35, "With what kind of body do they come?"). Here in Matt. 21:23 these two meanings coalesce. The question assumes that there are different kinds of authority and that Jesus *is* exercising authority of some kind (this is implied by the second question, "Who gave you this authority?"). It asks, "What is the nature of the authority you exercise?" The second question presupposes three possible sources: Jesus' authority is derived from God, from Satan (see 4:9; 9:34; 12:24), or from himself.

"These things" appears to refer to the provocative acts of the royal entry and the cleansing of the temple. It is probable, however, that Matthew subsumes under "these things" the entire public ministry of Jesus. One hint of this is the reference in verse 23 to Jesus' teaching. The combination of "authority" and "teaching" takes us back to the conclusion of the Sermon on the Mount: "He taught them as one who had authority" (7:29). His forgiveness of the paralytic's sins likewise manifested his authority (9:6), as did his healing of the centurion's servant (8:8–9) and his empowerment of the disciples (10:1). The authority issue has been present from the beginning, and all who were confronted by Jesus had to answer the question for themselves: Is this authority from God or not? (see the contrary responses at 9:33–34; 12:23–24).

From the very fact that they pose the questions it is clear that the questioners have already answered their own queries. They seek not information but an opportunity to trap Jesus by means of his response. At first glance Jesus' answer appears to be a clever ruse to escape the trap. He poses a counterquestion they cannot answer without getting themselves into trouble. His question, however, is to be seen not so much as an evasion as an *indirect* response. If they are able to acknowledge that John's call to baptismal repentance was truly authorized by God, they will have no difficulty in recognizing the source of his

245

authority. If, on the other hand, they admit that they cannot see the hand of God in John's ministry, they will demonstrate their incapacity to accept the answer he would give them.

Jesus does not seize the moment as an opportunity for preaching the gospel. The hour is too late for evangelism. The chief priests and elders of the people have appeared before him only to prepare the case against him. The next time he and they meet, Jesus will be brought before their council to be judged (26:47, 57). In the meantime he pronounces judgment upon them by means of three parables.

Modern readers find themselves in the position of Jesus' questioners. Confronted by Matthew's portrait of Jesus, they are compelled to ask the question, What is the nature of Jesus' authority, and what is its source? While Matthew provides an unambiguous answer to this question (see esp. 11:25–30; 28:16–20), an external answer of this kind does not relieve us of the necessity of forging our own response.

Our question prompts the counterquestion: Was John's ministry from God or just another instance of humans playing with religious ideas? Those who have allowed themselves to become imbued with the spirit of scientism, that is, the faith that no reality exists beyond the bounds of the physical universe, can grant no room in their worldview for God's intervention in human affairs. Jesus can be for them nothing more than "the greatest moral teacher who ever lived." Other readers of the Gospel, including some who think of themselves as agnostics, find themselves confronted by a mystery they cannot bring under their control. Jesus becomes for them the window through which they see God.

The Parable of the Two Sons (21:28–32)

In Mark's Gospel the parable of the wicked tenants immediately follows the challenge to Jesus' authority. Between these two passages Matthew inserts a parable that is not found elsewhere. He apparently regards it as a bridge joining the two; it continues the previous discussion by means of a reference to John the Baptist and anticipates the following parable by employing the vineyard metaphor.

246   The ancient manuscripts present a fascinating set of major disagreements on this passage, as can be seen by English readers through a comparison of the RSV and the NEB. The order of

the sons is reversed, so that in the manuscripts represented by the NEB the correct answer to Jesus' question is "The second." It is probable that this alternate order reflects an allegorical interpretation of the parable in the ancient church: Jews claimed to be obedient to God but rejected the gospel, but Gentiles, who had refused to obey God, repented and accepted the gospel. The order represented by the RSV is to be preferred. The story is less contrived if the father turns to a second son for help when the first son refuses.

In terms of structure a parallel is provided by the story of Nathan and David in II Samuel 12; Nathan's parable must not be separated from its context, because the unit includes David's response and Nathan's immediate denunciation, "You are the man" (II Sam. 12:7). In Matthew's setting the parable of the two sons presupposes the rejection of Jesus' authority on the part of the hearers. They correctly identify which son in the parable does what his father wants and then are denounced for playing the role of the disobedient son. As religious leaders, they claim to be faithfully obedient to God, but they are blind to the fact that authentic obedience includes responding in faith to the new things God is doing. As in the preceding passage, this withholding of faith in God is exemplified in their reaction to John the Baptist. Their refusal to see God at work in John's ministry anticipated their rejection of Jesus. The sinners in Israel, who had carelessly ignored the demands of their religion, will take their place in the kingdom, while Jesus' adversaries will be shut out.

In verse 32 we find the strange expression "the way of righteousness." It is unlikely that Matthew understands this as meaning only that John lived a righteous life. There is probably a connection between this phrase and the discussion at 3:15, where Jesus submits to baptism with the explanation, "For thus it is fitting for us to fulfil all righteousness." The way of righteousness thus includes not only John's proclamation of God's demand and the threat of judgment but also the sacrament of baptism, which dramatizes the need for the renewal of God's people as well as personal renewal.

The tax collectors and harlots who *believed* John (not "believed *in* John") accepted as true his threats of imminent judgment, repented of their sins, and underwent baptism (see the parallel in Luke 7:29–30). Even this miracle of renewal did not impress the religious leaders; it did not cause them to change

247

their minds (a better translation of the verb in v. 32 than "repent") and believe what John was saying.

Although the context applies this parable of judgment to Jewish religious leaders, Matthew probably intended a wider application as well. Christians too can become blind to what God is doing in the world around them. How easily "church work" degenerates into little more than simply maintaining the institution, with no excitement concerning what God's active grace is doing and consequently no enthusiasm for evangelism and renewal! We say that we are going to work in the vineyard, but instead of harvesting the grapes we spend our time rearranging the stones along the path!

The Parable of the Wicked Tenants (21:33–46)

Like the preceding parable of the two sons and the following parable of the king's wedding feast, 21:33–46 is a parable of judgment. It is the centerpiece of Jesus' threefold response to the religious leaders who question his authority (21:23–27).

In its present form the story is clearly allegorical, but the significance of the vineyard is not certain. Since the description of the vineyard echoes many of the details in Isa. 5:2, where the vineyard symbolizes Israel, it is natural to assume a similar meaning here. In this case the tenant farmers stand for Israel's religious leaders, who, despite their alleged loyalty to the Torah, fail to give God his due by believing in God's present activity in the ministries of John and Jesus (see comments on 21:23–27, 28–32). Although they are charged with the responsibility of leading Israel in the way of righteousness (see v. 32), they have in fact rebelled against God and will be replaced.

While this is a plausible understanding of the allegory, two considerations count against it, at least as far as Matthew's perspective is concerned. The vineyard, which in verse 41 is to be taken from the wicked tenants and given "to others," is interpreted in verse 43 as referring not to Israel but to the kingdom of God. It is not suggested that God will remove Israel's present leadership and provide it with more faithful leaders. Rather, "the kingdom of God" will be taken "from you" and given to *a nation* that will produce the fruits of the kingdom. Two corporate entities are involved. The "you" addressed consists not only of the opponents mentioned in the context but of all who follow their leadership in rejecting John and Jesus. The "nation"

248

to whom the kingdom will be transferred is the church. Although *ethnos* ("nation") when used in the plural means "Gentiles," it is by no means suggested that the kingdom is being transferred from Jews to Gentiles. The church, for Matthew, is neither Jewish nor Gentile but a "third race" that transcends the old distinction.

"The kingdom of God" is used here in an unusual way. It refers not to the age to come but to a special relationship to God's sovereignty, that is, divine election, including the privileges and responsibilities of being God's elect people. God's purposes in salvation history had been effected in and through Israel up to this time. As a consequence of its rejection of the Messiah, Israel is now to be "decommissioned"; its elect status as "light to the Gentiles" is to be taken over by the church.

This understanding is supported by a second consideration. The key feature of the allegory is not the cheating of the tenant farmers but their violent treatment of the owner's emissaries, including his son. It is generally agreed that reference is made here to the tradition that Israel has always persecuted the prophets sent to it by God (see I Kings 19:10, 14; II Chron. 24:18–22; 36:15–16; Acts 7:51–53; Matt. 23:29–39). The currency of the tradition is attested by Josephus and *The Lives of the Prophets.* Although Matthew's context addresses the parable specifically to "the high priests and elders of the people" (v. 23) and "the high priests and the Pharisees" (v. 45), the tradition of the persecution of the prophets, especially when taken with verse 43, suggests that behind these leaders stands "this generation," that is, rebellious Israel (see comments on 23:36).

On first impression the Scripture quotation in verse 42 appears out of place and irrelevant. It is often viewed as a later insertion. Before we submit to this proposal, it is incumbent on us to consider its function in the structure of the passage. Like the preceding parable, this one manifests the same structure as Nathan's; it issues in a self-incriminating response from the audience and culminates in a judgment by the parable maker, equivalent to Nathan's "You are the man" (II Sam. 12:1–7). In Matthew's version this final element could be supplied by verse 43, but there is some doubt about its status, since it is not found in the parallels in Mark and Luke. In these other Gospels as here, the initial denunciation is provided by the quotation. 249

The most probable explanation for the use of Ps. 118:22–23 in this passage is a wordplay in Hebrew involving the words for "son" and "stone" (cf. Lam. 4:1–2). This wordplay assisted Christians in gathering proof texts about "the Son, the Stone" from the Hebrew Scriptures. In I Peter 2:6–8 three different stone texts are reproduced together, including the one found here. The function of the text as a denunciation of the audience, then, is to prove from Scripture that the rejection of God's Son by the Jewish leaders is negated by God. A "stone" rejected by the "builders" will be given a role exceeding all others.

Verse 44 is omitted or placed within square brackets in many translations because of its omission from some important ancient manuscripts. Recently this issue has been reevaluated, and many now argue that it is an authentic part of Matthew's Gospel, not a scribal interpolation taken from Luke 20:18. It appears to be an allusion to two more stone passages, namely, Isa. 8:14–15 and Dan. 2:44–45. At the present time the Son is a stumbling block to many in Israel; when he returns in glory to judge the world he will crush all opposition. It suits the narrative setting that the references to the Son in verses 42, 44 are both indirect; only in the trial before the high priest will Jesus publicly acknowledge that he is the Messiah.

This "parable of the passion," with its emphasis on the murder of God's Son by Israel's leaders (the Romans are nowhere in sight!) and the consequent transfer of Israel's privileges to the church, must be treated with great care by Christians. What began as a prophetic critique designed not to damn Israel but to provoke repentance became in the course of Christian history an anti-Judaism which was sinfully perverted into anti-Semitism. Jews were reviled with the hated nickname "Christ killers." Popes and bishops taught that the Jews, because they had killed Christ and rejected his gospel, were a reprobate people, incapable of a spiritual life and thus not fully human. It ought not to surprise us that the ultimate result of this kind of thinking was the "final solution" of the Nazi gas chambers.

There are two ways of interpreting this passage that will avoid encouraging anti-Semitism. The first is to hear it as a piece of prophetic invective addressed by a Jew to fellow Jews. If we feel that Matthew has himself abandoned all hope of Israel's repentance, we must hold his pessimism in check by referring to Paul's optimism in Rom. 11:25–36. The second approach is to focus attention not so much on what the passage has to say explicitly about Jewish leaders as what it implies about Christians. The "others" to whom the vineyard is given over in verse

41 are also accountable to the owner. They too are charged with the heavy responsibility of producing the fruits of the kingdom (v. 43). The punishment of others is cause not for rejoicing but for fear (see Rom. 11:20–21).

The Parable of the King's Wedding Feast (22:1–14)

This third parable in the series of Jesus' responses to the challenge to his authority (21:23–27) is likewise a parable of judgment. It differs from the first two most noticeably by its concluding emphasis on the judgment of *Christians*.

In its Matthean form the parable, like the immediately preceding parable of the wicked tenants, can be characterized as an allegory of salvation history. The king is clearly God; the wedding feast for his son represents the messianic banquet (cf. Rev. 19:7–9). Those sent to invite the guests are God's prophets, including Christian missionaries. The reference to the mistreatment of the king's slaves recalls the tradition concerning Israel's violent treatment of God's prophets (see comments on 21:33–46; 23:29–39). The burning of the rebels' city seems to be an allusion to the destruction of Jerusalem by the Romans in 70 C.E., an event that Christians regarded as God's punishment upon Israel for its rejection of Jesus and the gospel. The invitation offered to others, "both bad and good," signifies the Gentile mission of the church.

Matthew's form of the story (cf. Luke 14:15–24) stresses the parallels between this allegory and the preceding one. The defiant refusal to participate in the wedding feast corresponds with the tenants' withholding of the owner's share of the fruit. In both, the leading actor sends out two sets of slaves (note the parallels between 21:34, 36 and 22:3, 4). The messengers are violently rejected in both (21:35–36; 22:6). In each, there is a severe judgment, but whereas in the first it is merely predicted, in the second it occurs as part of the story.

It is often proposed that verses 6–7 constitute a post-Matthean interpolation. Indeed, the narrative makes more sense if they are omitted. How bizarre to conduct a war while the roasted oxen wait to be eaten! The scholarly consensus, however, continues to regard these verses as authentic to Matthew and to accept them as evidence that the First Gospel was written after 70 C.E. While the verses do not fit well into the story, they are important to his allegory concerning salvation history

251

and the transfer of Israel's privileges to the church (see comments on 21:43).

The most remarkable feature of the allegory is that the king's slaves, obeying the command to go to the roads leading from the city, gather together everyone they find, "both bad and good." It is sometimes proposed that these adjectives refer to social ranks, but in view of Matthew's emphasis on ethics, it is best to take them in their usual sense. There is extensive evidence in the First Gospel that its author was deeply distressed by the mixed state of the church. In his view, there were too many false prophets and false disciples whose practice did not accord with their profession (see 7:21–23). Two parables about this problem have already appeared: there are weeds growing among the wheat (13:24–30, 36–43); the Gentile mission is like a great net that gathers "rotten" fish along with good ones (13:47–50). Matthew now makes an addition to the wedding feast parable to remind Christians that they are by no means exempt from the judgment that fell on those who rejected Jesus and the gospel.

The supplemental parable of the guest without a wedding garment is offensive to uninstructed readers. Why should the king be so incredibly harsh to a poor man who has hastily been brought from outside the city, who presumably had no opportunity to borrow a clean tunic fit for the occasion? And why should the king ask, "Friend, how did you get in here without a wedding garment?" After all, was it not the king who told his slaves to bring in everyone they could find? The answer to all such questions, of course, is that this is not an ordinary story but an allegory. The wedding feast is not the church but the age to come. The required garment is righteousness, that is, behavior in accordance with Jesus' teachings (see 28:19). The man is speechless because he has no defense; he accepted the invitation of the gospel, but refused to conform his life to the gospel.

The attached saying, "For many are called, but few are chosen," should not be taken as a forecast of the proportion of the saved to the damned. Its function is not to frighten Christians with the thought that the statistical odds are against them but to encourage vigorous effort to live the Christian life.

The Tribute Question (22:15–22)

Christians concerned about political issues and church-state relations eagerly approach this passage, hoping to find a principle to guide them through the maze of contemporary controversies. We must be careful, however, not to draw from the passage more than it contains.

According to Matthew and Mark, the question about paying the Roman tax is brought to Jesus by a coalition of Pharisees and Herodians. We know little about the latter, but their name suggests that they were a secular political party that supported the right of Herod the Great's successors to rule Palestine. By necessity they were pro-Roman, since no one could rule any segment of the Mediterranean world without Rome's approval. The Pharisees, on the other hand, tended to be quietists who resented the Roman occupation but accepted it as a necessary evil; they counseled submission as long as Rome did not interfere with the practice of religion. These diverse groups are brought together in this incident by their common opposition to Jesus. Their intention is to place Jesus on the horns of a dilemma. If he argues against paying the tax, they will be able to accuse him to Pilate of anti-Roman activity. On the other hand, if he supports the tax, he will be bound to lose some of his support in the general population, for whom the tribute was not only an economic burden but also a hated symbol of lost freedom.

It should be noted that the question, while profoundly political, is phrased in religious terms: "Is it permitted . . . ?" (cf. 12:2). The question can be paraphrased: "Does it accord with Torah to pay tax to Caesar or not?" One facet of the legal question involves God's ownership of the land of Israel: "The land shall not be sold in perpetuity, for the land is mine" (Lev. 25:23). Since Caesar is a usurper, is it not an act of disobedience to God to pay a tax to this pagan ruler?

Instead of taking the baited hook by discussing the legal niceties of the issue, Jesus calls for a Roman coin, knowing that the tax can be paid only in Roman currency. When a silver denarius is presented to him, he asks, "Whose image is this, and whose inscription?" Most probably the head of the coin showed the head of the reigning emperor, and the tail an inscription that identified him as "Tiberius Caesar, Son of the Divine Au-

253

gustus, Pontifex Maximus," that is, as high priest of the pagan Roman religion. Exodus 20:4 prohibits "graven images" of any kind. Yet here, in the most holy space in the holy land, Jesus' adversaries promptly produce a coin that violates the dictates of their religion! The hypocrisy is obvious. They are happy to do business with Caesar's coins. Why then should they raise a religious question about giving Caesar his due?

Since the question posed by the opponents is sufficiently answered by the object lesson and the first half of Jesus' epigram, special weight must be attached to the second half, *"and to God the things that are God's."* Perhaps we should imagine Jesus pausing in the middle of the sentence, so that the full force of the conclusion will be felt by his audience. Although there is strict parallelism between the two halves, they are by no means of equal significance, because Caesar's role is so vastly inferior to God's. That is, Jesus is not saying, "There is a secular realm and there is a religious realm, and equal respect must be paid to each." The second half practically annuls the first by preempting it. In Jewish religious thought, foreign kings had power over Israel only by permission from God. Tax may be paid to Caesar because it is by God's will that Caesar rules. When God chooses to liberate his people, Caesar's power will avail him nothing.

Since the time of Tertullian interpreters have pondered the possibility that the saying implicitly refers to humans as God's coin, bearing his image. Since men and women are created in the image of God (Gen. 1:27), they belong to him as surely as Caesar's coins belong to Caesar. To God must be given back what is his. This may be fanciful, but the conclusion is sound. In the second half of his epigram Jesus demands far more of his followers than in the first half. In the Sermon on the Mount, Jesus warns, "You cannot serve God and mammon" (6:24). Here he is saying, in effect: If Tiberius wants a few denarii, give them gladly, because giving them up will remind you that a person's life does not consist in the abundance of his or her possessions (see Luke 12:15). What counts above all else is living in accordance with the Father's will.

Was the trap successful after all? Did Jesus lose the support of the crowd because of his apparent lack of concern for their economic distress? No such suggestion is made by the text, but later in the story, when the crowd is offered two nominees for procuratorial pardon, their vote goes to Barabbas, a hero in the ongoing resistance against Roman domination (27:15–23).

254

In all likelihood the First Gospel was written for a diaspora church of Jews and Gentiles that had little sympathy for the Jewish resistance movement in Palestine. There was probably little need in such a context for the first half of the epigram. Newly converted Gentiles, however, will have been impressed by the second half; it called for a total commitment unlike anything they had known in the pagan cults they had left behind.

Taxing authority is only the tip of the iceberg respecting the power a state exercises over its citizens. Does the state have the right to invade privacy in matters not directly related to the public safety? Can it legitimately define and enforce ethical standards in the areas of sexuality and reproduction? Modern Christians may find that Jesus' epigram provides little help in dealing with such questions. Perhaps it will only be as a result of pondering deeply the second half of the epigram that we will know when, in God's name, we must surrender our docility and actively resist the power of the state.

The Sadducees' Challenge (22:23–33)

"When you're dead, you're dead!" These words, heard often from modern lips, express succinctly the point of view of the Sadducees, one of the religious parties in Judaism in Jesus' day. According to Josephus, the Sadducees were strict constructionists in their interpretation of the laws of the Pentateuch, firmly rejecting the innovations of the Pharisees. God was, for them, very transcendent; he did not interfere with or predestine human behavior, nor provide postmortem rewards and punishments. Humans were thus compelled to take full responsibility for their actions in this world, since there was no other. They refused to believe in the resurrection of the dead, because they found no evidence of such a doctrine in the Books of Moses. (An unambiguous witness to the resurrection appears only in the latest book of the Hebrew Scriptures, Dan. 12:2, which the Sadducees probably did not regard as Scripture.) Wisdom of Solomon 2:1–11, in referring to wealthy people who oppress the poor because they fear no retribution after death, may be speaking of Sadducees.

Because these conservatives supported the status quo, they were favored by the wealthy landowners, including the few families from whom the high priests were chosen (see Acts 5:17). It appears, therefore, that the Sadducees, although

255

they are not named as such in chapters 26–27, were a primary force in the termination of Jesus' ministry. They apparently perceived him as a serious threat to the status quo (see John 11:47–50).

In this passage their hostility is cloaked in a legal question, by which they hope, like their predecessors in verses 15–22, to discredit Jesus before at least a part of his audience. They present him with a case which, in their opinion, displays the absurdity of the belief in the resurrection. The legal issue concerns the application of the law of levirate marriage to the world to come. When a married man dies without begetting a son, his brother is obligated to marry the widow and thus provide the deceased with a posterity (Deut. 25:5–10). If seven brothers successively have the same woman as wife, who will lawfully have sex with her in the new age after the resurrection?

The Sadducees assume that Jesus will concur with the popular expectation that the new age will be like this one but much better. The Syriac *Apocalypse of Baruch*, written near the end of the first century, promises, "And women shall no longer have pain when they bear, nor shall any suffer torment when they yield the fruit of their womb" (*II Bar.* 73:7). *First Enoch* 10:17 suggests that the righteous will beget thousands of children in the coming age. Because it is not always clear in such texts whether this glorious time will follow or precede the resurrection of the dead, there were probably many who expected to participate in sexual pleasure after the resurrection.

Jesus promptly dismisses this popular view. The life of the resurrection will be totally different. It will be life in the body (this, of course, is the meaning of the resurrection of the dead in distinction from immortality of the soul), but it will by no means be a continuation of bodily existence as we now know it. The bodies of the resurrected will resemble the bodies of angels.

More important than the specifics of this response is the theological foundation Jesus lays for it. He denounces the Sadducees for being ignorant of the Scriptures. Apparently he is referring not to Old Testament texts about life after death, of which there are very few, but to the combined testimony of the Scriptures to the *power of God* (v. 29). Any trustworthy belief in the resurrection must be based not on wishful thinking or on a theory about the immortality of the soul but only on the doctrine of God. Life after death is not to be regarded as a

256

detached doctrine, an item on an à la carte menu of theological beliefs that can be taken or left. The resurrection of the dead is to be seen as an inference drawn from the doctrine of God.

Many different Old Testament texts might have been selected to make the point. Jesus carefully chooses a text from the Torah, since the Sadducees honored it above the Prophets and perhaps did not accept the Writings as authoritative. To modern readers the proof appears unconvincing. A superficial reading suggests that Jesus is proposing that the one who declares, "I *am* the God of Abraham and the God of Isaac and the God of Jacob" (Exod. 3:6) means to tell us that he is currently their God, which indicates that they are not dead but alive. This would indicate that they are alive in some sense, but it would not support the belief in the resurrection of the dead, since their bodies were believed to be in their graves. The real significance of this text, which occurs in the story of the burning bush that opens a new chapter in God's relationship to Israel, lies in its recollection of God's covenant love for the patriarchs. In the exodus narrative this covenant love, which seemed forgotten during long generations of slavery in Egypt, is renewed with demonstrations of power. The point is clear: those with whom God chooses to relate in covenant love he does not abandon. The creator of the universe has the power to maintain relationships with his chosen even beyond the portal of death (cf. IV Macc. 7:19). Jesus, who here instructs his mortal enemies regarding the nature of God, prepares to go to his death in the firm conviction that his Father is stronger than death.

The God of the Sadducees, ancient and modern, is too small. Such a God is little more than a theoretical principle, to be honored in formal worship but safely ignored at other times. Powerless over death, the Sadducees' God can justly be called "the God of the dead." The Christian faith in the resurrection of the dead is soundly based in the revelation of God's power and covenant love. It is strongly reinforced by the experience of the resurrection of Jesus.

The Double Commandment of Love (22:34–40)

The requirement that we love God and neighbor has become so prominent a feature of Christianity that we are apt to take it as axiomatic. If a superficial appropriation is to be avoided, we must struggle to discover what this juxtaposition of

257

Deut. 6:5 and Lev. 19:18 meant to early Christians like Matthew. Here it is especially important to remember that what is implicit is as significant as what is explicit.

Although Matthew places the passage in the same location in the series of temple disputes as Mark does (see Mark 12:28–34), it can be said that the Matthean context is different. In Mark the pericope carries less weight simply because the Second Gospel as a whole gives less prominence to Jesus' teaching. While the story itself is told with much more detail in Mark, in that version the focus rests on the wisdom with which Jesus answers the scribe's question, not on the significance of the answer as a recapitulation of Jesus' teaching. By adding verse 40, "On these two commandments hang the whole law and the prophets," Matthew takes us back to the very beginning of Jesus' teaching ministry, to the programmatic statement in 5:17–20, which opens with the words, "Do not suppose that I have come to destroy the law and the prophets; I have not come to destroy but to fulfill." The rest of the Sermon on the Mount, especially the antitheses of 5:21–48, illustrated how Jesus "fulfilled" the law in the spirit of the prophets. Just as the Golden Rule served as a summary of the Sermon on the Mount, so now the double commandment of love, coming at the end of the final series of disputes with his opponents, recapitulates Jesus' teaching ministry as a whole. The references to the law and the prophets in 5:17 and 22:40 bracket Jesus' ministry to Israel as the God-authorized end-time teacher.

Whereas in Mark the question is put by a scribe who is impressed with Jesus' responses to his adversaries and who praises the answer to his own question (Mark 12:28, 32–33), there is no room in Matthew's Gospel for a friendly scribe. He sees all Jewish teachers through the lens of the bitter persecution suffered by Jewish-Christian missionaries. As a result, the honest question becomes instead another devious attempt to entrap Jesus. Perhaps the Pharisees of Matthew's narrative, like the Sadducees of the preceding passage, are trying to tempt Jesus into making a statement that will eliminate a part of his popular support. Possibly Matthew is thinking of a view common in some circles of first-century Judaism that, since all commandments are of equal importance in God's eyes and are to be observed solely for God's glory, it is sinful to argue that some are more important than others on the basis of some merely human standard of judgment.

Literally translated, the question of the "expert in the law" reads: "Teacher, what kind of commandment in the law [is] great?" The omission of the definite article before "great" leaves the question open-ended. The answer, however, indicates that the question is understood as asking for "the greatest and most important commandment" (v. 38). Jesus refuses to name only one; to the command to love God he attaches Lev. 19:18, identified in Matthew as being "like" the first (v. 39). We should probably see "like" as meaning more than "similar in structure" or even "similar in importance." Implied is a similarity in theological depth and an interrelationship.

It is a mistake to suggest that the purpose of this passage is to show that Jesus was the first to bring these two commandments together as a summary of human obligation. There is evidence that this had been done already. The *Testament of the Twelve Patriarchs* refers frequently to loving the Lord and the neighbor, for example, *Testament of Issachar* 5:2, "But love the Lord and your neighbor, and show compassion for the poor and the weak." Indeed, in Luke's Gospel the identification of these two as the greatest commandments is attributed not to Jesus but to the lawyer who questions him (Luke 10:27)! The collocation by Jesus is significant only if we plumb its depths.

One way to begin this process is to ask, Is the double commandment to be described as an ethical maxim or as a theological statement? Simply by asking the question we become aware of the interpenetration of theology and ethics in Jesus' response. A second approach is to ask, In what sense are these *commandments*? Strictly speaking, a commandment refers to specific kinds of behavior that can be required or prohibited. Is love something that can be commanded? A third angle of vision is provided by the reference to "the law *and* the prophets." In what ways do the prophets transcend the particularity of the Torah's commandments? In Micah 6:8 the obligation laid upon Israel by its relationship with God is summarized in three requirements: doing righteousness, loving loyalty, and walking humbly with God. A distant parallel to this occurs in Matt. 23:23, where Jesus describes "the weightier matters of the law" as consisting of justice, mercy, and faithfulness, that is, forms of behavior demanded by the prophets but beyond legal regulation.

259

Again, we can gain a deeper appreciation of the theological significance of the double commandment when we ask, Are these two injunctions set side by side merely to indicate that human responsibility involves two parallel but separate spheres of accountability, or are they interrelated? A preliminary answer is provided by Jesus' treatment of the Sabbath law. Presumably Jesus regarded the Fourth Commandment as a particular manifestation of the broader requirement of love for God, and yet he argued that observance of the Sabbath should not take precedence over human need (12:1–14). Love for neighbor must teach us how to love God! Conversely, his radicalization of neighbor love to include enemies makes sense only to those whose love for God empowers them to imitate the Creator's generosity and thus display that they are his children (see comments on 5:43–48). Truly to love God is to love the neighbor; truly to love the neighbor is to love God (cf. I John 4:20–21).

In an age when the word "love" is greatly abused, it is important to remember that the primary component of biblical love is not affection but commitment. Warm feelings of gratitude may fill our consciousness as we consider all that God has done for us, but it is not warm feelings that Deut. 6:5 demands of us but rather stubborn, unwavering commitment. Similarly, to love our neighbor, including our enemies, does not mean that we must feel affection for them. To love the neighbor is to imitate God by taking their needs seriously.

Who Is Father to the Messiah? (22:41–46)

On first impression this passage presents Jesus as teaching that it is incorrect to conceive of the Messiah as the Son of David. Such an understanding is obviously erroneous in view of the important role played by the title "the Son of David" in the First Gospel, beginning with the opening verse. Since the Davidic Sonship of Jesus is taken for granted by Paul (Rom. 1:3) and the author of Revelation (3:7; 5:5; 22:16) as well as by Matthew, Mark, and Luke (John 7:42 is ambiguous), and since we have no knowledge of any group in the early church that *denied* this claim, we should assume that Jesus himself mounted no argument against the prevailing view that the Messiah would be a descendant of David. Indeed, there is no reason to doubt the tradition that Joseph's family claimed David as its progenitor (just as Paul's family traced its origin to Benjamin, Phil. 3:5), especially in view of the fact that relatively little is made of this tradition in the New Testament as a whole.

260

While not denying the Davidic Sonship of the Messiah, Jesus draws on Scripture (Ps. 110:1) in order to point to a weakness in the prevailing view. This verse from the psalm is quoted and alluded to more often in the New Testament than any other verse in the Old Testament and is echoed in the Apostles' Creed ("and is seated at the right hand of God"). It is the most important scriptural building block in the construction of New Testament Christology.

It has sometimes been argued by scholars that Jesus could not have employed this verse, because it had no messianic significance in contemporary Judaism and could therefore prove useful only after Easter when it was seized upon as a way of talking about Jesus' exaltation by resurrection. This is an argument from silence and intrinsically dubious. There is good evidence that this psalm was employed by the later Maccabean rulers as a propaganda tool in support of their claim to be priest-kings (they could not claim descent from David). Since their reputation became increasingly tarnished, there is every reason to assume that their religious opponents will have proposed a very different interpretation of the psalm, namely, that it spoke of the future Messiah. Even if this assumption could be proved false, however, there is no basis for arguing that, had Jesus been the first to treat this verse as a messianic proof text, his audience would have instantly rejected his interpretation. The probability that the psalm was already perceived in this way is supported by the fact that it was so interpreted by the targum (the Aramaic translation) of the psalm and by the later rabbis despite the church's appropriation of it for Christology.

It is impossible to prove or disprove that Jesus used the psalm as a means of interpreting his own role. If Jesus did regard himself as the Messiah (as this commentary assumes; see comments on 27:37), he may well have found Ps. 110:1 helpful in reconciling this conviction with another, equally strong conviction, that he was called to love his enemies, not destroy them (5:43–48). That is, Ps. 110:1 attributes a passive role to the king, who is to sit at God's right hand until *God* makes his enemies his footstool.

The weakness in the traditional understanding of "the Son of David" to which Jesus points in this passage is that the Messiah is too narrowly conceived as a conquering hero like David, who, with God's help, will destroy Israel's enemies. Psalm 110:1 suggests that the Messiah will be a very different kind of king, one whom even David must call "My Lord." Whose son, then, is he? The basic text of Israel's messianic hope is Nathan's oracle to David. Of David's progeny it is promised, "I will be his father, and he shall be my son" (II Sam. 7:14). While it is not wrong to say that the Messiah is David's son, it is more important to recognize that he is God's Son, that is, that he will have a unique relationship to God. In this connection we remember Jesus' use of *Abba* as a means of addressing his Father in heaven (see comments on 26:36–46). In his whole ministry Jesus has displayed how he understands the Messiah's role: he is a spiritual leader who seeks through word and deed to communicate God's love for the lost sheep of the house of Israel and to help them become children of the heavenly Father (5:45). If he must die to remain faithful to this role, he will do so. None of this, of course, is explicitly stated in the passage. The question addressed to nonfollowers (Pharisees, according to Matthew) intends only to provoke reflection concerning what it means to refer to the Messiah as the Son of God, one whom even David must call Lord.

When we examine its context we can gain insight into Matthew's understanding of the passage. It is the final item in the series of disputes in the temple that began with a question about Jesus' authority (21:23–27). This in turn was prompted not only by his cleansing of the temple but by the triumphal entry and his healing ministry in the temple, when he was hailed as the Son of David (21:9, 15). The humble king has arrived in his city, and the leaders of the people have refused to acknowledge his authority, because they cannot conceive of the Messiah in Jesus' terms. While Jesus refused to answer the question about his authority in 21:27, he tacitly answers it here, although his opponents cannot perceive it. It is as the Father's unique Son that he has the authority to exercise his messianic ministry (cf. 11:25–30).

While Matthew employs the title "the Son of David" more often than any other New Testament writer, for him it is clearly subordinate to "the Son of God." It is God himself who announces at the baptism that Jesus is his beloved Son (3:17), and this declaration is repeated at the transfiguration (17:7). The shortened title "the Son" plays an important role in 11:25–30 and in the trinitarian baptismal formula in 28:19 (see also 24:36). Matthew probably understands this title as pointing to Jesus' fulfillment of the Emmanuel prophecy of 1:23, that is, "the Son of God" designates Jesus as "God with us." While "the Son of

262

David" may be appropriately used with respect to Jesus' restricted role as the Messiah sent to the lost sheep of the house of Israel (15:24), "the Son of God" bespeaks his universal Lordship as the one in whom the Gentiles will hope.

This concluding challenge silences all opponents, indicating that the time has come for Jesus to deliver his farewell speech to Israel.

Matthew 23:1–39
The Messiah's Valedictory Address

Like the other great discourses in Matthew, chapter 23 is a composition of the Evangelist in which he draws on his various sources to make a connected whole. As in all the other instances, this discourse is occasioned by a passage in Mark (12: 38–40). Because chapter 23 does not conclude with the usual formula ("And when Jesus had finished," 7:28; 11:1; 13:53; 19:1), and since it is followed not by narrative but by another long discourse (chaps. 24–25) that is completed by the formula (26:1), many scholars argue that Matthew 23–25 constitutes a single discourse (rounding out the number of major discourses to five), with a change of location and audience occurring in the middle (24:1–3) just as in the parables discourse at 13:46, where Jesus leaves the crowds at the lakeside, enters a house, and speaks to his disciples alone. The common denominator uniting chapter 23 with chapters 24–25 is the theme of judgment.

Chapter 23 must be interpreted with great caution, so that it may not be used in support of modern anti-Semitism. All too easily its scathing denunciation of the scribes and Pharisees is perceived as eternally damning all Jews and Judaism. Modern Jewish scholars interested in the New Testament and interfaith dialogue rightly complain that this chapter is unfair in its wholesale condemnation of the Pharisees, the founders of modern Judaism. That some Pharisees were pious frauds is admitted on all sides—they are roundly condemned in the early rabbinic writings—but to suggest that Matthew 23 accurately describes people like Hillel, Shammai, and Jochanan ben Zakkai, first-century progenitors of modern Judaism, is manifestly unjust. Paul tells us that he was a Pharisee before his Damascus experi- 263 ence. Josephus claims to have been a Pharisee. It is unlikely that the generalizations of this chapter would fit either of them.

It must be recognized that in its present form chapter 23 is a piece of religious polemic, created not by Jesus but by the author of the Gospel. There need be little doubt that many of the individual sayings go back to Jesus, who was by no means averse to criticizing his religious opponents, but the original context of the individual sayings has been lost. In the Matthean composition their force is greatly intensified; the whole becomes a powerful invective aimed at Jewish Christianity's archrival in the competition for the religious allegiance of Jews in the postwar period. Comments concerning the difficulty of interpreting this polemic to modern Christians will be made at the end of the treatment of this chapter.

Christian and Pharisaic Teachers Contrasted (23:1-12)

The first section of this polemical chapter has three levels of application. The focus is on teachers of religion and their responsibility for rank-and-file members. At the first level, there are criticisms made by Jesus of his religious opponents (many of whom were probably not Pharisees). In the course of time these sayings were understood as directed primarily at the Pharisaic teachers who, after the disastrous war with Rome of 66–73 C.E., sought to reconstruct Jewish ethnic identity by extending and consolidating their influence in the synagogues of Palestine and the diaspora. Jewish-Christian missionaries who proclaimed a crucified and resurrected Messiah found in these Pharisaic teachers their most determined adversaries and rivals, and consequently reapplied Jesus' sayings to this new situation. In Matthew's editing, however, a third level of application appears: the sayings are applied to Christian teachers, who are thereby warned not to be like the teachers Jesus condemned. Indeed, it has been argued that the bitter conflict lies in the past for Matthew; his real concern in this polemical chapter is to address the problem of Christian leadership that has fallen short of the ideal required by Jesus. Seen from this perspective, verses 6–12 are by no means to be seen as an aside in a chapter condemning the Pharisees but as a passage expressing the goal of the whole discourse. This probably overstates the case. While Matthew is profoundly concerned about leadership in the church, he is also determined to present a theological statement about Israel's rejection of the Lord's Anointed. The polemic of Matthew 23 must be read as theology, not just as moral exhortation.

Fundamental to the passage is the problematical statement with which it opens: "The scribes and the Pharisees sit on Moses' seat; therefore do whatever they teach you and follow it" (vv. 2–3a). This statement stands in such stark contrast to passages sharply critical of the teaching of the Pharisees (15:1–20; 16:5–12) that it appears inauthentic to many scholars. If a genuine saying of Jesus underlies these verses, the original version may have suggested that in general terms the Pharisees' perspective on religion was to be preferred to that of the Sadducees or the Essenes. Whatever the origin of the statement, it is obvious that Matthew does not find it as problematic as do many modern scholars! For him, it does not negate the rejection of Pharisaic teaching in the earlier passages but merely establishes the level of accountability to which the Pharisaic teachers must be held. They were granted responsibility for leading Israel at the dawn of the messianic age, and they failed.

In the succeeding verses four different criticisms are made of the Pharisaic teachers. First, they do not practice what they preach. This, of course, is an attack to which teachers in any religion are vulnerable, since none are capable of fully exemplifying the ideal they proclaim. It is safe to assume that Matthew perceives this criticism as one that Christian teachers must take seriously. Those who teach whatever Jesus commanded (28:19) must live the teaching.

The second criticism, articulated in verse 4, is difficult to understand, especially in view of verse 3: "Do whatever they teach you and follow it." Whereas this preceding verse was prized by Pharisaic Christians, verse 4 reflects the point of view of less rigorous Jewish Christians (cf. Acts 15:10). Presumably reference is made here to the fact that the Pharisees stressed consistency in observance. It was, for example, not enough to keep the Sabbath "in a general way"; it was necessary to define carefully which weekday activities constituted work and were therefore prohibited on the Sabbath. Many ordinary Jews were probably irritated by such consistency and regarded the Sabbath rulings of the Pharisees as a burden imposed by the interpreters, not by Scripture itself. Although Jesus observed the Sabbath, he insisted that his ministry to the ill took precedence

265

over the Sabbath rulings of the rigorists (see comments on 12:1–14). He offered an easier yoke and a lighter burden (11:28–30). Perhaps this criticism, like others in the group, was aimed by Matthew at *Christian* teachers who were urging followers of Jesus to observe the Sabbath and the other ritual laws in accordance with the Pharisaic interpretation.

Little need be said concerning the third criticism (v. 5). The hypocrisy of a piety that seeks the adulation of other people rather than the glorification of God has already been soundly denounced in the Sermon on the Mount (6:1–6, 16–18).

Closely connected with the "public relations piety" of verse 5 is the lust for recognition and honor castigated in verses 6–7. This criticism is presented in the form of a woe in Luke 11:43. Matthew's version adds the clause "and to have people call them *rabbi.*" This Hebrew term, which literally means "my great one" or "my master," was used in the earlier part of the first century as a polite form of address in speaking to any Jewish teacher, such as John the Baptist (John 3:36) or Jesus (John 1:38; Matt. 26:49). Only after 70 C.E. did the practice develop of using *rabbi* as a technical term to designate those of the Pharisaic tradition who had been trained as teachers and set apart by ordination. Presumably it is used here in its nontechnical sense.

Although the audience of verse 1 includes "the crowds," verses 8–12 are clearly addressed to the disciples alone, who here represent for Matthew not rank-and-file believers but Christian teachers. In the Greek the opening word of verse 8 is emphatic and contrastive: "As for *you,* however, you are not to be addressed as 'Rabbi.' " It is unlikely that any of Jesus' disciples were so addressed during his lifetime, but this habit may have emerged soon after Easter when the earliest followers assumed the responsibility of transmitting to new believers the traditions about Jesus. It must have been natural to address the next generation of Christian teachers in the same way. Since they were performing an essential task, what wrong could there be in honoring their function by addressing them as "Rabbi"?

While the importance of the function is indispensable, it must not be used as an excuse for a self-aggrandizement that harms the fellowship. Only one is to be so honored; all others are brothers and sisters, that is, equals bound together by mutual affection and respect. This ideal of the church as an unstratified society is firmly espoused by Paul. Social historians

266

have contrasted Paul's churches with other clubs in Greco-Roman society in which members bolstered self-esteem by the use of a wide variety of grandiose titles. The apostle refers repeatedly to leadership *functions* without stressing the *persons* who fulfilled these functions. Instead, he implores his converts to abandon selfish ambition and humbly treat others as superior (Phil. 2:3; Rom. 12:3, 16).

Verse 10 virtually repeats verse 8, using a Greek rather than a Hebrew word for teacher and making explicit the fact that the only real teacher in the church is the Messiah. In contrast with verses 8 and 10, verse 9 employs the active voice of the verb: "And call no one your father on earth." It is generally agreed that reference is made here not to one's male parent but to a religious authority. Some rabbinic leaders were addressed as *Ab*, "Father." Although Paul uses "father" as a metaphor for his relationship with the Corinthian Christians (I Cor. 4:15), it seems unlikely that he or other Christian teachers were so addressed. Possibly, therefore, verse 9 alludes to the practice of some Jewish Christians of appealing to Jewish authorities on certain matters such as Sabbath observance instead of depending wholly on Christ who had interpreted for them the will of their Father in heaven. For the meaning of verses 11–12, see 20:20–28.

This passage is perennially relevant. It is not a mortal sin for clergy to be addressed as "Reverend," "Father," "Doctor," or "Pastor." The eagerness of laypeople to exalt ordained persons by the use of honorific titles, however, intensifies the minister's responsibility to work diligently at breaking down the barrier between clergy and laity.

Seven Woes Concerning the Pharisaic Teachers (23:13–33)

The use of the woe formula to express divine displeasure is common in the prophetic literature. Isaiah 5:8–23 contains a series of six woes. The woe can employ the third person ("Woe to those who . . ."), as in Isaiah 5, or the second person, as in Amos 5:18: "Woe to you who desire the day of the LORD!" The use of the second person does not imply the presence of the objects of the woe, as can be seen in Jesus' woes against two Galilean towns (Matt. 11:21). Since 23:1 limits the audience to the crowds and the disciples, we must not assume that Matthew conceives the Pharisaic opponents as auditors of the woes.

Because a similar series of woes against the religious antagonists is found in Luke 11:42–52, it is believed that the source used by Matthew and Luke contained such a series, which each Evangelist edited in his own way. In Luke there are six, three concerning Pharisees and three about "lawyers." This division recalls the distinction between ordinary Pharisees, the lay members of a religious movement, and their "scribes," that is, the "clergy" who were expert in the Pharisaic interpretation of the law, whom Luke calls lawyers for the sake of his non-Jewish readers (in Greco-Roman society a scribe was commonly a clerk who wrote letters for the illiterate for a fee). In Matthew's version this important distinction is forgotten; the Pharisaic laymen and their scribes are lumped together and characterized as a group by the pejorative "hypocrites."

Although the idea of conscious dissembling may be present in the statements about the "hypocrites," we must remember that the noun and the corresponding verb did not always bear this meaning. When Paul accuses Peter and Barnabas of "hypocrisy" in Gal. 2:11–14, he does not mean that their behavior had been dishonest but rather that it had been inconsistent with their Christian faith. While Matthew may regard some of the Pharisees as genuinely hypocritical, that is, as pretending to be religious when they have no real faith, he probably intends the pejorative to indicate that what they do and teach is in serious tension with the faith they received from the law and the prophets. Supportive of this understanding is his repeated use of "blind" as a description of the opponents (vv. 16, 17, 24, 26); they are blind to the inconsistency between their interpretation of the law and the law's real intent.

Most of the woes are thus more concerned with the teaching of the Pharisaic scribes than with their practice. This is most obvious in the case of the opening woe (v. 13). It is not by their behavior, good or bad, that the scribes lock people out of the kingdom but by their teaching. When the people were attracted by Jesus' ministry ("Can this be the Son of David?"), the Pharisees declared, "It is only by Beelzebul, the prince of demons, that this man casts out demons" (12:23–24; see also 21:15). By their public refusal to acknowledge that Jesus is the one to whom the prophets witnessed, the Pharisaic scribes demonstrate that they are incompetent interpreters of Scripture. Similarly, the second woe (v. 15) accuses the teachers of going to great lengths to convert a Gentile (perhaps a prominent person, such as Flavius Clemens of Rome or King Izates of Adiabene?) from paganism to a false form of Judaism, presumably by teaching him or her to focus on nonessentials, as illustrated in the third and fourth woes.

The third woe (vv. 16–22) must be read in the light of Jesus' rejection of oaths in 5:33–37 (see also James 5:12). The use of inappropriate oaths was rampant among ordinary people. In one reported instance a man swore "by the life of the fig-picker"! Early rabbis attempted to help people understand the distinction between valid and invalid oaths and to keep the promises made with a proper oath. Jesus was impatient with such distinctions, believing that they distracted people from the central issue, honesty. Every oath, whatever its wording, is a declaration to which God is the supreme witness, who will be the final judge of our language (see also 12:36–37).

At the explicit level the fourth woe (vv. 23–24) is concerned not with teaching but with practice. The opponents are chastised for paying so much attention to such trivial matters as the tithing of garden herbs (which goes well beyond the explicit tithing requirements of Deut. 14:22–23) that they neglect the law's central demands: justice, mercy, and faith. It is possible that this trio of nonlegal obligations reflects Micah 6:8: "And what does the LORD require of you but to do justice, and to love kindness, and to walk humbly with your God?" In the Greek translation of Micah the Hebrew word translated "kindness" by the RSV is rendered by *eleos* ("mercy"), one of Matthew's favorite words for summarizing the moral requirements of the Old Testament (see 9:13; 12:7). Since the trio is concerned primarily with interpersonal relationships (ethics), the third word should perhaps be understood as meaning not faith in the sense of humble confidence in God (as suggested by Micah 6:8) but *faithfulness* in human relationships. Although these verses explicitly criticize the Pharisees' practice, we are surely justified, in view of the context, in seeing here an implicit attack on their teaching. It is assumed that they teach others to imitate their careful tithing of garden herbs and thus draw attention away from God's *moral* will.

The fifth woe (vv. 25–26) reflects a scribal debate within Pharisaism about whether the inside and the outside of cups and plates were independent regarding uncleanness, that is, whether the inside was contaminated when the outside became ritually unclean and vice versa. These verses reflect the perspective of 15:1–20: it is not eating with unwashed hands that renders a person unclean but acting immorally. Instead of debating these fine points regarding the purity of dishes, the religious opponents should be concerned with ethical behavior. The preposition *ek* in the last clause of verse 25 should perhaps be given a causal rather than a partitive sense: "they are full *from* [i.e., on the basis of] robbery and self-indulgence" (see NEB, TEV). In this case, the plate and the cup are not metaphors for the hearts and minds of the Pharisees but should be taken as meaning "Your tables groan with ill-gotten gains." Verse 26, however, does treat the cup metaphorically: "First cleanse your heart, and then your behavior will reflect your inner purity."

As in the fourth and fifth woes, an attack on the teaching of the Pharisees is merely implicit in the sixth woe (vv. 27–28). Here the metaphor of a beautiful grave monument is used to contrast the opponents' reputation for uprightness with their inner hypocrisy and lawlessness. The last word in verse 28, *anomia,* translated "iniquity" by the RSV, is often used with this general sense, but its derivation from *nomos* ("law") may be significant in this context. The opponents who claim the right to expound God's law are guilty of *lawlessness,* because they stress minutiae and neglect the weightier matters of the law. This is the essence of their hypocrisy. Understood in this way, verse 28 serves as a summary of the first six woes.

The seventh woe (vv. 29–31) is different in kind from the first six. It attacks neither the teaching nor the personal ethics of the Pharisees; rather, it accuses them of their solidarity with earlier Israelites who had persecuted God's prophets. The logic is strained, to say the least. Why does the honoring of dead prophets with monuments constitute evidence of concurrence with those who murdered them? One would infer the very opposite. To honor the memory of Lincoln, Kennedy, and King is to condemn their murderers. What we encounter in this woe is the rhetoric of polemic, not reasoned argument. The underlying idea, however, is obvious. The opponents are charged with manifesting the same negative attitude toward God's messengers as was exhibited by those who killed the prophets of earlier generations. The legendary tradition that Israel had always persecuted its prophets was well established in first-century Judaism (see comments on 21:33–46). In rejecting Jesus and his

270

disciples, the opponents are continuing the tradition. They will "fill up the measure," that is, complete the number of acts of rebellion that will bring upon them God's final judgment.

The Final Condemnation (23:34–39)

In Luke the woe concerning building the tombs of the prophets is followed immediately by a saying that Jesus attributes to another speaker in the past: "Therefore also the Wisdom of God said, 'I will send them prophets and apostles' " (Luke 11:49). In Matthew's version the saying is attributed to Jesus himself, and thus it refers more emphatically to the mission that his followers will conduct among their fellow Jews: "I am sending to you prophets and sages and scribes." Whereas the wisdom saying in Luke reports the negative reception in general terms, "some of whom they will kill and persecute," in Matthew this is expanded to include specific forms of persecution that were referred to in the mission discourse: "some of them you will flog in your synagogues and harry from town to town" (see 10:17, 23). By alluding in this way to the opening and closing lines of 10:17–23, Matthew perhaps intends that the whole paragraph about the persecution of Jewish-Christian missionaries be recalled. In this editing of the wisdom saying the Evangelist suggests that, while it may have originally referred to the ancient prophets (cf. II Chron. 36:15–16), he understands it as finding its ultimate fulfillment in the Christian mission to Israel. The violent rejection of the gospel will bring to an end the period of God's long-suffering with the murder of his messengers. Now divine vengeance will be wrought "on this generation." In this last phrase of the wisdom saying a subtle transition is made between the earlier part of the chapter, a condemnation of the Pharisees as teachers of Israel (see 23:2), and the conclusion, which pronounces judgment on the people as a whole. Because they have followed the Pharisees in rejecting Jesus and his missionaries the whole nation is doomed.

The Jerusalem saying (vv. 37–39) is found in a very different context in Luke (13:34–35). The Third Evangelist seems to have understood it as referring to the triumphal entry, at which time people greet Jesus with the shout, "Blessed is he who comes in the name of the Lord!" (Luke 19:38). By placing it as the capstone of the Messiah's valedictory address, Matthew gives the saying a much more pessimistic tone. God's punishment of Is-

271

rael for the rejection of Jesus and his messengers will include the abandonment of "your house" (v. 38). It is not clear whether Matthew understands this as referring to Jerusalem, the temple, or the nation as a whole, since each of these indirectly involves the others. The verse is especially ironic if Matthew hears in it an echo of Jer. 12:7, "I have forsaken my house, I have abandoned my heritage; I have given the beloved of my soul into the hands of her enemies." What God had called "my house" has been demoted to "your house." In view of Matthew's addition to the parable of the king's wedding feast in 22:7, it is probable that the Evangelist regarded 23:38 as anticipating the destruction of Jerusalem and the temple by the army of Titus in 70 C.E.

Because of the context in which Matthew has set it the final verse of the chapter is to be taken as referring to judgment, not to evangelism. Unlike Paul (see Romans 9–11), Matthew does not anticipate the conversion of Israel in the final moments of history. When they greet his return in glory with the acclamation, "Blessed is he who comes in the name of the Lord" it will be not with joy but with the gloom of the condemned who are compelled to honor their judge (cf. Phil. 2:10–11). Following this final word of condemnation, the Messiah literally abandons the temple and prophesies its destruction (24:1–2).

What is the intention of the bitter polemic of Matthew 23? While its narrative function is polemical (according to 23:1 it is addressed to the crowds and the disciples), it is contained in a book for Christians, not for Jews. From this perspective it is possible to view it primarily as apologetic rather than as polemic. It seeks to provide a theological explanation for the unhappy fact of history that the one whom Christians honor as Israel's Messiah was rejected by Israel, and those who subsequently announced his resurrection were violently rebuffed. The passage attempts to come to terms with this challenge to the church's faith by explaining, first, that the people had been misled by false teachers and, second, that the rejection of Jesus and his messengers was simply the final instance in a long history of Israel's mistreatment of God's prophets. Nevertheless the reverse side of this apologetic is undeniably polemic. The passage portrays Israel as bereft of God's healing presence.

While Matthew's negative theology concerning Israel is historically understandable in view of the unhappy experience of Jewish-Christian missionaries, his presentation of God's deselection of Israel must be placed within the broader context of

Paul's reflections on this question. Paul contended that Israel's negative response to the gospel can by no means deter a faithful God from pursuing his plan for Israel, "for the gifts and the call of God are irrevocable" (Rom. 11:29). The "hardening" that has come upon Israel provides the opportunity for taking the gospel to the Gentiles; when the full number of the Gentiles has entered the church, "all Israel will be saved" (Rom. 11:26). At that point, Matthew's polemic will have been superseded.

Matthew 24:1—25:46
The Discourse About the Messiah's Glorious Coming

The final collection of Jesus' teaching (an expanded form of Mark 13) is often referred to as "the apocalyptic discourse." The adjective "apocalyptic," derived from the Greek verb *apoka-lyptō* ("reveal, disclose"), is used by scholars of a genre of Jewish literature that flourished from 200 B.C.E. to 135 C.E. These apocalypses, of which only two were admitted to the biblical canon (Daniel and Revelation), purport to disclose divine secrets concerning God's plan for the denouement of history and the final judgment. Their intended function is to strengthen believers to remain faithful in difficult times by dramatizing the hope that God will indeed come and redeem his people. Despite its brevity, the apocalyptic discourse fulfills the same function. Although it speaks of a series of future events climaxing in the arrival of Jesus in glory, its emphasis is on exhortation to faithfulness, not on the disclosure of heavenly secrets. This is indicated not only by the amount of space devoted to parables about faithful waiting but also by the large number of imperatives scattered throughout the discourse.

In Matthew as in Mark the discourse is occasioned by an observation of the disciples concerning the impressiveness of the temple buildings. The complex on the temple mount, the result of Herod the Great's ambitious building program, was justly regarded as one of the most famous of the ancient world. Like a latter-day Jeremiah, Jesus predicts its total destruction (cf. Jer. 7:14). There is wide variation in the reports of Jesus'

273

prediction about the temple (see John 2:19; Acts 6:14), and Mark designates the version presented at the trial before the high priest "false testimony" (Mark 14:57–58; see comments on Matt. 26:61). Although uncertainty concerning the original wording must remain, there need be little doubt that Jesus made such a prediction. Implicit in the prophecy, as is explicit in Jeremiah's, is the conviction that the destruction will represent God's punishment of his people for their sin. In Matthew this understanding is indicated by the context; 24:2 must be read as the sequel to 23:34–39.

Since the focal point of Jesus' teaching was the arrival of the kingdom, his followers must inevitably have interpreted the temple saying as an *apocalyptic* prophecy, that is, the destruction of the temple will have been anticipated as a sign that God was about to come and establish his rule. After the resurrection experience assured them that Jesus was glorified at God's right hand (see comments on 26:64), many will have awaited the temple's annihilation as a prelude to the Messiah's glorious return.

Thus understood, the temple saying provides the basis for the apocalyptic discourse, which addresses two fundamental concerns of early Christians: When will Jesus come in glory, and what are we to do in the meantime? The structure, accordingly, is relatively simple: *(a)* events prior to the great tribulation (24:3–14); *(b)* the abomination and the great tribulation (24:15–28); *(c)* Jesus' coming in glory (24:29–31); *(d)* the time when all this will happen (24:32–44); *(e)* three parables about faithful waiting (24:45—25:30); and *(f)* the judgment of the pagans (25:31–46).

Events Prior to the Great Tribulation (24:3–14)

In Mark the discourse is introduced by the disciples' request, "Tell us when this will be, and what will be the sign when all these things are about to be accomplished" (Mark 13:4). That is, the basic question concerns not the coming of the Messiah in glory but the destruction of the temple. Nevertheless the reference to "all these things" implies that the temple's toppling will be part of a complex of apocalyptic events that will include Jesus' return. The burning of the temple by the Romans required a reassessment of this expectation. Matthew, accordingly, edits the disciples' request in order to distinguish clearly

274

between this past historical event and the apocalyptic signs and events that for him still lay in the future: "Tell us when this [the destruction of the temple] will be, and what will be the sign of your coming and the completion of the age." In what follows, no answer is given to the first of these two questions, since it is no longer of any interest to Matthew's readers; all attention is paid to the second.

It should not be too quickly assumed that some or all of the experiences prophesied in verses 5–14 had already occurred when Matthew wrote. The extensive history of the period by Josephus reports no incidents about persons claiming to be the Messiah, and Christian writings likewise provide no evidence of anyone pretending to be Jesus redivivus. It is probable, therefore, that the prediction of verse 5 remained unfulfilled. The same is true of verses 6–7. The Pax Romana had been reestablished at great cost in the war in Palestine. No other ethnic group in the Mediterranean basin dared to challenge the Roman military might. These verses contain a traditional apocalyptic motif, namely, that internecine strife will become rampant as the end of the old age approaches (a contemporary parallel can be found in *IV Ezra* 13:30–31). It presupposes the collapse of the Roman Empire. Earthquakes and famines were likewise stock items in apocalyptic portrayals of the future. This first group of signs is summarized by the notice that as a group they constitute "the beginning of the birth-pangs" (v. 8), that is, the violent pains accompanying the birth of the age to come out of the old age. These events will occur by divine necessity ("must be" in v. 6 seems to echo the Greek translation of Dan. 2:28, 45) but do not signal the Messiah's arrival. The end is not yet.

Matthew extensively revises the next paragraph, because he has already used Mark 13:9–13 in his missionary discourse at 10:17–22. By removing these verses from Mark's apocalyptic discourse, Matthew suggests that the persecution experienced by Christian missionaries at the hands of Jews is not an eschatological sign but simply part of the history of the church (this commentary assumes that the mission to Israel belongs largely to the past for Matthew; see comments on chap. 10). In the space left by the removal of the Markan verses, Matthew places several important motifs. In place of Jewish persecution, there is now a bloody Gentile persecution. Christians throughout the empire must have been severely shaken by news of Nero's

275

arbitrary and brutal punishment of Christians as scapegoats for the fire of Rome. Having already experienced the animosity of former friends and family as a result of their adoption of the Christian life-style (see I Peter 3:14–16; 4:3–4), Christians everywhere must have trembled at the expectation that verbal persecution might soon become transposed into pitiless violence, with or without the participation of the government. As far as we can tell from the evidence, however, there was no extensive persecution involving murder or execution from the time of Nero's bloodbath to Trajan's reign in the early second century (the alleged persecution under Domitian in the period 90–96 C.E. seems to be the figment of later imagination). We should assume, therefore, that the predictions of apostasy, betrayal, and hatred of verse 10 are likewise unfulfilled except for isolated cases.

Verse 11, on the other hand, apparently refers to a real and pressing danger as far as Matthew is concerned, since he has already warned his readers to be on the watch for false prophets (7:15–20). By this term he apparently means not people who make false predictions about the future but those who claim divine inspiration and thus the right to exercise religious leadership in Christian congregations yet whose lives are not in conformity with Jesus' ethical teaching (7:21–23).

This "lawlessness" of verse 12, modeled by the false prophets and imitated by their followers, constitutes in Matthew's view the most severe threat to the church, a threat far more serious than persecution. One of its worst effects is that "the love of the many" will grow cold. The standard translations take the genitive in this phrase as subjective, "most people's love," but in view of the way "the many" serves at Qumran as a designation for the total membership of the sect, we should consider the possibility that the genitive is objective: "the love for all the other members of the Christian fellowship." A religion that revels in exorcisms and healings but sits loose to the life-style challenge of the Sermon on the Mount easily degenerates into a pious self-centeredness that shows scant concern for the little ones in the congregation (see 18:1–14). To share in the age of salvation, one must *endure* (v. 13; cf. 10:22). This involves not only enduring persecution and other trials without giving up one's faith but also persisting in love despite all the hostility love encounters (see I Cor. 13:7: love *endures* all things).

The final verse of this section is in some respects the most

276

important for Matthew. He has expanded the brief comment of Mark 13:10, "And the gospel must first be preached to all the Gentiles," and moved it from its location in the middle of the paragraph on persecution to this climactic point, reinforcing its importance by the added note: "and *then* the end will come." For decades many in the church had been in a waiting mode, ever hopeful that Jesus' return was imminent. By the time the First Gospel was written, probably during the last two decades of the century, the church found it necessary to consider the possibility that the end might be many years hence. Matthew provides a theological explanation for the delay: it is a time for mission. The waiting must be active, not passive. All the Gentiles must be confronted with the gospel. Not until this task has been fulfilled can the eschatological drama move to its denouement.

The Abomination and the Great Tribulation (24:15–28)

When the mission to the Gentiles has been completed, the end will occur (v. 14). The final sign is the great tribulation, which itself is inaugurated by "the abomination of desolation."

It is sometimes argued that for Matthew the events of verses 15–21 have already occurred: "the abomination of desolation" refers either to the siege of Jerusalem or to the final capture of the temple by the armies of Titus and the offering of pagan sacrifice on the holy site; the flight that follows is either the migration of the Jerusalem church to Pella east of the Jordan prior to the siege or the escape of refugees following the fall of the city; the great tribulation of verse 21 describes the desperate situation in Palestine in the months following the Roman victory. All of this is most improbable. The flight of which verses 16–20 speak is not any historical event, and most certainly not the escape of refugees from the burning capital in the summer (not winter) of 70 C.E. It is not clear why Matthew's version adds "nor on a Sabbath" in verse 20, since it seems to acknowledge that the flight will take place whether it is winter or on a Sabbath or not, but it certainly indicates that the event has, for Matthew, not yet taken place; there would be no point in praying about a past event. No, it is best to treat these various events as representing familiar apocalyptic motifs.

277

"The abomination of desolation" (Dan. 12:11) referred to the setting up of a pagan altar on top of the high altar in Jerusalem (see I Macc. 1:54, 59). It may have been given a new application when Caligula attempted to have a statue of himself set up in the Jerusalem temple. Perhaps during the war with Rome some Jewish Christians used the phrase in fearful anticipation of the pagans' victory celebration. Christians probably understood the phrase in supernatural rather than natural terms, however. Second Thessalonians 2:3–4 speaks of the *revealing* of "the man of lawlessness," who "takes his seat in the temple of God, proclaiming himself to be God." This supernatural figure symbolizing all evil will be destroyed by Jesus at his glorious return (II Thess. 2:8). It seems likely, therefore, that Matthew understands the abomination of desolation as referring to some supernatural Antichrist. Because this ultimate manifestation of rebellion against God's authority will call down fire and brimstone from heaven as in the judgment of Sodom and Gomorrah, the motif of the abomination is followed by the motif of eschatological flight, which seems to have as its paradigm Lot's flight from Sodom (Gen. 19:17); the righteous will escape the judgment of the wicked only by hastily abandoning the condemned city (cf. Luke 17:32).

The motif of the "great tribulation" (v. 21) is probably inspired by Dan. 12:1: "And there shall be a time of trouble, such as never has been since there was a nation till that time." No details are given concerning this period of suffering. In contrast to the lurid depictions of Revelation, there is here only the notice that the duration of the tribulation has been cut short "for the sake of the elect." This notion may indirectly reflect another feature of the Sodom story. In Gen. 18:32 God assures Abraham that the presence of as few as ten righteous persons in the wicked city would secure for it a reprieve. In verses 23–28 Matthew combines material from Mark 13:21–23 with sayings found in Luke 17:23–24. The main point is obvious: Christians in Antioch and more distant cities need not be disturbed by rumors that Jesus has already returned and is hiding somewhere in Palestine. Like a bolt of lightning that illuminates the whole sky, his coming will be a supernatural event witnessed by all, whatever their location. The prophesied rumors presuppose that the Christ will be a purely human being, one who may conceal himself in an inner chamber. The promise is that Jesus, while fully human during his earthly life, will return

278

in supernatural glory that is beyond concealment. The statement about the carcass in verse 28 makes the same point: the glorified Jesus will be as obvious to the world as carrion to sharp-eyed vultures.

Jesus' Coming in Glory (24:29–31)

The end prophesied in verse 14, which will arrive immediately after the great tribulation (v. 29), will be marked by awesome celestial portents. Here Matthew's source draws on Old Testament prophecies concerning the day of the Lord, especially Isa. 13:9–10; 34:4. Israel's prophets spoke of "the day of Yahweh" as a day of divine vengeance on human sin (see, e.g., Isa. 13:6, 9; 34:8; Joel 1:15; Amos 5:18; Zech. 14:1; Mal. 4:5). Christians were able to appropriate these texts as referring to Jesus, since the Greek word *kyrios* ("lord") designated for them both the Lord Jesus and the Lord God. Paul writes about "the day of the Lord" with reference to Jesus' final coming (I Thess. 5:2; II Thess. 2:2; I Cor. 1:8; 5:5; II Cor. 1:14). Thus the astronomical catastrophes associated with the day of the Lord in the Old Testament are taken here as signaling the coming of Jesus.

"The sign of the Son of man" in verse 30 has puzzled many. Some have proposed that the verse prophesies that Jesus' cross will appear as a portent in the sky. This is not impossible, but it is more likely that the sign is the Son of man himself. In Isaiah 11, a passage that profoundly influenced messianic ideas, it is prophesied: "On that day the root of Jesse shall stand as an *ensign* to the peoples" (Isa. 11:10); "He will raise an *ensign* for the nations" (Isa. 11:12). In the second of these clauses the Greek translators employed *sēmeion*, the word translated "sign" in Matt. 24:30. We can paraphrase verse 30*a:* "And then shall appear in the sky the messianic sign of Isaiah 11 in the person of him who calls himself the Son of man." (For Matthew's understanding of "the Son of man" as Jesus' self-designation, see the Introduction.) It will be the appearance of the Crucified himself that will prompt the mourning of "all the tribes of the land" (v. 30*b*). The allusion here is to Zech. 12:10–14, where all the families of Israel mourn for one "whom they have pierced" (see also Rev. 1:7). In Matthew's understanding, the mourning is probably negative; the guilty look fearfully at the one who will avenge the killing of the Messiah.

Verse 30*c* alludes unmistakably to Dan. 7:13: "I saw in the

279

night visions, and behold, with the clouds of heaven there came one like a son of man, and he came to the Ancient of Days and was presented before him." In Daniel it is made clear that this man-like figure (in contrast to the four beasts mentioned earlier, who represent four successive world empires) symbolizes "the people of the saints of the Most High," that is, a purified Israel (see Dan. 7:14, 27). By the first century C.E., however, we have evidence that Dan. 7:13 was interpreted as referring to the Messiah. In *IV Ezra* 13:2–3 we read: "And this wind brought a human figure rising from the depths, and as I watched, this man came flying with the clouds of heaven" (NEB). Later in the chapter the author explains that the man from the sea stands for the eschatological rescuer whom God calls "My Son" (13:25–53). Although the journey on the clouds in Dan. 7:13 is from earth to heaven, apocalyptists like the author of *IV Ezra* and John the Divine had no difficulty in conceiving the figure as coming to earth (see Rev. 1:7). Early Christians found in Daniel's prophecy an important way of expressing their conviction that Jesus the Crucified would return as the glorified Messiah (see also 26:64). The last phrase of verse 30, "with power and great glory," is perhaps a short paraphrase of Dan. 7:14.

In view of Matthew's special interest in the last judgment (see comments on 7:21–23), it is remarkable that this short passage says nothing about Jesus coming to execute judgment on the wicked (apart from what is implied in the mourning of v. 30). The concluding verse is entirely positive: the Messiah will instruct the angels delegated to him by God to gather his "chosen ones" from every corner of the earth. The great blast of the trumpet here signals redemption, not judgment (see Isa. 27:13; *Pss. Sol.* 11:1; I Thess. 4:16; I Cor. 15:52).

The Time When All This Will Happen (24:32–44)

Instead of having Jesus dwell further on the exciting changes that will accompany his return in glory, the discourse now shows Jesus addressing the pressing question: When will all this happen? Thus a transition is provided between the eschatological predictions of the first half and the exhortations to faithful waiting that will dominate the last half of the discourse.

The brief fig tree parable relates primarily to verses 15–28; "all these things" in verse 33 looks back to the list of "signs" that will immediately precede the end. It provides no further clue concerning when the end will arrive but merely assures the readers that when they witness the final signs they will know that they need not wait much longer. The fig tree produces new foliage later than other deciduous trees in Palestine; the time between the appearance of leaves and the fig harvest is thus relatively short. When other trees are garbed in spring growth the stark fig branches appear dead. The final appearance of leaves provides assurance that there will indeed be a harvest.

Although no exact date (such as the destruction of the temple) is suggested, verse 34 solemnly promises that Jesus will return while some of his contemporaries are still alive (a reprise of 16:28). Since this prediction was not fulfilled, several proposals have been made with the intention of understanding the saying as still to be fulfilled. Some have argued, for example, that "this generation" refers not to Jesus' contemporaries but to the Jewish nation or to the church. The linguistic evidence in favor of such proposals is not impressive. Since some of Jesus' contemporaries were still alive when the First Gospel was penned, this prediction had not yet been falsified. The trustworthiness of the promise is underscored by a saying about the eternal validity of Jesus' teaching: "Heaven and earth will pass away, but my words will never pass away" (v. 35). It is possible that this saying originally had a very different context, where it referred not to eschatological predictions but to ethical instruction (compare the statement of 5:18 concerning the eternal validity of the Torah).

Did Matthew firmly believe that Jesus would return before the last of his contemporaries had died? We cannot answer this question. What we do know is that Matthew regarded the "delay" as a time of grace. God was postponing the last judgment so that many more might have a chance to hear and accept the gospel. It was a time for worldwide evangelism (24: 10; 28:19).

From the first days after the resurrection to our own time there have always been some Christians who were not satisfied with uncertainty concerning when the "second coming" will occur. In Luke's narrative of the ascension the disciples ask the risen Jesus, "Lord, will you at this time restore the kingdom to Israel?" His response is firm: "It is not for you to know times or seasons which the Father has fixed by his own authority. But you shall receive power . . . and you shall be my witnesses . . . to the end of the earth" (Acts 1:6–8). Not all have accepted

281

this counsel. Instead of concentrating on the task, they have tried to calculate the times. Drawing on apocalyptic prophecies from Daniel and Revelation, they have insisted that events in their own day were the fulfillment of biblical predictions and that Jesus was about to return. The fact that all previous interpretations have been falsified by the continuing "delay" of the second coming does not deter some in our own time from boldly continuing along the same path. The spiritual arrogance that presumes to pry into God's secret plan is roundly condemned by Matt. 24:36. Not even the Messiah knows when the end will occur! Not even the highest archangels are privy to the Father's intention! How foolish it is for humans to think they can play with biblical numbers and ambiguous prophecies and discover what was hidden even from Jesus!

Verse 36 has a second, still more important message for us. Since the emergence of the docetist heresy at the end of the first century there have always been Christians who have had difficulty believing that Jesus was fully human (it is probably for this reason that many ancient manuscripts of Matthew omit the phrase "nor the Son"; see the KJV). They have reasoned that when the Second Person of the Trinity came to live among us he must have retained his supernatural knowledge and power. He was not moved by ordinary human emotions and was incapable of anxiety because he knew the outcome of all future events. The Nicene and Chalcedonian creeds attempt to correct this misconception by insisting that Jesus was fully human as well as fully divine, that is, his divinity does not compromise his humanity at any point whatsoever. He was a genuine human being like us, or his death on the cross was a cruelly deceptive sham. The gospel testimony provides strong support for this view: Jesus did not know all things.

The remaining sayings of the paragraph stress the unexpectedness of Jesus' return. It will be as unexpected as the flood, which caught a careless and unprepared generation off guard. The same point is implicit in the picture of two men in the field and two women grinding meal; they are busy with their daily occupations when the Messiah arrives, and then it is too late to prepare oneself for the kingdom. Only those who are ready will participate. Although verses 40–41 may refer to the "rapture" described in I Thess. 4:17, a very different verb is used; the word here translated "taken" normally means "receive"; those who are ready are received into the Messiah's kingdom. In

282

verse 43 we encounter one of the favorite images for the unexpectedness of the Messiah's coming. In addition to the Gospel parallels, see I Thess. 5:2, 4; II Peter 3:10; Rev. 3:3; 16:15.

Three Parables About Faithful Waiting (24:45—25:30)

Most of the parables in the First Gospel are gathered in three collections, chief of which is the compilation in chapter 13. The remaining two consist of three parables each, all of them concerned directly or indirectly with the final judgment. The first trio (21:28—22:14), addressed to Jesus' opponents, warns of the judgment that will fall on those who reject him and his message. The second trio, appended to the apocalyptic discourse, reminds Christians that they too are accountable for their response to Jesus. The fact that they have accepted the gospel while others have rejected it is no cause for complacency, because genuine acceptance is a lifelong project. It is good to look forward to Jesus' coming in glory, but Christians must never forget that the day means judgment for them as well as for others. Only those who endure to the end will be saved (24:13).

The three parables of this final discourse are concerned with three different kinds of accountability that Christians must face up to as they prepare for the glorious day.

The Parable of the Slave Left in Charge (24:45-51)

There is a certain correspondence between the first of the final group of parables and the first of the earlier trio, the parable of the two sons (21:28-32). In both there is a sharp contrast between obedient and disobedient forms of behavior, and both are aimed at religious leaders.

The consensus that the parable is directed at religious leaders is based on the detail that the slave is set over the household to give the other slaves their food at the proper time. It appears likely that the allusion to food is intended as an allegorical reference to spiritual nourishment. The parable warns leaders not to grow slack in their ministry to other Christians simply because the day of reckoning seems to have been postponed.

283

The parable concludes with a harsh punishment. Verse 51*a* means literally "and he will be cut in two." It is not necessary, however, to take the verb so literally. It is probably a hyperbole of a kind common in everyday speech ("I'll break every bone in your body!"). A second element of the punishment, while not sounding as brutal, is just as severe: the faithful servant will be placed "with the hypocrites." This is probably intended as a reminiscence of the denunciation of chapter 23. Christian leaders who betray their master's trust will fare no better than "the scribes and Pharisees," the "hypocrites" whose lives (including teaching as well as conduct) do not conform to the faith they profess (see comments on 23:13–33). The point of the parable is clear. Those appointed to spiritual leadership in the church must treat their responsibility with the greatest seriousness (cf. 18:6–9).

The Wise and Foolish Virgins (25:1–13)

It has become customary for modern English translations to render *parthenoi* as "girls," "maidens," or even "bridesmaids" (NRSV). The NIV follows the KJV in translating the word literally: "virgins." Since a common Greek word for "young women" was available, Matthew's choice of the word meaning specifically "virgin" was perhaps deliberate because of its symbolic value. In II Cor. 11:2 Paul compares the Corinthian congregation to a virgin: "I promised you in marriage to one husband, to present you as a chaste virgin to Christ" (NRSV).

By appending the parable to the apocalyptic discourse, Matthew demonstrates that he regards it as further commentary on the sayings of 24:42–44 concerning being watchful and ready for Jesus' return. It is probable, therefore, that certain details of the parable are allegorical for Matthew. The virgins represent Christians who await the bridegroom, Jesus the Messiah (for the bridegroom metaphor, see also 9:15; John 3:29; it is implicit in II Cor. 11:2; Eph. 5:27; Rev. 19:7, 9). The bridegroom's delay (v. 5) alludes to the fact that Jesus has not returned as soon as many had hoped. The marriage feast symbolizes the life of the age to come. The closed door stands for the last judgment.

Less certainty, however, surrounds the allegorical significance of the key element in the story—the extra oil that the wise virgins have and the foolish do not—since this is not a stock metaphor. Luther urged that the oil represents faith. Spiritual piety has also been proposed. In view of 24:12, "the love of the many will grow cold," it is possible that the oil that causes the

284

lamps of the wise virgins to continue to burn brightly is enduring love (see I Cor. 13:7–8). The most popular suggestion is that
Matthew regards the oil as standing for good works. Support for
this proposal is found in several earlier passages. At the beginning of the Sermon on the Mount, Jesus' followers are urged to
let their light so shine that people will see their good works and
glorify their Father in heaven (5:16), and at its conclusion a
parable contrasts wise and foolish builders (the same adjectives
as in 25:2), comparing them to hearers who do or do not do what
Jesus says (7:24–27). The entreaty of the foolish virgins, "Lord,
Lord, open to us" (25:11), is reminiscent of the false Christians
of 7:21–23, who address Jesus as "Lord, Lord," but fail to do the
will of the heavenly Father. Finally, a parallel is seen between
the virgins without oil and the guest without a wedding garment in 22:11–14; what is lacking in both cases must be good
deeds.

Attractive as this proposal is, it is flawed by the fact that it
is in tension with other details of the story. One commentator
justly asks, Do good deeds burn out before the final judgment?
Can they be bought at the store? (Susan Marie Praeder, *The
Word in Women's Worlds,* p. 96). It is better to take the oil not
allegorically but parabolically. The main point of the story is
that the foolish virgins are not ready when the great moment
finally arrives. Undoubtedly Matthew understood being ready
as involving a tireless performance of good works, but he surely
included other obligations as well: abstinence from bad behavior (15:19), love for enemies (5:44), love of other Christians
(24:12), forgiveness of others (18:21–35), unhesitating faith (21:
21), loyalty to Jesus (10:32), and love for God (22:37).

Also dubious is the allegorical interpretation of the sleeping
(v. 5) and rising (v. 7) of the virgins as alluding to death and
resurrection. While this proposal, unlike the suggestion about
the oil, has the advantage that a stock metaphor is involved
("sleep" is a frequent metaphor for death; see 27:52), it spoils
the story to conceive of the dialogue of verses 8–9 and the
departure to the stores as occurring after the resurrection. The
sleeping of the virgins is simply a narrative detail that fills in the
time between the commencement of the waiting and the bridegroom's arrival. Despite the attached command "Watch!" (v.
13), the sleeping of the foolish virgins is not the source of their
problem, since the wise sleep also. Being watchful means being
ready at all times, whether waking or sleeping.

285

INTERPRETATION

Whatever may have been its earlier application, in Matthew's use the parable refers to rank-and-file Christians—not to church leaders as in the preceding parable, nor to people with special gifts as in the following one, but to ordinary followers of Jesus who must persevere in their doing and being until Jesus comes, no matter how long the delay may be. It is those who endure to the end who will be saved (24:13).

The Parable of the Talents (25:14–30)

The third in the series of judgment parables focuses not on the accountability of church leaders as does the first (24:45–51), nor on the general responsibilities of ordinary Christians as does the second (25:1–13), but on the obligations of those who have been granted special gifts.

As with the preceding parables, we can assume that several of these details have allegorical significance for Matthew. According to verse 15 the servants are entrusted with large amounts of money (contrast Luke 19:11–27). A talent was equivalent to approximately 6,000 denarii, that is, the earnings of a day laborer for twenty years (see 20:2). In Luke each slave is given one mina (approximately 100 denarii). The use of talents instead of minas not only gives added interest to the story as story but undoubtedly has allegorical meaning; the immensity of the sum is intended to remind us of the preciousness of the gifts that God has entrusted to our care.

Whereas each slave gets the same amount in Luke, in Matthew the three are given different sums, "to each according to his ability" (v. 15). This detail suggests that Matthew regards the entrusted money as representing different gifts, not something shared equally by all Christians, such as the gospel or the gift of life. The differing gifts are wisely conferred; no servant is given more than he is capable of handling. Even the one with the least ability is given a significant responsibility, an honor for which he should be grateful. To be entrusted with a mere quarter of a million dollars is not something to be resentful over!

In Luke instructions are given by the departing slaveholder: "Do business with these until I come back" (Luke 19:13, NRSV), but in Matthew the determination of what is to be done with the money is left to each person's initiative. Concerning the first slave Matthew reports: "Immediately the one who received five talents went off and worked with them and gained five more." No attempt is made to describe how the slave dou-

286

bled his money; all emphasis is laid on the fact that he *worked*. The allegorical significance of this detail is not certain, but probably the Evangelist understands it as referring to Christian service.

The first and second servants are rewarded for their faithful labor with a warm commendation and an invitation, "Enter into the joy of your master." This probably takes us beyond the parable setting (a rich man settling accounts with his slaves) into Christian expectation regarding the Messiah's victory banquet. Jesus' worthy servants are invited to join him at table in the kingdom of heaven (the verb "enter into" is the one used in 18:3 with respect to entering the kingdom of heaven).

Despite this reference to the joy that faithful servants will share with their master, the parable gives far more attention to the negative example and disastrous fate of the third slave. For this reason it is justly called a parable of judgment. Of central importance is the dialogue between the unfaithful slave and his master. The slave rationalizes his failure to do anything with the talent entrusted to him by blaming his master! His master is a harsh and rapacious businessman, a "sharp dealer" who extracts far more from a business transaction than is his proper due ("reaping where you did not sow, and gathering where you did not winnow"); the master's assignment is therefore no privilege or honor but a terrifying responsibility because failure may entail severe punishment. By burying the talent, he has preserved the capital for his master. "Look, you have what is yours!" With these words taken from commercial language the servant disclaims any further responsibility for the money. He may even be expecting to be commended for showing such prudence and returning the capital intact. The slaveholder answers the unproductive slave using his own words against him (except that the adjective translated as "harsh" or "hard" is dropped as inappropriate in an allegorical allusion to God or the Messiah). Whereas the slave characterized himself as being (justly) afraid, the master calls him *lazy*. At the very least the slave should have taken the trouble to place the money in a safe investment with bankers, so that a small profit would have been made.

The parable makes no attempt to examine the causes of the slave's laziness, but one factor is evident from the dialogue: the slave has no love for his master. He is really interested only in himself, and consequently security, not service, is his goal.

287

There is not the slightest trace of gratitude that his master trusted him with so great a sum. Respect for his master is limited to a grudging acknowledgment of power.

If we are correct in taking the phrase "to each according to his ability" as indicating that for Matthew the parable challenges Christians to make full use of the gifts that God has entrusted to them, the portrayal of the third servant reminds us that love for our master must be demonstrated in faithful and untiring service to other people.

It is routine for Christians to excuse themselves by protesting that their gifts are too modest to be significant. This parable insists that the gifts are precious and are to be exploited to the full. "As *each* has received a gift, employ it for one another, as good stewards of God's varied grace" (I Peter 4:10; see also I Cor. 12:7; Eph. 4:7).

The Judgment of the Pagans (25:31–46)

It is customary to interpret this passage in universal terms: at the last judgment all will be judged on the basis of how they have treated the needy and distressed. This understanding has inspired generations of Christians to pay closer attention to their sins of omission instead of concentrating exclusively on sins of commission (adultery, dishonesty, bad temper, lying, etc.). This passage reminds us that what we don't do also gets us into trouble!

While this interpretation provides a very needed corrective by placing such a high priority on service to the poor and distraught, it involves several problems that must be acknowledged. First, there is nothing specifically Christian about the passage so interpreted. Even the ancient Egyptians believed that such good deeds would win them life after death. Faith plays no role. Second, this view ignores the fact that the preceding chapters suggest other grounds for judgment. Jews will be judged on the basis of their rejection of the Messiah (23:29–39). Christians will be evaluated regarding their faithfulness to Christ, their performance of assigned tasks (24:45–51; 25:14–30), and their avoidance of bad behavior, as well as on the basis of their good deeds (25:1–13). Matthew certainly does not wish to suggest that Christians have no other obligation than to help the needy. Third, while the phrase "all the nations" could theoretically mean "everyone," this is most improbable for

288

verse 32. If this had been Matthew's meaning, he should have written *pantes* ("all"), because *ethnē* ("nations") had in Jewish Greek become a technical term designating non-Jewish individuals. It rendered the Hebrew *goyyim,* which by the first century regularly meant "Gentiles." Even the KJV correctly translates the term in 10:5, "Go not into the way of the Gentiles," where it is not a question of foreign nations but of Gentile neighborhoods in Galilee and its environs. Unless the context clearly indicates otherwise, it is proper to take *ethnē* in each of its occurrences as meaning Gentiles rather than collective national entities (see esp. 24:9, 14; 28:19). Translators shrink from so rendering it in 25:32, because it is assumed that the judgment involves all human beings. This is an unjustified presupposition. Jewish and Christian apocalyptic writings often speak of two or more judgments, sometimes explicitly differentiating the judgment of Israel from the judgment of the Gentiles. Paul apparently makes such a distinction in Rom. 2:1–11 ("the Jew first, and also the Greek").

If "all the Gentiles" excludes Jews, it must also exclude Jewish Christians and therefore Christians in general, who will be judged according to the criteria established by the Sermon on the Mount and other teachings of Jesus. "All the Gentiles" thus refers to pagans who are neither Jewish proselytes nor converts to Christianity.

A number of ancient Jewish texts express concern for "righteous Gentiles." Jews living in contact with pagans were not slow to observe that, despite their idolatry, some pagans were genuinely good people. Was it fair for them to be eternally damned? Paul echoes this concern in Rom. 2:14–16, where he suggests that Gentiles who have no relationship to Torah may yet fulfill its ethical requirements and thus be excused. Matthew's use of "the righteous" in the concluding line of the passage may reflect this perspective on the problem of righteous pagans.

Scholars who interpret "all the nations" as referring to pagans usually understand "the least of these my brethren" as a reference to Christian missionaries. Matthew regularly uses *adelphoi* ("brothers [and sisters]") as a designation for members of the Christian fellowship except in the few instances where it refers to blood brothers. "Least" is similar to "little" in 18:6, 10, 14, where reference is made to vulnerable members of the fellowship. Perhaps what "the least of these my brethren" and

289

"the little ones" have in common is poverty. In the case of missionaries it is voluntary poverty; they have abandoned their usual vocations and "travel light," as prescribed by Jesus in 10:8–9, and are thus totally dependent on the hospitality of those among whom they proclaim the gospel. The passage is intended by Matthew to encourage these vulnerable missionaries by announcing that pagans will be judged on the basis of how they treat these "least" of Jesus' followers. Strong support for this interpretation, it is argued, is found in 10:40–42: "He who receives you receives me, and he who receives me receives him who sent me. . . . And whoever gives to one of these little ones even a cup of cold water because he is a disciple, truly, I say to you, he shall not lose his reward."

This may well be a correct interpretation of "the least of these my brethren," but questions still remain. There is less cause for astonishment on the part of both "the blessed" and "the cursed" if it is a matter of how they have treated Christ's announced representatives. They *know* how they have treated the missionaries! The motif of astonishment is much more credible if those addressed had no notion that the persons they helped or refused to help had any relationship to the one whom Christians proclaimed as the judge of the living and the dead. Second, if Matthew is concerned about the problem of the righteous Gentiles, it seems improbable that he would limit the good deeds worthy of divine reward to those performed for Christians. Such a self-serving restriction does not fit well with Matthew's high moral vision as reflected in the Sermon on the Mount and elsewhere. While Jesus expresses solidarity with his messengers in 10:40–42, the same kind of language is used regarding children in 18:5: "Whoever receives one such child in my name receives me"; here, as in the parallel in Mark 9:37, "child" is to be taken literally (see also Matt. 19:14). It is not because of a faith relationship but because of their vulnerability that Jesus identifies himself with children. It appears more probable, therefore, that Matthew intends "brothers" in 25:40 to be taken in a much broader sense than is usual in his Gospel: the poor and the distressed, whoever they may be, should be regarded as Jesus' brothers and sisters.

There is nothing uniquely Christian about the idea of Jesus' solidarity with his messengers; it reflects the Jewish *shaliach* principle: "A man's representative is as the man himself." What is distinctive about Matt. 18:5 is the notion that vulnerable

290

children who have no conscious relationship to him are none-theless his "representatives." In 25:31–46 this remarkable prin-ciple is extended to include all the world's powerless and needy.

Because of this solidarity principle, the good deeds per-formed by pagans are not treated as atoning for their sins, nor as evidence that they imitate God, but as indicating *a relation-ship with Jesus!* Although they knew it not, the righteous pa-gans were serving him by helping those with whom he identified. Although their case is anomalous, they are in a lim-ited sense "in Christ" (to borrow Paul's language) by means of this service. They are "anonymous Christians."

If this understanding is correct, the passage offers encour-agement to Christians who participate in dialogue with mem-bers of non-Christian faiths. If some are disappointed that the usual interpretation has been abandoned, they need only re-member that no less is expected of Jesus' confessing followers than of "the righteous pagans."

The Messiah's Ill-Treatment and Execution

MATTHEW 26:1—27:66

Central to the Christian story, according to I Cor. 15:3, is that "Christ died for our sins in accordance with the scriptures." The apostle is here satisfied with the bare fact (plus its interpre-tation), but undoubtedly in oral presentations he and others provided details about the events that culminated in the cruci-fixion. The passion narrative was probably the earliest con-nected sequence of oral traditions about Jesus (as distinct from individual anecdotes transmitted without any connection to a sequence of events).

There are fascinating differences in detail in the four writ-ten versions of this complex of traditions. Although Matthew and Luke seem to be following Mark's version most of the time, their additions and subtractions are significant. John's passion narrative is independent, yet it parallels Mark's at many points

291

and agrees with Matthew or Luke in various details. Behind the four can be seen a common core.

None of the Gospel passion narratives pretends to be an objective historical account. All are firmly rooted in certain basic facts, but their intention is to *interpret* history, not simply to report it. Powerful theological motives are at work in the telling of the story. One is indicated by Paul's phrase quoted above: "according to the scriptures." Over and over again the way the story is told is colored by important texts from the Old Testament, by means of which early Christians were assured that what had happened to Jesus was in accordance with God's plan of salvation. As we read Matthew's passion narrative we will be watching carefully for indications of the Evangelist's theological appropriation of the traditions.

Matthew 26:1–16
The Plot Thickens

Whereas Mark's passion narrative begins abruptly with the plotting of Jesus' enemies, Matthew provides a formal introduction that sets the tone for what ensues. In verse 1 he supplies his customary formula as a transition between the preceding discourse and the following narrative (see 7:28; 11:1; 13:53; 19:1), adding, however, one word: "When Jesus had finished *all* these sayings." This may be meant to indicate that Jesus' teaching ministry has now been completed and it is time for him to die (for a possible parallel, see Deut. 32:45–52).

In verse 2 Jesus solemnly announces the beginning of his passion, using the present tense of the verb, "the Son of man *is being delivered up*" (a future formulation was employed in 17:22; 20:18). A direct connection with Passover is indicated. Although Matthew does not explicitly exploit the motif, we can assume that, like Paul, he saw theological significance in the fact that it was at Passover, not at some other time, that Jesus was "sacrificed" in Jerusalem (cf. I Cor. 5:7: "For Christ, our passover [lamb], has been sacrificed"). It was customary for the procurator to station extra troops in Jerusalem at Passover because of the excitability of the crowds at that time. This unrest was probably due to the widespread expectation that the Mes-

292

siah would appear at Passover. Christians were mindful of the fact that the Messiah had indeed appeared at Passover, not in glory but in shameful humiliation, enthroned on a cross.

It is only after Jesus has made this announcement that his enemies can plot his death (v. 4). Here and throughout the passion narrative the Pharisees, his primary opponents in the earlier chapters, are noticeably absent. The culprits are "the chief priests" (meaning not only the reigning high priest but members of the few priestly families from which the high priest was selected) and "the elders of the people" (replacing Mark's "scribes," perhaps to implicate the people as a whole through these representatives).

The word in verse 4 translated "stealth" in the RSV and the NRSV, "secretly" in TEV, and "in some sly way" in the NIV, literally means "by deception" and may refer to both verbs. We could paraphrase: "and they deliberated how they might arrest and kill Jesus on a trumped-up charge." This suggestion, while attractive, is rendered unlikely by verse 5, where the concern is not the excuse for an arrest but its publicity; "not during the feast" means "not in the presence of the Passover crowds," from which the conspirators fear a violent reaction (see also Luke 22:6).

Whereas in Luke the leaders' plot and the offer of assistance by Judas are combined (Luke 22:2–6), in Matthew (as in Mark) these are separated by the anointing in Bethany (vv. 6–13). The intention seems to be to present this story as a bright foil to the dark plotting of the enemies and Judas.

No interest is shown in the woman's motive. Enticing is the conjecture that the woman means to anoint Jesus as king (see I Sam. 10:1; 16:13; I Kings 1:39; II Kings 9:6), but nothing in the text supports this proposal. Does the woman intend to anoint his body for burial, as Jesus suggests? This, too, cannot be demonstrated from the text; it looks, rather, as if Jesus announces the significance of her act as something unknown to her. Matthew shows no interest in naming a motive. Presumably he, like his readers ancient and modern, regarded the anointing simply as an act of love.

In Mark objections to this lavish "waste" of money are raised by unnamed spectators (Mark 14:4; in John 12:4 it is Judas who decries the gift). Matthew implicates "his disciples." As often in the First Gospel, the disciples, in their weaknesses and strengths, represent Christians in Matthew's church. The

293

voiced objection is soundly based on concern for the poor. Although almsgiving was encouraged at all times, there was a special emphasis on giving to the poor during Passover week.

Jesus defends the woman by maintaining that she has done a "good work" ("a beautiful thing," RSV and NIV, misses the point). The rabbis discussed the relative importance of two kinds of "good works": giving money to the poor and burying the dead. The latter was given a higher priority, because it could not, like almsgiving, be done at any time but only at the required time, and also because it involved personal service, not an impersonal gift of money. "The poor you have with you always" is by no means a cynical, anti-utopian statement but a simple recognition that giving to the poor is an ongoing obligation, not one that has to be done at the right time or not at all. Without knowing it, the woman has performed the superior "good work" by preparing his body for burial at the right time.

The last verse of the paragraph promises that the unnamed woman will be remembered wherever "this gospel," that is, the story about Jesus that culminates in the passion narrative, is proclaimed. Sad to say, her name, like the names of many other women mentioned in the Gospel (8:14; 9:18, 20; 15:22), was not remembered. Like the tomb of the unknown soldier, this nameless woman stands for many who responded to Jesus' ministry with enthusiasm and who served him with love (see 27:55).

The women of the passion narrative come off much better than the men. They are more loyal and unselfish, and braver. Here the contrast is shocking. The men quibble over the legitimacy of a generous act of love, while the woman manifests the true spirit of discipleship!

The contrast is even sharper between the woman, who cannot qualify as a member of the Twelve because of her gender, and Judas, whose treachery is underscored by the note "one of the Twelve" (v. 14). She lavishes her money on a gift for her Master; he bargains away his teacher for a paltry thirty pieces of silver. The value of the contract is uncertain, since Matthew does not specify the denomination of the coins. It is postulated that Tyrian shekels (a shekel was worth about four denarii, i.e., four days' minimum wage) are meant because of the probable allusion to Zech. 11:12 here and in 27:9. In the Zechariah passage the amount is spoken of sarcastically as "the lordly price" (Zech. 11:13). Whereas in Zechariah the shepherd is paid thirty shekels, in Matthew Israel's shepherd (a common metaphor for the king—see Ezek. 34:23) is sold for this amount.

294

As in the case of the woman, no attempt is made to supply a motive for Judas' treachery. In view of John 12:6 it is often suggested that the motive was nothing more complicated than lust for money, yet this seems improbable in view of the modest size of the bribe, the subsequent return of the money (27:3), and the fact that Judas had doubtlessly already made a considerable financial sacrifice by leaving all to follow Jesus. Others propose that Judas was angered by his master's refusal to assume the role of a conquering hero, but Jesus' posture must have been obvious from the beginning in view of his teaching about nonresistance and love for enemies (5:38–48). Yet another proposal is that Judas hoped to compel a miraculous event of redemption by forcing God to come to Jesus' aid. Matthew is less interested in such speculations than we are. He is apparently content to grant that there is a mystery about evil that is beyond human fathoming. "The heart is deceitful above all things, and desperately corrupt; who can understand it?" (Jer. 17:9).

Matthew 26:17–75
The Night of the Messiah's Arrest

The story of Jesus' last night has many scenes, beginning with the disciples' preparation of the Passover seder and concluding with the sorry tale of Peter's denial. The mood throughout is somber, yet the story is shot through with the conviction that what is happening is not mere happenstance or blind fate but in some mysterious way the outworking of God's plan for the world.

The Last Supper (26:17–30)

The brief narrative about the preparations for Jesus' last meal with his disciples manifests little interest in historical questions. Modern Christians are apt to ask: Did Jesus have a personal relationship with the owner of the "upper room" (Mark 14:15) from previous visits to the city? Is the information concerning the location kept secret because Jesus does not want the meal to be interrupted by his enemies? It is pointless to pose such questions to the text. The passage is concerned simply to present Jesus as in charge of the situation and the disciples as

295

obedient. Matthew reinforces this impression by subtly changing Mark's question, "Where is my guest room, where I am to eat the passover with my disciples?" (Mark 14:14), to a royal statement of intention: "I will keep the passover at your house with my disciples" (v. 18). To this the Evangelist prefaces another passion announcement: "My time *(kairos)* is at hand." Although *kairos,* meaning "special time" or "season," is often used in a general, unemphasized sense, here it is surely used with theological force. Jesus' *kairos* is the focal point in God's salvation history. It is the time of his being "delivered up," which begins with the betrayal and arrest but is consummated on the cross (see 17:22; 20:18; 26:2, 45; Rom. 8:32).

The RSV translators seem to have been influenced by Leonardo da Vinci's famous painting of the Last Supper in verse 20, "he sat at table"! There is no mention of a table in the Greek text, and the verb means "reclined" (the NIV translates correctly). Although Jews sat at tables for ordinary meals, on festive occasions it was customary to imitate the Greco-Roman practice of reclining on low sofas or cushions. At Passover this became a requirement, to remind participants that the exodus had made them as free as any in the pagan world. That Jesus reclined at this meal is made even clearer in John 13:23, where it is reported that the beloved disciple "was lying close to the breast of Jesus."

It is only after the meal has commenced that Jesus announces that one of his closest followers is about to *deliver* him *up* (using *paradidōmi* as in 17:22; 20:18; 26:2, 45). The scandal is intensified by the fact that the traitor, despite his nefarious conspiracy, nonetheless shares the meal. Eating together implied "friendship," that is, the renunciation of hostile intentions. The cultural standard reflected in Ps. 41:9 (cited in the parallel at John 13:18) is implicit in the narrative: "Even my bosom friend in whom I trusted, who ate of my bread, has lifted his heel against me." The disciples' response as reported by Mark 14:19 is expanded by Matthew in two significant ways: the loyal disciples address Jesus as *Lord* one after another (instead of in chorus), and Judas is then marked as the traitor by calling his master "Rabbi" instead of "Lord" (see also 26:49). In the First Gospel it is usually unbelievers who address Jesus as "Master," "Teacher," or "Rabbi" (see 22:24, 36; for a possible exception, see 8:19).

Judas' question is as hypocritical as his kiss in Gethsemane.

He knows the answer! Jesus' response, "You said it," is a qualified affirmative that places responsibility on the speaker: "Your
own words point to the truth" (see also 26:64; 27:11). There is
no expression of outrage from the other disciples (and no indication of an exit by Judas), because Jesus' foreknowledge of the
betrayal indicates that it is part of the foreordained way of
suffering he must follow: "The Son of man goes *as it is written
of him*" (v. 24). Matthew supplies no hint concerning which
scriptural passage is in mind. One possibility is the Greek translation of Isa. 53:12, in which "delivered up" occurs twice: "because his soul was delivered up unto death, and he was
numbered among the lawless; and he bore the sins of many, and
on account of their sins he was delivered up."

Although the Last Supper is a seder, Matthew feels no need
to refer to the four cups of wine, the bitter herbs, and the other
elements of the traditional Passover meal. Not even the roasted
lamb is mentioned. There is, however, an allusion to the dip-
ping into a bowl (v. 23); following the first cup of wine and the
recital of the *kiddush* (sanctification), each participant dipped
a vegetable into salt water, as a way of recalling the crossing of
the sea in the escape from slavery. A piece of *matzah* (unleav-
ened bread) was then consumed in recollection of the haste
with which Israel left Egypt. An indispensable feature of the
seder, then as now, was the interpretation of these various details of the meal, a responsibility that fell to the father of a
household or to the host in a larger gathering. Jesus naturally
assumed this role. Imagine the startled response of the disciples
when the host, taking the *matzah*, made no mention of the
ancient exodus but instead solemnly declared, "This is my
body." Implicit in this radical reinterpretation of the Passover
matzah may be seen the announcement: "By means of my
imminent death a new exodus will occur."

After the main course (the lamb) was eaten, a second cup
was served. This was the most important of the four, because it
was the occasion for narrating the exodus story and reciting
prayers for the future redemption of Israel (which was anticipated as a reprise of the liberation from Egypt). In many house-
holds there may have been a prayer for the coming of the
Messiah, since it was widely believed that the Lord's Anointed
would appear at Passover. A first-century rabbi is reported to
have said, "On this night they were saved; on this night they
will be saved."

It was probably this second cup which Jesus reinterpreted for his followers (see I Cor. 11:25, "after supper"). As we seek to understand the cup word it is important to remember the double orientation of the second cup of the seder: it looks back gratefully to God's past saving act and eagerly anticipates the future redemption. The cup was filled with red wine, symbolic of the blood of the "passover"; the blood of lambs, sprinkled on the doorposts and lintels of Israelite homes, had been the means by which the avenging angel had "passed over" Israel (Exod. 12:13). The phrase "the blood of the covenant" is not used in this part of the exodus story. It does occur, however, in a later chapter (Exod. 24:8) in connection with the covenant at Sinai. Since the acceptance of God's laws at Sinai was part of the exodus event in the broader sense, there may have been a tendency to expand the phrase "the blood of the covenant" to include the passover blood. Jesus' word, however, makes no reference to the past but is focused exclusively on the future: "This is *my* blood of the covenant, which is poured out for many" (Mark 14:24). Implicit is a reference to God's future saving act: just as the blood of the passover lambs had been a sign of salvation at the beginning of Israel's history, so Jesus' blood, when "poured out for many," would be the sign of God's end-time saving work. Also implicit is the notion that this covenant will in some sense replace the prior covenant and therefore be "new" (see I Cor. 11:25; Jer. 31:31–34). Although Matthew does not insert the word "new," he clarifies the function of "my blood of the covenant" by adding "for the forgiveness of sins." The deliverance to be effected by the Messiah's death will not be like the first exodus; it will deal not with slavery to Pharaoh or any other external enemy but with slavery to sin (cf. Matt. 1:21).

Although Jesus' death inaugurated a new covenantal relationship between God and the human race, sin and death are still real enemies. The final saying of the Last Supper reminds us that our orientation is still toward the future when "the kingdom of my Father" will be fully established. Like the seder, the Lord's Supper is a grateful remembering, but it is also a joyful anticipation (cf. I Cor. 11:26).

Theologians speak of the Lord's Supper as the sacrament of the real presence of Christ. This important truth must be balanced by another. In a certain sense it is the sacrament of the real absence of Christ. The eucharistic service forcefully re-

298

minds us that Jesus was violently removed from our midst. Despite his spiritual presence (18:20; 28:20), he is our absent Lord. During his absence we continue to walk the way of the cross, accepting heartache and suffering as unavoidable ingredients of discipleship (see 16:24). We look forward to his coming in the kingdom of his Father, when suffering will be no more (Rev. 21:3–4).

The Prophecy of Desertion and Denial (26:31–35)

This transitional passage prepares the readers for the disciples' flight (v. 56) and Peter's denial (vv. 69–75) by reporting that Jesus foresaw these scandalous events and regarded them as elements of God's mysterious plan as announced in Scripture.

The exact meaning of the first part of Jesus' statement in verse 31 is uncertain (lit., "you will all be scandalized in me"). The same construction in 11:6 is translated by the RSV: "And blessed is he who takes no offense at me" (similarly, in 13:57), but here the RSV reads: "You will all fall away because of me." Perhaps the best parallel is provided not by 11:6 and 13:57 (despite their use of "in me") but by 13:21: "when tribulation or persecution arises on account of the word, immediately that person *is scandalized*"; the context suggests that the believer in question, lacking the power to endure, ceases to be a believer and drops out of the fellowship (see also 24:10, where persecution is again the occasion for being "scandalized"). Consequently the NEB boldly translates: "Tonight you will all fall from your faith on my account" (REB: "lose faith because of me") and the NRSV has: "You will all become deserters because of me this night." The disciples had come to believe that Jesus was the long-awaited Messiah through whom God would establish the golden age. This night (and on the morrow) this faith would be shaken to its foundations. How could Jesus be the Messiah if he refused to exercise divine power against his enemies? And how could God be worthy of worship if he abandoned this holy man to disgrace and suffering? Their disillusionment would be profound.

The prediction of the collapse of the disciples' faith is supported by a quotation from Zech. 13:7. In the Hebrew and Greek versions of Zechariah the opening verb is imperative ("*Strike* the shepherd"), but here in Matthew (as in Mark 14:27) the action is attributed to God: "*I will strike* the shepherd." The

299

deepest mystery of the passion story is that God uses the evil actions of Jesus' enemies and his faithless disciples to accomplish the purposes of salvation history.

As in the primary passion announcements (16:21; 17:22–23; 20:18–19), this prophecy of the disciples' apostasy is accompanied by a prediction of the resurrection (v. 32). The promise "I will go before you to Galilee," which will be reiterated by the angel in 28:7, assures the disciples that their desertion will not be permanent. In Galilee they will be restored to fellowship with Jesus, although on an entirely new basis.

Peter's bravado is understandable, almost admirable. "Even if I must die with you, I will not deny you" (v. 35). Because of Jesus' prophecies of desertion and denial, however, the readers know that this brave promise is ill-founded. It is based on Peter's ego, not on a power beyond his own. We are thus prepared for the next scene, in which Jesus prays earnestly and Peter sleeps.

Gethsemane (26:36–46)

The Gethsemane narrative makes a significant contribution to a sound Christology by reminding us that Jesus was a genuine human being. As Nicene Christians we affirm both the divinity and the humanity of Jesus, but our reverence tends to cloud the distinction and we "divinize" the human nature. There are Christians who refuse to believe that Jesus could be anxious or fearful, "because he was God." This docetic tendency is theologically dangerous because it deprives Jesus' death of its saving significance. If Jesus was not fully human, the cross was an empty pantomime.

The dominant theme running through the passion narrative is predestinarian: "The Son of man goes as it is written of him" (26:24). With equanimity Jesus announces Judas' betrayal, the disciples' desertion, and Peter's denial, because everything that happens will be in accordance with God's plan. The Gethsemane narrative offers stiff resistance to this picture by reminding us that Jesus is free to rebel against God's will. He does not go to the cross as God's robot. If he submits to shame and torture rather than running away, it is because he learns through prayer to subordinate his will to God's.

300

By the standards of martyrological narrative, both Jewish and Christian, the Gethsemane narrative is not very edifying.

It does not portray Jesus as a hero of the faith who refuses to flinch even when faced with the severest torture. Neither is he presented as a powerful mystic who can rise above pain, numbing his senses by concentrated adoration of God. Instead, he appears as a normal human being, capable of fear and anxiety: "Distress and anguish overwhelmed him, and he said to them, 'My heart is ready to break with grief' " (vv. 37–38, REB). This unheroic description is supported by Heb. 5:7: "In the days of his flesh, Jesus offered up prayers and supplications, with loud cries and tears, to him who was able to save him from death."

Two further details in the gospel narrative underscore the humanity of Jesus. First, he is portrayed as falling on his face (v. 39). It is not a Stoic philosopher who here contemplates his fate! Second, he expresses bitter disappointment that his closest followers prove incapable of agonizing with him: "What! Could none of you stay awake with me for one hour?" (v. 40, REB). The Gospels are not interested in probing deeper into the psychological pain Jesus experienced, but since he was truly human, he must have suffered that night almost as much from his friends as from his enemies. He expected nothing but the worst from Caiaphas, but did Peter really love him so little?

The Epistle to the Hebrews, in the passage quoted above, continues: "Although he was a Son, he learned obedience through what he suffered; and being made perfect he became the source of eternal salvation to all who obey him" (Heb. 5:8–9). Was Jesus not sinless? Surely he did not have to *learn obedience?* How could he *become perfect* through suffering? Such questions indicate that we do not recognize that obedience is dynamic, not static. Jesus had not been disobedient, but he could not become "obedient unto death" (Phil. 2:8) until he was genuinely tempted to save his life by ignoring God's will.

Jesus prays, "My Father, if it is possible, let this cup pass from me" (v. 39, NRSV). "Cup" is a metaphor for death. In the Hebrew Scriptures it appears most frequently as the cup of God's wrath (see comments on 20:22). In asking "if it is possible," Jesus is speaking not of the chance of a physical escape to the barren hills outside the city but the possibility of God establishing his kingdom without requiring the Messiah to suffer public shame and an excruciating death. God is all-powerful. Can he not destroy evil without making his Son its victim? Apparently the answer to this troubled question was no. There was no other way.

301

The prayer begins with the words "My Father." In Mark's earlier version the address is *Abba* (Mark 14:36). This affectionate Aramaic word, used normally only by little children (compare our "Daddy"), was so characteristic of Jesus' approach to God that both Mark and Paul assume familiarity with it on the part of their Gentile, Greek-speaking readers (Rom. 8:15; Gal. 4:6). Matthew, perhaps because he writes for a later generation that no longer prizes Aramaic words and phrases, gives only a translation. He nevertheless reproduces something of the intimacy of the original by adding "my." The depth and intensity of Jesus' relationship to his Father is not explored by the Gospel writers, but it is reflected in this prayer: "Yet not what I want but what you want" (v. 39, NRSV).

For the sake of his readers Matthew supplies words for a second prayer (Mark 14:39 reports that Jesus used the same words): "My Father, if this cannot pass unless I drink it, *thy will be done,*" quoting the Lord's Prayer. The Evangelist reminds us that praying "as Jesus taught us" can be costly when a serious decision is being contemplated.

Matthew stresses that Jesus prayed three times. Perhaps he anticipates the fact that Peter will deny Jesus three times. The sleeping Peter does not prepare himself through prayer for his time of testing, despite Jesus' warning, "Watch and pray that you may not enter into temptation" (v. 41). The word *peirasmos* can mean either "temptation" or "testing." It appears in the Lord's Prayer: "And lead us not into *peirasmos*" (6:13). Verse 41 does not suggest that by watching and praying we can evade all situations in which we are tempted to put our desires before God's will. To be human means to be tested in this way. As in the Lord's Prayer, the goal of the admonition is not escape but victory (see comments on 6:9–13). We can paraphrase: "Be on your guard and pray for divine help that you may resist temptation when put to the test."

The second half of verse 41 is easily misunderstood by readers accustomed to the body-mind dualism of the Greeks. "The mind is willing but the body is weak" is an incorrect interpretation, because it ignores the fact that in Hebrew thought "the flesh" was a way of speaking of the whole person, body and mind. Thus Paul includes among "the works of the flesh" sins that we associate with mental activity (enmity, strife, jealousy, anger, etc., Gal. 5:20–21). "The flesh" designates human beings in their vaunted independence from God. The saying of Jesus

302

by no means suggests that the human spirit is always eager to serve God but is handicapped by bodily fatigue. Peter's real problem lies not in his tired muscles but in his "double-mindedness"; he has not yet learned "to will one thing" (Kierkegaard). The "willing spirit" refers to the potentiality for a relationship with God that has been placed by God within each of us. The psalmist cries: "Create in me a clean heart, O God, and put a new and right spirit within me" (Ps. 51:10). This "spirit" inclines us to serve God, but our fleshly minds are intent on serving ourselves (cf. Rom. 7:18). Only through prayer can this uneven conflict be resolved in favor of God's Lordship.

By emphasizing the real humanity of Jesus, the Gethsemane narrative presents him as a model that ordinary Christians can follow. We can learn from him to stand the test by praying frequently and earnestly that our wills be aligned with our Father's will. This is the practical point of the narrative. Its theological message is even more important. It suggests that Jesus' most important sacrifice was not his blood but his obedience. The Epistle to the Hebrews, which draws on sacrificial language more extensively than any other New Testament writing as a way of talking about Jesus' saving death, indicates that "blood" and "sacrifice" are but metaphors for the obedience that was Jesus' real offering to God (see Heb. 10:5–10). The same theological point is made by Paul: "For as by one man's disobedience many were made sinners, so by one man's obedience many will be made righteous" (Rom. 5:19). For Christians, the Garden of Gethsemane is the reversal of the Garden of Eden.

Jesus Is Delivered Up (26:47–56)

From the time of the second passion announcement (17:22–23) the readers have been awaiting the dread moment when Jesus the Messiah will be "delivered up" into the hands of men who will kill him. Since 24:14–16 they have known that this will happen whenever Judas finds an opportune time. The moment now arrives, but not before the Messiah has won his victory over temptation in the garden. Nor does it catch him by surprise. Majestically Jesus announces: "Arise, let us be going; look, the one who delivers me up is drawing nigh" (v. 46). Jesus does not wait to be hunted down; he advances to meet his betrayer, who arrives on the scene precisely as the announcement is made.

303

The arrest scene contains three focal moments. The first is the shocking detail of the hypocritical kiss; a gesture of affection or honor (see Luke 7:45) becomes the token of betrayal (cf. II Sam. 20:9–10). Matthew's version of Jesus' response is an incomplete sentence and therefore puzzling. Earlier English translations understood it as a question: "Friend, why are you here?" (v. 50, RSV, following KJV). It has now become common to treat it as a statement, with a verb in the imperative added: "Friend, do what you are here to do" (NRSV, REB). In view of Matthew's emphasis on Jesus' foreknowledge of the betrayal, it is hardly likely that he would intend a question here, unless perhaps a sarcastic one: "Friend, are you really here to honor me with a kiss?"

The second moment occurs when one of the disciples slices off the ear of a slave of the high priest (v. 51). In Mark it is "one of the bystanders" who commits this violent act (Mark 14:47), but Matthew states clearly that "one of those with Jesus" is responsible. (John 18:10 identifies the culprit as Peter, the victim as Malchus.) Mark makes nothing of this detail, proceeding as if it had no effect. For Matthew it provides the occasion for further teaching from Jesus on the subject of nonviolence: "Put your sword back into its place; for all who take the sword will perish by the sword" (v. 52). The Messiah who taught "Do not resist one who is evil" (5:39) now lives his creed. The ethical motif is subordinate to a christological one, however; Jesus' relationship to God ("My Father") is such that he *could* request twelve legions of angels to inflict violent punishment on his enemies (v. 53), but he will not do so, because he is determined to follow his God-appointed path of suffering as prophesied in Scripture (v. 54). These verses may serve an apologetic function, responding to the question, "How could Jesus of Nazareth have been the Messiah in view of the fact that he was powerless against his enemies?" Jesus had access to spectacular power, we are assured, but renounced its use because God's way of dealing with sin is through weakness.

The final moment comes in Jesus' self-defense: "Have you come out as against a *lēstēs?*" (v. 55). Josephus regularly uses this term with reference to the Jewish guerrilla fighters, who were often guilty of committing armed robbery in support of their cause. Jesus notes that if he were a political threat, they could easily have arrested him in the temple, where he made himself conspicuous by *sitting* to teach (see comments on 5:1). The fact that he made no effort to hide himself was evidence that he was not a hunted revolutionary. While Jesus later refuses to defend himself before the authorities, whether Jewish or Roman, he makes this defense before the "crowd" sent to arrest him. The defense is then dismissed as essentially irrelevant because everything that is happening to him is in accordance with scriptural prophecy. This includes the flight of the disciples, which he had already predicted in verse 31 on the basis of Zech. 13:7. Separated from his followers, the Messiah must face the last hours of humiliation and suffering alone.

Jesus Before the High Priest's Council (26:57–68)

Volumes have been written about this passage because of the many historical problems it poses. It is argued that the Jewish high court would not have convened at night, in a private home, on the eve of a major festival. Defenders of the historicity of the tradition maintain that the alleged irregularities are accounted for by the fact that this was an extraordinary situation requiring secrecy and haste. Yet Luke seems to have had doubts about the account; he sets the trial before "the council of the elders of the people" *(presbyterion)* on Friday morning, presumably in its regular meeting place, although none is specified (Luke 22:66–71). Both Luke and John report that Jesus was taken to the home of the high priest following his arrest (Luke 22:54; John 18:24; to this, John prefaces a hearing before Annas, the high priest's father-in-law), but there is no trial of Jesus before a Jewish court in the Fourth Gospel.

The central issue of the scholarly debate is whether Jesus received the sentence of capital punishment from a competent Jewish court on the legal charge of blasphemy. It has often been assumed that the claim to be the Messiah constituted an act of blasphemy according to the legal definition of that crime. Unfortunately, we do not know how the crime was defined in the first century. Presumably it was not defined so narrowly as in the Mishnah at the end of the second century *(Sanhedrin* 7:5), yet it must be insisted that a relatively narrow definition must have prevailed at a time when the Sadducees controlled the high priesthood. According to Josephus, the Sadducees were more severe in their punishments than the Pharisees but "strict constructionists" in their interpretation of the laws. The pertinent Old Testament passages are Exod. 22:28, "You shall not

305

revile God," and Lev. 24:16, "He who blasphemes the name of the LORD shall be put to death; all the congregation shall stone him." That is, the crime of blasphemy consisted of public language in which God was cursed or insulted. The intent of the law was not to enforce theological orthodoxy but to maintain public decency. It is obvious that Jesus was not guilty of such a crime. The Christian claim that Jesus was the Messiah and had been exalted to the right hand of God was apparently not treated as blasphemy by the high priest during the post-Easter mission (see Acts 4:21). Undoubtedly Christian preaching about Jesus was regarded by many as "blasphemous" in the nontechnical sense, but it was not punished as a capital crime. The British scholar J. C. O'Neill proposes that, while it was not an act of blasphemy to proclaim Jesus as the Messiah, it was an established Jewish tradition that no man could publicly claim to be the Lord's Anointed before God had acted to identify him as the Messiah; to do so constituted a serious infringement of God's prerogative and therefore blasphemy *(Messiah: Six Lectures on the Ministry of Jesus)*. This proposal is the most satisfactory of the various defenses of the blasphemy charge, but it suffers from a lack of positive evidence that the legal definition of blasphemy included such violations of God's prerogatives.

Fortunately we are not required to resolve all the historical issues raised by this passage. We can proceed on the assumption that a historical kernel underlies the passage but some details may derive from Christian reflection. It seems likely that Caiaphas interrogated Jesus, perhaps in the presence of those who advised him on important matters, and that Jesus was accused of blasphemy in a nontechnical sense, but that the capital charge brought against him before Pilate was rather that he claimed to be "King of the Jews" (see comments on 27:11).

The main point of the story for Matthew is theological. It provides the ultimate confrontation between Jesus and the official leaders of Israel (Caiaphas the high priest, the scribes, and the elders, v. 57) on the subject of his messianic status. Here Jesus makes a public confession, which draws the unanimous condemnation, "He deserves death." In this scene is fulfilled the first part of the prophecy of Ps. 118:22: "the stone which the builders rejected" (see Matt. 21:42); for the fulfillment of the second half, we must await the resurrection.

306

In anticipation of the climax of the rejection motif, which has permeated the Gospel from the birth narrative on (see 2:3), the trial scene begins ominously with the statement, "And the chief priests and the whole council were trying to find *false testimony* against Jesus so that they could have him put to death" (v. 59). The implication is that they knew it was impossible to find a valid accusation, but since they were determined to get rid of the "deceiver" (27:63), they had to fabricate a charge that would justify a capital sentence. The assumption of Jesus' innocence is then reinforced by the report that, although many false witnesses were produced, none of them presented an accusation, however spurious, that would hold up in court (v. 60). Finally two came forward with a *true* but *insufficient* charge (Matthew carefully omits Mark's identification of this as false testimony, Mark 14:57): "This man said, 'I am able to destroy God's temple and build it in three days'" (v. 61).

The tradition that Jesus made a prophecy about the temple appears in remarkably different forms. In addition to the Markan parallel to this passage (Mark 14:58) and the echo of it at Matt. 27:40, see Mark 13:2 (Matt. 24:2; Luke 21:6); John 2:19; and Acts 6:14. There can be no doubt that Jesus made some such prediction, but in view of the diversity of the evidence, it is no longer possible to reconstruct the original saying. For our purposes, however, it is sufficient to observe how Matthew uses the tradition. First, he alters Mark's "I will destroy" to "I *can* destroy." By the time Matthew wrote, the temple had been burned by the Romans. His version is therefore satisfied with attributing to Jesus the divine power required for such a task. Mark contrasts the old and new temples by two adjectives, "made with hands" and "not made with hands," in order to indicate that the eschatological temple will be a divine product. Matthew drops the adjectives but nonetheless implies that the temple Jesus will build will be supernatural, since it will be constructed in a three-day period. Presumably some Christians, taking their cue from the Qumran use of "temple" as a metaphor for the community of believers, saw in the saying a prediction of the creation of the church through the resurrection of Jesus on the third day. Matthew leaves us no trace of this understanding. He apparently regards the temple saying as relevant to this context, because only the Messiah could claim such supernatural power. It is not clear whether Jews of the first century, like the authors of the later targums, expected the Messiah to rebuild the temple. In any event, Caiaphas is represented by Matthew as perceiving a messianic reference in the saying, yet

307

acknowledging at the same time that this evidence in itself is too indirect to secure a conviction without corroborative testimony from the defendant. He therefore asks Jesus for comment. When the prisoner refuses to cooperate, Caiaphas makes explicit what was merely implicit in the charge that Jesus had uttered the temple saying: "By the living God I charge you to tell us: Are you the Messiah, the Son of God?" (v. 63, NEB, REB).

The question is formulated in confessional terms. Instead of asking Jesus, "Do you say that you are the Messiah?" (cf. Luke 23:2), Caiaphas echoes Peter's confession of 16:16. The symbolic importance of the query is indicated by Jesus' answer. Whereas Mark presents Jesus as responding with a straightforward assent, "I am," Matthew substitutes an indirect affirmative, "You said it." In view of verse 65, it is clear that Matthew intends this to be taken not as an evasion but as a positive response (just as at 26:25), but he prefers the indirect affirmative as a means of emphasizing the role of the questioner and thus underscoring the irony. It is Jesus' primary enemy, the high priest, who correctly formulates the confessional statement with which he and his whole people should be acknowledging the Messiah!

It is sometimes argued that Jesus' response in verse 64*b* means that the high priest's formulation is inadequate: "*You* use the titles 'Messiah' and 'the Son of God,' but I am more than these designations suggest; I am the heavenly Son of man." This is to misread both this passage and the Gospel as a whole. Nowhere does Matthew suggest that "the Son of man" is the title of a heavenly being. Consistently used as Jesus' self-designation, it conveys nothing concerning his identity to friend or foe (see 16:13 and Introduction). Moreover, it does not function as a title in this passage. Jesus is not represented as saying, "I am the Son of man." In the subsequent narrative Jesus is mocked because he claimed to be the Messiah (v. 68), not because he asserted that he was a heavenly figure. Nor does the narrative audience assume that he is speaking about a heavenly personage distinct from himself. The passage presupposes that the hearers are aware of Jesus' habit of referring to himself in this indirect way. What the audience hears is: "Yes, I am the Messiah, the Son of God; but I tell you, despite what you may think of me in my present humiliation, right now a new era is starting, and one day you will see me 'seated at the right hand of Power' in fulfillment of Ps. 110:1 and 'coming on the clouds of heaven' as prophesied by Dan. 7:13." (See comments on 23:39 and 24:30 regarding the future "seeing" of Jesus by his enemies.)

308

Matthew has already demonstrated at 22:44 and 24:30 how important these two proof texts were to Christian thinking about Jesus. In this climactic statement they are brought together. He whom God has chosen as his "right-hand man" (Ps. 80:17) will be exalted through death and resurrection to a place at God's side, where he will await the time appointed for his coming to rescue the elect and judge the wicked.

Jesus' "blasphemy" is promptly pronounced worthy of capital punishment, and his judges proceed to mistreat the condemned Messiah in outrageous ways symbolizing the full extent of their rejection of his God-given status. By attributing to the councillors the derisive command, "Prophesy to us, you Christ! Who is it that struck you?" (v. 68), Matthew indicates that he regards it as a common Jewish understanding that the Messiah will possess prophetic powers. The terms "prophet" and "Messiah" are not mutually exclusive terms (see 21:9–11; John 6:14–15).

Two additional points require our attention. First, it is often insisted that Jesus was put to death because the Pharisees regarded him as attacking the law of Moses. Although the murderous hatred of the Pharisees is mentioned in 12:14, we found that Jesus' interpretation of the Sabbath did not exceed Jewish tolerance limits. The same proved true of his treatment of divorce (5:31–32; 19:1–9) and the purity and food laws (15:1–20). Since they were denounced by the Sadducees for altering the laws, it is exceedingly improbable that the Pharisees would have persuaded Caiaphas and his council to condemn Jesus on such a basis. Moreover, Pharisaic involvement in the condemnation of Jesus is not supported by any of the relevant texts. The united affirmation of the passion narratives of all four Gospels that Jesus was condemned as a messianic pretender is to be accepted as historically probable. There is no need to resort to the flimsy hypothesis that he was killed because of his teaching about the law.

Second, Christians must not be misled by narrative details suggesting that the Jewish system of justice was hopelessly corrupt. The narrative is shaped by Christian faith to make a theological point. Here as elsewhere in the Gospel, Matthew is struggling with what was for him a major theological problem: How could Israel reject God's Messiah? As the changes he makes in Mark's narrative indicate, he is not interested in merely reporting but in interpreting history. We must be careful, therefore, not to use his faith narrative as the basis for

309

making historical pronouncements concerning "what the Jews did to Jesus." This issue will be discussed further in connection with 27:11–26.

Peter's Apostasy (26:69–75)

There can be little doubt regarding the historicity of Peter's denial, which is reported with minor variations in all four Gospels. No one in the early church would have created such an embarrassing story about Jesus' most prominent disciple. Presumably the story was transmitted by Peter and others as a shining example of the victory of divine grace over human sin. Peter's restoration is presupposed by the tradition of a special resurrection appearance (Luke 24:34; I Cor. 15:5). John 21 presents a dialogue in which the risen Lord asks Peter three times, "Do you love me?"—a detail reminiscent of Peter's threefold denial. The "happy ending" is not reported by Matthew but is implicit in 16:17–19.

Peter's downfall is presented as a negative example. In 10: 32–33 Jesus declares: "Everyone therefore who acknowledges me before others, I also will acknowledge before my Father in heaven; but whoever denies me before others, I also will deny before my Father in heaven" (NRSV). The saying implies persecution, much of which will be unofficial, as in Peter's case. Even in front of serving girls his courage fails him and he denies having any relationship to Jesus. No explanation of Peter's denial is offered in this passage, because it has already been suggested in the Gethsemane scene, where Peter sleeps despite the warning, "Watch and pray that you may not enter into temptation" (26:41). There it was stressed that Jesus prayed three times and that Peter slept three times. The fruit of those earlier failures to pray are now the three refusals to acknowledge his Lord.

As in Mark 14:53–72, Jesus' appearance before the high priest's council is "sandwiched" into the story about Peter; the disciple's arrival is mentioned in verse 58. By beginning verse 69 with a verb expressing continuing action ("was sitting"), Matthew suggests that the two scenes in different parts of the high priest's palace have been occurring simultaneously rather than consecutively. Three times Jesus is confronted by a verbal threat (false witnesses, valid witnesses, Caiaphas); three times Peter is similarly tested (two serving girls and the bystanders).

Whereas Jesus bravely makes "the good confession" (see I Tim. 6:12–13), Peter plays the coward and denies.

By means of a few editorial alterations (compare Mark 14:66–72), Matthew develops the threefold denial into a powerfully climactic series. In the first, Peter merely denies "before all" (compare "before others" in 10:32–33) that he knows what the girl is talking about. In response to the second girl's question he takes an oath and declares, "I do not know the man" (a formula used by Jesus in 7:23 for disassociation from unfaithful disciples, "I never knew you"). By guaranteeing his denial with an oath, Peter is also disobeying Jesus' injunction, "Do not swear at all. . . . Let what you say be simply 'Yes' or 'No'; anything more than this comes from evil" (5:34, 37). The third instance should fill the readers with horror. The verb translated "curse" is regularly transitive and not reflexive, that is, in all other instances it takes a direct object other than the speaker. The rendering of the RSV, "Then he began to invoke a curse *on himself*" (so also NIV), cannot be defended linguistically. It represents an attempt to soften a statement that was as unacceptable to Matthew's first readers as to us. The object is euphemistically omitted but implicit because of the context; Peter cursed Jesus as a way of firmly disassociating himself. We may compare Paul's concern in I Cor. 12:3 regarding the possibility that Christians may excuse their cowardice in a situation of testing by saying, "It was the Holy Spirit that moved me to declare 'Jesus be cursed!' " Early in the second century Pliny, the Roman governor of Bithynia, reported to the emperor Trajan that when people are brought before him accused of being Christians he insists that they curse Jesus, because he has heard that a genuine Christian can never be induced to do this.

We must read this story from the perspective of Matthew's first readers, many of whom faced informal persecution of the kind here depicted. (Apart from the brief incident in Rome under Nero, we know of no widespread governmental persecution until that reported by Pliny.) Great pressure was placed on them by Matt. 10:32–33 and by their fellow Christians to speak out bravely when challenged about their religious affiliation. The Epistle to the Hebrews is very harsh in its judgment of those who apostatize under pressure (Heb. 6:4–6). Why, then, was Peter, the foremost apostle, so easily excused for his apostasy? Matthew's answer is perhaps to be found in 12:32: "And whoever says a word against the Son of man will be forgiven;

311

but whoever speaks against the Holy Spirit will not be forgiven, either in this age or in the age to come." Peter had not yet experienced the resurrection and the gift of the Holy Spirit, and so was not yet a "Christian" in the full sense of the term. If he had denied Christ later in his life, he would have committed the unforgivable sin.

As well as providing a fearful example of what happens to Christians who do not pray for divine help, the passage serves to confirm Jesus' messianic status by illustrating that his prophecy of 26:34 has come to pass. This is emphasized by the literal repetition of the prophetic saying (omitting only its introduction). This stress on Jesus as prophet intensifies the irony of verse 68, where Jesus' enemies mock him with the taunt, "Prophesy to us, you Christ!" Without realizing it, the mockers are putting into words the truth about the prophetic Messiah whose prophecies do come to pass!

Matthew 27:1–66
Condemned, Ill-treated, Crucified

Despite the fact that a new day (Friday) has dawned, the passion narrative continues without any obvious break in the action. Indeed, Matthew's language in verse 1 is sufficiently vague that the reader is left uncertain whether the reported meeting is simply a continuation of the one related in 26:57–68 or a more formal assembly held in a proper meeting place at a legal time for the purpose of regularizing the decision made during the night. Apparently the issue is unimportant to Matthew. He devotes little space to the daytime meeting and stops short, as in 26:66, of stating explicitly that the judges handed down a verdict requiring capital punishment. We should regard such a sentence as implied, however, since Jesus prophesied in 20:18 that the high priests and scribes would condemn him to death, and in 27:3 Judas learns that Jesus has been condemned. The function of the verse is to prepare for the transfer of the prisoner to Pilate's jurisdiction (v. 2).

The Death of Judas (27:3–10)

The death of Judas is related very differently in Acts 1:15–20. The only detail in common is the purchase with the betrayal money of a piece of land which became known as "the field of blood." There is no need to worry about which of the two accounts more accurately reports what happened to Judas. Both assure us that Jesus' betrayer came to a bad end. More important is what the story means to Matthew.

Especially significant is the fact that Matthew has inserted the story into the middle of the narrative about Jesus' trial before Pilate. Since this is historically inappropriate (the chief priests who are in Pilate's presence according to vv. 2, 12 are in the twinkling of an eye transferred to the temple in v. 3), we must assume that Matthew's purpose is theological. Just as Peter's denial is juxtaposed with the trial before Caiaphas for the purpose of contrasting Jesus' brave confession with Peter's cowardice, so now Judas' behavior is meant to cast light on what is done by the chief priests and Pilate in the Roman trial. Judas appears on the scene at this juncture in order to remind us that Jesus is *innocent* (v. 4). He thus prepares for Pilate's finding that Jesus is innocent and has been brought before him only because of envy (v. 18). The return of the betrayal money by a remorseful Judas symbolizes the assignment of primary responsibility to the Jewish leaders. While they openly deny their guilt ("What is that to us? See to it yourself," v. 4), they are compelled to concede that they cannot receive the money as a temple offering, because it is "blood money." With these words they acknowledge their guilt and prepare the readers for the shocking acceptance of responsibility in verse 25 that constitutes the climax of the Roman trial. Similarly, the idiom translated "See to it yourself" by the RSV and more idiomatically "That's your responsibility" by the NIV becomes a boomerang that returns upon them from Pilate's mouth in verse 24, " 'I am innocent of this man's blood,' he said. 'It is your responsibility!' " (NIV).

Although the narrative might have seemed more historically apt had Matthew placed it after Jesus' death or burial, its position here serves another purpose. Because of proximity the story about Judas constitutes a foil to the one about Peter. Both disciples are guilty of a serious sin against Jesus, but whereas Peter manifests genuine repentance by remembering what

313

Jesus said and by weeping bitterly, Judas is merely "seized with remorse" (NIV, REB). The verb *metameleō* in verse 3, translated "repented" by the RSV and the NRSV, must be carefully distinguished from *metanoeō*, the verb regularly used in the New Testament for genuine repentance or "turning around" (the meaning of the corresponding Hebrew verb). *Metameleō* means "regret" or "change one's mind" and so can be used of God in Heb. 7:21. Judas recognizes that he has made a serious mistake, but he fails to throw himself on the mercy of God. Instead, he lamely "atones" for his sin by returning the tainted money. Still worse than Judas' sin of betrayal is the collapse of his faith in the God of grace whom Jesus had proclaimed to him.

The juxtaposition of Peter and Judas may have been more meaningful to early readers than to us. During times of persecution, both formal and informal, some Christians denied their allegiance to Christ, and others, still more cowardly, attempted to save themselves by turning informer against their brothers and sisters in the church. These two stories would suggest to such readers that those who denied Jesus might perhaps repent and be restored (except where the harsh judgment of Heb. 6:4–6 prevailed), whereas those who betrayed other Christians could never again be accepted in the church.

Two additional motifs may be briefly noted. Like the story about Peter, this story illustrates Jesus' status as a true prophet; Judas' sorry end is the fulfillment of the prediction of 26:24. More important, it constitutes a fulfillment of Old Testament prophecy, thus showing again that everything that happens to Jesus is in accord with God's plan. Matthew emphasizes this through the use of his customary fulfillment formula (see comments on 2:13–23). The quoted Scripture is not found in any one Old Testament passage but is a complicated adaptation and conflation of phrases in Zech. 11:13 and allusions to Jeremiah. The whole is attributed to Jeremiah, perhaps so that readers will see the allusions (Jer. 18:1–2; 32:6–15; and 19:1–13 have been proposed) or perhaps because Jeremiah was regarded as the prophet of bloodshed and judgment.

The Trial Before Pilate (27:11–26)

314

The function of this passage is primarily theological rather than historical. Its intention is not to report that Jesus was sentenced to crucifixion by the Roman procurator (in v. 26, Matthew carefully avoids saying that a death sentence was formally handed down by Pilate) but to exhibit the theological conviction that Israel, the Messiah's own people, assumed full responsibility for his death and therefore warranted the judgment of 21:43, "Therefore I tell you, the kingdom of God will be taken away from you and given to a nation producing the fruits of it."

The trial narrative begins abruptly with Pilate's question. We are not told what prompted the procurator to formulate the charge in this way. Luke attempts to remedy this deficiency in Mark's account (Mark 15:1–2) by providing a Jewish accusation: "We found this man perverting our nation, and forbidding us to give tribute to Caesar, and saying that he himself is Christ a king" (Luke 23:2). Matthew is not interested in the historical background. In all four Gospels Pilate asks Jesus, "Are you the King of the Jews?" (see Mark 15:2; Luke 23:3; John 18:33). In each Gospel this question anticipates the notice on the cross that identifies Jesus' crime (see comments on 27:37). In the First Gospel this title has already been used by the Gentile Magi in 2:1–2.

Jesus' response is studiously ambiguous. Whereas the same expression must be taken as an indirect affirmative in 26:25, 64, here it must retain its ambiguity. From Matthew's perspective it would be false for Jesus to answer in the negative; the title is valid even though it is a Gentile version of "the king of Israel" (see 27:42). On the other hand, if the response is clearly positive, Jesus has confessed to the crime and there is no reason to continue the trial. As in the previous instances of the idiom, "You say so" (v. 11, NRSV) makes the questioner an unintentional witness to the truth concerning which he asks.

From this laconic response to the great cry of dereliction on the cross Jesus says nothing (contrast Luke 23:38–41, 43; John 18:34–37; 19:11, 26–28). Matthew does not develop the motif of the silence of Jesus. Presumably Isa. 53:7 lies in the background (see Acts 8:32). From Matthew's point of view it would be theologically inappropriate for Jesus to speak in his own defense because the charge is a valid one (he *does* claim to be king of Israel) and, more important, because he goes to his death in accordance with his Father's will (26:36–46).

Scholars continue to debate the historicity of the tradition reported in verse 15 concerning the custom of releasing a prisoner each Passover (see also Mark 15:6; John 18:39). Josephus makes no allusion to such a custom, and it is omitted by Luke.

Although the practice appears incredible to modern minds, it clearly did not appear so to Matthew, Mark, and John, all of whom assume that their story will be believed by their readers. Even if the amnesty program is exaggerated by being treated as an annual affair, however, there is no need to doubt the possibility that it lay within the military governor's power to release an individual prisoner as a conciliatory gesture. Pilate may have found it politically expedient to appease public hostility by pardoning one revolutionary while persisting in his intention to crucify others (see v. 38).

The Greek form *Barabbas* represents either "son of the father" or "son of our teacher" in Aramaic. It is probable that the person so identified also had a proper name. In some ancient sources this name is provided: Jesus. This was a common name in the first century (see Col. 4:11), as might be expected, since the Greek *Iēsous* represented "Joshua" (see Acts 7:45; Heb. 4:8). Since it is much more likely that pious scribes would omit "Jesus" as a name for Barabbas than that they would add it, its appearance in verse 16 is probably authentic. Whereas Mark portrays Barabbas in dark hues as a rebel "who had committed murder in the insurrection" (Mark 15:7), Matthew is satisfied with a noncommittal modifer, *episēmos*. In its only other use in the New Testament, at Rom. 16:7, it is usually translated by a positive adjective meaning "famous," whereas here it is customary to employ "notorious" or its equivalent. What this divergence indicates is that the word itself is neutral; Matthew probably means by it "prominent" or "well known." The crowd demands Barabbas not because he is especially bad but because his exploits are well known. In view of Matthew's wordplay in 1:21 ("You shall call his name Jesus, for he will save his people from their sins"), the crowd is offered a poignant choice. Which Jesus do they want, one who will strive to save them with his sword or one who will give his life for their sins? Although for Matthew this choice was uniquely offered at a single point in salvation history, Christians must confess that it symbolizes a continuing situation. We are still tempted to choose Barabbas over Christ.

There is a tendency in the Gospels to exonerate Pilate from responsibility for the death of Jesus—a tendency that leads eventually to the canonization of both Pilate and his wife in the Coptic church. It is permissible to be skeptical of this feature of the tradition in view of Pilate's record of dealing harshly with

316

suspected revolutionaries (see Luke 13:1). We need not assume, however, that Pilate, after interrogating Jesus, must have regarded him as a genuine threat to Roman control. Certainly the Gospel offers no hint that the governor viewed Jesus' movement as subversive; no attempt was made to find and execute Jesus' most important followers. If Pilate concurred with Caiaphas on the need for removing the Nazarene, it must have been because he recognized the possibility that Jesus could be used as a figurehead by a revolutionary movement (see John 6:14–15).

In any event, it is *theologically* important to the Evangelists to transfer as much of the responsibility as possible from Pilate to the Jewish leaders. Matthew contributes to this ongoing project by adding several verses to the narrative he receives from Mark 15:6–15. In verse 19 he inserts an anecdote about Pilate's wife, who, like the Gentiles of the birth narrative (2:12), is warned (by God) in a dream. Pilate accedes to this divine warning and refuses to take responsibility for Jesus' death. The hand-washing scene is probably inspired by Deut. 21:6–7; Ps. 26:6; 73:13 (hand washing seems not to have been a rite of innocence in pagan society). Echoing the disclaimer of the high priests and the elders in 27:4 ("That's your responsibility!" NIV), Pilate announces to the crowd, "I am innocent of this man's blood. . . . It is your responsibility!" (v. 24, NIV). In verse 25 this responsibility is willingly accepted by "the people as a whole" (correctly translated by the NRSV). Again, this is a theological rather than a historical note. Matthew does not mean merely "the whole crowd" (TEV) that happened to be present; in that case he would have used his favorite expression, "the crowds" (see v. 20). For him, *laos* ("people") is a term reserved for Israel, God's special people in the old dispensation (see 2:6). Israel as a whole assumes the guilt of Jesus' death with the ominous declaration "His blood be on us and on our children!" (v. 25).

Since this text has been so sinfully misused in Christian history by those who cried "Christ killers!" and murdered and pillaged as "avengers of Christ's death," it is imperative that we understand Matthew's intention. He surely does not mean the words as a self-curse, as if Israel were collectively declaring: "We acknowledge that we are accursed murderers and that all our descendants should be treated as murderers." The statement gives voice rather to the theological conviction that Israel

317

as a whole has rejected its Messiah in a final and definitive way and in consequence deserves to be deselected as God's special people. Understood in this way, verse 25 is to be viewed less as an attack on Jews as an apologetic for the Gentile mission and for the church in which Gentiles now predominate (cf. 21:43). Nevertheless the "left hand" of this apologetic is inevitably polemical. Matthew's anti-Judaism must be countered with the more positive appreciation of God's irrevocable relationship to Israel articulated by Paul in Romans 11.

Mocked by Gentiles (27:27–31)

Pilate's alleged innocence is somewhat compromised by the behavior of his soldiers, who treat Jesus without any of the respect attributed to their commander in the preceding scene. The mocking by Gentiles is a fulfillment of the third passion announcement in 20:19, where it is prophesied that the chief priests and scribes will "deliver him to the Gentiles to be mocked and scourged and crucified."

The passion narrative as a whole is parsimonious in detail. In contrast to later martyrological narratives the Gospels are reticent concerning many of the indignities Jesus suffered. No attempt, for example, is made to portray the frightful flagellation with leather lashes, to which pieces of bone and balls of lead were attached. The brutal suffering is left entirely to the imagination of the readers. In this scene, by contrast, vivid details are supplied, probably in part because of their ironic significance.

Matthew substitutes a scarlet *chlamys* (a short cloak worn over the shoulders by soldiers) for Mark's royal purple robe (Mark 15:17), which would hardly have been available to ordinary soldiers, and adds the reed scepter to enhance the royal caricature. For Matthew and his readers the scene is full of profound irony. The one whom the soldiers mock is indeed the king of kings, at whose name every knee will bow (Phil. 2:10–11).

In his comment on this passage Calvin appropriately suggests that the amazing love exhibited in Jesus' willingness to accept such insults on our behalf should move us to "secret meditation, not fancy words" (*A Harmony of the Gospels*, vol. 3, p. 189).

The Crucifixion (27:32–44)

Matthew's story of the execution of Jesus contains remarkably few details. No mention is made of the pounding of the nails into hands and feet, the racking pain, the desperate thirst. Indeed, the process of fastening Jesus to the cross does not even obtain a clause of its own but is reported laconically in verse 35 by means of a solitary participle (lit., "having crucified"). Unlike the earlier Jewish and later Christian stories about religious martyrs, this story makes no reference to the courage, self-control, and faith of the victim. The narrative says astonishingly little about Jesus, who remains entirely passive (except for tasting and rejecting the insulting gift of wine mixed with gall in v. 34) until his one and only utterance, the loud cry of abandonment just before his death (v. 46, followed by a wordless cry in v. 50). What details are given concern not the victim but the *spectators.*

The first to be mentioned is Simon the Cyrenian, who is portrayed positively in this paragraph. He is probably known as a Christian to Mark's readers (Mark 15:21 identifies him as the father of Alexander and Rufus), but Matthew apparently regards this information as unnecessary for his readers. No explanation is offered for the Cyrenian's impressment; we are not informed, for example, that Jesus is too weak from the torture of the lashes to carry the crossbeam himself. Simon, like the women who are mentioned only after Jesus' death (vv. 55–56), is a silent spectator of the salvation-historical drama.

The soldiers are negative spectators, not only because they are cruel executioners but because they fulfill the prophecy of Ps. 69:2 (as rendered by the Septuagint) concerning "David's" enemies: "And they gave me gall as my food and for my drink they gave me sour wine." This is no humane act (as it is in Mark 15:23) but a malicious trick! The appropriation of the condemned man's clothing by the executioners was standard practice, but it is reported in language borrowed from Ps. 22:18, again to show that the soldiers are "David's" enemies as prophesied. The fact that the soldiers are not neutral but hostile observers enhances the Christian confession they will make after Jesus dies (v. 54).

Also hostile are the two brigands who are crucified with Jesus, "one on the right and one on the left" (v. 38). The signifi-

319

cance of their placement is indicated by the preceding verse, which announces Jesus' crime and ironically declares the truth: "This is Jesus the King of the Jews." The two brigands on left and right constitute the king's retinue! They are perhaps presented as caricatures of James and John, who requested these positions of honor, assuring Jesus of their willingness to share his cup but who instead of dying with him forsook him and fled (20:20–23; 26:56). The "thieves" are identified as *lēstai*, the word used by Josephus to designate Jewish freedom fighters, many of whom committed violent robbery to support the nationalist movement. How ironic that the king who preached nonviolence and love of enemies (5:38–48) dies with violent men as his "court"! They firmly reject the role thrust upon them, however; in verse 44 they join the spectators in reviling their king.

Because Simon, the soldiers, and the brigands are given no lines to say, their roles are decidedly less important than those of the two main groups of observers presented in verses 39–43. Here we reach the heart of the passage. The first speakers are identified as "passersby" (v. 39). Since a Greek participle meaning "those standing by" would seem to be a more natural choice for Matthew to make, it has been suggested that the Evangelist may intend an allusion to Lam. 2:15, "All those who pass by snap their fingers at you; they hiss and wag their heads" (REB). In any event, we are probably meant to see another allusion to the "passion psalm," Ps. 22:7: "All who see me mock at me, they make mouths at me, *they wag their heads.*" In their speech these unnamed enemies draw on material from the Jewish trial (26:57–68). The claim that Jesus is the Messiah and the saying about the temple are brought into yet sharper juxtaposition than at the trial; it is in effect acknowledged that the declaration about being able to destroy and rebuild the temple constitutes a messianic claim. The dual claim is challenged in the form of a temptation reminiscent of Satan's challenge in 4:3, 6: "If you are the Son of God . . . ." Just as the devil tempted Jesus to draw on the supernatural power available to him in order to meet his physical need for food (v. 3) or to demonstrate his status (v. 6), so the passersby challenge Jesus to prove that he is the Messiah by "saving" himself from death on the cross through the exercise of the supernatural power with which the Messiah is to be endowed (see Isa. 11:4).

The climactic group of spectators is constituted by the chief priests, scribes, and elders—namely, the leaders who condemned Jesus at the Jewish trial. The motif of "saving" reappears, this time not in an imperative but in a derisive comment: "He saved others; he cannot save himself" (v. 42). The first clause probably refers to Jesus' healing ministry (the verb "save" is often used in the miracle stories, as in 9:21–22, where the verb is translated "made well"). The second clause suggests that Jesus is nothing more than a faith healer and by no means the Messiah, "the king of Israel," since he has no power to rescue himself from crucifixion. In verse 43 Jesus is reproached with words influenced by Ps. 22:8: "He committed his cause to the LORD; let him deliver him, let him rescue him, for he delights in him!" Matthew's wording does not agree exactly with either the Hebrew text or the Septuagint. It may borrow in part from the statements about the sufferings of the righteous man who calls himself a son of God in Wisd. Sol. 2:12–20. The allusion to the passion psalm is clear enough, however. These spectators, too, are "David's" enemies in accordance with prophecy. Their derision of the Lord's Anointed is in accordance with the divine plan.

The theological problem that shapes this passage into a portrayal of the spectators rather than the victim must have been a pressing one for Jewish Christians: How could Jesus of Nazareth be the Messiah when he proved so utterly helpless against the Romans? The two mocking speeches contrast Jesus' claim with his apparent weakness. Those who became Christians had to face this challenge from family, friends, and acquaintances. It was not an easy question to answer. Matthew's crucifixion scene attempts to answer it by showing that the indignities Jesus suffered as Messiah were all in accordance with the prophecies of Davidic psalms. Israel had expected an all-powerful Messiah, but God had sent one who would renounce the use of force against his enemies and submit instead to suffering and death, for "the Son of man came not to be served but to serve, and to give his life as a ransom for many" (20:28).

The Death of the Messiah (27:45–56)

As intimated at the beginning of the preceding section, the story of the crucifixion and death of Jesus must be carefully distinguished from accounts of the glorious deaths of martyrs. There is a startling contrast between the description of the

321

martyrdom of Eleazar in Second Maccabees and the story related by Matthew. When compelled to eat pork, Eleazar
bravely refuses and willingly goes to his death after making a
bold speech of defiance. When he is on the point of dying from
the blows he has received, he groans aloud and declares, "It is
clear to the Lord in his holy knowledge that, though I might
have been saved from death, I am enduring terrible sufferings
in my body under this beating, but in my soul I am glad to suffer
these things because I fear him" (II Macc. 6:30; see also the long
story of the martyrdoms of seven brothers in II Maccabees 7).
Whereas the martyrdom stories are designed to edify and for-
tify believers, the gospel narrative is meant to humble and awe.
Instead of providing an uplifting oration, Jesus' last word presents the readers with an excruciating question: "My God, my
God, why have you forsaken me?"

To many interpreters it seems impossible that Jesus' life
should have ended with such a question or that the Evangelist
should have understood it so. They propose, therefore, that
Jesus (and the Gospel writers), in thus quoting Ps. 22:1, intends
to refer to the whole psalm, which ends on a very positive note.
Instead of a cry of dereliction, it is a triumphant declaration of
faith in God. This evasion is precluded by two facts. First, Luke
apparently had difficulty in understanding the cry in this way
and consequently substituted a more edifying word ("Father,
into thy hands I commit my spirit!" Luke 23:46). Second, the
context in Matthew (as in Mark) contradicts the "positive" interpretation; the bystanders hear not an affirmation of confidence in God but a desperate cry for help.

At the other extreme are a few interpreters who take this
final cry as evidence that Jesus lost his faith in God and looked
back on his lifework as a total failure. Given what we know
about Jesus' faith, this is intrinsically improbable, and given
what we know of the Evangelist's faith, we can assume that such
a shout of bitter despair would never have been included in the
traditions about Jesus.

A context for interpretation must be sought in the psalm
itself and in the wider Old Testament background. Men and
women of faith did not consider it inappropriate to argue with
God. It is not unfaith but faith that permits Job to call God's
322 justice into question (e.g., Job 9:13–35). The psalmist reproaches
God for unresponsiveness: "O my God, I cry by day, but thou
dost not answer; and by night, but find no rest" (Ps. 22:2). It is

a common complaint, but the intensity of the rebuke is directly proportional to the depth of the faith from which it springs. Only those who have great confidence in God can be disappointed when God remains aloof. Although Ps. 22:1 questions God, that challenge is raised within the context of faith: *"My God, my God, why . . . ?"*

Did Jesus really feel abandoned by God? Matthew believes that he did and retains the troubling question because it points to the deepest mystery of the saving event. In Deut. 31:17 God forecasts the sinfulness of Israel and declares, "Then my anger will be kindled against them in that day, and I will forsake them and hide my face from them." Matthew regards Jesus as sinless (see 3:13–15); if Jesus is abandoned by God, it can only be because he is giving his life as a ransom for sinners (20:28). Separation from God is the price of sin. Jesus is paying that price on behalf of others. The darkness that covers the land for three hours while Jesus dies (v. 45) probably symbolizes for the Evangelist the depth of human sin and God's judgment upon it. There is here perhaps a reminiscence of the prophetic promise that the day of the Lord will be one of darkness, not one of light (Amos 5:18; see also Amos 8:9). Although we cannot plumb the depths of Jesus' anguished cry, it firmly reminds us of his real humanity and compels us to meditate on the mystery to which it points: "For our sake he made him to be sin who knew no sin, so that in him we might become the righteousness of God" (II Cor. 5:21).

Although Matthew usually does not retain Mark's Aramaic phrases, he does in this case (with minor changes) because it is essential to the context. The bystanders mistake the first word *Eli* ("my God") for *Eliyyahu* ("Elijah"). (An earlier form of the tradition may have preserved an alternate form *Eliya*, which could more easily be confused with *Eliyyahu*.) Since they believe that Jesus is calling on Elijah for help, the gift of sour wine (in fulfillment of Ps. 69:21) is probably not to be seen as a humane gesture, since the psalm attributes the act to enemies, but as a mocking attempt to prolong Jesus' agony a few more minutes so as to give Elijah time to respond to the call. Verse 49 need not be taken as opposing this action (as suggested by RSV, NIV); it can be translated: "And the others were saying, 'Let us see if Elijah comes to save him' " (cf. NEB). For the significance of Elijah as an end-time figure, see comments on 11:14; 17:10.

Matthew takes over from Mark the dramatic sign of the

323

rending of the temple veil (Mark 15:38). Neither Evangelist provides an interpretation of the sign. We are not even informed whether it is the outer or the inner curtain that is affected (see Heb. 9:3). Since it is followed by a Gentile confession of faith in Jesus, we can surmise that it symbolizes for both Evangelists the dissolution of the cultic system that prevented Gentiles from having access to God. The note that the curtain is torn from top to bottom reminds us that God is responsible (we have here another example of the divine passive, where the actor is not identified for reasons of reverence). The torn curtain is God's first comment on the death of Jesus. Matthew adds three more, interconnected signs. The earthquake and the splitting of the rocks are indications of God's active presence (cf. Nahum 1:5–6). The resurrecting of the saints, prefiguring the general resurrection, suggests that the death of Jesus has conquered death and prepared for the final victory of those who die in faith. The temporal note of verse 53, "after his resurrection," is meant to prevent any misconception; Jesus will be the *first* to be raised from the dead. That is, Matthew does not mean to present the appearance of the saints as an *event* in the history of salvation but as a *sign* only.

The scene's real climax comes in the response of the Gentile soldiers. Whereas in Mark and Luke it is the centurion alone who responds, in Matthew he is joined by the soldiers under him. For these unbelievers the earthquake and the attendant events constitute a revelatory occasion inspiring sacred fear, just as the event of Jesus walking on the sea had aroused terror in the disciples (14:26). Like the disciples in 14:33, the Gentiles confess: "Truly this was the Son of God!" In so doing, they vindicate Jesus over against all the mockers who had employed the same title in derision while Jesus was dying. The soldiers represent the vast Gentile multitudes to whom the gospel will be preached after the resurrection (28:19).

The passage concludes with the brief notice that many women who had followed Jesus from Galilee were passive observers of Jesus' dying. Three are specified. After Mary Magdalene comes Mary the mother of James and Joseph. She is probably Jesus' mother, in view of 13:55, but it is puzzling that she is not so identified here and that she is subsequently referred to simply as "the other Mary" in verse 61 and in 28:1. While Mark 15:40 names the third as Salome, Matthew reads "the mother of Zebedee's sons" (exactly as at 20:20). The female

324

witnesses connect the crucifixion with the ensuing scenes of the burial (v. 71) and the resurrection (28:1–10).

The Burial of the Messiah (27:57–61)

According to Paul's statement in I Cor. 15:3–8, the early kerygma contained the statement, "and he was buried." Undoubtedly the function of this clause was to confirm the preceding statement, "Christ died for our sins in accordance with the scriptures." The burial attests the reality of the death.

This function is emphasized in Mark's account of the burial (Mark 15:42–47). When Joseph of Arimathea asks for Jesus' body, Pilate does not immediately grant his request but first summons the centurion in order to assure himself that Jesus is really dead. Perhaps Mark was reacting to the allegation of skeptics that the resurrection appearances were effected by a Jesus who had survived the trauma of crucifixion. By omitting this detail of Mark's story, Matthew indicates that this particular challenge to the resurrection story is not of concern to him. He is troubled by a very different allegation, namely, that the tomb was found empty because the body was stolen (28:13–15).

Consequently Matthew stresses different elements of the burial account. By identifying Joseph as a *rich* man (instead of a member of the council, Mark 15:43), the Evangelist probably means to suggest a fulfillment of Isa. 53:9, "And they made his grave . . . with a rich man in his death." Whereas Mark makes Joseph appear sympathetic to Jesus by describing him as "looking for the kingdom of God," Matthew makes a relationship to Jesus explicit: Joseph was "discipled" to Jesus (the verb is found also in 13:52 and 28:19).

It has been proposed that the story of the burial is legendary, on the assumption that the Romans would not have allowed an executed criminal to be buried privately; out of deference to Jewish scruples, the soldiers probably threw the bodies of the three victims into an open trench and covered them with earth (instead of leaving the corpses on the crosses to be eaten by vultures, as done elsewhere). Archaeological evidence to the contrary has been unearthed recently in a family tomb on Mount Scopus, which was discovered to contain the skeleton of a young male who had been crucified. Moreover, in view of Jesus' reputation as a holy teacher, it is not at all incredible that a pious Jew, moved by pity and respect for the dead rabbi,

325

should have undertaken to give him a proper burial; burial of a stranger was considered an important expression of true piety (see Tobit 1:17–19).

Although it is impossible for us to assess the accuracy of Matthew's claim that Joseph was a disciple of Jesus (did he perhaps become a Christian later?), the point he makes is clear: Jesus' body was not treated with contempt by enemies but was given personal care by one of his own circle. Matthew underscores Joseph's pious devotion to Jesus by describing the linen cloth as *clean* and the rock-hewn tomb as *his own* and *new* (vv. 59–60).

Two of the women mentioned in 27:55–56 reappear here (why the mother of James and John is absent is not explained). The first witnesses of the risen Jesus link the three narratives of the death, burial, and resurrection. Because they know that he truly died and was truly buried, their testimony to his rising is all the stronger.

The Guard at the Tomb (27:62–66)

Matthew is the only source for the tradition that the tomb was placed under surveillance on the suspicion that the disciples would attempt to steal the body and fabricate a resurrection story. From a historical perspective the tale has little to commend it. It is improbable that Jesus' enemies expected his disciples to concoct such a plot or that they would have been concerned about such a possibility had they heard of it. As it turned out, the public response to the message of the resurrection was far from overwhelming. Moreover, had there been a serious concern, the authorities would surely have taken charge of the corpse immediately instead of waiting until Saturday morning when the body could already have been stolen. And there was no need for Roman soldiers (28:14 clearly implies that the soldiers are accountable primarily to Pilate, not to the chief priests); a unit of temple police would have sufficed.

Such considerations serve to point out that this narrative is being told for apologetic reasons. The story is a rhetorical response to a rumor that, according to Matthew, is still making the rounds in his day (28:15). The rumor, in turn, is a response not so much to Christian preaching that Jesus was alive as to the story of the empty tomb. The ancient world was not as skeptical about appearances of dead persons as we are (see Acts 12:15).

326

Matthew is thus preparing in advance for his defense of the women's discovery of the empty tomb.

The Pharisees, who have been absent from the passion narrative proper (their last appearance was at 22:41), now reappear, again in conjunction with the chief priests as at 21:45, probably because they alone can "remember" that Jesus prophesied his resurrection "after three days." Since Matthew has carefully changed Mark's "after three days" to "on the third day" in each of the three passion announcements (16:21; 17:23; 20:19), his use of the Markan formulation here serves to draw our attention to 12:40, the only "announcement" of the resurrection uttered in public: "For just as Jonah was three days and three nights in the belly of the sea monster, so for three days and three nights the Son of Man will be in the heart of the earth" (NRSV). Since the Pharisees are included in the audience at 12:38, they can be represented as remembering the veiled prediction.

The irony in verse 65 is surely intentional: "Go, make it as secure *as you know* (how to)." Pilate's words anticipate the futility of human efforts to confine Jesus to his tomb. Those who attempt to do so know nothing of the power of God.

God's Vindication
of the Crucified Messiah

MATTHEW 28:1–18

Matthew 28:1–15
The Empty Tomb

The resurrection of Jesus is an affront to many scientifically trained minds. While the disciples' feeling that Jesus was still present with them "in spirit" is credible, the story of the empty tomb is dismissed as a pious legend. The church's celebration of Easter is sometimes perceived by such persons as an embarrassing fraud.

It must be conceded from the outset that, conceived as a matter to be submitted to a jury, the case is seriously flawed. The discrepancies in the story as submitted by the four Evangelists are substantial. Who first discovered that the tomb was empty? When? How and when was the stone rolled from the mouth of the tomb? And the introduction of an angel or angels does not increase the credibility of the story. These factors have been used by the "defense lawyers" to support the argument that the earliest Christians cannot have conspired to create the legend out of nothing; in this case they would have made certain that their testimonies agreed. Unfortunately, this argument does not impress the jury. Variations in other stories about Jesus demonstrate that early Christians were not terribly concerned about accuracy of detail. The "prosecution" asks: Regardless of the disagreements, is there any truth in the underlying story that the tomb was found to be empty?

Matthew's attempt to bolster the story by introducing "hostile witnesses," the detachment of Roman soldiers guarding the tomb, will not be convincing to the jury. As verse 15 suggests, this subplot seems to have been inspired by a Jewish rumor that the disciples stole the corpse (see comments on 27:62–66). While the existence of the rumor need not be doubted (it is reported by Justin Martyr a century later), this fact does not prove that the tomb was empty but only that Jews were aware of the story.

The fact of the matter is that the case was not meant to be brought to the jury. It is a faith story, intended not for unbelievers but for believers, because it is not so much about Jesus as it is about God, whose activity is not subject to the scrutiny of a law court. For this reason, the event is less problematic to Pinchas Lapide, a believing Jew, than to some Christians (*The Resurrection of Jesus: A Jewish Perspective*). To this orthodox rabbi it is by no means inconceivable that the God of Elijah and Elisha raised Jesus of Nazareth from the grave! Although Christians will assess the theological significance of the narrative differently, their point of departure must be the same: What is this story telling us about *God?*

Approached from this perspective, the Easter event is properly seen as God's comment on Good Friday. It is not just a "superlative miracle," like the raising of Lazarus, but the resurrecting of *the crucified Messiah* (see v. 5). Jesus' cry of dereliction from the cross is answered. His obedience to the

328

uttermost is honored by his Father (see 26:39). It is only in the light of God's affirmation that the disciples are able to understand Jesus' death as a victory instead of a tragedy. While the cross seems to annul Jesus' Messiahship, the resurrection confirms it. It is then possible to interpret the cross as the central event of God's salvation history.

At the other end of the continuum from the skeptics are Christians who miss the point of Easter by treating it as automatic. For them it is a foregone conclusion that Jesus arose because he was divine. Such talk deprives Good Friday of its significance; if the rising was due to Jesus' "nature," then his death on the cross was an empty charade. No, the resurrection is understood by Matthew as God's act. For this reason, the verb in verse 6 should be taken as a true passive: "He has been raised" (correctly rendered by NEB, REB, and NRSV; cf. I Cor. 15:15; I Peter 1:21). Only because Jesus was as dead as any mortal can be was the resurrection a meaningful statement about salvation history.

Even in Matthew's version of the story, with its addition of the Roman soldiers, the empty tomb is presented not as *proof* but as a *sign* of the resurrection. That the sign is ambiguous is indicated by the negative interpretation given to it by Jesus' opponents (v. 15). Even the positive witnesses, however, do not come independently to a proper understanding; the emptiness of the tomb must be interpreted for them by an angel. This feature of Mark's narrative (Mark 16:5–7) is enhanced by Matthew in several ways. The angel's arrival is accompanied by an earthquake (as was Jesus' death; see comments on 27:51). The angel rolls back the large, sealed stone and sits on it (perhaps to ridicule the futile efforts of Jesus' enemies to confine him to the tomb). The angel's appearance is described in terms reminiscent of Dan. 7:9; 10:6. These details all point to the majesty and power of God, the unseen leading actor in the drama. Nevertheless the focus of the narrative in Matthew's enhanced version, as in Mark's simpler one, is on the *message* of the angel: "He has been raised." To Mark's statement Matthew adds the clause "as he said," reminding us that Jesus had foretold his resurrection in each of the passion announcements (16:21; 17:23; 20:19), even though this part of the prediction was never appropriated by the disciples.

329

The angel's speech includes a message for the disciples. The first statement, "He has been raised *from the dead*" (the italicized words are absent from Mark 16:7), is perhaps an indication that Matthew, like Paul, regards Jesus' resurrection as the initial instance of the end-time general resurrection of the dead (see I Cor. 15:20–21). Such a view is supported by the fact that in 27:53 the resurrected saints are represented as appearing only after Jesus' resurrection even though their tombs were split open at the time of his death. Jesus' resurrection is thus portrayed as an eschatological event; it ushers in a new era.

The second part of the message for the disciples recalls 26:32: "But after I am raised up, I will go before you to Galilee." It thus prepares for the appearance that will be described in the closing verses of the Gospel. Despite his strong interest in Peter, Matthew omits the reference to him in Mark 16:7, "Tell his disciples *and Peter.*" Although both Luke 24:34 and I Cor. 15:5 mention a special appearance to Peter, nowhere in the New Testament is this encounter described. Perhaps Matthew's omission is meant to suggest that, regardless of Peter's primacy, the risen Christ belongs to the church as a whole, not to individuals.

Mary Magdalene and "the other Mary" (apparently Jesus' mother, in Matthew's view; see comments on 27:56), who witnessed Jesus' death (27:55–56) and burial (27:61), are now witnesses to the empty tomb and the angel's message. They run from the sepulcher "with fear and great joy"; their awe at the power of God does not inhibit their elation that their crucified Messiah has been raised from the dead. Neither Mark nor Luke reports an appearance to the women. Here Matthew is closer to John; the Fourth Gospel narrates an encounter between Mary Magdalene and the risen Jesus (20:11–18). The encounter scene in Matthew is little developed. Jesus addresses the two women with the customary Hellenistic greeting *chairete.* The English translators have difficulty finding an appropriate rendering. "Greetings" (NIV, NRSV) is accurate enough, but the effect is weak. The TEV, attempting to get behind the Greek to what Jesus would have said in his native Aramaic, substitutes "Peace be with you." While not an accurate translation, this is surely more edifying than "Greetings," which in today's vernacular becomes "Hi there!" While Matthew is using a stereotyped form, he may intend his readers to take the word still more literally. The verb means "rejoice" (the same imperative form, *chairete,* appears with this sense in Phil. 4:4). It is appropriate that the risen Lord's first word be not simply "Greetings" but "Rejoice!"

As Matthew presents it, Jesus' message for the disciples is little more than an echo of what the angel has already said in verse 7. There is one significant addition, however. "Disciples" is replaced by "brothers." In view of the following passage, we must take this not as a reference to his siblings but to the eleven apostles (v. 16). The substitution indicates Jesus' forgiveness of the ten who forsook him (26:56) and the one who denied him (26:69–75).

Since women were not regarded as competent witnesses in Jewish courts, it is clear that their presence in this narrative guarantees that it was not created to impress outsiders. The story is cherished by the faith community, in which women play an indispensable role as witnesses to the power of God.

As in the passion narrative, great restraint is shown in the telling of the resurrection story. Unlike the later *Gospel of Peter,* none of the New Testament writers dares to describe Jesus' emergence from the tomb. Despite his readiness to paint the angel with the vivid colors of apocalyptic, Matthew refrains from giving a verbal portrayal of the risen Messiah. The mystery must not be trivialized by idle words. This awed restraint reminds us that the resurrection is not a carefully constructed myth but an inexplicable event. The story is credible only because God is credible.

Matthew 28:16–20
"Enlist All the Gentiles as Disciples"

The importance of this passage to a proper understanding of the First Gospel can hardly be exaggerated. At one level it is simply another of several appearance narratives that give substance to the witness claims of the earliest kerygma, "he appeared to Cephas, *then to the twelve"* (I Cor. 15:5). As in Luke 24:36–51 and John 20:19–23, this narrative relates an encounter of the Twelve (now eleven) with the risen Messiah, who sends them forth as his heralds. It is possible that a common story of the commissioning of the Twelve underlies these three, very different accounts. In any event, it is clear that each of the Evangelists describes the commissioning from the perspective of his own theology. It is therefore imperative to note the details with which Matthew tells this climactic story.

331

Although Luke strictly limits the resurrection appearances to the Jerusalem area (Luke 24:49), Matthew follows Mark in locating the commissioning encounter in Galilee (Mark does not include an appearance story, but the Galilean encounter is promised in 14:28; 16:7). The Fourth Gospel accommodates both traditions; it locates the commissioning scene in Jerusalem but supplements it with an appearance to Peter and six other apostles in Galilee (John 21). Whereas John (explicitly, 20:19) and Luke (implicitly, 24:33) locate the primary encounter in a room, Matthew places the appearance on "the mountain." Mountains have played a significant role in the First Gospel. Both the final temptation (4:8) and the transfiguration (17:1) occur on "a (very) high mountain" (no definite article). In certain references to a mountain the accompanying definite article seems to bear no special significance (see 14:23; 15:29). The one instance in which *"the* mountain" seems to be stressed by the Evangelist is 5:1, the introduction to the Sermon on the Mount (see comments on 5:1). It is possible, therefore, that Matthew wants us to see in 28:16 a reference to the Messiah's inaugural address.

This possibility is rejected by many commentators for lack of evidence. Certainly the common English rendering of the clause provide little support for the hypothesis. The Greek, however, is not nearly so straightforward as the unanimity among translators would suggest. The adverb translated "to which" in most modern versions normally means "where" (see KJV). The pronoun rendered "them" is not the object of the verb; it is in the dative case, which means that something was done *to* or *for* them. The verb itself is ambiguous. Its basic meaning is "put in order, arrange." From this origin it develops secondary meanings such as "appoint" (see KJV) and "command." If we take the verb in verse 16*b* in this latter sense, we can translate the verse: "And the eleven disciples went to Galilee, to the mountain where Jesus laid down rules for them." If this interpretation of verse 16 is accepted, the disciples' return to the site of the Sermon on the Mount reinforces Matthew's heavy emphasis on *doing* the will of the Father in heaven as interpreted by Jesus the Messiah (see esp. 7:21–27).

The motif of hesitation or doubt of verse 17 may have been traditional in resurrection narratives, a by-product of the motif of uncertainty regarding Jesus' appearance (the two on the road to Emmaus do not immediately recognize Jesus, and in Luke

24:16 the disciples think it is a spirit; see also John 21:4). The disciples' doubt is dispelled not by what they *see* but by what they *hear*. As in chapters 5–9, Matthew strongly subordinates seeing to hearing obediently what Jesus says (see comments on 4:23).

The Great Commission is prefaced with one of the most important christological statements in the First Gospel: "All authority in heaven and on earth has been given to me." This recalls the similar declaration of 11:27: "All things have been handed over to me by my Father." In the comments on that verse it was suggested that the subject there is Jesus' *revealing* authority, while in 28:18 his *ruling* authority is in mind. Some scholars see here an allusion to Dan. 7:13–14. Others point to Ps. 2:8. It is not clear that verse 18 echoes either of these passages. With greater confidence we can assert that the fundamental idea underlying verse 18 is the conviction that Jesus the Messiah has been exalted through death and resurrection to "the right hand of God" as predicted by Ps. 110:1 (see comments on 22:44; 26:64; see also Acts 2:34–35; Rom. 8:34; Eph. 1:20; Col. 3:1; Heb. 1:3), where he sits and reigns "until he has put all his enemies under his feet" (I Cor. 15:23, also alluding to Ps. 110:1). According to Matthew, Jesus is not waiting passively in heaven for his glorious arrival as judge and king but is already exercising his Lordship as God's plenipotentiary Son. The Great Commission is thus founded on Jesus' *present* Lordship (note the "therefore" of v. 19).

The target of the commission is "all the Gentiles." In most translations we find instead "all nations." This does not correspond with the normal function of *ethnē* in the New Testament as a whole or in Matthew (see comments on 25:32). Greek-speaking Jews regularly used *ethnos* in the plural as a way of speaking of non-Jewish individuals (the equivalent of *goyyim* in Hebrew). Clearly it is individuals who are meant in verse 19; it is not possible to baptize a nation but only the individuals who comprise it. This interpretation does not necessarily exclude Jews as prospective disciples. What verse 19 explicitly does is remove the restriction of the earlier Galilean mission ("Go nowhere among the Gentiles," 10:5). Perhaps Matthew believed that the mission to Israel must continue until Jesus returns in glory (see 10:23), but in view of 21:43 this seems dubious. The mission to Israel, attended by persecution and frustration, has been unsuccessful (see the comments on 10:17–42). While Jew-

333

ish converts are by no means excluded, the focus of the church's mission, Matthew seems to suggest, must henceforth be the Gentile world.

The most remarkable feature of Matthew's commissioning statement is the absence of any call to preach the gospel! Correspondingly, there is no demand for faith as a precondition for baptism. Matthew apparently can take for granted that the missionaries will proclaim the good news and call for faith (see 24:14; 18:6); what he cannot take for granted is that the converts will treat seriously Jesus' moral demands. He is deeply distressed by the number of so-called converts who think they can attend the Messiah's wedding feast in the shabby rags of their old pagan morality (see 22:11–14). What is stressed, therefore, is that the Gentiles must be *discipled* (the verb *mathēteuō* is used here, as in 13:51; 27:57, not the more common noun *mathētēs*, "disciple"). What this means is explored further in verse 20: "teaching them to observe everything that I commanded you." As we saw in the Sermon on the Mount, Matthew's Jesus does not present himself as a legislator laying down a new code of laws to replace the Mosaic corpus but rather as the God-authorized, final interpreter of Torah. To do what Jesus teaches ("my words," 7:24) is to do the will of the Father in heaven (7:21). The tense of the participles ("baptizing," "teaching") does not indicate that the Gentiles must be discipled before they are baptized, or baptized before they are taught. It looks as if Matthew perceives baptism as occurring in the middle of a discipling-and-teaching process that must continue indefinitely.

Nothing is explicitly said in the commission about building the church (see 16:18), but its emphasis on Jesus' teachings clearly points in the direction of nurturing a community. A great many of the individual sayings in the Sermon on the Mount and elsewhere in the Gospel have particular relevance to the Christian fellowship. The Gentiles are not to be converted to a philosophy but to a unique way of *living together* in the Messiah's community, a way prepared not by the risen Lord but by the earthly Jesus. The church is not to be cut loose from its historical moorings by an appeal to charismatic revelation (again, see 7:21–28).

334

The triadic baptismal formula used to be considered a later interpolation but is now generally accepted as authentic. Triadic references to Father, Son, and Holy Spirit occur in other

New Testament writings, with variations in the names used (see I Cor. 12:4–6; Eph. 2:18; 4:4–6). It should not be assumed, however, that such formulations reflect the developed Christology of Nicaea. For Matthew, "the Son" is a functional rather than an ontological term; it identifies Jesus as the miraculously born Messiah who was destined from birth to be exalted to God's right hand.

In Luke's Gospel the last word about Jesus speaks of separation: "While he was blessing them, he withdrew from them and was carried up into heaven" (Luke 24:51, NRSV). In Matthew, by contrast, the last word promises Jesus' continued presence. "I am with you" is a formula ascribed to God in the Old Testament, sometimes with reference to an individual (Gen. 26:24), sometimes addressed to the people as a whole (Hag. 1:13). The attribution of the formula to the risen Jesus reminds us at the conclusion of the Gospel that Jesus is still Emmanuel, "God with us." To him God has delegated responsibility for leading and protecting the new people of God (see Isa. 41:10).

God with us

In its context the promise of verse 20 is addressed to the missionaries of the gospel. This conforms with the portrayal of Jesus as the great missionary in 13:37 ("The one who sows the good seed is the Son of man"). The disciples who go into all the world with the gospel are instruments of *Jesus'* activity (see also 10:40).

It would be a mistake, however, to regard the promise as restricted to the missionaries. The last word is surely for the church as a whole and for all its constituent congregations. In 18:20 Jesus' presence is promised for times of judgment and discipline in the church. Here the promised presence is for empowerment. As in 8:23–27, the little ship of the church, battered by life's storms, knows that it is never left to depend on its own resources. The Lord Jesus is with it "all the days, right up to the consummation of the age." It is not certain why Matthew chooses to write "all the days" rather than the simple adverb "always." We may guess that the phrase is intended to emphasize the *daily* nature of the supporting presence—"day by day by day."

The continued existence of the church despite its myriad sins of commission and omission provides the surest evidence that the promise has been kept.

SELECTED BIBLIOGRAPHY

1. For further study

BEARE, F. W. *The Gospel According to Matthew: Translation, Introduction, and Commentary by Francis Wright Beare.* San Francisco: Harper & Row, 1982.

DAVIES, W. D. *The Setting of the Sermon on the Mount.* Cambridge: Cambridge University Press, 1964.

DAVIES, W. D., and DALE C. ALLISON, JR. *A Critical and Exegetical Commentary on the Gospel According to St. Matthew.* 3 vols. Edinburgh: T. & T. Clark, 1988–.

GUNDRY, ROBERT H. *Matthew: A Commentary on His Literary and Theological Art.* Grand Rapids: Wm. B. Eerdmans Publishing Co., 1982.

HARRINGTON, DANIEL J. *The Gospel of Matthew.* Collegeville, Minn.: Liturgical Press, 1991.

HILL, DAVID. *The Gospel of Matthew.* London: Oliphants, 1972.

KINGSBURY, JACK D. *Matthew as Story.* 2nd ed., rev. and enl. Philadelphia: Fortress Press, 1988.

MEIER, JOHN P. *The Vision of Matthew: Christ, Church, and Morality in the First Gospel.* New York: Paulist Press, 1979.

2. Literature cited

BROWN, ROBERT McAFEE. *The Bible Speaks to You.* Philadelphia: Westminster Press, 1955.

CALVIN, JOHN. *A Harmony of the Gospels Matthew, Mark and Luke.* Translated by A. W. Morrison. Calvin's Commentaries. Edited by David W. Torrance and Thomas F. Torrance. 3 vols. Grand Rapids: Wm. B. Eerdmans Publishing Co., 1972.

CULLMANN, OSCAR. *Peter: Disciple—Apostle—Martyr.* Translated by Floyd V. Filson. Philadelphia: Westminster Press, 1953.

DERRETT, J. DUNCAN M. " 'Where Two or Three Are Gathered in My Name . . .': A Sad Misunderstanding." *Expository Times* 91 (1979): 83–86.

DONALDSON, TERENCE L. *Jesus on the Mountain: A Study in Matthean Theology.* Sheffield: JSOT Press, 1985.

HARE, DOUGLAS R. A. *The Son of Man Tradition*. Minneapolis: Fortress Press, 1990.

———. *The Theme of Jewish Persecution of Christians in the Gospel According to St. Matthew*. Cambridge: Cambridge University Press, 1967.

JEREMIAS, JOACHIM. *The Parables of Jesus*. Rev. ed. Translated by S. H. Hooke. New York: Charles Scribner's Sons, 1963.

KINGSBURY, JACK D. *Matthew: Structure, Christology, Kingdom*. 2nd ed. Minneapolis: Fortress Press, 1989.

———. *The Parables of Jesus in Matthew 13: A Study in Redaction-Criticism*. London: SPCK, 1969.

LAPIDE, PINCHAS. *The Resurrection of Jesus: A Jewish Perspective*. Translated by W. C. Linss. Minneapolis: Augsburg Publishing House, 1983.

LUZ, ULRICH. *Matthew 1–7: A Commentary*. Translated by W. C. Linss. Minneapolis: Augsburg Publishing House, 1989. The translation of *Matthew 8–17* is forthcoming in 1994.

MANSON, T. W. *The Teaching of Jesus*. Cambridge: Cambridge University Press, 1931.

O'NEILL, J. C. *Messiah: Six Lectures on the Ministry of Jesus*. Edinburgh: Cochrane Press, 1980.

PRAEDER, SUSAN MARIE. *The Word in Women's Worlds*. Wilmington, Del.: Michael Glazier, 1988.

SCHWEIZER, EDUARD. *The Good News According to Matthew*. Translated by D. E. Green. Atlanta: John Knox Press, 1975.

SIGAL, PHILLIP. *The Halakah of Jesus of Nazareth According to the Gospel of Matthew*. Lanham, Md.: University Press of America, 1986.

SPEAKMAN, FREDERICK B. *Love Is Something You Do*. Westwood, N.J.: Fleming H. Revell Co., 1959.